ROUTLEDGE LIBRARY EDITIONS: SCIENCE FICTION

Volume 3

THE WORLD OF SCIENCE FICTION, 1926–1976

THE WORLD OF SCIENCE FICTION, 1926–1976
The History of a Subculture

LESTER DEL REY

Routledge
Taylor & Francis Group
LONDON AND NEW YORK

First published in 1980 by Garland Publishing, Inc.

This edition first published in 2021
by Routledge
2 Park Square, Milton Park, Abingdon, Oxon OX14 4RN

and by Routledge
52 Vanderbilt Avenue, New York, NY 10017

Routledge is an imprint of the Taylor & Francis Group, an informa business

© 1980 Garland Publishing, Inc.

All rights reserved. No part of this book may be reprinted or reproduced or utilised in any form or by any electronic, mechanical, or other means, now known or hereafter invented, including photocopying and recording, or in any information storage or retrieval system, without permission in writing from the publishers.

Trademark notice: Product or corporate names may be trademarks or registered trademarks, and are used only for identification and explanation without intent to infringe.

British Library Cataloguing in Publication Data
A catalogue record for this book is available from the British Library

ISBN: 978-0-367-74838-8 (Set)
ISBN: 978-1-00-315980-3 (Set) (ebk)
ISBN: 978-0-367-74839-5 (Volume 3) (hbk)
ISBN: 978-0-367-74896-8 (Volume 3) (pbk)
ISBN: 978-1-00-316011-3 (Volume 3) (ebk)

Publisher's Note
The publisher has gone to great lengths to ensure the quality of this reprint but points out that some imperfections in the original copies may be apparent.

Disclaimer
The publisher has made every effort to trace copyright holders and would welcome correspondence from those they have been unable to trace.

THE WORLD OF
SCIENCE FICTION:
1926-1976
THE HISTORY OF A SUBCULTURE

by Lester del Rey

GARLAND PUBLISHING, INC.
NEW YORK & LONDON

Copyright © 1980 by Garland Publishing, Inc.

All rights reserved. No part of this work covered by the copyright hereon may be reproduced or used in any form or by any means—graphic, electronic, or mechanical, including photocopying, recording, taping, or information storage and retrieval systems—without permission of the publisher.

Library of Congress Cataloging in Publication Data
Del Rey, Lester, 1915-
The world of science fiction, 1926-1976.
Includes index.
1. Science fiction, American—History and criticism.   I. Title.
PS374.S35D4   813'.0876   75-4065
ISBN 0-8240-1446-4

Printed on acid-free, 250-year-life paper
Manufactured in the United States of America

To my wife, Judy-Lynn,
who inspired this book—
many and many a time!

ACKNOWLEDGMENTS

THIS BOOK might never have been possible without the devotion and unexpected generosity of Edward and JoAnn Wood, well-known fans and experts in almost every aspect of science fiction. When I first began this work, my difficulties were multiplied by the fact that a fire had recently destroyed most of my library of magazines, books and reference works. Knowing this, the Woods volunteered to check every fact against their own extraordinarily complete library. This was a time-consuming and onerous task, but they did far more than I could expect; each chapter was not only checked and double-checked, but was returned to me with copious notes, suggestions and helpful questions. Such accuracy as exists in this work must be credited to them; and any remaining errors can only be those I may have made in rewriting. They have earned more thanks than I can render, both for the time and effort involved and for the pleasure of their friendship over the years.

I am also indebted to the many fans of science fiction, too numerous to credit properly, who have labored with little or no recompense to prepare the indexes, guides and collections of data on the world of science fiction. No other fandom that I know has provided so much valuable scholarship for the researcher.

And finally, my thanks to my publishers who waited through the long delays—with unfailing kindness, if not always with patience!

—Lester del Rey
New York City
1978

CONTENTS

Foreword   xi

PART I   Background
1. What Science Fiction Is   3
2. The Beginnings of Science Fiction   12
3. The Rise of the Pulps   21
4. The Third Source   30

PART II   The Age of Wonder (1926–1937)
5. The Magazines of Hugo Gernsback   43
6. The Dawn of *Astounding*   52
7. The Crucial Years   61
8. The Active Fan   71
9. The Shaping of the Future   80

PART III   The Golden Age (1938–1949)
10. Campbell's *Astounding*   91
11. The War and the Bomb   102
12. A Proliferation of Magazines   114
13. Science Fiction in Books   128
14. The Growth of Fandom   138
15. Reshaping the Future   148

CONTENTS

PART IV The Age of Acceptance (1950–1961)

16	The Quest for Magic	161
17	The Big Boom	169
18	And the Collapse	181
19	The Magazine Business	189
20	Wider Horizons	198
21	FIAWOL or FIJAGH?	207
22	Watershed	216

PART V The Age of Rebellion (1962–1973)

23	The Survivors	229
24	The Torch Passes	239
25	Rebellion: The New Wave and Art	249
26	Enter: Academe	263
27	The Big Con Game	271
28	The Fifth Age (1974–)	279

PART VI Parallels and Perspectives

29	Fantasy	291
30	Buck Rogers and Mr. Spock	304
31	Glossary	316
32	Themes and Variations	327
33	Utopias and Dystopias	341
34	But What Good Is It?	348
35	Mene, Mene, Tekel . . .	357
36	After *Star Wars*	369

Appendices	379
Index	393

FOREWORD

SCIENCE FICTION is far more than a form of literature. To many of its readers, it is to some degree a way of life. Readers and writers together form a sort of extended family, in which a high degree of interaction and feedback exists. In many ways, this forms a genuine subculture where the books and magazines that make up the easily recognizable part are firmly rooted in a complex of activity and background tradition. A body of accepted beliefs and conventions has developed, with a specialized jargon for many occasions. To some extent, science fiction has developed its own ethics and values. And its literary focus is often only marginally related to that of most other literature. Understanding all this requires a reasonable sophistication from reader or student.

Recently, a number of books have been published which attempt to cover science fiction; a few are excellent, but many are marred by lack of familiarity with the subject as a whole. Among the best works are indices and encyclopedias compiled by informed, long-time readers. There are also bibliographic and biographic studies, some unfortunately less accurate than might be desired. Nevertheless, these have been of great assistance to the librarian, teacher, anthologist and "completist" fan (the reader who tries to collect everything dealing with some part—or all—of the field).

So far as I can discover, however, there is no book which can serve as a guide to the interaction of the field as a whole for the student or newer reader who finds the literature and associated activities confusing as well as fascinating.

This book is an attempt to correct that lack. It is intended as a guide to the major forces in the subculture of science fiction, to help the reader understand the history of the field and the related developments that have shaped the literature. I have written it as if it were to be used by some researcher a century hence, who might know that something called science fiction once existed but who would need a key to unlock it for future research and help him select an area for his interest. (Of course, such a researcher would almost certainly not be so ignorant of how to learn about the field; libraries are already collecting works of authors and volumes of reference, with many of the books printed to endure for centuries. Still, an initial guide might be helpful.)

This, then, is an introductory book. It is not complete; a definitive history of science fiction would take a work of many volumes. And while I have made every effort to be accurate, no general guide to such a complex field can hope to avoid all error or bias. The chaotic development and many strong personalities which have affected the field impose too many difficulties. Experts may find errors, and I can only crave enlightenment from them.

I am not a final authority on any aspect of the field. But I have been fortunate in having nearly a lifetime of experience in most of the areas that will be covered. I have been reading science fiction for nearly fifty years and writing it for forty, with stories in most of the major magazines and dozens of books to my credit. I have edited five magazines, acted as associate editor for a group of other magazines, and am currently consulting editor to one of the largest publishing houses dealing in science fiction, as well as book-review editor of the magazine with the largest circulation in the field. I have acted as literary agent, story doctor to well-known writers, and advisor on television series. I have lectured widely, taught at workshops and one university, and been guest of honor and toastmaster at world science fiction conventions. I became an active fan in 1935 and have enjoyed the friendship of a great many readers, fans and professionals in the field. I have also dealt professionally with many of the leading artists. For most of my life, science fiction has been my world.

The years of close participation and study have taught me a deep respect for science fiction as the thing it is, with no wish to apologize for what it is not. I am well aware of its faults, as I've indicated, perhaps all too often, publicly; but I am even more aware of its genuine virtues.

Science fiction is unique among all categories of literature in the devotion it has inspired among its readers. I share that devotion as ardently now as I did when I first discovered the field in 1929 and began my efforts to understand it. My hope is that I can convey some sense of that devotion and part of that understanding to those who may read this book.

PART I

Background

CHAPTER 1

What Science Fiction Is

MOST PEOPLE seem to think that science fiction is some kind of wild futuristic trash, full of giant insects, invading monsters, mad scientists, robots out of control, and violent action in which seminude girls are always being rescued by excessively masculine heroes equipped with strange ray guns. These concepts are probably derived from the movies, television, comic books, and the covers of the more sensational magazines.

In reality, most science fiction bears little resemblance to that. It has used all of those themes, and some of the stories have involved an excess of action for action's sake. But much of it has used plots no more violent than can be found in most other literature. Its aliens are seldom monstrous and by no means always hostile. A great deal of it has concerned itself quite seriously with the problems of people of all kinds under the stress of an unusual environmental or cultural challenge. It usually takes place in the future, but there are many exceptions.

Even the devoted aficionado—or fan—has a hard time trying to explain what science fiction really is. People have been trying to define it since the first magazine of science fiction appeared. So far, there has been no fully satisfactory definition.

The trouble comes from the fact that there are no easily delineated limits to science fiction. It is a branch of literature which concerns itself with all time, from the remote past to the farthest future; it isn't limited to any one locale, such as Earth, but roams freely across the galaxy and beyond. And it deals with characters who may be animal, vegetable, or mineral—human beings, sentient plants, or metal robots; it may even use a whole intelligent planet as its protagonist.

Science fiction also embraces all other categories of fiction. (A category is a division used by publishers to indicate what part of the book-buying public will be attracted by a particular book.) Some of the great science fiction classics were originally published and accepted as mainstream literature. A number of Westerns have appeared in science fiction guise—usually not very good, but there have been exceptions. Isaac Asimov's *The Naked Sun* is valid as a detective mystery, yet it is unquestionably science fiction. And Peter Phillips' "Mana" was a ghost story, though no reader doubted it was science fiction.

Various attempts have been made to define science fiction as stories that could not be written without science concepts behind them. That would eliminate such stories as Harry Harrison's *Make Room! Make Room!* and a number of others, but would include such novels as Sinclair Lewis' *Arrowsmith*. True, the ideas of science play a part in much science fiction; but science need not be involved.

When asked for his definition, Frederik Pohl stated that science fiction was what he bought as an editor. He was then asked: "What kind of stories do you buy?" His wry answer was: "Science fiction!" Other attempts at definition have been equally guilty of defining the thing in terms of itself, though many have been less honest in recognizing the trick.

Some attempted definitions indicate that science fiction deals primarily with extrapolation. That is a nice, impressive word to describe the process of taking known trends or fads and carrying them forward to their ultimate development—often to absurdity; the trouble with using trends is that many of them reach a peak and then decline, rather than increasing steadily.

To some extent, extrapolation is a useful tool for science fiction. The idea of space travel came from carrying forward the theories of Hermann Oberth to the point where rocket travel would become an engineering fact; and Einstein's formula which showed that matter and energy were equivalent led to stories of atomic power. (Eventually, of course, later writers borrowed the devices without the need to do the extrapolating for themselves.)

Extrapolation proved to be a good way of obtaining the material for satirical novels. Frederik Pohl and C. M. Kornbluth, in *The Space Merchants*, used the tendency of advertising to become increasingly important and exaggerated it to show a world completely dominated by advertising agencies. This was in the heyday of the trend toward extrapolation, before it peaked out. But even then, only a minority of the stories depended on the process.

I found no satisfactory definition during most of my professional career, though I spent considerable time trying to find one. Finally, in 1971, I was able to develop one which seemed to fit the facts. It is reasonably short and includes most of what I consider science fiction, while excluding nearly all stories that do not belong in the field.

Science fiction is an attempt to deal rationally with alternate possibilities in a manner which will be entertaining.

Unfortunately, some of the key terms in that definition are ones which require considerable explanation to clarify them to one who is not already familiar with the subject. There are four such elements, which I shall take up somewhat out of order.

The one which is probably easiest to cover is the idea that science fiction is primarily meant to be entertaining. There may be objections to this from a few writers who consider themselves writers of serious literature or who feel that their stories are particularly significant and relevant. The fact remains, however, that publishers print such works primarily for readers who want to find entertainment in their reading. After all, its serious or informational content must be secondary, since it deals with things which cannot be happening in the normal course of human world events. A science fiction story may have other virtues, but it is read by most for its value as entertainment.

As fiction meant to entertain, the stories usually follow the patterns found to work best for other popular fiction. They are usually strongly plotted and center around one or more characters who undergo stress from inner or exterior conflict; and there should be a resolution which satisfies the reader. (Unlike most other popular fiction, however, there is no strong demand that the story must end happily. It must achieve something, but that is another matter.) All the common rules of fiction apply to science fiction; in fact, they apply even more strongly, since the writer must create acceptance, rather than find it in an already common background.

Science fiction must deal with what the reader can accept as possibilities. While it probably evolved from fantasy to some extent, science fiction is not considered straight fantasy by its readers, and hence should not involve ideas that are known to be impossible. A story need not be probable from what we know, but it should be justified until it seems possible within the framework of the idea being used. Scientific knowledge is taken as a major part of its background, and may be violated only by the use of some plausible theory to account for the story's divergence from what is known. Magic won't work—unless it can somehow be fitted into the structure of known science and acceptable theory.

There are a number of science fiction ideas which seem to violate the need for possibility, however. Time travel is accepted as a perfectly valid basis for a story, as is the idea of traveling faster than the speed of light through some mysterious "hyperspace." Those ideas are not possible according to what is known—in fact, they seem clearly impossible. But they were justified very carefully in early stories in the field. Now they are merely conventional devices, accepted as means to facilitate the development of a story.

The writer should know the difference between science-fiction conventions and science fiction ideas. When time travel or any other convention is used as the basic idea of a story, it must still be justified.

Telepathy and other extrasensory abilities, referred to in science fiction as psi powers, are really highly speculative. But telepathy was originally a necessary convention to make communication with aliens possible without holding up a story for months while languages were exchanged.

Attempting to deal rationally with any idea is the basic methodology of science fiction. A story must be rationally developed. Once a writer has presented a reader with his essential postulate, or the element which is not part of known and accepted reality, he must develop it as rationally and fully as a good scientist should develop his theories. In a sense, the writer has made a promise to the reader: accept the premise which I have tried to justify and I will then follow through as logically as I can. A good story requires that the writer try to discover every ramification of his original idea and build a world, society, or situation as completely as possible without violating the limits of his original assumption or dragging in conflicting ones.

It must be admitted that there are stories which pay little heed to rationality. These are usually referred to as pseudoscience stories, or as science fantasy. They usually appropriate some world or situation developed by science fiction and then use this as mere background for fantastic events.

Perhaps the most important element in distinguishing science fiction from other literature is that it should deal with something alternate to our reality. All other requirements might be found in a good detective story. (Certainly many mystery stories have no more probability than much of science fiction.) Science fiction often takes place in the future, which is removed from our current reality; but many stories also deal with alternate presents or pasts. It is the word *alternate* which distinguishes science fiction, no matter where or when it is supposed to occur. Science fiction must show us an alternative past or present that is different from what we know and accept, or take us to a future which is not simply like the present.

The story of Ab the Caveman, told about cavemen as we best know them to have been, is not science fiction. However, if we discover that Ab never evolved here but was really the descendant of people from some alien world, we have science fiction. (Or we have something like the seriously proposed idea in Erik von Däniken's books, but that was meant to convince, not to entertain.) However, if we are assumed to be descendants from that alien race, some theory should account for the anatomical evidence linking man to other Earthly mammals.

A story of social friction in the present resulting from the Civil War is mainstream. But one like Ward Moore's *Bring the Jubilee*, telling of a present in which the South won the War Between the States, is science fiction. A novel by Alan Drury, in which the story is set in some near future essentially the same as our present, is not science fiction, though it would be if he had conceived of a world not like the one we now know.

So we have rationality in handling, alternate possibility as a theme, and entertainment as the intent in our definition of science fiction.

There is another and simpler way of describing science fiction, as I realized fairly recently. It has the disadvantage of not distinguishing between science fiction and fantasy, however. (Fantasy is currently considered to be an attempt to deal rationally with alternate *impossibilities*.) But the distinction between the two is constantly becoming less apparent in many novels. The two categories seem to be merging gradually, so perhaps a definition that covers both is not without its uses.

In some ways, this shorter definition seems to describe modern science fiction better than the previous one.

Science fiction accepts change as the major basis for stories.

Most other fiction is based upon the world as we perceive it and as we believe it to have been. Such literature exists in the *now* of the writer and reader, and the object is to illuminate that eternal now. A writer of the mainstream is usually judged according to the degree of reality shown in his story, under the dictum that fiction should hold up a mirror (perhaps deliberately distorted) to reality.

Even historical and Western fictions deal with stories of that eternal now. With rare exceptions, they follow our current concepts of reality, giving only token gestures toward history. Thus our current concept of romantic love—only a few hundred years old—is grafted onto the age of so-called chivalry, when the attitude toward romance and love was not at all the same.

Science fiction, to a noticeable extent, rejects the unchanging order of things. It states implicitly, if not explicitly, that the world of the story is different from the accepted present or past of the reader. The change may be in science, environment, attitude, morality, or the basic nature of humanity. But it must have this change in the story as a basic part of the idea.

The reader is required to step out of his present

frame and adjust to other frames of reference. This requires considerable mental flexibility, which gives science fiction a comparatively limited and specialized readership, though one that is growing rapidly at present.

This need for effort and flexibility on the part of the reader should refute the claim that science fiction is "escapist" literature—a means of letting the mind escape from the pressures of daily life by turning to some vicarious emotional outlet that requires less thought and effort. A reader who is intent on a magazine or anthology which demands that he accept a new frame of reference for each story is hardly seeking to avoid thinking. In fact, the entertainment of science fiction comes less from vicarious emotions and more from the enjoyment of ideas than is true for other fiction.

True, the reader does "escape" from the world he knows. But he does so only by accepting a considerable challenge to his mental agility. For that matter, a man who is intently reading a work of Shakespeare or Turgenev is also "escaping" from the real world immediately around him and from thoughts of his personal affairs.

As C. S. Lewis pointed out in his thoughtful *An Experiment in Criticism,* the matter of such "escape" is dependent on the intent of the reader far more than on what he reads. Anyhow, playing chess is also a means of escape to anyone except the professional chess player; nobody seems to regard that as "escapist," however.

In fact, there seems to be some evidence that the reading of science fiction may actually make dealing with reality somewhat easier and develop attitudes that are necessary in the modern world. Alvin Toffler's *Future Shock* indicates that most people have severe difficulty in adjusting to the rapidly changing nature of the world. Their eternal now refuses to fit change, and they are confused. Science fiction, in demanding repeated acceptance of change from story to story, may well serve as a training exercise for the needed mental flexibility.

This does not indicate that science fiction can or should prophesy the future before it arrives. Despite what has been claimed at times, science fiction does not attempt to prophesy. As Frederik Pohl has stated repeatedly, science fiction does not deal with *the* future; rather, each story presents *a* possible future, not necessarily a probable one. Reading science fiction gives no insight into what will happen; it can only help the reader to be ready for whatever may occur.

Of course, science fiction has predicted such things as atomic power, space flight, air pollution and heart transplants. But that should not be surprising. Science fiction derives many of its ideas from the early speculations of science and preliminary work done in laboratories. Most of the predictions of science fiction were made by taking some idea from science and speculating on how it could be developed into engineering reality.

For every accurate prediction, there were probably a hundred that did not come true. And even the accurate ones were often wrong in details. Nobody predicted that space flight would be so costly that it would have to be funded by the government. Almost nobody predicted that Mars would be covered with craters.

In the final analysis, science fiction is largely based upon the asking of a single question: What if . . . ? What if men found a way to live forever? What if men suddenly met an alien race? What if men were able to go back in time and change history?

The rules and requirements of science fiction have been worked out to keep such speculations from flying off into wild fantasy and to help make the answers an author may find both interesting and believable to the reader.

CHAPTER 2

The Beginnings of Science Fiction

THERE HAVE BEEN many proposals for the first story of science fiction. My own feeling is that it probably began before the invention of writing. Perhaps when Ab the Caveman was using a bent sapling to operate a snare, he noticed how the released sapling sprang back with the force of many throwing arms. Thereupon he anticipated the development of the bow by dreaming up a tale of how some Super-Ab beyond the sky went about killing mammoths by hurling a spear from a bent length of wood.

Placing credit for the first story depends somewhat on the definition of science fiction being used. If a use of science as we know it is involved, then we are limited to the age of our science. If we accept the body of known and hypothesized facts of the world as the equivalent science of the day, we can go back a good deal farther.

In that case, science fiction is precisely as old as the first recorded fiction. This is the epic of *Gilgamesh*. The most complete version we have of this story is nearly 3,000 years old, and it probably has origins a thousand years earlier. Unlike most written material of the time, it seems to have been intended as a work of fiction.

Gilgamesh was a legendary king of Ur and the epic tells of his wondrous deeds and his search into a strange land for the secret of immortality. It anticipates the use of the superman hero, the trip beyond the world of reality and the possibility of immortality through drugs; it involves a long search for knowledge and understanding. It would be very easy to transpose all of it into quite acceptable science fiction by replacing the gods and monsters with alien beings; indeed, little change would be needed in the attitude of Gilgamesh toward the mythical creatures.

Another possibility is the *Odyssey*, since Homer dealt with the wonders of his world in accordance with the facts then known and believed. But *Gilgamesh* is closer in devices and feeling to our modern fiction than is the epic of Homer.

Certainly the first known interplanetary tale was *The True History* of Lucian of Samosata, written about 175 A.D. Lucian's hero went to the Moon, where he found intelligent, nonhuman beings. The works of Hellenistic mathematicians, such as Aristarchus of Samos, had established the beginnings of real astronomy. Lucian was aware of the fact that the Moon is just another world which circles a spherical Earth. The distance of the Moon and its diameter had been determined with reasonable accuracy, and Lucian used all such known science. He did not know that no air existed between the Earth and the Moon for most of that distance, and his device of having a ship lifted by a waterspout and carried to the Moon on a whirlwind seemed quite possible to him. It would be almost fifteen hundred years before a better piece of science fiction could be written.

Roman writers, so far as we know, produced nothing remotely related to science fiction. Despite their background of myth, they tended to be rather practical in their outlook, with little love of fantasy. After the fall of Rome, literature gradually developed the medieval romance, filled with much wonder and little rationality. Most of this was allegorical, rather than thoughtful. *Orlando Furioso*, written at the end of this reign of imaginary wonders, does contain a section in which a man flies to the Moon, but it is difficult to label it as science fiction.

What might be called science fiction began with *Somnium* (1634), by Johannes Kepler. Kepler was a great pioneer astronomer, who first established the mathematical principles to explain the orbits of the planets. But he was also an astrologer and mystic. As the title indicates, this story takes place in a dream, where a spirit carries Kepler to the Moon and planets. The picture given of the Moon is excellent, but most of the work is taken up with Kepler's philosophical ideas, and the story is incredibly dull by modern standards.

Bishop Francis Godwin wrote the first story in English of flight into space. His *The Man in the Moone* (1638) has birds pull a raft through space to the Moon. But he anticipated Newton's theory of gravity and had the pull of the Moon much lighter than that of the Earth.

In 1650, another *Voyage to the Moon* appeared, by Cyrano de Bergerac. He seems to have been in real life the superb swordsman, poet and wit who is the hero of Edmond Rostand's play, complete with an extremely large nose. His tale is quite a lively one, and his lunar creatures are interestingly described. He has a number of inventions, including a talking machine, used by the Lunarians. In the beginning, he suggests a number of ways to make the trip; rockets are suggested for the first time, as are hot-air balloons and the use of a parachute for descent. The means actually used, however, is the rubbing of his body with beef marrow, which draws the narrator upward according to some popular belief of the time!

Jonathan Swift's "Voyage to Laputa" in *Gulliver's Travels* (1726) is a rather bitter diatribe against the scientists of the Royal Society. Gulliver is taken onto a flying island in the sky, where he finds all concerned with studies and none possessing good sense. But the story is of interest because Swift correctly stated that Mars has two tiny moons (at approximately the right distance from the planet). It wasn't until 1877 that Asaph Hall was the first to sight those moons through his telescope. Swift's prediction was almost certainly a lucky guess, but it has led to all sorts of speculations.

It was in the nineteenth century that the story involving speculation on science became an important part of literature. This shouldn't be a cause for surprise; science had been developing for some centuries, but was only then beginning to affect the lives of the average man. This was the century that produced the railroad, the telegraph and telephone, and eventually the motorcar.

Mary Wollstonecraft Shelley's *Frankenstein* (1817) was the first novel to use the new discoveries about the power of electricity. Dr. Frankenstein is shown as a scientist who attempts to create a man from parts of corpses, bringing the creation to life by electricity. He succeeds, but his "monster" is turned into a savage creature by the prejudices of the world and rebels against him.

Brian Aldiss, in his history of science fiction (*The Billion Year Spree*), suggests that *Frankenstein* is the first true novel of science fiction. There is some merit in his argument, but I cannot accept it completely. While the gadgetry and initial sympathetic treatment of the monster do suggest the development in later stories, the novel is really little more than a reworking of the ancient tales of the Golem—a creature raised from dirt or slime by cabalistic use of the Name of God, who then turns on his creators. The use of electricity is little more than a substitute for the spells from the Kabala. Nevertheless, it is a fascinating book, a good deal better than the movie that was made from it.

In America, Edgar Allan Poe was probably the first

to write what might be called science fiction. He was a great innovator as a writer, the originator of the detective story and a strong influence on many other types of literature. A number of his stories bear touches of science fiction. The one showing the closest resemblance is "The Unparalleled Adventure of One Hans Pfaal" (1835), which deals with a voyage to the Moon by balloon. Apparently convinced that such a conveyance would not work, however, Poe never finished his account of what Hans Pfaal was to find on the Moon.

Fitz-James O'Brien also wrote a number of stories of science fiction. The best known is "The Diamond Lens" (1858), which tells of a man who ground a marvelous lens from a diamond, enabling him to see into the world of the microcosm. He sees a beautiful girl living on an atomic world in a drop of water. In the end, he watches her die as the water evaporates. The ending may be scientifically ridiculous, but the story inspired a great many later ones, among them Ray Cummings' popular *The Girl in the Golden Atom* (1919).

Then we come to Jules Verne, whose stories did more to establish the tale of wonderful voyages and marvelous scientific gadgets than the work of any other writer. Many of his novels are still regarded as classics, particularly by those who have not read them!

Jules Verne (1828–1905) was educated as a lawyer but switched to writing plays, with indifferent success. Then, in 1850, he sold a story about a balloon ascent in which a madman tries to take over control; it was an instant success. Thereafter, he produced a great many stories of thrilling events, somewhat improbable dangers and hairbreadth escapes. Some of these involved voyages to strange parts of the world.

In 1864, he published *Journey to the Center of the Earth*, using the idea that the Earth is hollow, with a world inside our world—a theory having some popularity at the time. As men descend farther into the

Earth, they find traces of older and older life forms. The story is really a chance to expound on the theory of evolution of life. Verne was a good researcher into the more popular expositions of science and mechanics, and this afforded him a chance to use a great deal of material from his researches.

His next voyage was even more extraordinary—A *Trip from the Earth to the Moon* (1865). This is made by having men in a giant shell shot from a huge cannon that is dug into the ground. Verne obviously researched it thoroughly, and there are excellent details in his working out of the ballistics problems. But he sloughed off the fact that the men would be turned to jelly by the tremendous acceleration, simply having them floating in water to take up the shock. The details of the trip to the Moon and the nature of the Moon are well done.

This story was completed by a sequel in 1870, *Round the Moon*, in which his travelers swing around the Moon, seeing active volcanoes on the far side; they then head back for Earth, to land in the ocean and be rescued—not too unlike the rescue of our astronauts.

His most famous novel is probably *Twenty Thousand Leagues Under the Sea* (1870), in which a man is captured by a mysterious Captain Nemo and taken into a marvelous submarine for a voyage under the oceans—even to the South Pole and to buried Atlantis. The details of the submarine are marvelously complete.

It is probably this story which established Verne as a prophet. But little prophecy was needed, since engineers were already working on the problem of such a vessel. It is an ingenious story, perhaps his best, and his skill in taking rough ideas and turning them into fiction must be admired, but there is no real prophecy. Even the periscope, which he is said to have invented, was used by the *Turtle*, a primitive submarine invented and used during the American Revolution! (That craft also used a screw propeller.)

Verne was at his best in descriptions of machinery and suspense plotting. His style is lacking in grace and his characterization is usually primitive. (In *Hector Servadac*, published in 1877, he has men caught up in a comet and carried through space; one of the men is a Jew who might serve as a model for the later caricatures of Jews used by the Nazis in their propaganda.) Nevertheless, his contributions to science fiction are immense.

In 1865, the same year Verne was having men shot from a gun to the Moon, Achille Eyraud published *A Voyage to Venus*, which uses rocket propulsion to drive the ship through space. Eyraud understood the basic principle and detailed it quite well, though he thought the exhaust could be caught and used again. So far as I know, this was the first time rockets were actually used in space.

In *The Brick Moon*, Edward Everett Hale gave us the first story to use an artificial satellite. This was a four-part serial beginning in the October 1869 issue of *Atlantic Monthly*. His brick structure is accidentally shot into space with men aboard. As it continues to circle the Earth, supplies are shot up to keep those on board alive, and all is going well at the end of the story.

About this time, the dime novel type of publication discovered a form of science fiction known as "invention stories." This began with *The Steam Man of the Plains* (1868), by Edward F. Ellis. It proved so popular and long-lasting that Harry Enton was asked to do a series of similar books, the first of which was *Frank Reade and the Steam Man of the Prairies* (1876). Enton continued with others, but proved incapable of anything original, and the series was turned over to Luis P. Senarens (writing under the pseudonym of Noname). In 1898, he retired Frank Reade and began telling the exploits of an inventor son in *Frank Reade Jr. and his Steam Wonder*. Thereafter, the stories appeared regularly, until hundreds of these tales of marvelous inventions had appeared. Much later, the same basic approach was used in the *Tom Swift* series by "Victor Appleton," beginning in 1910.

Mark Twain's *A Connecticut Yankee in King Arthur's Court* (1889) is a tale of travel back through time and an attempt to change the past, and remains an excellent story, even today.

But it was H. G. Wells who did more to make acceptable literature of science fiction than any previous writer. From the time his *The Time Machine* was published in 1895, he dominated the field. Even most people who look on science fiction with contempt have read some story of Wells with enjoyment.

Herbert George Wells (1866–1946) was the son of a tradesman. He studied biology under Thomas Huxley and gained a genuine appreciation for science. He began as a teacher, but soon switched to writing as a full-time occupation. He was one of the founders of the British Fabian Society and retained strong socialist beliefs throughout his life. He was the author of several "straight" novels, often bitter or didactic, and of *The Outline of History*, as well as coauthor of *The Science of Life*. But it is for his science fiction that he is best remembered.

The Time Machine is the story of a man who invents a device to carry him into the future. His first stop is 800,000 years ahead, where he finds man divided into weak but charming aesthetes and grim and ugly underground workers who prey on the aesthetes. He then goes on thirty million years, until he finds Earth dying as the sun fades. It is a bitter story, but splendidly written, with a strong mood and almost poetic insights.

He followed this with *The Island of Dr. Moreau* (1896), dealing with a scientist's attempt to alter heredity, and *The Invisible Man* (1897), which is still being used for movie and television stories. Then in 1898 *The War of the Worlds* appeared, firmly establishing him as the master of the field. This is the story of a Martian attempt to take over Earth, foiled only by the fact that our germs find no resistance among the Martians. It is told with such detail that it seems to be actually happening before the reader.

When Orson Welles updated the story and laid it in New Jersey for a radio broadcast in 1938, hundreds of people did believe that it was happening and clogged the roads in their attempts to escape the invading Martians.

More stories followed quickly, including *The First Men in the Moon* (1901). But there is a growing bitterness in them. He does not paint glorious futures, but usually ones where man's inability to control technology or his base desires brings him to ruin. Wells' *Men Like Gods* (1923) is a utopian novel of a world where men have taken the right course and developed an almost perfect world, using the machine properly, rather than being mastered by it. But the modern Earthmen who are rotated into that wonderful world are unable to adapt to it. Apparently, to Wells, utopia is not for present-day mankind.

Wells also wrote a great many short stories, many of which are even more skillfully done than his longer works; the bitterness is less prevalent in them. But in whatever length, he dominated the field through the excellence of his writing and the detailed vision and understanding he brought to his subjects.

Jack London's *The Iron Heel* (1907) is more bitter than Wells could ever be, with a stronger socialist bias. It is the story of a dictatorship, and in some ways it is quite prophetic of the Nazi methods to appear later in real life. But it has almost none of the insight into humanity that Wells displayed.

J. D. Beresford's *The Hampdenshire Wonder* (1911) is a novel with a quiet, restrained demonstration of such human sympathy and understanding. It is one of the earliest stories of human mutation into a potential superman. For many years, it has been considered one of the great classics of science fiction by those fortunate enough to have read it.

By this time, however, the emphasis on science fiction was shifting from books to magazines. Most of Wells' stories were first published in magazine form, though his reputation was assured through book publication. But for most of the development of science fiction after *The Time Machine*, it is necessary to study the history of the magazines.

CHAPTER 3

The Rise of the Pulps

ALTHOUGH MAGAZINE PUBLISHING goes back at least to 1731, when *Gentleman's Magazine* was founded, it wasn't until *Blackwood's Magazine*, in 1817, that fiction was featured regularly in periodicals. Very little of the fiction published in *Blackwood's* was even remotely science fiction, though George Tomkyns Chesney's *The Battle of Dorking* (1878) may have been the first future-war story, a type of fiction that soon became popular. It tells of the conquest of Britain by the Prussians, and was intended as a serious criticism of England's military preparedness.

Through most of the nineteenth century, the magazines were intended for the well-to-do, well-educated section of society. They featured serious essays as much as fiction, and were priced beyond the normal ability of the less-affluent to pay. America had *Harper's*, *Scribner's* and the *Atlantic* as examples of such magazines.

For the less-educated or poor, there were the dime

novels (which usually sold for five cents or less)—thin little booklets of about 32 pages, featuring sensational melodrama with little attention to writing style or plausibility. Many of these were aimed at younger readers.

By 1891, however, a number of factors contributed to a change in this situation. The Linotype had made it possible to set copy far more quickly and cheaply than the older method of handsetting. Wood-pulp paper had been invented; it was distinctly inferior in surface and lasting quality to what had preceded, but it was far less costly. And there was now an active middle class that was able to read easily and with leisure for the pleasure magazines could bring.

The first magazine to aim for this market was *The Strand Magazine* in 1891, which published both fiction and articles. Its success was assured when it contracted to buy a series of stories about Sherlock Holmes. This was an English magazine, but it soon had an American edition. It was followed almost at once by *The Idler*, and then by *Pearson's Magazine* in 1896.

In America, *McClure's Magazine* began publishing in 1893, using many stories reprinted from *The Idler*. Among these was Rudyard Kipling's "With the Night Mail" (1905). This story, with its 1912 sequel, "As Easy as A. B. C.," presents a world in which the mail service runs giant dirigibles and rules much of the world. It is complete with a well-developed future culture, including its own convincing slang.

The Strand published A. Conan Doyle's *The Lost World* (1912), the first major story to use a lost world where dinosaurs and other ancient beasts still live. The hero, Professor Challenger, also appeared in a number of other science fiction stories, including the classic "When the World Screamed" (1929), which tells of a great hole bored into the Earth, so deep that it touches the living creature whose shell is our planet.

Pearson's published *The War of the Worlds* and

most of the science fiction works of H. G. Wells. The magazine also presented J. Cutcliffe Hyne's *The Lost Continent* (1899), which tells of the end of Atlantis —long a popular science fiction theme.

The first all-fiction magazine was *The Black Cat*, which began publication in 1895. This later gained a reputation as a fabulous magazine, and has even been credited with being the first science-fiction magazine. This is incorrect. The magazine used all sorts of off-trail fiction along with some minor fantasy and science fiction. Little of its fiction is remembered today.

The real beginning of all-fiction magazine publishing came with the entrance of Frank A. Munsey into the field. In 1882, he began a children's weekly called *The Golden Argosy, Freighted with Treasures for Boys and Girls*. This was changed to an adult fiction magazine, under the title *The Argosy*, in 1896. In 1905, he added *The All-Story Magazine*, and *Cavalier Weekly* in 1908. These all sold for 10¢ an issue and were huge magazines, running to 192 or more pages each; they appeared in what became the standard pulp size of 7 x 10 inches. They also featured serials running usually to six or more installments, often with more than one serial running in a magazine at the same time.

Munsey was also the originator of the specialized, single-interest magazine. In 1906 he began *The Railroad Man's Magazine* and later *The Ocean*, which featured only sea stories. But these were not very successful. It was left for Street and Smith to succeed with such a magazine—*Detective Story Magazine*, founded in 1915.

Argosy and *All-Story* both welcomed science fiction adventures, the latter using *A Columbus of Space*, by Garrett P. Serviss, in 1909. Serviss was one of the few writers, aside from H. G. Wells, to have a background in science, having majored in it for four years at Cornell. His story of the first flight to Venus has a ship powered by atomic energy derived from uranium, and some of the descriptions of Venus are quite moving. The book is still remarkably readable.

It was left to *Cavalier*, however, to scoop its sibling magazines. It published Serviss' *The Second Deluge* (1911), the story of the Earth being flooded by water from space, with survivors building a great ark. And in 1912, it began publishing *Darkness and Dawn*, by George Allan England, the first of a trilogy which was to include *Beyond the Great Oblivion* and *The Afterglow* in 1913. (All appear together in book versions under the title of the first.) This is the story of two who survive a catastrophe that ruins civilization and wake to a monstrously changed world. Its appeal lies in the marvelous descriptions and the sustained mood, as well as the sense of reality conveyed by the writing.

All-Story's great discovery of February 1912 was a story entitled (in magazine form) *Under the Moons of Mars*, by Norman Bean. This is a landmark in the history of science fiction publishing and the beginning of a whole new category of such stories.

Norman Bean—or Normal Bean, as he had intended his pseudonym to appear before it was "corrected"—was really Edgar Rice Burroughs, and the story later appeared in book form as *A Princess of Mars*.

Edgar Rice Burroughs (1875–1950) had previously done a little of everything, from serving in the cavalry to acting as an advertising salesman for a patent-medicine firm. He had made no success of anything he tried; probably in desperation, he tried writing fiction, feeling that he could write stories at least as good as those he saw in the magazines where he had placed most of the advertisements. In this, he proved right. By the time of his death, he estimated that his writing had earned him ten million dollars. Fifty-nine of his books had seen print, with 35 million copies sold in North America and countless more in translations into most of the major languages of the world. Additionally, many movies had been made from his stories, and his

Tarzan was a highly successful cartoon strip, syndicated all over the world. Probably more people have read his stories than have read the works of any other writer, except as required by school courses. As I write this, almost all of his books are still in print and selling very well indeed.

From the literary point of view, he was not a great writer. Many of his books were hastily done, and they were designed to tell a story, with other details discarded happily as unimportant. Yet he was a great natural storyteller, with considerable skill. For his Tarzan books, he developed a technique of repeated cliffhanging incidents that somehow did not interrupt the flow of the narrative. Yet in his first-person novels (such as those laid on Mars), he was meticulous in telling the story from the single viewpoint, without such breaks.

John Carter is the hero of *A Princess of Mars*. He is a fighting man, as well as a Virginia gentleman. Trapped in a cave by hostile Indians, he is overcome by some gas. From there he is astrally projected to Mars, where mysteriously he finds himself in a body exactly like his own. (This was never explained—nor do most readers ever question it, so smoothly is it handled.) He is captured by giant, green, six-limbed Martians. As a result of his Earthly muscles and fighting skill, he rises to be a chieftain among them. Then he flees with Dejah Thoris, a Princess of the great Martian city of Helium—who is totally human, except for her red color and ability to lay eggs! The rest of the story is a tale of pursuit, danger and love. In the end, villainy sabotages the air machine that gives Mars a breathable atmosphere. Only John Carter can repair it. He does so, with his last gasp for breath—and wakes up back in the cave on Earth. At the end, he is still gazing at Mars, wondering if he can ever return to his beloved Dejah Thoris.

More than sixty years after the story was published—

and after a great many imitations of it—it sounds trite and full of bathos. But the reaction of the readers at the time was one of wild enthusiasm, and a demand for more.

Burroughs gave them more, after some correspondence with *All-Story*'s editor about higher rates. The next work was *Tarzan of the Apes*, which is not science fiction of any kind, but which somehow captures the same sense of the different and marvelous. In 1913, he provided the demanded sequel to John Carter's unhappy fate in *The Gods of Mars*, which he also left with an ending that demanded yet another sequel. And in 1914, he began another series, entitled *At the Earth's Core*, about Pellucidar, a world which lies inside the crust of Earth, with its own sun and a panoply of savage beasts and more savage men from the dawn of time.

These stories established a type of fiction which came to be known as the scientific romance. Science fiction had been rather barren of warm human emotions; it depended on marvels and trips to strange lands, or on some trick with science or technology. But Burroughs used his science fiction background as a setting for a love story. He did not slight local color and detail—he had a gift for making them seem real. But fighting and love were the twin themes of most of his work. Nothing could have been more popular.

All-Story had fallen on hard times. The editor had handled Burroughs badly; he had suggested a novel and then rejected it, to follow by rejecting the sequel to the first Tarzan story. There had also been endless bickering about the rate of payment. Burroughs took his stories elsewhere, and *All-Story* lost its great exclusive.

In 1914, *Cavalier* was combined with *All-Story*, which then became a weekly publication under the direction of Robert H. Davis. Davis, according to many writers who worked for him, was one of the really great editors, one who could teach technique, supply ideas, and engender tremendous enthusiasm. Certainly many of his discoveries became leading writers in later years. He patched things up with Burroughs (though not enough to become his exclusive publisher) and went about gaining new science fiction talent.

Many of the stories he obtained were scientific romances, with considerable debt to Burroughs. In 1915, Charles B. Stilson gave him *Polaris of the Snows*, a romance laid in the Antarctic, and its sequel, *Minos of Sardanes*. The trilogy ended with *Polaris and the Goddess Glorian*, published in 1917.

The real discovery of that year, however, was A. Merritt, whose short fantasy "Through the Dragon Glass" involves a strange Oriental mirror and the man who looks through it to discover a beautiful girl in a garden beyond the glass. The story is slight, but the writing is outstandingly effective. This was followed in 1918 by "The People of the Pit" and "The Moon Pool." The latter involves strange, ancient ruins on a Polynesian island and a monstrous creature that comes to take people into some mysterious place beyond the Pool when the moonlight is bright. It is completed in *The Conquest of the Moon Pool*, where a small group of people follow the creature into the inner world. Its strength lies in convincing characterization and an intense emotional appeal to the reader's sense of both beauty and horror. His *The Metal Monster* (1920) uses the most clearly science fiction theme of any of his stories, involving a sentient metal that has fallen from space and threatens human life. It tilts very heavily toward pure horror.

As an editor of Hearst's *American Weekly*, Abraham Merritt had no need to supplement his income by his writing and could take his own good time. Between "The Face in the Abyss" (1923) and its concluding sequel, nine years passed. But the two parts, published in book form as *The Face in the Abyss*, form what may be his best work. This is the story of a hidden valley in

Central America where a race of technologically advanced people have hidden away, guided and ruled by the last of the snakelike creatures who shaped all men. The Snake Mother has the head and arms of a beautiful woman and is the essence of feminine mystery. There is also a fascinating villain, imprisoned in the side of a cliff, and a richness of background rarely seen in any fiction. Through all this runs a forbidden romance between an American and a girl of the old race.

After this, Merritt turned more and more toward straight fantasy. His *The Ship of Ishtar* (1924) involves a ship that sails a timeless sea, a pawn for the goddess Ishtar and the evil god Nergul, while a modern man and a priestess of Ishtar try to work out their love against the background of the battling gods. His *Dwellers in the Mirage* (1932) is laid in another lost valley, and deals with the worshippers of an ancient god who resembles the kraken. *Burn Witch Burn* (1932) deals with an evil witch who animates dolls with men's souls; and his final *Creep, Shadow* (1934) blends modern witchcraft with the legend of the sunken, evil city of Ys.

In 1938, the readers of *Argosy* voted Merritt their favorite writer of all time.

In 1918, J. U. Giesy began another scientific-romance trilogy with *Palos of the Dog Star Pack*, which even imitates Burroughs' use of astral projection to get the hero to Sirius, the dog star. And in 1919, Ray Cummings began his long career with *The Girl in the Golden Atom*, in which a scientist manages to shrink himself down to a world that is part of an atom of gold, where he naturally meets a princess, falls in love, etc.

All-Story was combined with *Argosy* in 1920, eventually to produce the *Argosy Weekly*, and Bob Davis was let go. But one name must be mentioned. Murray Leinster, whose work remained popular in science fiction for more than fifty years and who was rightly named "the Dean of science fiction writers," published

"The Runaway Skyscraper" in 1919; this is a story of a skyscraper and crew carried back through time. The next year, his "The Mad Planet" appeared.

Argosy continued publishing a great deal of science fiction for many years. When the Munsey empire broke up, after the death of Frank Munsey, the magazine was bought by Popular Publications. It was gradually changed into a higher-class men's magazine. But as late as 1950, I sold them a story of a robot in a laboratory on the Moon.

During this period, a great many other magazines used science fiction to some extent. *Blue Book* often featured such material, as did most of the better adventure magazines, with the exception of *Adventure*. Even some of the slick magazines (the classier magazines, devoted mostly to women readers, depending on advertising, and paying far more than other magazines) used occasional science fiction. As an example, *The Saturday Evening Post* published Lord Dunsany's "Our Distant Cousins"—a story of a man who flies to Mars to discover that the human Martians are only food for the dominant race there. And the specialized horror-fantasy *Weird Tales* began using science fiction by such writers as Edmond Hamilton and Jack Williamson.

But the male adventure pulps were probably the major influence on science fiction from 1895 to 1925, and particularly the ones published by Frank Munsey. Most of the writers who would provide science fiction for the next twenty years grew up reading such stories, and their ideas of what science fiction should be were naturally conditioned by what it had been.

It wasn't an unnatural development. Basically, adventure fiction seeks to use the action of men with strange occupations or in exotic locations to provide the sense of the unusual that most readers seem to want. To a major degree, adventure is the conflict between man and his environment. Thus these stories involve men who dig tunnels, fight fires, or seek rubies

30   THE WORLD OF SCIENCE FICTION

from the eyes of heathen idols. They take place back of the beyond, or where the average reader is unable to go.

But the world was becoming too well known, and men's occupations were becoming far from adventuresome. The movies (and later, television) made all the Earth accessible to the viewer, and machinery took the glamour out of most work.

There was still the future, however, where men might walk on strange worlds, or face alien invaders—or almost anything.

Inevitably, adventure science fiction developed. It was time for the magazines to take the one further step toward publishing issues that would have nothing but science fiction.

CHAPTER 4

The Third Source

NOT EVERYONE could agree that science fiction should be a further extension of adventure fiction, however. There were still some of the more thoughtful readers who bemoaned the cheapening of science fiction into scientific romances and wanted to get back to the sociological material of H. G. Wells and other writers before the day of pulp fiction. They had little influence. But there was a third source of opinion as to what science fiction should be.

This came from the hobbyists, who had found that in the field of technology there were many areas where they could tinker with new ideas, build variations on known devices, and generally turn science and gadgetry into things to be exploited for their personal pleasure.

There was never quite such a period for them as that which began about 1900. (There probably never would be again after a few brief decades, since the advance of science and the cost of equipment soon went beyond their means, financial or intellectual.) Men all over America—and the technological world—were building new models of motorcars, or motorized bicycles; some even succeeded in doing such a good job in their small garages that they became manufacturers. Others were building strange devices that could fly, after a fashion. There wasn't even the need at first to have a license to build or fly experimental aircraft. All that was needed was some kind of fairly light engine, wood to be shaped into frames, and fabric to stretch over the wings. After all, the Wright Brothers had begun in a bicycle shop. Why couldn't others do as well? A few did, a few were killed, and a great many more dreamed about it and studied what technical literature there was.

It was a period when almost every man had to be his own motor mechanic, unless he was rich enough to hire a trained chauffeur. Those early engines were unreliable; a standard sight along the road was an auto with its hood up (in front or back) and a man in soiled driving coat working busily at it. Before long, most men felt they were pretty good engineers, and their minds began to turn to such mysteries as chokes, spark advance, gearing, and a thousand other mechanical details.

It was into this world that Hugo Gernsback came. He was born in Luxembourg in 1884 and came to the United States in 1904, where he immediately became involved with the infant science of radio. He built and marketed the first home radio set in 1905, and began publishing a catalogue filled with bulky condensers, detectors made of galena—or more cumbersome devices of powdered iron—and all the paraphernalia that would enable a tinkerer to satisfy that urge!

Radio was mostly a mystery at that time. But the idea of sending words through the air in code which could be picked up and read miles away fascinated a great many people.

In 1908, Gernsback started a magazine which would explain some of the mystery. He called it *Modern Electrics*; electronics was a term not yet heard, and most people referred to radio as wireless. The response to the magazine was excellent, and Gernsback was now a publisher.

But he was still very much a hobbyist at heart. During the following years, he had some eighty patents assigned to him. He also designed innumerable ways to make sets simpler and cheaper for other hobbyists. So far as I can learn, he was the first to combine regeneration with a reflexive circuit; through this trick he was able to combine radio-frequency amplification at its maximum, detection, and audio amplification into a single-tube (a tetrode, as I remember) set, which could just pick up a signal and play it over a loudspeaker, if the room were quiet.

As late as 1947 or 1948, he devised a tricky television antenna which could sort out ghosts and bad signals and deliver a picture under impossible conditions. I built one and it worked, though it took a lot of attention each time the station was changed. And his answer to my letter concerning it was as enthusiastic as his replies must have been when he first began publishing.

But Gernsback was interested in far more than radio. He was fascinated with anything involving science or engineering. The future, to him, was a time when all the things he could dream up would come true and make Earth a paradise for man. He could not let his visions go unpublished.

In 1911, *Modern Electrics* published the first part of a twelve-part serial by him with the tricky title of *Ralph 124C41+*, which is supposed to be the name of the hero. It is subtitled "A Romance of the Year 2660," and it details the life of a man at that marvelous time and the adventures he has.

As fiction, it is simply dreadful. I doubt that anyone today could get through it unless required to do so. The character is worse than wooden, the writing is stilted and forced, with conversations devoted mostly to explaining things that everyone at that time must already know. The plot is mostly a series of events that help to move from one marvelous device to another.

But never mind that. It is one of the most important stories ever written in the science fiction vein. It is a constant parade of scientific wonders—but they are logically constructed wonders, with a lot of keen thought behind them. The novel forecasts more things that really came true than a hundred other pieces of science fiction could hope to achieve. There is television (which was named by Hugo Gernsback), microfilm, tape recording, fluorescent lighting, radar—in fact, most of the things that did eventually make up our future. (There are also impossible gadgets, but they seemed logical at the time.)

The readers, who were themselves filled with technical dreams, were almost literally carried into the future. It was like a trip into such a world, with no need to have marvelous adventures; the romance of the story for its readers lay in the marvels themselves.

Greatly encouraged by the response from the enthusiastic readers, Gernsback began using more fiction in his magazine, whenever he could get a story that suited his ideas. He carried this policy over when he changed the name of his magazine to *The Electrical Experimenter* in 1913. About 1915, he began writing a series of spoofs, based upon real science, which were "The Scientific Adventures of Baron Munchhausen."

Radio, as a field, grew rapidly. Many of the hobbyists were now licensed operators or hams, banded together into an organization, and serving very creditably to advance the young science of radio. There were also dealers and mechanics, as well as engineers. To take advantage of this growing audience, Gernsback brought out *Radio News* in 1919. *The Electrical Experimenter* was converted to *Science and Inventions,* which embraced a far larger section of the readers interested in hobbyism and technology. Now he could report on all the fascinating developments in the field of science—not so much abstract science, however, as the science of making things work. He seems rarely to have considered science as an intellectual discipline, but rather as a means to building a brighter world for mankind's use. In this, he was in close sympathy with most of his readers.

Science and Inventions was an attractive magazine, with bright covers showing some recent development or some speculative possibility. (Many of those covers were done by Howard V. Brown, who later did most of the early covers for Street & Smith's *Astounding Science Fiction.* Another of Gernsback's artists was Frank R. Paul, who became the most admired of all science fiction artists.)

The science fiction stories that appeared in the magazine proved so popular that Gernsback decided to run a special "scientifiction" issue, as he called it; this was obviously a shortening of scientific fiction, and was Gernsback's favorite term for this type of literature. The August 1923 issue of *Science and Inventions* carried six stories, and again the readers were enthusiastic.

He continued using "scientifiction" in his magazine. One of Ray Cummings' best stories, *Tarrano the Conqueror,* began in the July 1925 issue of *Science and Inventions.* This is a story of a dictatorship and interplanetary war in the twenty-fifth century, with far better realization of the character of the dictator than could be found in most such fiction.

Gernsback had sent out a letter before this to 25,000 people—presumably to all of his subscribers—querying them about interest in a magazine containing nothing but science fiction. The response must have come as a surprise; despite the enthusiasm for the fiction he had published, the answers were largely unfavorable. For the moment, he gave up; but not for long. In 1926, without queries, he announced that he was issuing the first magazine devoted solely to "scientifiction."

As a result of this decision, when he died in 1967 he was known as the "father of science fiction," despite all the claims that might have been advanced for Verne or Wells having right to that title.

Perhaps Gernsback was not exactly the "father of science fiction." The origin of such literature is obviously spread over many centuries and belongs in tiny increments to many men. But certainly Gernsback was the father of magazine science fiction and was largely responsible for making a viable category of it. He founded the first seven magazines in the United States to use science fiction exclusively. And he spread the faith by contests, slogans, and a readers' league. He began the reader columns that brought readers together. Unquestionably, science fiction as a distinct category of literature begins with Hugo Gernsback.

The world of science fiction, as I use the term, begins with and owes a permanent debt to Gernsback.

The many books could not establish science fiction fully; they were priced out of reach of most readers and they also tended to disappear into the mainstream. To develop, science fiction had to remove itself from the usual critics who viewed it from the perspective of that mainstream, and who judged its worth largely on its mainstream values. As part of that mainstream, it would never have had the freedom to make the choices it did—many of them quite possibly wrong, but necessary for its development.

The adventure magazines offered somewhat more freedom, but there were pressures to conform even there. The readers were already asking for a large measure of romance in their science fiction; in effect, they were asking that most of it become little more than regular pulp stories laid against more exotic backgrounds. Also in the magazines, writers had to satisfy editors who were judging the stories for their exciting nature, just as they would judge any other story submitted. Plot had to supersede rationality, and science fiction needed a chance to develop more logic and less of the standard plot devices. Only after it had developed its own virtues could it afford to take up the disciplines of other fields.

Finally, the hobby magazines were no safe place for the evolution of science fiction. Generally, the readers wanted too much of the exact opposite of the requirements of the adventure magazines. There was no incentive there to use real human beings, to try fiction that might not involve gadgets, but be as validly science fiction as any technological story.

It was only when science fiction stood on its own feet, catering to its own special readers, that there was an opportunity to grow and shape itself. It was only in its own magazine that it had a chance to attract the writers who would never have the courage to dare a market like *Argosy*, where they would be competing with the best pulp writers of the day. Many of those new writers were bad—but many of them somehow contributed ideas that science fiction needed.

Critics and many writers now may cry large tears over the long period when science fiction was in "the ghetto"—more on that later—but without that fact of being apart from other fields, it would have remained just a special case of some other kind of fiction.

Before I get into the history of science fiction as it began in 1926 and evolved for fifty years, some explanations are in order.

This book is essentially a story of the evolution of science fiction in the United States. This is manifestly unfair. There was a great deal of science fiction published in Russia long before 1926. According to Willy Ley, there was even a magazine devoted exclusively to science fiction from 1903 to 1923, called *World of Adventure*. My friend John J. Pierce gave me a set of books translated from the Russian which devotes an entire volume to citing early works of science fiction. And Russian science fiction is still appearing in Russia.

However, until recently, Russian science fiction had almost no influence on the development of our modern science fiction. The language barrier and the political separation created a break that was almost leakproof. And the world of science fiction, as most of the readers outside Russia know it, developed primarily within the magazines published here. (The readers were far more international, since many of our magazines were disseminated across the globe. Hence, the feedback between readers and American magazines is actually somewhat multinational.) It was fairly late in our history before even England could find ways to publish science fiction magazines economically; most of the British influence was strongly felt, however, because their writers were published here.

Germany had a great deal of science fiction activity before Hitler began to rise. But that, through translations, has become part of our legacy. And the same is true for France and other European countries outside of the Russian sphere.

Hence, while I regret this limitation, as I regret all nationalism, I do not apologize for it, but simply accept its necessity.

Finally, before taking up the actual history, I wish to point out that the division into four historical periods or ages of twelve years each is not at all arbitrary, nor is it designed only for my convenience. As I first noticed when preparing a speech for a meeting honoring John W. Campbell for 25 years of editorship, science fiction really does divide into duo-decades. As I said then,

"The basic nature of the fiction, the type of magazines, the writers, and even the fan activities, all seem to change markedly from period to period."

This is even borne out by the number of issues in any given year. In the first period (The Age of Wonder, 1926–1937) the number of issues per year increases steadily to a peak in the fifth year. In each succeeding age, the same thing happens, except that the peak occurs regularly in the fourth year of each duodecade. (The first period doesn't deviate too radically, obviously; and that slight variation may have been caused by the fact that this period began with a partial year.)

Actually, I have no idea why the statistics are as they are. Even sun-spot cycles won't account for this pattern, since they come in eleven-year periods! Nevertheless, it seems that each age begins with mounting enthusiasm that soon peaks, then gradually declines until another age begins the cycle all over.

The ages are chosen because of many events that shape them. The first begins with the initial publication of a magazine devoted to science fiction. The second takes off from the beginning of the editorship of John W. Campbell, who radically altered the course of the category's development. The third begins with the introduction of two new magazines which broke Campbell's effective monopoly and also altered the field in many ways. The fourth age begins with a less clear demarcation, but it involves an attempt to set science fiction on a radically different course, some effects of that effort still being noticeable.

Now, if the cyclic pattern holds true, we should be into a fifth age. It is still too early to be sure whether that is the case, or whether we have finally broken the pattern. I suspect that the growing influence of books and the weakening of magazines in the field will tend to negate any radical change to a new age; publishing books is necessarily a more conservative business than issuing magazines. Hence, tentatively, I have simply attached a final chapter onto the fourth age to indicate these last few years.

Nothing is certain about the long history of science fiction, however. Hugo Gernsback had a logical and carefully planned course in mind for the literature, but events conspired to wrest control from his hands. John W. Campbell taught many fine writers to see science fiction as he saw it; then, apparently, he changed his mind in many respects. All we can do is to begin and trace the course the field has followed.

PART II

The Age of Wonder

(1926-1937)

CHAPTER 5

The Magazines of Hugo Gernsback

THE FIRST ISSUE of a magazine devoted exclusively to science fiction was the April 1926 *Amazing Stories*. Hugo Gernsback had no intention of letting it be mistaken for just another pulp publication. It was the size of a sheet of typing paper, 8½ x 11 inches; it contained 96 pages of contents, but was made to seem double that thickness by using bulkier paper. There was a colorful cover by Frank R. Paul, showing skaters on a frozen world with Saturn looming huge in the background. It featured prominently stories by Jules Verne, H. G. Wells and Edgar Allan Poe. And the price was 25¢, more than double that of most adventure magazines.

Gernsback had originally thought of calling the magazine *Scientifiction*, his choice of terms to describe the stories. But a poll of readers had been so discouraging that he resorted to a catchier title.

All the stories included were reprints of previously published ones. It wasn't until the third issue that he found new stories to include, and reprints were the chief material during the first two years of the magazine's existence.

On the contents page was a picture from the tomb of Jules Verne, showing the writer rising from his grave. Below that was the motto: "Extravagant Fiction Today—Cold Fact Tomorrow!" This was to remain as a permanent feature of the magazine under Gernsback's management.

The idea of using mostly reprint material was probably based on a number of factors. Obviously, Gernsback couldn't hope to get enough material from writers to keep the magazine on his schedule of regular monthly publication. Probably he was also reluctant to pay what new stories from known writers would have cost. And finally, by using well-known stories, he could attract the readers who had heard of them but had no chance to find them in most libraries and could not afford to buy books in those days.

Anyhow, the scheme worked. By 1927, the magazine was said to have at least 100,000 readers. The first year featured works by such writers as Wells, Verne, George Allan England, Garrett P. Serviss and Murray Leinster. Serials were used from the first issue, sometimes as many as four running at once, as in the October 1926 issue.

As Gernsback stated in his first issue, he intended to bring out stories which would not only entertain, but would also instruct about science. But there were few such stories available, and the first consideration was profit. In 1927, the magazine began printing the stories of Merritt—hardly instructive, but very popular. It also used H. P. Lovecraft's "The Color out of Space;" and among the new stories were a few by A. Hyatt Verril and Miles J. Breuer, who wrote extensively for Gernsback for several years.

In 1926, Gernsback sent out a questionnaire to his readers, asking what they would think of having the magazine issued semi-monthly. He announced that 498 readers were opposed, 32,644 were in favor of the idea. Those figures seem to be somewhat doubtful, and are probably loaded in various ways; if 3,000 responded to a questionnaire, it would be a heavy return. Certainly, Gernsback was not convinced by the results. But in 1927, he did give the readers a bonus in the form of *Amazing Stories Annual*, with more pages, for double the price. This featured a new story by Edgar Rice Burroughs, *The Mastermind of Mars*, complete in the issue. Gernsback had approached Burroughs, asking for a story with a heavier science content, and Burroughs had obliged.

There was also a new feature in the January 1927 issue. Gernsback had been amazed at the letters sent in by readers. Now he began "Discussions," a column where some of the letters could be published. He also printed the address of each correspondent, which gave readers a chance to write to each other or locate fellow fans who lived in the same area. This may have been one of the most important events in the history of science fiction.

There was no *Annual* in 1928, but Gernsback replaced it with four *Quarterlies* at 50¢ each, running to 144 pages. And the magazine was beginning to get more new stories from writers who soon became regular contributors. There were Edmond Hamilton and Jack Williamson. David H. Keller, M.D., contributed stories of psychological and sociological interest, and soon became one of the most popular authors.

August was the outstanding issue. This contained the first installment of *The Skylark of Space*, by Edward Elmer Smith, Ph.D., and Lee Hawkins Garby. (Actually, Mrs. Garby had helped only briefly at the inception of the novel.) This proved to be one of the most important novels in the development of science fiction. It is the first "space opera" in which men go outside the Solar System to meet alien races, engage in struggles, and generally reach the maximum limits of exotic adventure. There is also a strong conflict between Richard Seaton, who invents the great spaceship from which the novel draws its name, and a fascinating villain, Blacky DuQuesne, who always manages to follow Seaton and threaten him.

The story remains one of the great classics of the field, and is almost required reading for anyone who tries to understand the history of science fiction. It is, however, hardly an example of good writing. The characters are mostly stock—except for DuQuesne; conversations are incredibly stilted; and stylistically, the author achieves his effects by constant overuse of adjectives and hyperbole, and by giving exaggerated importance to every event. Still, somehow it moves—once one can adapt to the writing, it is a stirring tale of wonder, unlike anything that had gone before. (In defense of Smith's style, however, it seems to be necessary to the effect of wonder he achieved; I've tried writing it into normal form, and the story no longer works.)

This novel was begun by Smith in 1915; he finished it in 1919, and then had it rejected by every magazine and book publisher to whom he sent it.

Smith was a chemist, working for food industries, so he had a good knowledge of science, though he often disregarded that for the story. In later years, he became one of the best-beloved writers of science fiction—justifiably, since he was one of the most kindly and gracious of men to his fans and fellow writers.

In the same issue, there was another story that made history. This is "Armageddon, 2419 A.D.," by Philip Nowlan. It is the story of Anthony Rogers, who wakes up in the future in the middle of a war between the overlords from Asia who have conquered America and the American survivors of that conquest.

This became the basis for the popular comic strip, *Buck Rogers in the 25th Century*. After the story appeared, a newspaper syndicate asked Nowlan to adapt it. It appeared daily for years, drawn from scripts provided by Nowlan. Hence, the frequent claim that science fiction is "that Buck Rogers stuff" is somewhat untrue; the correct statement would be that Buck Rogers was a comics version of that science fiction stuff.

The next year, 1929, began normally. There were no outstanding stories or new discoveries in the magazine, though Philip Nowlan had a sequel to his story in the March issue. "The Airlords of Han" was as well received as the first story. (The book version contains both long novelettes under the title of *Armageddon, 2419 A.D.*) But in the Spring *Quarterly* was *After 12,000 Years*, by Stanton A. Coblentz. Coblentz had already established some reputation as a poet, and his story marked the reintroduction of satire into science fiction. It is one of the author's better novels, telling of a man who awakes in the future to find the world ruled by a race of insects.

Then disaster struck Gernsback and his Experimenter Publishing Co. It is said that this was caused by Bernarr Macfadden, who was motivated by spite when Gernsback refused to sell his magazines. Whether that is true or not, three of Gernsback's creditors suddenly filed to have him declared bankrupt in February 1929. Under New York State law, that was sufficient to have bankruptcy declared. (Eventually, Gernsback paid back all his creditors at the rate of $1.08 on the dollar, so it hardly seems his business was insolvent.)

Gernsback sold his magazines to Teck Publications. The editorship of *Amazing Stories* eventually fell to T. O'Conor Sloane, Ph.D. Sloane, who had been at least nominally editor under Gernsback, was 77 years old at the time. And while he had been an able scientist at one time, his ideas were somewhat behind the times. He repeatedly chided his readers for taking space flight seriously, for example. But the magazine continued. How much of the material used after May 1929 was bought while Gernsback controlled things is impossible to say. At the time, payment was no more than one-half cent a word. (Smith was said to have received only $75 for *Skylark!*) And since that pittance was paid only after—sometimes long after—publication, material could be held for years without incurring expense.

John W. Campbell, Jr., was the discovery of *Amazing* in January 1930. His first story, "When the Atoms

Failed," is a long novelette that assumes atomic power and goes on from there. This was followed in April with "The Metal Horde," then in June with "Piracy Preferred," about huge air transports and a pirate with the secret of invisibility and a gas that can make men unconscious, even through walls of steel. This was the beginning of the famous Arcot, Wade and Morey stories, which soon came to rival the novels of Edward E. Smith in popularity. In November, "Solarite" continued the series with a flight to Venus. And the Fall *Quarterly* had a novel-length story called *The Black Star Passes*, in which an invading world attacks Earth with strange weapons, to be overcome by the wonderful scientific inventions of the heroes.

Campbell was only nineteen when he sold his first story, and still going to college. He was majoring in science at M.I.T. (From which he flunked out because of difficulty with German, not from difficulty with the math and science courses. He finished his education at Duke University.) His stories are filled with invention followed by more inventions, all marvelously justified by the latest theories of advanced science.

May brought a story by Edmond Hamilton, *The Universe Wreckers*, a three-part serial which increased Hamilton's growing reputation. August saw the long-awaited sequel to E. E. Smith's first novel—*Skylark Three*. This goes far beyond the original and is somewhat better written, while losing none of the sweeping visions that the readers wanted. With a new and wonderful ship, Seaton flies hither and thither through the galaxy, meeting a race that is trying to conquer all others and pursued by DuQuesne, until in the end it seems that DuQuesne has met his just deserts.

The Spring *Quarterly* carried another of Campbell's epic series, *Islands of Space*. The series finished in the Spring-Summer 1932 *Quarterly* with the longest and strongest of the stories, *Invaders from the Infinite*. In this, Arcot, Wade and Morey take off into space, get into an interstellar war, go back through time, and make further inventions, including a thought amplifier. With it, Arcot can literally create anything he can imagine. The story left the readers gasping—science could go no further. By this time, Campbell and Smith were the favorite writers in the reader polls.

The advent of Neil R. Jones as a major writer of the day came in 1931. His "The Jameson Satellite" in the July 1931 *Amazing* is the first of many stories about Professor Jameson. In it, Jameson is buried in a ship in orbit around the Earth. But the cold of space preserves his brain. Millions of years later, he is discovered by a wandering race of robots, the Zoromes, who put his brain into a metal body such as they have. He takes off to explore the universe. (And he does so, in other stories that were eventually collected in five books.) In general, the stories were ahead of their time.

The major change apparent in *Amazing* under the new ownership was in the art. Most of the previous artwork inside the magazine and on the cover had been done by Frank R. Paul. Now his place was filled by Leo Morey, who had done some work for the magazine. Unfortunately, the old four-color covers were replaced with three-color reproductions. Without the black plate, there was a lack of crispness and full contrast to the covers from then on.

Paul went with Gernsback, who had not been idle. When his magazines were sold, Gernsback immediately created Stellar Publishing Company, with a replacement title for each of his former magazines. He solicited subscriptions for these; obviously, the readers had a considerable confidence in him, since he received enough orders to put him back in business.

In place of *Amazing Stories*, he planned two new magazines: *Science Wonder Stories*, to begin with the June 1929 issue; and *Air Wonder Stories*, to begin in July. "The Reader Speaks" replaced "Discussions." And as an added gesture to his readers, he began a policy of opening each story with a drawing and short biography of the author. He also planned on bringing out *Science Wonder Quarterly*.

Most of the authors were happy to have the new magazines as markets, and many showed more loyalty to Gernsback than to the original magazine.

There was a new editor for the magazines. David Lasser was a young man, much more aware of both modern trends in science and modern styles of writing. Under his aegis, the type of stories bought and the level of writing showed considerable improvement.

In many ways, however, *Science Wonder Stories* was simply a continuation of the former magazine. A few new authors began to appear with some regularity: Ed Earl Repp, Harl Vincent and Raymond Z. Gallun. The November issues saw the first two stories by Gallun, "The Space Dwellers" in *Science Wonder* and "The Crystal Ray" in *Air Wonder*. Gallun shortly became one of the better writers and contributed much to the evolution of science fiction.

The Fall 1929 *Science Wonder Quarterly* had an unusually effective cover by Paul, showing three men in spacesuits, tethered by air lines to a rocket. Scientifically, it would have been much better had the rocket not been blasting with full force, since the pressure of such acceleration would have snapped the lines immediately. But nobody seemed to mind. Inside was a short novel by Edmond Hamilton, *The Hidden World*, based on the old hollow-Earth idea, this time with strange creatures rising from inside the Earth to menace all humanity.

The feature novel, however, was a translation of Otto Willi Gail's *Der Schuß ins All*, now entitled *The Shot into Infinity*. This is perhaps the first novel to deal with a trip to the Moon in really scientific terms. Gail was fully familiar with the rocket theories of Hermann Oberth, and he followed them carefully, using a step-rocket of several stages. In this case, Gernsback had found a story with entertainment and science that was both correct and instructive. The story had a wide influence on science fiction and probably was the source of most writers' knowledge of rockets for the next two decades.

This, incidentally, was the first science fiction magazine I ever read. I'm happy to see it before me now as I write, and I can still feel some of the excitement I derived from reading Gail's story.

It turned out that *Air Wonder* was too specialized and that *Science Wonder* was somewhat discouraging to readers who thought it another magazine of science. Gernsback solved the problem by combining them as *Wonder Stories* for the June 1930 issue. Meantime, he had started *Scientific Detective Stories* in January 1930; the title was changed to *Amazing Detective Tales* in June. But the magazine only lasted ten issues, until the October issue.

In June 1930 *Wonder* ran "The Time Ray of Jandra," by Raymond A. Palmer. Palmer was a very active fan and, so far as I know, the first of the ardent fans to become a professional writer. It was an event that was later duplicated over and over by others. The next month, "The Red Plague" appeared, by P. Schuyler Miller, another fan who became an excellent writer and later ran a continuous book-review column for more years than anyone else in science fiction.

Apparently, Gernsback was having troubles with the cost of the magazine, however. In November he shifted from the large size to the standard 7 x 10–inch pulp format. But a year later, in November 1931, the large size was resumed.

December 1931 saw the first story by Clifford D. Simak, "The World of the Red Sun." And in the same issue was the beginning of *The Time Stream*, by John Taine. Taine was really Eric Temple Bell, a well-known mathematician, who wrote many quiet but forceful stories of discoveries. This novel is unique, however. It tells of the people in an almost utopian future who are threatened with rebellion. They learn to swim back through time, and to occupy other minds in various periods. And whenever they are, they take their conflicts and loves with them. It is a confusing story at times, but oddly compelling, and is still one of the great classics from the period.

CHAPTER 6

The Dawn of *Astounding*

Now LET US LEAVE GERNSBACK and the magazines that originated with him and go back a bit in time, as science fiction permits us. So far we have left the pulps and followed what grew out of the hobby magazines. But in those days, the pulps could not be dismissed.

One chain of such adventure pulps was owned by William Clayton. As such magazines went, they were above average. Authors were treated by the Clayton magazines considerably better than in most other publishing houses. A standard rate of payment was two cents a word, and payment was promptly on acceptance. Thus an author who sold a normal 5,000-word story would receive $100 within a few weeks of submission. In a period when an office worker might make $15 a week and sirloin steak sold for 30¢ a pound, that was not to be sneered at.

But to make this rate of payment profitable, Clayton had to exercise considerable ingenuity in cutting other costs. At the time being covered, he was publishing thirteen magazines. Covers, which were one of the expensive items of printing, were usually put through the press in lots of four. For economy, he needed to eliminate one magazine or add three more. It didn't make sense to cut back.

Harry Bates, an editor at Clayton Publications, tells the story in a historical note at the beginning of Alva Rogers' *A Requiem for Astounding*. According to him, Clayton suggested they add a historical-fiction magazine with a title that Bates loathed. While supposedly thinking it over, he went to a newsstand and began looking for some alternative. His eyes spied *Amazing Stories*. The next day he suggested that the magazine be science fiction, to be called *Astounding Stories of Super-Science*. Clayton liked the idea and made Bates the editor. And thus science fiction became part of a pulp chain.

Bates had a difficult time filling the magazine on the short notice he was given. He found that most science fiction writers of the day couldn't write well enough for even the standards of the pulp adventure readers. And still fewer could plot the fast-action stories he needed. He emphasized "super-science" in the title, but he wanted adventure fiction against alien backgrounds.

The first issue of *Astounding* came out January 1930. For a cover artist and illustrator, Bates had turned to H. W. Wessolowski, another artist whose work had been used by Gernsback. (Later his work was usually signed "Wesso," under which name the readers came to know him.) It is a scene of a terrified girl in the background, with a gallant hero frantically fighting off a giant beetle—the type of illustration now referred to as a BEM (bug-eyed monster) cover. It illustrated the first installment of *The Beetle Horde*, by Victor Rousseau, a writer of considerable reputation in the field. But the story is of a type that has always drawn justified sneers from outsiders. It involves a mad scientist setting loose great numbers of man-sized beetles in an attempt to destroy the world.

The rest of the contents was a sadly mixed business.

Ray Cummings had a story, and was to become a regular contributor, with numerous serials appearing in the next few years. Murray Leinster, by now, was an experienced writer both as Leinster and under his real name of Will F. Jenkins; he had sold stories to almost every type of market, but loved science fiction best. Among others whom Bates would use as regular contributors was S. P. Meek. There was also a considerable amount of fantasy in the magazine, simply because Bates couldn't get enough of what he wanted.

As time went on, Bates did build up a stable which included the above names and Harl Vincent, Sewell Peaslee Wright, Arthur J. Burks (a high-production pulp writer who could turn out stories of any kind on demand), Charles Willard Diffin and Nat Schachner. Nathan Schachner became the most prolific of all science fiction writers within a few years.

The magazine quickly began attracting a special new audience of readers who were more interested in the dramatic covers featuring human conflict than they had been in the machines so common to the other magazines. Many of them who were basically adventure readers soon became addicted to science fiction. And a large percentage of the Gernsback-type readers also joined the *Astounding* audience. The magazine was not highly profitable at the rates authors and artists were paid, but its success satisfied Clayton.

A fairly typical example of a lead story for the magazine was Nat Schachner's "Slaves of Mercury," in which a couple of men return to Earth from space and find their planet has been taken over by dreadful monsters from Mercury. Naturally, being heroes, they find a resistance movement and lead it to victory through pages of capture, hairbreadth escapes and much blood and gore. Certainly those who consider science fiction to be trashy material would feel justified on reading this story.

In February 1931, the name of the magazine was

shortened to *Astounding Stories.* (Curiously, the last two issues of the magazine to be published by Clayton reverted to the longer title.)

In that same month, the first story by a writer called Anthony Gilmore appeared. "The Tentacles from Below" was a pretty standard piece of fiction for the time. But the name of the author soon became one of the most famous to be associated with the magazine.

In November, Gilmore appeared again, this time with a long novelette entitled "Hawk Carse." The title seemed curious for this magazine, which loved such words as "brood," "spawn," "menace," and "brigands" in its titles. I remember wondering why Bates hadn't changed the title; it was quite a while before I could find that he hadn't changed it because he was responsible for it. The story sets up a hero named Hawk Carse whose job is catching dangerous criminals and who has a secret farm on Mars full of special devices, such as the spaceship in which he travels. Pitted against him is a wily Oriental villain named Ku Sui, who keeps the brains of great scientists in a container, all hooked up so that their combined mental power can provide him with the means for taking over control of the planets.

Obviously, this was a case of adapting the stories about the insidious Dr. Fu Manchu to adventure science fiction. But few of the readers commented upon this; rather they were delighted, and began asking for more from Gilmore. Perhaps many of them did recognize the similarity but didn't care. The story was better written than most, and there was considerable gusto to it.

Gilmore appeared again with Hawk Carse and Ku Sui in March 1932 to tell "The Affair of the Brains." The central part of this story, of course, revolves around Hawk Carse's attempt to free the imprisoned brains from the control of Ku Sui. As a result, he is able to get them to work with him.

May saw "The Bluff of the Hawk." And the series apparently finished with "The Passing of Ku Sui." My impression is that each story was a little better than the one that preceded it. Certainly the readers grew steadily more enthusiastic.

But the great question among readers was: "Who is Anthony Gilmore?" Readers wrote in to the letter department demanding to know the secret, but Bates would not divulge it. Ray Palmer, in one of the amateur fan magazines, warned his readers not even to try to guess—some secrets could not be divulged. In all probability, he and a few others had been let in on the secret, but sworn not to tell.

Why it was such a secret is even more mysterious. *Astounding* had an associate editor named Desmond Hall, who had written several stories, none outstanding, under his own name. Anthony Gilmore was simply a collaboration between him and the editor, Harry Bates. There was nothing underhanded in their selling to their own magazine, either. William Clayton knew the truth and was one of the biggest admirers of the stories.

The mystery surrounding the stories helped to boost the reputation of the magazine, however. If that was the intent in clouding it with mystery, Bates was good at guessing the reader reactions; but he never admitted his reason.

Years later, Bates wrote a fifth Hawk Carse story without assistance from Hall—"The Return of Hawk Carse," July 1942 *Amazing*. It was greeted with a great deal of advance enthusiasm. But time had dimmed the luster. It was no longer the right atmosphere for Hawk Carse. Obviously, however, the enchantment of the stories remained for some readers. In 1952, the four stories from *Astounding* were collected in a book entitled *Space Hawk*.

A rather curious fact is that science fiction seems to

have the power to convert professional editors. Harry Bates was no fan of the literature when he began editing *Astounding*. To him, it was not much different from any other category of fiction, except for being rather more poorly written than the examples he found in the other pulp magazines. Yet in two years, he began writing it. And for many years after he stopped being an editor, he continued to write science fiction under his own name. Some of his stories can be called classics. This same conversion happened in at least two other cases later.

In 1932, America was in the middle of what has been called the worst depression it ever suffered. Some ten million workers had lost their jobs, and many were dying of hunger. This was the period that saw the beginning of the Bonus March on Washington, since the only hope was for early payment of veterans' benefits; there was no workman's compensation or general unemployment relief then. The 20¢ an issue that *Astounding* charged was a lot of money in those days, particularly for the younger people who made up a large element of the audience for the magazine.

Yet this was only a small part of the trouble the magazine faced. I cannot discover precisely the cause, but the whole chain of magazines was suffering internal financial difficulties. It may have been that Clayton had invested in stocks—which had become comparatively worthless—or perhaps there was difficulty in securing loans needed to meet the outlays. But all the magazines owned by Clayton were operating on tight budgets. (They might have survived if Clayton had been willing to cut his rates to authors, though that seems doubtful. But this Clayton refused to do to the end. He did resort finally to paying on publication, but this was just before the final decision to stop publication.)

The first sign was the lack of a July 1932 issue. Up

until then, the magazine had maintained a regular monthly schedule. But the next issue was that of September, after which it went bimonthly.

The last issue was that of March 1933. Apparently, when the magazine was set, no one knew that it would be the final issue, since there was an announcement that the next issue would feature a new novel by Edward E. Smith with the intriguing title of *Triplanetary*.

Smith had indeed written the novel and sold it to Bates, just at the time payment was scheduled only after publication. As a result, the story was returned to him and he never enjoyed the comparatively large check he must have anticipated.

It was a complete surprise when the magazine appeared on the stands again with the October 1933 issue.

Street and Smith Publications was one of the oldest and biggest of the magazine chains at that time. They had pioneered the idea of the specialized magazine. And in 1933, they had carried this specialization so far that several of their magazines concerned the exploits of a single hero, such as *The Shadow* or *Doc Savage*. But they had no magazine of science fiction.

The closest they came was with *Doc Savage*, written at that time by Lester Dent under the house name of Kenneth Robeson. Many of the early *Doc Savage* exploits involved science fiction situations. Doc and his friends discovered a place where dinosaurs still existed, foiled villains who had incredible scientific devices, and swam under water for hours without needing to breathe by the use of a superscientific oxygen pill. But these devices were only the trimmings used to bring an element of the unique into the chasing of various villains. To the real science fiction reader, they were sometimes amusing, but they did not satisfy the craving.

Hence, when Clayton folded, Street & Smith acquired *Astounding*. It must have seemed to them that the adventure slant of the magazine suited their regular policy. They turned it over to one of their regular editors, F. Orlin Tremaine. They also acquired the services of Desmond Hall, and he served as an assistant to Tremaine for the first year of putting out *Astounding*.

The first issue was not very promising. About all that remained the same was the price of 20¢. There was a nondescript cover by some artist who was not named. There was no serial; and while a great many fans often wrote indignant letters about having to wait for succeeding installments of serials, those same fans wanted long stories with full development. Instead, there were eleven stories, and several of them were not science fiction at all, but simply not very good fantasy. About the only names most readers could recognize were those of Nat Schachner and Anthony Gilmore. The Gilmore story was "The Coffin Ship," and while perhaps the best in the issue, it had nothing to do with Hawk Carse.

The November issue was little better. Again there was the mixture of too little science fiction and too much fantasy. Jack Williamson had a rather good story, "Dead Star Station," about an old man who has never been allowed to test his great invention properly. Interestingly, its dead star has some similarity to the much later neutron stars and black holes. Murray Leinster also had a story in the issue. But his "Beyond the Sphinx's Cave" has more fantasy than science fiction in it. It deals with the idea that once upon a time the ancient gods of the Greeks were perhaps aliens from space who possessed the wondrous weapons that made them seem godlike. Even then, this idea was hoary with age.

Probably the most appealing thing in the issue was a page announcing a forthcoming story. In large, heavily leaded type, it announced: "The Next Issue of Astounding Stories WILL CONTAIN a story that will awaken MORE CONTROVERSY than any story ever published in a SCIENCE FICTION MAGAZINE." The story was to be "Ancestral Voices," by Nat Schachner.

When the December issue appeared, it did indeed represent a great improvement. There was a serial by Charles Willard Diffin—not too good a one, but definitely science fiction, with an alien menace to be conquered. There were several other stories that were clearly science fiction, and only two that could be called fantasy. And then there was the story by Schachner, the first of what Tremaine called "thought variants."

"Ancestral Voices" turned out to be an interesting story as far as its premise was concerned, and was generally praised by the readers. Looking back on it, however, it doesn't stand up well. It deals with the old paradox of time travel: What happens if a man goes back and kills his own grandfather? Schachner sends his hero back into the remote past, where he does indeed kill his grandfather. The result is that the hero disappears, along with all the other descendants of the man. And the promised shock that was supposed to cause so much controversy is the fact that those descendants represent not only whites, but blacks and every other race, occupation, class, and so on.

The story does not, however, resolve the paradox upon which it is based. If the man goes back in time and kills his grandfather then he can not have been born—but if he has never been born and does not exist, then he can not kill his grandfather; therefore, his grandfather is not killed, and the man does exist, to go back and . . . Round and round it goes. Later, science fiction learned to fudge the paradox by supposing alternate time tracks, so that he was born on one track, but crossed over in going back so that he killed his grandfather on another track. Another answer sometimes suggested is that his grandmother may have been cheating a bit on his grandfather; but that's also story cheating. As with any true paradox, there is no logical solution—unless one rules out all time travel, which is probably the logical approach. That would make a lot of good science fiction impossible, however.

Anyhow, *Astounding* was back in favor with the readers, who were now content to wait for the further improvements which the editor promised them.

CHAPTER 7

The Crucial Years

ASIDE FROM *Astounding*, the magazines were in trouble. The Great Depression was lasting far longer than anyone had feared, despite Roosevelt's efforts to patch things up. The economy had begun to stabilize at a level of depression that might have been bearable if there had been any end in sight. About the only sign of good humor left seemed to be the slogans that pleaded, "Prosperity, come home—all is forgiven!" Most people no longer thought of a glorious future.

There was little specific evidence of trouble for the magazines, yet. But *Amazing* abandoned cover paintings for several months in 1933, then skipped an issue, combining August with September 1933. In October, for the first time, it went to the smaller size of other pulp magazines; it never went back to the larger format. *Wonder* also resumed the smaller size in November 1933. It also abandoned cover paintings, reduced the number of pages, and tried other experiments that failed to work. The last *Wonder Stories Quarterly* was Winter 1933; *Amazing Stories Quarterly* limped along until the Fall 1934 number.

Probably most of the trouble at *Amazing* came from the uninspired editing of T. O'Conor Sloane, who was now over eighty years old.

The stories he published were mostly mediocre at best, and some caused considerable complaint. When Joseph W. Skidmore wrote "The Romance of Posi and Nega," published September 1932, it might have been considered amusing. This is a love affair between Posi, the positron or nucleus of an atom, and Nega, the negative electron circling it. Skidmore's science was long out of date, since no scientist really believed in the simple solar-system type of atom. The neutron had been discovered in 1931, but this was completely overlooked. And the story is mostly endless talk—since, obviously, nothing can really happen. Posi, in his stock masculine superiority, lectures Nega endlessly about atoms and space from his misconceptions. And Nega goes all coy and feminine, in a rather dripping sort of cuteness. It should never have seen print. But all right, that was only one story.

Only it was more! It turned out to be a series. They appeared again in January 1934 in "Adventures"; January 1935 in "An Epic"; and then went on later in 1935 for "A Saga" in May and "A Legend" in October.

In the November 1934 issue, another story set a new low. This is "The Moon Waits," by L. L. G. Sullivan. It involves a great tube built between Earth and the Moon. That solves all the difficulties of space travel, because men can ride up and down it by means of compressed air.

Hundreds of readers wrote the editor, pointing out that the story was totally ridiculous. The only way such a tube could be built that way would be by having the Moon stand still over one spot on the Earth, and then finding a way to keep the Earth from rotating! Also, of course, the compressed-air idea wouldn't work; the pressures required would be so high that nobody could exist in the tube, even if the tube could stand such pressures. Sloane admitted that the story wasn't quite scientific, but replied that it had seemed such an interesting idea that he felt it deserved publication.

(Years later, another writer of high skill and reputation wrote about spiders spinning webs between Earth and the Moon; but at least that wasn't supposed to be scientific, and it appeared in a magazine that mixed real fantasy with its science fiction.)

For a time, *Amazing* got by mostly on the stories by Campbell and Smith. John W. Campbell had three short serials appearing between March 1933 and November 1936. One of these is an exceptionally good example of his ability to start with one assumption about physics and build a whole catalogue of wonders from that. This is *The Mother World,* or *The Contest (Conquest) of the Planets;* the title went through strange changes from installment to installment during its appearance in 1935.

Edward E. Smith sold *Triplanetary* to *Amazing* after its return to him, and it began in January 1934. This was the beginning of the ideas that eventually were to appear in his "Lensman" stories, and it is one of his best-written novels to that date.

Little else of real merit appeared, and even the faithful began to desert *Amazing.* In August 1935, it went bimonthly, a schedule which it maintained for the remainder of Teck's ownership. Shortly before the April 1938 issue appeared, Teck Publications went out of business.

Wonder Stories did well with stories in 1933. There were two series in that year that were greatly liked by the readers. At that time, there was a good deal of discussion about something called Technocracy—a sort of political idea which included the claim that only engineers should be permitted to govern, because only they knew enough about the modern world. Nat Schachner seized on the idea for a series of stories. "The Revolt of the Scientists" began in April 1933, followed immediately by "The Great Oil War" and "The Final Triumph." Reader response was excellent.

In March 1933, Laurence Manning began another series about a man who awakes from suspended animation only at long intervals to explore the world. "The Man Who Awoke" tells of a civilization based on forests after twentieth-century man has depleted and polluted the Earth. (It still reads like good prophecy.) Each time he awakes, he finds radical changes, until in "The Elixir," in the August issue, he finally finds a society which seems to offer hope for the future. The stories were collected in 1975 to make a paperback book, entitled *The Man Who Awoke*; after slight editing, they read well now. Manning was a thoughtful, careful writer who did far too little fiction.

In November 1933, Gernsback replaced David Lasser with a new editor. A young fan named Charles Hornig had been publishing a fan magazine, *The Fantasy Fan*, which Gernsback liked so much that he called the young publisher in to edit *Wonder*. Hornig was just seventeen.

The result was not good, though how much blame attaches to Hornig is hard to discover. He later claimed that Gernsback insisted on passing on all stories. In any event, the policy for stories to be bought altered quickly to encourage those with cute or slight ideas, and the level of contents fell quickly. Richard Vaughan's serial, *Exile of the Skies*, was one of the best space adventures of the period; but since it began with the January 1934 issue, it must have been one purchased by Lasser. There were a few other bright moments, such as *The Green Man of Graypec*, a serial by Festus Pragnell that began July 1935. But generally, the quality declined.

There was one outstanding exception to this. July 1934 had a story that is still considered a classic, "A Martian Odyssey," by a new writer named Stanley G. Weinbaum. This was followed in November by an equally good sequel, "Valley of Dreams." Together, the stories tell of the strange life found by the first expedition to Mars. These are truly alien creatures, and among them is an intelligent birdlike creature named Tweel, apparently part animal, part vegetable, but certainly one of the most appealing aliens ever described. Weinbaum's aliens are like none ever before seen in science fiction, and his writing is far better than the average then. These two stories were enough to establish him immediately at the top of the list of favorite writers.

But other stories were rather dreary. One set tells of a race of huge-headed, puny people who are totally decadent and selfish. But in the end, everything changes for the better when they finally discover a forgotten plant and learn to brew coffee!

With the November 1935 issue, *Wonder* went bimonthly. Its final issue under Gernsback was the March–April 1936 one.

The magazine was then sold to Standard Magazines, a chain which called all their publications thrilling. Hence, *Thrilling Wonder Stories* appeared in August 1936. It was now edited by Mortimer Weisinger, a long-time active science fiction fan.

The magazine was no longer the same. It was deliberately slanted to a lower age group, far more frankly designed to use action stories than *Astounding* had ever been, and it included a comic strip inside it. The comic insert was soon dropped, but it had already helped to give the magazine a bad reputation with the older readers.

Weisinger did his job well, within the limits imposed on him, and the magazine continued its bimonthly publication with considerable success in appealing to the readers for whom it was intended.

Over at *Astounding*, things were going in quite another direction, as 1934 proved to be a banner year, one of the most impressive in the history of the magazine. Tremaine's editorial skill and his demand for new ideas—thought variants—combined to bring new life to the magazine. There was no more fantasy. The covers were turned over to Howard V. Brown—another of the artists who had previously done work for Hugo Gernsback—and he produced a steady stream of really excellent ones.

January featured "Colossus," by Donald Wandrei. This is the story of a man who builds a device that can reach unthinkable velocity. But as his speed increases, he also expands greatly in size. At the end, he bursts through our cosmos into another in which our entire universe is only a single atom. The story was brilliantly done to hold the reader spellbound, and it won great approval. Many readers knew that Wandrei had completely reversed the relativistic formula; it's true that mass increases with velocity, but size does not—in fact, length shortens as mass increases. Still, the story was impressive and much-praised.

The same issue held a story by Nat Schachner that showed how well he could write when not pressed. This was "Red Mask of the Outlands," which tells of an unusual autocratic state and the scamp-hero who rebels against it. Even then it was not a fresh theme, but Schachner made it seem so. Of all his stories, this has remained one of my favorites.

February began *Rebirth*, a serial by Thomas Calvert McClary, who was a top writer in the adventure field. Its theme is that all mankind is put to sleep; when they awaken, all have lost their memories. The story is about the way they slowly recover the knowledge needed to attain a better civilization.

In March, *Astounding* increased its size from 144 to 160 pages with no increase in price. That month Jack Williamson had "Born of the Sun," in which the sun hatches into a winged creature of fire.

April was a splendid month for the reader. Harry Bates appeared with "A Matter of Size"—one of the best stories ever written of shrinking men down to tiny stature. Jack Williamson began a six-part serial, *The Legion of Space*, which was hailed as an outstanding example of space opera. It deals with a gallant trip across space to a horrible alien world, to save the one secret that mankind needs to survive. The trip across the alien planet is gripping. And the comic-sympathetic picture of Giles Habibula as fearful spaceman and partly reformed thief is one no reader seems to forget.

To add to everything, there was the first section of Charles Fort's *Lo!* Fort was an iconoclast who sought every bit of evidence that might upset all the standard beliefs of science. He collected his findings into four books: *The Book of the Damned, New Lands, Wild Talents* and *Lo!* Material from these books has been a source for a number of science fiction stories. The books make excellent reading, even if one rejects the theories Fort throws in—as Fort urges the reader to do!

June saw Murray Leinster's "Sidewise in Time," the first story in the magazines to suggest the idea that the past must have branched into multiple, parallel presents as a result of decisions which could go either way.

August brought Edward E. Smith's long-awaited *Skylark of Valeron*, which outdid anything Smith had tried before, as well as finding what seemed a final solution to the problem of DuQuesne. The story was illustrated by a new artist, Elliott Dold, who became the regular interior artist, and whose strong black linework was different from anything done before in science fiction.

Dold had previously illustrated a magazine of which he was the editor. This was *Miracle Science and Fantasy Stories*, which lasted for only two issues, April–May and June–July 1931.

Astounding also changed its type style and format to give the readers an extra 25,000 words in each issue. It was now not only the cheapest but also the largest magazine in terms of content.

October had "Bright Illusion," by C. L. Moore.

Catherine Moore had previously done work for *Weird Tales*, some of which had a strong science fiction element. This story is really fantasy. A man stumbles on an alternate world, where he meets a girl with whom he falls in love; but then he discovers she is masked by illusion and is indescribably alien. Their fate, before the strange god of the alien world, is unforgettable.

In November, there was "Twilight," the first story by Don A. Stuart, which was then remarkable for its mood and atmosphere. This is the sad, haunting story of a man who has visited the far future and seen its bitter end. The identity of the writer was held a deep secret, but finally he was revealed to be John W. Campbell—the man who wrote all the hard-science stories that totally lacked mood! Campbell told me that he found his model in the first chapter of *The Red Gods Call*, a rather routine adventure novel with a powerful first scene. Be that as it may, Stuart went on to do all the things for which Campbell was not noted.

In December, Raymond Z. Gallun had "Old Faithful," another story like nothing the readers expected. This tells of a Martian scientist whose desire for knowledge drives him to desert his own world and find a means to journey to Earth. The trip kills him—but he dies happy as he studies the human beings before him. In spots there is some crudity to the writing, but the story hit the readers with unusual emotional power.

In the same issue, John W. Campbell's *The Mightiest Machine* began, another of the hard-science space novels. In this one, the heroes burst out of our universe into another, where they find an eon-long war going on between humans and creatures resembling satyrs. It involves enormous space fleets, worlds being moved, and everything the space opera buff can want. In my opinion, it is the best of this type of story; it is also the last where technology transcends everything else. (The issue also contained "Atomic Power," by Don A.

Stuart and "The Irrelevant," by Karl van Campen—both stories really by Campbell.)

Tremaine could never quite equal the wonders of 1934 after that. But 1935 was a highly successful year. None of the stories stood out quite so strongly as those of 1934, but the average remained very high in comparison to anything that had been done earlier.

His first move was to obtain the stories of Stanley G. Weinbaum. Starting with January, seven of Weinbaum's stories were published during 1935. None was quite as good as "A Martian Odyssey," but any one of them could be considered unusually good. Don A. Stuart had six stories during the year. By now, under his two names, Campbell was acclaimed as the two best writers for the magazine. And in March, Murray Leinster had "Proxima Centauri," which tells of a generation-long flight to another star, with mutiny coming from boredom. This is the first example in the magazines of a closed-cycle spaceship in which a voyage can last hundreds of years, with generations growing up inside the ship.

Weinbaum died of cancer in December 1935, at the age of thirty-three, cutting short the most promising career of any science-fiction writer. But Tremaine still had a few of his stories to publish in 1936. He also published H. P. Lovecraft's *At the Mountains of Madness*, beginning in February 1936, and "The Shadow out of Time" in June—two of the most detailed stories of the Cthulhu Mythos; this is a weird-horror cycle, but with considerable science-fiction material. And John W. Campbell began "A Study of the Solar System"—a series of eighteen articles, which set the precedent for the later use of science articles in the magazines.

During the year, *Astounding* also made a surprising concession to the wishes of the readers. For a long time, letters had been protesting the uneven edges which made the magazine appear messy and also made turning the pages difficult. These appeals for trimmed edges had been brushed aside casually on the grounds that trimming would increase the cost too much. In February, Street and Smith gave in, with no prior fanfare such as might have been expected. From then on, the edges were neatly trimmed.

Though there were few outstanding accomplishments in 1937, it was another good year. Wesso returned to take over some of the covers, doing a much better job than previously. In March, Willy Ley began the first of many articles with a survey of developments toward space travel. Ley had fled Germany, disgusted with the behavior of the Nazis. But he already had a superb command of English, though he always retained a strong accent.

Two of Don A. Stuart's best stories were published during 1937. "Forgetfulness" appeared in June. This is the story of a great spaceship that comes to Rth in the far future. Once, long before, the men of Rth had visited the alien planet and set them upon the road to technological civilization. They find the men of Rth now to be only simple, pastoral people, with none of the legendary greatness. At their request, they are shown an ancient museum that still contains working machinery. But when they ask how it works, the answer is always that the Rthmen have forgotten. They are filled with pity and plan to save these poor descendants of the great race by taking them over and working with them. But in the end, they discover that the men of Rth have forgotten only because they no longer need crude machinery; they are an adult race and have put the devices of childhood behind them, as the aliens find to their consternation. To me, this novelette manages to condense all the dreams of science fiction into one story with great effect.

"Out of Night," in October, is another story of an alien race that has taken control of Earth, some four thousand years before. But the ancient Sarn Mother is a splendid ruler, and her conflict with the rebels among the Earthmen bears little resemblance to most other such tales.

Then, in September, F. Orlin Tremaine ceased to edit *Astounding*. He remained as a supervisory editor, but the real task was to go to another man.

The man selected as editor was John W. Campbell. And the next age of science fiction belongs to him.

CHAPTER 8

The Active Fan

THE FIRST TWELVE YEARS saw a great deal of activity on the part of the devoted readers, or fans, but during most of that time there was little effort made to organize them. Only the beginnings of what fandom later became was achieved. Yet even before they were organized, the fans were a significant part of the world of science fiction, and nobody was more aware of that than Hugo Gernsback. At various times, he offered prizes and some form of honor to the readers who were most active.

But no great incentive was needed. Science fiction seems to have a tendency to encourage a fair number of its readers to become somewhat fanatic on the subject, and most other readers show more enthusiasm for the field than they do for any other interest that takes so little direct attention on their part.

The real beginnings of active fandom came with the introduction of a letter column in *Amazing Stories*. It gave the readers a chance to be heard—and to see proof in the printed letters that the things they wrote would actually be read by the editors. The comments they made on the stories—and those were frequent and vigorous—turned out to be important to the authors. (Usually, authors of magazine stories get no word, aside from a check or rejection slip; occasionally they may meet someone who comments on a story they have written, but such personal remarks are apt to be tempered. In the magazines, uninfluenced by direct confrontation with the authors, the fans felt quite free to state their opinions in no uncertain terms.)

I know by my own experience and the comments of other writers that such a collection of reader criticism does influence the authors. Aside from remarks about the author's own stories, the comments on other stories often show what type of fiction gets the best reaction, and can help writers to determine their choice of later ideas or ways of presenting them. For some reason, science fiction fans tend to be less polite than others in such letters, which makes their comments far more valuable.

The letter columns also gave the fans a sense of their importance, and made them far more active. Any writer of letters who actually saw his words in print became much more deeply involved with science fiction.

Since the addresses were usually printed together with the names of the writers, other fans were encouraged to write to the man who had his letter published. In some areas, such as the larger cities, the addresses made it possible for fans to find friends with similar interests. This was the original nucleus of organized fandom.

I found, during the period around 1935 when I was what is called a letterhack, that I received quite a few letters from other readers. And one of my oldest friends, Milton Rothman—who was a prominent fan at the time—met me because of seeing my letters.

There is an impression that such fans are usually maladjusted, introverted youngsters. (Some of those "youngsters" were in their sixties!) There is probably some truth in that idea. Withdrawn people are more likely to turn to fiction as a replacement for the social life they do not have. On the other hand, anyone who loves reading enough to devote a considerable amount of attention to it simply doesn't have as much time for minor socializing as one who reads very little. Which is cause and which effect is sometimes hard to determine.

I've known a fair number of fans who do not seem to have had any serious social problems or maladjustments. A few have even been active in sports and outdoor affairs.

A poll made in the late thirties indicated that the average age of the fans was twenty. The "average" fan was supposed to be white, male, and probably somewhat more intelligent than the general level of the population, though hardly the genius he liked to believe himself. This would be changed considerably today, but at the time there were very few blacks or women in fandom. Another poll indicated that there were not more than a few hundred really active fans. This may also have been true, though the number is considerably greater now. If so, that small number had an influence far greater than they were entitled to, though the results of that influence were generally good.

A rather large percent of the writers were themselves fans. Usually, their letters to the editor did not get published, because they were professional. But when a story was particularly good, the editor usually received considerable mail from the other writers. And a great many writers numbered fans among their closest friends.

Hugo Gernsback helped to encourage the tendency of the fans to organize into groups. In 1934, he used the pages of *Wonder Stories* to begin something called the Science Fiction League. Paul drew up an emblem, and there were to be chapters in the cities and corresponding chapters for those who were isolated. Of course it was intended to increase the reader loyalty to his magazine and probably to help boost his circulation. One of the ideas behind the League was that the fans should do everything they could to promote science fiction.

There was a surprising response to the idea. Quite a few chapters of the League were founded and began regular meetings, while soliciting more members through the pages that Gernsback kept open for League activities. Most of the groups fell apart in a year or so —but some continued in existence long enough to turn into fan clubs that lasted for decades. Long after the League had become no more than a memory, the organizing impetus it gave to fandom continued—in fact, it has never ceased.

Today, the emblem of the League is still in use. A group of readers who were active during the first twelve years is now called First Fandom, with the old League emblem appearing on their stationery and on badges and neckties the members wear. The members meet at world conventions and at a couple of other science fiction get-togethers. They give an award each year to some old-time writer or editor who has endeared himself to them. And they still talk chiefly about science fiction. Most of them would happily admit that science fiction has been a good influence on their lives.

The names of some of the early fans rank high among the science fiction professionals of today. A number became writers: Frederik Pohl, Robert Bloch, James Blish and Damon Knight among others. Some turned to editing: Charles Hornig, Mortimer Weisinger, Ray Palmer, Frederik Pohl (again), Donald Wollheim, Robert Lowndes, Sam Moskowitz—and in England, Walter Gillings and the late Ted Carnell. These are only the names that come easily to mind.

By 1932, there was even a printed fan magazine devoted to the world of science fiction. It included (together with the inevitable notice about delayed publication!) news about authors, brief biographies, a history of science fiction, book reviews, news about future stories in the magazines, a readers' column, and even advertisements. This was *The Time Traveller*, edited by Allen Glasser with the help of Mortimer Weisinger, Julius Schwartz and Forrest J. Ackerman, who is often referred to today as Mr. Fandom himself. It was supposed to be monthly, and sold for 10¢ an issue or $1 per year. The circulation must have been less than 200, so it obviously ran at a loss, being intended as both a hobby and a way of promoting science fiction. At the time, it was listed as "Science Fiction's Only Fan Magazine."

In September 1932, *Science Fiction Digest* appeared, with Maurice Z. Ingher as editor. Weisinger and Schwartz were now joined by Raymond A. Palmer as associate or managing editors. This publication had a set of departments somewhat similar to those of *The Time Traveller*. But one of the more interesting bits was a column speculating on just who Anthony Gilmore might be. The closest guess was Harry Bates and Arthur J. Burks. But this was eliminated because Burks had denied it.

After sixteen issues, the *Digest* was changed to *Fantasy Magazine* and continued until 1937. It was edited by Julius Schwartz, with Palmer as literary editor and Ackerman as "scientifilm editor." The issue I have before me is the Fourth Anniversary one. The paper is yellow with age, but the magazine still impresses me with the amount of material it contains and the work that must have gone into preparing it.

There was also an increasing number of little fan magazines (the term fanzine had not yet been coined) which were put out by readers who did not have access to the editors for news and could never hope to afford to have their publications printed. These were often done on a hektograph; a few were mimeographed, but they were rare at first. They might have a circulation of ten to thirty, and were intended to give the "publisher" a forum to express his opinions about science fiction and perhaps offer his friends a similar opportunity.

Many of these were designed to be exchanged with other fans who put out similar publications.

Inevitably, the idea of sending them to one address from which they could be mailed to each member arose. Such amateur press associations were not uncommon in other fields. H. P. Lovecraft spent a considerable amount of time writing and publishing *The Conservative* for a literary amateur press association.

A survey in 1937 showed that there were about 30 such publishers, whose usual circulation ran from 20 to 35 copies. Some of these agreed to join together to form the Fantasy Amateur Press Association, or FAPA for short. Thus each member would get all the publications, and each would have a chance to reach every other member with his bulletin. There was a great deal of variation in what was considered a publication; in some cases, a single sheet of paper would suffice, while more ambitious members might run off twenty pages of copy for a mailing.

In time, this became so popular that there was a waiting list for membership. (Membership was limited to a number that made convenient mailings possible. Collating any mailing was itself a major task.) Eventually, there were several such APAs.

Science fiction was the central subject of FAPA—at least for some years. But other topics were freely discussed, from politics to music, Freud and Ezra Pound. And there were many hot arguments exchanged, with each side trying to outmaneuver the other verbally. The waiting time between mailings gave plenty of opportunity to think up new arguments and marshal them into the best form for presentation.

Much of this had no direct effect on science fiction. But quite a few members got their first experience at putting their ideas into print in this manner. It was probably a good training ground for those who later got into real editing and writing. Certainly James Blish thought so, and he remained active in at least one APA for many years after he was an established writer.

A more restricted activity was that of collecting. Most readers who discovered science fiction magazines after they had already been publishing for some time tried to obtain earlier issues. (I didn't start reading the magazines regularly until 1931. But I was soon haunting the used-magazine stores in search of all that I had missed.) From there, it was only a short step to wanting the older books that were mentioned from time to time in the letter columns. And some fans began trying to obtain everything that had ever been printed which could be called science fiction.

If they began such active collecting during the first age of science fiction, they were lucky. Back issues could often be found at less than half the original price. Even the rare ones could usually be purchased for no more than $1 each. And since no dealers were looking for science fiction, used-book stores might have the desired volumes among the miscellaneous oddities which sold for 10¢ a copy. That contrasts oddly with the prices now being asked.

Forrest J. Ackerman is one of the fans who has an enormous collection. He recently was forced to move into a new home to house it safely. Oswald Train is another fan with such a collection. And there are many more. It is through the efforts of such fan activity that a full record of science fiction will be preserved. (Ackerman plans to leave his collection to a university, I understand. It should be invaluable for future students.)

Most activities of present-day science fiction fandom

were going on, even in this early period. There were no "world science fiction conventions," yet. But there were signs already that such might come.

A number of New York fans took a bus to Philadelphia to meet with a group of fans there in 1937. The meeting lasted only one day, but during the course of it suggestions were made to hold larger meetings in the future. When the first convention actually was held a couple of years later, the fans who made the trip were among those instrumental in organizing it.

The local clubs were only getting started. One of the oldest was the Philadelphia Science Fantasy Society, which was founded in 1935. Another informal club met in Milwaukee, but this was composed mostly of professionals—Weinbaum, Ralph Milne Farley, Robert Bloch and Raymond Palmer. Los Angeles had one that began as a chapter of the Science Fiction League but remained in existence after the League became nonexistent.

But the one that attracted most attention was the Futurians, a group of New York fans and a few from nearby. This was not exactly a club. Rather than meeting at some regular interval, the members were constantly in touch with each other. Most of them had belonged to the League, but difficulties arose about that. Somehow, difficulties always arose in any group of New York fans who formed anything like a club, or between competing clubs. Some of the squabbles made a large part of the written history of fan activities.

Sam Moskowitz in 1954 brought out a book, *The Immortal Storm*, which covers the 1930 to 1939 period. It is a record of feuding, organizing, counterorganizing, and general turmoil.

In the matter of the League, something typical happened. A number of fans, with Donald A. Wollheim as the leading one, were kicked out of the League by Gernsback for their activities—one of which seems to have been the organizing of a rival to the League. The petty squabble took on the nature of a major upset in all fandom if one judges by the severity of Gernsback's reactions and the countless manifestoes that circulated at the time.

Part of the trouble lay in the fact that politics somehow got mixed up in fan affairs in New York. This was a time when a large percentage of the young men of the nation were severely discontented with the lingering depression and the government's apparent inability to do anything about it. Few actually became communists, but many felt strong sympathies for a movement that seemed to preach brotherhood, propose solutions, and endorse all that was good in theory. Quite a few college students at the time joined the YCL—the Young Communist League.

Some of the Futurians were strongly leftist in their beliefs. Others—or at least, others associated with them—had the typical American fear of anything that smacked of being "red." They carried their beliefs over into their opinions of what science fiction should be and how clubs should be organized, and there was a fairly constant struggle for power among many of the New York fans. Most of the old feuds are long since dead, and previous enemies are now good friends. But it was a bitter blow to the idea that all science fiction fans are true brothers together!

In the long run, the Futurians made their mark on science fiction—not as a club, but through the efforts of the members. Many of them became some of the leading editors and writers in the years to come.

And somehow, despite all the eruptions of furor, most of science fiction fandom went on growing and becoming more active.

CHAPTER 9

The Shaping of the Future

THE MOST IMPORTANT aspect of the first period of science fiction was the rapidity of its evolution.

Certainly the stories that were representative of the best to appear in *Astounding Stories* under the editorship of Tremaine were often unlike those in Hugo Gernsback's early issues of *Amazing Stories*. "Twilight," one of the most popular stories of 1934, would have seemed pure heresy much earlier; C. L. Moore's "The Bright Illusion" would have been rejected as a wild mixture of fantasy and nonsense. On the other hand, such gadget stories as Bob Olson's various "fourth-dimensional" efforts, which were once popular in *Amazing*, would have seemed totally unacceptable to the readers of 1937; they were stories of mere gadgets, based on a misunderstanding of the laws of mechanics and whatever rules could be derived for any physical fourth dimension.

This rapid evolution could not have occurred without the appearance of the specialized magazines. To those who bewail the past "ghettoization" of science fiction, I suggest that the present general acceptance of the literature would have been impossible without such a past.

Previously, for those capable of discovering them, there had been scattered stories that might be called science fiction, printed as books with no distinguishing label to set them apart from other, more conventional novels, or appearing as shorter works that were buried among conventional stories in general magazines. But to the reader who desired such literature, science fiction could only be found by a great deal of time and patience spent in browsing through material that did not interest him.

The appearance of magazines wholly devoted to this literature brought it within the immediate reach of any reader who cared to look over the magazine racks. And many who had not known of their desire for such stories discovered them through the gaudy covers that caught their attention.

Writers also found a ready market to which they could direct their writing. (Not a very good market at first, even as pulp markets went. But still a godsend to those who were not interested in doing other fiction, but were properly hesitant about aiming for the few slots for their work in general magazines, or in doing books that might be rejected for their subject matter.)

Above all, the magazines provided a ready market for a great many short stories. The demands of this market were not so great as to frighten even writers unsure of their skills. Editors could take a chance on a story which might fail in one respect, but seem to succeed in another. If the readers didn't like that story, there were still many others, so its publication did not spell disaster to any given issue. The short story has always been the natural training ground for new writers. They could learn faster by doing many 5,000-word stories than by writing a few novels. And editors could afford to request rewrites and make suggestions when a story wasn't quite right but seemed promising.

Of course, many more stories could appear in short form during any period of time than if only novels were considered. And this larger number made for much faster evolution.

In a sense, this was a program of inbreeding—a

method often used by plant and animal breeders to speed development. A single interest was gathered in one place, and those possessing it were exposed to each other. Each writer was constantly exposed to the work of every other one. Many ideas were tossed into the hamper, and some of them were quickly seized on by other writers for further development. Other ideas were quickly abandoned—losing their novelty or proving unsuitable for other reasons.

This was a form of feedback among writers, and it proved very influential on the field. There was also a strong feedback between writers and readers, both through the letter columns and through personal contacts. There was no long wait for critical comments that seldom came from established critics and reviewers. As soon as a story appeared, enthusiastic comments —both pro and con—began to flood into the editor's office. The magazines were a sort of link that made the connection between writer and reader (who might well be another writer).

It was as if the first life had crawled out of the sea of normal fiction and found a whole continent waiting to be taken over by science fiction that must adapt to fill all the ecological niches. In another way, it was like the early days of radio, when the hobbyists discovered it and "ghettoized" themselves into carrying this new technology far beyond what the technically trained had foreseen.

It was a time for enthusiasts to take over a field. Readers and writers became almost fanatic. And the result was the fastest evolution that ever affected any type of literature, so far as I can determine.

That was fortunate, since science fiction needed to evolve rapidly if it was to survive.

In the first few years of magazine science fiction, many of the stories were crude, at best. Few established writers could waste their time on work which promised so little reward. This left the field open to new writers. And even the more skilled authors who did try science fiction found serious problems in dealing with the fiction.

There was a tendency to slight the necessary background or to stuff it into huge expository passages that stopped the story. In some cases, this was done by having one character turn to another and begin explaining a machine that both characters had grown up with in that future. Or others might discuss a whole history of something which they would have taken for granted; it was as if a modern man were to tell the whole history of the auto before beginning a trip. The easy way around these troubles with background was to lay the story in the near future, but the readers wanted further vision.

Somehow, bit by bit, methods were discovered for dealing with the problems of background and development necessary for a story laid in some alien culture or strange future. No one writer found the answer. But many contributed some part of it, and later writers absorbed the tricks as they read the successful stories. Eventually, the better writers were able to develop a complicated background in a short story without stopping the story or seeming to orate.

This was a skill that had never been developed to any great extent in the mainstream or most other fiction, simply because there was no need for it; such fiction generally shared a common background with which the readers were familiar.

In science fiction, Gresham's law about money did not apply by analogy; in the long run, good writing tended to drive out the bad. Part of this tendency was again due to the fact that there was a strong participation of the readers in shaping the fiction—and one demonstrated constantly in the letters to the editor. Most of the writers who appeared at the beginning of the age of wonder were selling few stories at the end. Their type of writing had been replaced by writing that was at least considerably better.

There was another factor leading to improvement. At the beginning, there was very little accepted background for the ideas and devices needed to make fiction about the future work. Each writer tended to be limited by what he personally knew or could devise. But in time, a familiarity with many other men's ideas emerged—a sharing of useful background. One story could build upon something in another, and a bit of useful thought could be shared in many other stories where it applied. The details of space flight no longer had to be developed separately by each writer who wanted to go to another planet.

When Edward E. Smith broke through the barrier that had kept the stories confined to the Solar System, many other writers seized on the possibilities suggested. When Weinbaum rejected the alien monsters or too-human aliens from other planets, he made the other writers realize how bad their previous conceptions had been.

In 1931, John Campbell had Arcot, Wade and Morey travel to other suns, to find human beings almost like themselves with whom they instantly allied against evil alien monsters. But in 1937, as Don A. Stuart, he made his invading Sarn completely alien in form, but highly sympathetic to the reader—and he gave them a psychology which was neither human nor that of evil monsters.

A number of devices and conventions were adopted because they were necessary to avoid holding up everything in a story while time passed or an explanation could be found. Thus, special relativity makes flight at the speed of light or greater impossible. (Despite the fact that this was well known by science in 1926, it took quite a while before most writers became aware of it.) That meant that a writer must either allow for decades or centuries of travel to reach another star—or he must find some way around the limitation on velocity.

In early stories, considerable space was devoted to explain how rapid travel between stars was possible. Most of the methods boiled down to one, however: if faster-than-light travel through space was impossible, men had to find some kind of space where that rule didn't apply. Eventually, this was simply called hyperspace and became a conventional device used by most writers. The readers quickly accepted it, because the explanation for it all had been flanged up in previous stories. And writers were freed to concentrate more on care in writing and less on devising trickery.

As some of the crudity of too many early stories was abandoned, the fiction became more accessible to readers who appreciated better writing—something that didn't seem to matter to most gadgeteers or very young readers in the past. Many of the more critical readers began to read and like science fiction, and some began writing it, bringing a further improvement in style.

Characterization improved considerably, too. Readers grew tired of mad scientists, helpless females who always had to be rescued, or heroes who acted without thinking. They objected to having aliens used simply as villains about to conquer Earth, pure evil without motive. They wrote long letters to let the writers know of their feelings.

The improvement was also partly due to the fact that the literature became popular enough to be taken up by regular publishers and turned over to editors who had experience with other fiction. They demanded stories that came closer to meeting at least normal pulp standards. Harry Bates appreciated the wealth of ideas in science fiction, but was shocked by the writing and wooden characterization. F. Orlin Tremaine was also a professional editor. Both men demanded better fiction technique—and since they paid best, the field came around to their standards.

A reader who picks up several magazines from the early years may find a few excellent stories (as several critics who once denied this have recently discovered). He will find quite a few ideas that are interesting, in themselves. But too many of the stories will seem nearly unreadable.

But the stories published from 1934 to 1937 are often quite different. Many of these are still being anthologized and admired today. There are still too many not worth reading, of course, but even the average shows improvement over earlier stories, at least to much nearer the general pulp level. (The best are far above that.)

The readers were not all approving of the change, however. To many, the originality—the sense of manifold wonders—had decreased markedly. Too much attention was being spent on style and on characterization—things which they could find in other fiction. They wanted the element of the marvelous that was unique to science fiction.

There was some truth in their complaints. There *were* fewer marvelous inventions and gadgets in the stories now. But some of this loss was inevitable. Time machines automatically became less marvelous as they were used more often; the surprise of going to the Moon wore thin after the twentieth flight. Part of the trouble was that the early stories had used up the more easily imagined sources of wonder.

By the mid-thirties, science fiction was beginning to give up marveling at every possible gadget. But there were still wonders to be found in subtler areas for those willing to accept them. Now writers were turning to attempts to understand their future cultures or their alien creatures. They were beginning to look deeper into their possible futures or to see them from different points of view, instead of centering their interests on devices that made it possible to see those futures. They were growing curious about the nature of an interplanetary society, instead of concentrating on the building of the interplanetary ships.

Stories that could explore such things well were still very much in the minority—as they will probably always be a minority among more routine efforts. And the change had not reached *Amazing* or *Wonder* to any major extent—though *Wonder* had made the first tentative steps toward the new type of science fiction under the editorship of David Lasser.

But in *Astounding,* this feeling of change was very strong. It was probably the cause of excitement among its readers, far more than the "thought variant" ideas that Tremaine had been pushing. There was a sense that something new was developing, which was itself enough to inspire some feeling of wonder.

Also, the readers were beginning to be influenced by books from outside the magazine field. Aldous Huxley's *Brave New World* (1932) stirred up a great deal of controversy with its anti-utopian world. Karel Čapek's *R.U.R.* had provided the word "robot"—though his artificial men would now be called androids; and his *The Absolute at Large* (1927) dealt with something that seemed to be God as a residue from atomic power—taking science fiction into the realm of religion. Olaf Stapledon produced a huge, philosophical history of a future in *Last and First Men* (1930). From the fan's view, his *Odd John* (1935) was even more impressive in its depiction of a strange superman and his conflicts with the normal world. Most science fiction readers heard of these books from friends or reviews in the magazines and adopted them as their own.

When Worlds Collide, by Edwin Balmer and Philip Wylie, began in 1932 in *Blue Book Magazine,* and was considered excellent science fiction by even the now somewhat sophisticated standards of the fans. (A sequel beginning in 1933, entitled *After Worlds Collide,* was equally popular.)

A study of the period makes it hard to accept the "ghettoization" of science fiction now frequently claimed by critics. A ghetto, of course, is a place to which people or things are restricted, either by law or economics. But science fiction was in no sense restricted. It appeared in mainstream books and general magazines. Many of the writers were well known in other fields of literature. And certainly the readers were never restricted in what they might read, nor was the readership confined to any given class, interest, or type. The word "ghetto" applies in this case no more than it does to an exclusive country club.

True, there was considerable contempt for most science fiction by those not devoted to it—and some of this contempt was justified by many of the stories appearing in the science fiction magazines. But that contempt was shared by most of the pulp magazines in all categories.

Rather than a ghetto, the magazines were a hothouse, encouraging the rapid growth and evolution of this type of fiction. And by 1937, science fiction was firmly established as a successful branch of commercial literature.

PART III

The Golden Age

(1938-1949)

CHAPTER 10

Campbell's *Astounding*

WHEN F. ORLIN TREMAINE was given directorship over several magazines, it became necessary for him to find another editor for *Astounding,* and his choice was John W. Campbell. Then, when Tremaine left Street & Smith in May 1938, Campbell assumed full authority for the magazine. Actually, he was responsible for the buying of stories considerably before that date.

John Wood Campbell (1910–1971) was one of the most popular writers in the field before he became an editor. But many of the readers were worried when his name replaced that of Tremaine, who had proved to be extremely capable. The fears were soon put to rest. The transition between editors was extremely smooth; by the time the magazine had used its previous inventory and began to depend solely on Campbell's selections, the readers were delighted.

February 1938 brought the conclusion of E. E. Smith's *Galactic Patrol.* In March came the first indication that there were to be alterations; the title of the magazine was changed to *Astounding Science Fiction.* Campbell felt that the old title was far too indicative of pulp-action stories, and meant in time to drop *Astounding* from it, leaving only *Science Fiction.* Unfortunately for his plans, the simpler title was chosen by another publisher before Campbell was ready to make the final break with the past.

In April, two stories showed the type of writing and writers Campbell would be using. L. Sprague de Camp had previously appeared with one story, "The Isolinguals," in September 1937, but his "Hyperpilosity" was far more typical of what Campbell wanted; it deals with a disease that suddenly makes all human beings grow lush coats of hair, and the consequences of that; it is told with the wry humor that would make de Camp's stories popular from then on. Lester del Rey* appeared for the first time with "The Faithful," a story of mankind's replacement by intelligent dogs who still revere man's memory. This story would never have been written except for the writer's knowledge that Campbell was the editor.

May introduced Charles Schneeman as a cover artist. Schneeman had succeeded Dold as the featured interior illustrator. His work was superior in its realistic handling of people and machinery, and his mastery of perspective was unequaled. But this was his first work in color. It illustrated Jack Williamson's serial, *The Legion of Time*; this deals with a war between two possible futures, with the man whose actions will determine which is to win forced to choose between the two fascinating women those alternate futures produce.

June brought Raymond Z. Gallun's "Seeds of the Dusk," one of his finest stories, dealing with Martian seeds trying to take over Earth when mankind is an old and tired race and other animals are intelligent; its strength lies in a marvelously maintained mood. Clifford D. Simak appeared in July with "Rule 18," a story of future football and the recruiting of a super-team out of the past. Simak had previously sold a few stories; but he felt that Campbell was an editor who would let him write the kind of stories he wanted to do—and time proved him right. Effectively, he was a new writer. In the same month, "The Dangerous Dimension" was

---

* As a writer of this book, I shall continue to use first person; but when dealing with myself as a writer and editor who played a part in the history I am describing, I shall use third person.

by a writer new to science fiction, though not to the adventure magazines—L. Ron Hubbard.

Another new writer appeared in August; Malcolm Jameson had "Eviction by Isotherm," a story based on climatic changes. And Don A. Stuart's "Who Goes There?" was almost certainly the finest of his career. This takes place in the Antarctic, where an isolated group of men discover a strange creature, preserved by the cold after an ancient spaceship disaster. When thawed, it comes to life—and can assume the shape and apparent character of any or all of them, or of their dogs. If that gets loose in the world, it can become all life. But how can they identify something that can be exactly like the men it has replaced? This was later made into a movie under the title *The Thing*, but so debased that it was simply another horror monster plot.

In September, Hubbard began a serial, *The Tramp*, about a little man who discovers he has strange mental powers. And Robert Moore Williams' "Robots Return" deals with five little metal men who come to Earth, to discover that their lost origin may have been from the strange protoplasmic life that has now vanished. Williams had previously sold two other stories to *Astounding* (one under the name of Robert Moore), and this story proved that he could have become one of the major writers for the magazine. But he decided that writing for Campbell was too demanding, and quickly turned to other markets.

L. Sprague de Camp's "The Command" was the first of several stories about Johnny Black, a charming and intelligent bear. This appeared in October. In December, de Camp's tale of a man who is forced to breathe under water, "The Merman," was featured on the cover. And Lester del Rey was back with "Helen O'Loy," the story of a beautiful and too-human robot who falls in love with one of her owners—and eventually, wins him. This is still regarded as one of del Rey's best short stories and continues to be reprinted.

All in all, 1938 was an excellent year, if not an outstanding one. Campbell was now firmly in control and beginning to develop a stable of his own writers: del Rey, Hubbard and Jameson were his discoveries; and de Camp and Simak were developing under his aegis into leading writers.

1939 *was* outstanding. This proved to be one of the great seminal years for science fiction and was to exert a strong influence on the future of the field.

It began quietly. Clifford D. Simak's first serial, *Cosmic Engineers*, began in February; this is a superscience epic in plot, spanning time and space to show the real masters of the galaxy, but the style is acceptably modern, without unnecessary hyperbole. The cover was perhaps more important, however, because it used Canadian-born Hubert Rogers' first painting. He did four covers during 1939 and soon became the regular cover artist and a favorite with the readers.

In March, Don A. Stuart made his last *Astounding* appearance with "Cloak of Aesir," a sequel to "Out of Night." And Malcolm Jameson had a warmly humorous story of a little ship that grows up and runs away to sea—"Children of the Betsy B." April saw the last of Jack Williamson's serials about the Legion of Space —*One Against the Legion*. Even the comic figure of Giles Habibula is not quite enough to make this seem fresh.

July was the turning point. It introduced two major writers. A. E. Van Vogt had "Black Destroyer," which hit the readers with more force than any other first story since E. E. Smith's initial appearance. It deals with a supervital, seemingly all-powerful catlike alien which attacks the crew of a spaceship. The efforts of the creature and the attempts by the men to control it make for extreme suspense, and the viewpoint of the alien is handled with great skill. Van Vogt became a major writer at once.

This was not the case with Isaac Asimov, whose "Trends" appeared in the same issue. Asimov had previously had two stories in another magazine, but he was still very much a product of Campbell's search for new writers, since Campbell had been guiding him and helping him to mature as a writer. "Trends" was the first story to suggest that the public might violently oppose rocket flight, as it had so often opposed other developments. It was a good story, but not up to Asimov's later work; it took time for him to become one of the magazine's top writers, but he was on his way.

August introduced Robert A. Heinlein, who is usually conceded to be the first among the best in science fiction. "Life-Line" is a story of the man who discovers a way to determine how long any man will live. The writing is excellent, the story smoothly handled—but Heinlein also had to wait for the full recognition he quickly earned from later stories.

Theodore Sturgeon appeared in September with "Ether Breather," about creatures who can distort television signals to make unmentionable things appear on the viewing screens. (The nature of television for public entertainment was excellently forecast.) It is humorous and the writing is clever and original. Sturgeon's talent was obvious from the beginning, though the story wasn't of sufficient importance to show his full abilities.

Three months had produced four top-name writers who would lead the field for years to come—Asimov, Heinlein, Sturgeon and Van Vogt! And, as it turned out, all were prolific during the next few years. Campbell's stable of writers was firmly established.

E. E. Smith began his second Lens serial in October with *Grey Lensman*, in which the great war between the forces of evil and those of good is shown to be far more complex than it seemed at first. This was some of the best writing Smith had yet done, and he admitted later that much of the improvement came from the long letters of rewrite suggestions sent him by Campbell.

In December, there was Van Vogt's "Discord in Scarlet," in which the crew of the *Beagle* discover another superpowerful alien creature. It was perhaps too much like the first story, but so well done that few readers noticed. And it proved that Van Vogt could repeat his success.

But 1939 was a busy year for Campbell in another respect. In March, he introduced a sister magazine to *Astounding. Unknown* (later retitled *Unknown Worlds*) was a fantasy magazine—the magazine that developed what came to be known as modern fantasy, free of nameless horrors, in which the object was to consider what would happen to fantasy situations in today's world. Although it only lasted for 39 issues, its final issue being October 1943, it gained a devotion from its readers that no other magazine can match—not even *Astounding*.

There was an additional triumph for Campbell. In August 1939, a British reprint of *Astounding* was issued; it wasn't exactly the same as the American edition, but it brought most of the same stories to the British fans. And the next month, a British reprint of *Unknown* was also launched.

The level of the previous year was maintained in 1940, though there was no major development in finding new writers. Heinlein's "Requiem," in January, was the story of a man who makes his fortune developing space travel, always intending to leave Earth; now he's old, and his heart won't stand the trip. But in the end, he finds a way to reach the Moon, happy to accept death as the price. The sentiment is saved from bathos by the quiet, simple writing that makes it seem true.

February brought *If This Goes On,* a short serial by

Heinlein, telling of a world taken over by a fundamentalist, theocratic dictatorship. Here Heinlein had a chance to display his ability to make his future worlds completely detailed and real. The issue also carried the first story of H. B. Fyfe. "Locked Out" is a problem story, dealing with the lone operator of a spaceship who gets locked out while making repairs and has nothing but his simple tool kit to use in finding a way inside. Fyfe later became a frequent contributor and his stories about a "Bureau of Slick Tricks" were always ingenious and amusing. Leigh Brackett also made her first magazine appearance with "Martian Quest." Brackett was an exceptionally skillful writer and her stories were colorful and adventuresome; but after a couple in *Astounding,* she went on to become a leading writer in other magazines.

In April, Malcolm Jameson's "Admiral's Inspection" was the first of several stories about Bullard, a space officer who rose eventually to commander. But the feature story was the beginning of L. Ron Hubbard's *Final Blackout.* This was a grim story of a Europe that has suffered total war for a generation, until only scattered remnants of its population remain. It tells of a small band who fight their way back to England, where conditions are so bad that they must still fight to survive and restore order—their own kind of order. It is an ugly story, but a moving one, with sustained tension. It was this novel that established Hubbard as a major science fiction writer.

Van Vogt's first serial began in September under the title *Slan!* This deals with a world after a war between men and supermen—or slans—in which any surviving slan is to be killed on sight; and the slans have sensitive tendrils which give them telepathic powers, but can easily be detected. Van Vogt bypassed the usual problem with such stories of making supermen believable by having his hero begin as a small boy. He is orphaned in the first chapter and on the run from then on, as he tries to find other slans and survive in the harsh world around him. It is a remarkable novel and became an instant classic. It was also one of the very few early superman stories which did not negate the value of superpowers by having the hero fail in the end.

Heinlein also had a story in September. "Blowups Happen" deals with a plant using uranium-235 to produce power. (Campbell's readers had been kept abreast of the early work with uranium done by Fermi and others; several editorials were devoted to the subject.) The problem is not to keep the reaction going—but to keep it from blowing up. Despite the fact that we now know blowups can be avoided, the story stands up well, particularly if other problems of nuclear fission are considered.

Harry Bates proved what a really good science fiction writer he was in October with "Farewell to the Master." This is a story of a ship containing a robot and a man. The man is killed, and the robot is seeking ways to return him to life. The ending is marvelous. This was later turned into the movie *The Day the Earth Stood Still*—one of the better science fiction movies, though it used only a little of the original story.

In December, Willy Ley had "Fog," one of his few pieces of fiction, under the pen name Robert Willey. After leaving Germany in disgust at the Nazi regime, Ley had been doing articles for *Astounding* since early in 1937. But his accounts of conditions in Germany after World War I so fascinated Campbell that Ley was asked to write a novelette on a similar background. The result was a story of tension and chaos, as various revolutionary forces fight for control of a city—and nobody really knows what goes on. The story's real importance, however, comes from the fact that Campbell used it to get at least two other major novelettes by somewhat roundabout means. These will be covered as they appear.

Heinlein seemed to stake out a claim on 1941 and

THE GOLDEN AGE   99

make the year his own. In January, he began a serial under the name of Anson MacDonald—*Sixth Column*. This tells of a future war in which Asiatics conquer America, with a small band of Americans using a new science cloaked in religious mumbo-jumbo to cover up their real purpose. The story may seem a bit jingoistic now, but it suited the temper of the times. It also led to other stories of science masked as religion.

In May, there was "Universe," considered by many to be the best story ever written of a ship designed to occupy generations in traveling to another star, with the ship a small world in which air and all supplies are recycled. In this case, the crew has apparently mutinied; certainly they have lost all sense of the original mission, and the routine of the ship has become something of a religious rite. There have also been mutations from the radiation of space. The story deals with one man's discovery of the true nature of the ship. As Anson MacDonald, Heinlein also had "Solution Unsatisfactory," which deals with a dust that can be used as a weapon, sowing the ground with radioactive contamination. It's grimly honest, and it fits in all too well with what we later learned of the fallout from atomic bombs. And finally, Campbell ran an announcement that all of the stories published under Heinlein's own name were laid in a single, integrated future history. He also published the chart of this future history. Others (including Neil R. Jones) had worked from a master plan. But this chart was more detailed about all future developments in science, devices, philosophy, and straight historical events than any writer had developed previously.

July brought another serial by Heinlein. *Methuselah's Children* describes a group who have been given extreme longevity by careful breeding of long-lived people, and what happens when the short-lived discover their existence and refuse to believe that there isn't more to the secret. This story introduces Lazarus Long, the oldest man of all, but the most youthful, who leads the Howard Families through space and back to find a solution. This is the same character who appears in Heinlein's 1973 *Time Enough for Love*; 32 years is a long time to wait for a sequel, but the readers never stopped demanding one. (Writers' attitudes change in thirty years, so it isn't surprising that some readers were not completely happy about the final story of Lazarus Long.)

Heinlein had two novelettes again in October. "Common Sense" appeared under his own name, and was a sequel to "Universe," in which the hero leads a rebel force to take over the ship and steer it to planet-fall. And Anson MacDonald's "By His Bootstraps" is a totally confusing but logical story of time running in circles, with the hero meeting himself in many ways.

Of course, there were other stories by other writers, and many of them were excellent. April brought "Microcosmic God" by Theodore Sturgeon. This is still hailed as a classic by many readers, though Sturgeon now seems bothered by some parts. (I tend to agree with the majority; it may have some flaws, but it easily transcends them.) It tells of Kidder, a scientist who retreats to an island where he develops a tiny race of Neoterics with a tremendously speeded-up time rate. Kidder communicates with them by teletype when they develop civilization, and they consider him their god. When he needs an invention, he asks for it; they thereupon spend all their efforts for generations (a day or so of his time) in developing it. When the world threatens Kidder, he asks for an impregnable shell of force around the island and seals them and himself inside. (I've often wondered what happens to them if he dies.)

In the same issue, Isaac Asimov had "Reason," his first story of robots that were forced to obey certain laws. These laws have become one of the hallmarks of science fiction. They are:

1. A robot may not injure a human being, or through inaction allow a human being to come to harm.

2. A robot must obey the orders given it by human beings except where such orders would conflict with the First Law.

3. A robot must protect its own existence as long as such protection does not conflict with the First or Second Law.

A great many other writers have accepted robots based upon such principles, though without stating them. Asimov has written dozens of stories about robots and these laws of robotics. (I don't use them; I object to the second law because (a) it's a slave-under-master law and (b) the conflicting orders in the real world would soon drive the robot to madness. But the results in Asimov's stories have been good, and he doesn't care what others think of them.)

Asimov was featured in September with "Nightfall," which was the story that established him as one of the major writers. This is laid on a planet where conditions are such that men can see the stars only once in a thousand years. The assumption is that they will then go mad—as, it turns out, they have repeatedly gone mad before, with civilization ending and having to start again. It's a powerful story.

In July, Van Vogt had "The Seesaw," which was a prelude to his later works about wonderful weapon shops. It only dimly foreshadowed what was to come, but it established the motto of the series: "The right to buy weapons is the right to be free."

In November, E. E. Smith began the third of his Lens novels, *Second Stage Lensman*, in which a woman becomes a wearer of the marvelous lens that can only be worn by men of super ability and honesty. And the struggle between the forces of good and evil spreads to an even vaster area.

Then, December 7, the Japanese bombed Pearl Harbor, bringing the United States into World War II and bringing troubles to the wonderful world of science fiction that John Campbell had created in only four years.

CHAPTER 11

The War and the Bomb

SINCE EACH ISSUE of a magazine must be planned months ahead of its appearance, the January 1942 issue of *Astounding* showed no evidence of the fact that the United States was now at war on two fronts. Instead, it proved Campbell's confidence by a change of size to 8½ x 11½ inches, with a considerable increase in the contents. This was meant to remove it from the action pulps and place it among more respectable magazines in the display racks.

April began a new serial by Heinlein, *Beyond This Horizon*, much praised at the time, though less tightly plotted than most of his work. It begins in a world where all men wear guns and duels are again popular, shifts to a fine exposition of how men might learn to control their offspring's characteristics, and ends with much ado about the proof of telepathy. Van Vogt had the first of a new series, "Co-operate—or Else!" Here mankind is threatened by the Rull, monstrous aliens, and has to convince a savage but intelligent catlike race to work in cooperation or have both men and cats destroyed. And a new department was begun. This was *Probability Zero*; it used very short fiction about ideas which seemed logical but couldn't work, and it gave many new authors a chance to appear in print. It continued through 1944.

Isaac Asimov had "Foundation" in May—the first story in a series that was to become the most popular in science fiction. This deals with the fall of a Galactic Empire and a foundation set up at one end of the galaxy, nominally to preserve knowledge in an encyclopedia, but actually to form the nucleus for a new empire. "Bridle and Saddle," the second Foundation story, appeared in June, as did "Proof," the first story by Hal Clement, who was to become one of the best writers of hard-science stories in the field.

September introduced Anthony Boucher to science fiction—he had previously appeared in *Unknown*—with "The Barrier." This story poses one of the knottiest problems of time travel: if time travel is developed, why are not we (and all the past) visited by such travelers? Surely if the invention is ever made, there should be evidence. But the major story proved to be Lester del Rey's long novelette, "Nerves." This is laid in a future industrial atomic plant during an accident that threatens to blow up half the continent. Campbell had suggested the idea, hoping to get something like Ley's "Fog," since the story was to be told from the view of the company doctor, who could only partly understand what was happening. Instead, he got a story of characters under stress and of extreme suspense, entirely unlike the previous work of the author. The readers paid the story the unusual honor of unanimously voting it the best in the issue.

George O. Smith appeared for the first time in October with "QRM—Interplanetary." Smith was an electronics engineer, and the story deals with communication between the planets by the use of a satellite around Venus—the first story to develop that idea. There were also novelettes by Jameson, Van Vogt and del Rey, but Smith's story was the most memorable and led to a long series that was eventually collected in a book under the title *Venus Equilateral*. It is still one of the finest examples of "engineering" science fiction.

The year closed with Van Vogt's "The Weapon Shops," a very sympathetic story of a man who has always been loyal to his Empress, but who is driven to buy a gun at one of the mysterious weapon shops—and who then discovers the true nature of his ruler. This set up the background that had only been hinted at in "The Seesaw."

On the surface, all was well with *Astounding*. But Campbell knew otherwise. Rogers had done his last cover for many years in August, and Schneeman would henceforth be missing; a large number of his artists had gone into military service. From now on, Campbell would have to depend mostly on William Timmins for covers; and while Timmins was sometimes very good, his work lacked the magic touch that had made Rogers so popular. To some extent, Paul Orban would replace Schneeman. Orban was a highly skilled black-and-white artist, but he was unfamiliar with science fiction. At first, readers protested against his work; in time, however, he came to understand the stories, and gained popularity—but only after some years.

Among the writers, Heinlein, Hubbard, de Camp, Asimov and Williamson were called to military service. And some others, such as Lester del Rey, would be too occupied with work in war plants to do much writing. The most important part of Campbell's hard-won stable of writers was now suddenly missing! And with so many young men who might have tried writing being drafted into the armed forces, the chance to find new talent was much diminished.

January 1943 showed one answer Campbell found for his problem, which was to pull some of his better fantasy writers into the pages of *Astounding*. Henry Kuttner had been very popular in *Unknown*, but among science fiction readers he was considered a mere hack writer; this rather unfair judgment was the result of some of his earlier and less skillful work. His name would not appeal to potential readers of *Astounding*; but they were used to seeing new names that often proved to be major talents. Hence, Kuttner's "Time Locker" appeared under the "new name" of Lewis Padgett; it deals with a somewhat mad scientist who can only work when drunk, but can't remember when sober what his inventions were for. In this, his name is Galloway; but the second of several amusing and fascinating stories to use the scientist names him Gallagher; Kuttner later explained that his real name was Galloway Gallagher!

Padgett also appeared in February with an entirely different type of story which has since been accepted as a classic—"Mimsy Were the Borogoves." This is a grim, chilling story of children who discover marvelous teaching toys from the future and soon evolve beyond their parents. In the same issue, Van Vogt's *The Weapon Makers* was the culminating serial about the weapon shops; it shows the same man to be behind both the shops and the forces of the Empress in their long struggle for supremacy. It is a complicated, multifaceted novel, and was better liked than anything by Van Vogt since *Slan*.

March featured "Clash by Night," a long novelette of the mercenaries who fight on the savage surface of Venus while the people who have fled our destroyed Earth stagnate in domes far below. It was by Lawrence O'Donnell—and was another name perhaps related to Henry Kuttner. Kuttner had married C. L. Moore, and they often pooled their talents in writing, until it is hard to discover who did what. This was probably mostly the work of Moore, however.

May brought another fantasy writer to *Astounding*. Fritz Leiber began with a major serial, *Gather Darkness*. This presents a world once wrecked and now taken over by an arrogant priesthood who use science to perform miracles for the ignorant masses. But a "witchcraft" has developed with its own miracles, determined to overcome the theocracy. It is a rich novel with fine characters and marvelous devices, and it led to a considerable body of other stories based upon the central idea of science being perverted to a religion.

Raymond F. Jones made his first major appearance in October with "Fifty Million Monkeys." Jones had previously had three short stories in *Astounding*, but this was his real debut. The story takes off from the idea that "fifty million monkeys typing at random will eventually produce all the works of Shakespeare"—a logical fallacy, of course. But in the story, the hero discovers that there are hitherto unknown laws to random chance.

All in all, Campbell managed to get through 1943 in fairly good shape, so far as stories were concerned. But there were further wounds from the war. *Unknown Worlds* vanished forever after its final appearance, the October 1943 issue. And *Astounding* had gone from giant to pigmy in size.

This was due to paper rationing. The war was making heavy demands on the supplies of paper, and the magazines were all being forced to cut back. For the smaller publishing houses, this was a major disaster. For large magazine chains, such as Street and Smith, it meant the dropping of magazines below a certain circulation in order to transfer paper to the others. *Unknown* had enjoyed a high reputation and a steady following, but it had never gained the circulation of *Astounding*; hence it was out.

Even that was not enough of a cut. In May, *Astounding* had been forced to revert back to its older pulp size. And in November, it became a digest, 5½ x 8 inches. In the long run, the new size was probably an advantage; but at the time, Campbell worried about justifying it to the readers.

Such paper and binding glue as were available were

of inferior quality, also. Within a few years, the glue grew brittle, letting the pages fall out; and the paper deteriorated rapidly. Most issues of this period can be read today only at the risk of total ruin.

1944 had its high spots, but there were not many of them. Clifford D. Simak's "City" appeared in May. This is the first of a series of stories (later issued as a book under the same title as this first story) which deals with man's retreat into the cities and his eventual disappearance. In time, the dogs take over Earth (along with some antisocial robots and colonies of ants), guided by an eternally loyal robot, who sees the dogs as capable of replacing man. This became one of the most admired series to appear in the magazine. Raymond F. Jones began a serial, *Renaissance*, in July. This was based on a seminal idea, often used in other stories. It tells of a separate tiny universe into which children are sent, having no knowledge of Earth, to develop their own civilization—and in time, to find their way back and save the mess that Earth has become. Frederic Brown was another fantasy writer who switched to *Astounding*. His "Arena" appeared in June, and uses the old idea of two warring races each selecting one champion to fight and decide the war; it is still an excellent story of suspense.

In August and October, Asimov found time to add two more stories to his Foundation series. In November, Theodore Sturgeon had "Killdozer"—a taut suspense story about a giant bulldozer possessed by an alien, inimical creature on a small island where a construction crew is isolated. The picture of that behemoth machine roaring and charging against seemingly puny human beings is genuinely frightening. (This is another story that evolved by steps out of "Fog." This time Campbell had suggested to Sturgeon that he do it in the mood of del Rey's "Nerves"—which partly derived from the Willy Ley story. Like del Rey, Sturgeon took the idea and created his own mood and story, however.) And December saw C. L. Moore back under her own name with "No Woman Born"—the story of a famous dancer so injured that her body must be replaced by one of metal. The gallantry of her fight to overcome her limits and the tendency to become isolated from the humans around her makes one of the finest stories Moore ever wrote.

The most sensational story, however, was a fairly minor one that appeared in March; this is "Deadline" by Cleve Cartmill, another fantasy writer Campbell had transferred. The plot is a routine one of future war, but it involves an atomic bomb made from U-235 and a trigger device to detonate it. Neither bomb nor trigger could work, as outlined; but the trigger device is similar to what was eventually used. (A device so obvious in its general design that any reasonably ingenious engineer might have thought of it, but one which had never been described in print before.)

Shortly after the story appeared, grim government men appeared in Campbell's office. They also quizzed Cartmill and even Paul Orban, who had illustrated the story! They were sure that the story proved that Cartmill had gotten a hold of restricted documents and was spilling government secrets. They were about to close down *Astounding*, apparently.

Eventually Campbell convinced them that no secrets had been stolen, and that putting a sudden end to stories about the possible use of atomic power would tip off the enemy far more surely than any number of science fiction speculations. Campbell retained his free hand. All that the investigation had done was to convince Campbell of what he had suspected, along with several of his writers—the government *was* working on an atom bomb.

Some of the same hush-hush foolishness attended the publication of del Rey's "Nerves." When the magazine appeared at Oak Ridge, it was immediately stamped secret, and the research workers were refused permission to read it unless they had top clearances. They had to go outside the government plant to buy the issue from the newsstands, where it was freely available. With such "secrecy," one wonders how the real secret was ever kept!

February 1945 carried the first of a new series by Lewis Padgett, "The Piper's Son." This deals with the problem of mutant supermen living among normal men. But unlike most other stories on this theme, it is not one about violent war for survival. This time the Baldies, or mutants, are joined by many normal humans in an attempt to find a means to cooperate. It makes for a less obvious suspense situation, but one which has a great deal more depth and reality. These stories were collected in a book under the title *Mutant* to make an excellent novel.

May saw "First Contact" by Murray Leinster. It deals with a meeting of two ships far out in the galaxy —one human, the other alien. And neither dares let the other return to its own planet for fear that it can be tracked to its home by the other. The problem is so well developed and the solution so ingenious that the story became the definitive treatment of man's first contact with an alien.

In August Van Vogt began his serial *The World of Null-A*—a novel so intricately complicated that it is impossible to describe—or perhaps to follow clearly. This was followed in November by Asimov's serial, *The Mule*, another Foundation story. This time, the great thousand-year plan to establish another empire is almost wrecked when a mutant develops powers for which no planning could allow and threatens to take over the Foundation.

In 1946, January saw the beginning of *The Fairy Chessman*, a two-part serial by Lewis Padgett about a grim war following atomic holocaust. April saw the debut of Arthur C. Clarke with "Loophole," followed by "Rescue Party" in May. The latter deals with aliens who come to Earth to rescue at least a few men from a cosmic disaster. They find great towers broadcasting a signal out into space—but no human life. They leave, regretting the end of what might have been a promising young race. The marvelous ending shows just how promising that race really was; the story remains an example of superb, classic science fiction.

In September, Lawrence O'Donnell (mostly, at least, C. L. Moore) had another classic in "Vintage Season"—the story of an almost perfect autumn and the strange people who come from the future to witness it—and to see what follows it!

The December issue was distinguished mostly by a new artist, Alejandro, who was to paint a number of future covers. Many of his covers were purely symbolic, and this type of art soon influenced other artists. (Sigmond had used symbolic covers for *Amazing* in 1933—but his work had not caught on generally.) Apparently, this was another attempt by Campbell to divorce *Astounding* from its pulp heritage, which he always tended to deny.

In March 1947, however, Hubert Rogers returned, and his covers were greeted with loud praise and much delight in the letter column of the magazine. In October, *Astounding* used the first of Chesley Bonestell's marvelous astronomical covers. These were to appear occasionally for several years.

In other ways, too, 1947 proved better for the magazine than the previous year. In March, William Tenn (who had previously appeared once) had "Child's Play," a story of wry humor and a new slant on life which was to characterize much of his later writing. This deals with a package missent from the future which contains a child's Bild-a-Man kit, with instructions for building a man. It remains one of the best examples of humor in science fiction. And Poul Anderson made his first appearance (in collaboration with F. N. Waldrop) in "Tomorrow's Children"—a story of postatomic Earth where a large percentage of the children are mutated in strange ways, and some means must be found to count and handle them. Anderson (this time alone) had a sequel in July—"Logic"—in which the hero of the first story discovers his own son is a mutant. Anderson soon became one of the most reliable and prolific writers Campbell discovered.

Another discovery was H. Beam Piper, whose "Time and Time Again" appeared in April, telling of a man who suddenly awakens in the body of his much younger self, with some hope of setting aright the errors that were made in his previous future.

In May, Lawrence O'Donnell (probably mostly Kuttner) began *Fury*, a sequel to "Clash by Night." In this story, we see the undersea domes where mankind has grown hopelessly decadent on Venus—and a marvelous character who tries to swindle mankind back to the surface for his own profit. But while he is using the people of the domes, another is using him to insure the very benevolent but harsh development of surface survival that the hero meant only as a come-on. The ending is truly memorable. (The Avon paperback uses the title *Destination Infinity*.) And there was a superb story by a new writer, T. L. Sherred. "E for Effort" deals with a device for viewing the past—and what happens when a movie is made of the true life of Christ! Unfortunately, Sherred wrote little after this, and nothing to equal this classic story.

In July, Jack Williamson had "With Folded Hands," about robots that come to save men from all harm—any harm, even the risk of a scratched finger. It is as if Asimov's laws of robotics were to be applied with absolute, judgmentless rigor.

November began the last of E. E. Smith's Lens novels, *The Children of the Lens*, in which four children discover the full nature of the forces of good and evil. Smith considered it his best novel, but most readers probably question his judgment.

In 1948, the January issue began another Foundation serial by Isaac Asimov, *Now You See It*. In this, the Mule is seeking the Second Foundation, which is supposed to be at the other end of the galaxy; its location is supposed to be a secret in all the stories, to be divulged only at the end.

March had a different kind of Asimov entry, an article entitled "The Endochronic Properties of Resublimated Thiotimoline." This resembled a serious science report, complete with bibliography. It deals with the property of a chemical which dissolves in water before it touches that water! Surprisingly, many readers took it seriously, though it was a gorgeous spoof on the type of paper Asimov—then doing graduate work in chemistry—saw all too often. There was also the beginning of Jack Williamson's . . . *And Searching Mind*, a sequel to his "With Folded Hands." In this, the too-protective robots are discovered to be involved in taking over control of all inhabited worlds. There is a small group who oppose them and an apparent traitor who seems free to do as he chooses, despite the robots. There is also a little girl with strange psi powers. The original story was excellent, but I found the serial too cluttered with extraneous developments.

In July, H. Beam Piper began a series of stories with "Police Operation," based on an assumption that time not only goes forward and backward but also sidewise; beside our world are an infinity of other worlds in which events have not proceeded quite the same. Those nearby are almost identical, but those farther away differ greatly. One world has learned to traverse through this "paratime" and to exploit other worlds and cultures. But in doing so, the rulers must police all the worlds and prevent any accidental discovery of the secret by others. This permitted Piper to use almost any setting or culture for his background without stepping out of his basic situation, and the stories were usually excellent.

THE GOLDEN AGE 113

1949 introduced one major new writer (though he had appeared previously in *Unknown*). This was James H. Schmitz. His "Agent of Vega," in July, was the first of several related stories. And his "The Witches of Karres," in December, was a delightful story of three little girls who are rescued by a spaceman—and who turn out to be witches, loaded with all kinds of extrasensory powers.

Hal Clement was back with a serial, *Needle*, in May. This was one of the first detective–science fiction stories Campbell used. It describes a creature with cells so tiny that it can slip into a human body without being detected. The trouble is that the outlaw it is supposed to catch has the same ability. Problem—who among humans carries the outlaw? Sprague de Camp's serial *The Queen of Zamba* began in August. This is one of de Camp's "Viagens Interplanetarias" stories, which are good-natured, amusing adventures somewhat like the sword-and-sorcery stories of fantasy.

And in November, after having covered only half of the projected thousand-year plan, the Foundation cycle ended with Asimov's serial *And Now You Don't*, in which the secret of the Second Foundation is supposedly revealed. But there was a good deal more to that issue.

A letter had appeared back in November 1948 in which reader Richard A. Hoen listed the stories and his ratings for the 1949 November issue. It was amusing, but nobody remembered it—except Campbell. He immediately set about making the prediction come true, announcing his plans to the writers listed and asking for stories. He got them, and the issue was almost the same as the one Hoen had described. There was no "We Hail" by Don A. Stuart, but its place was taken by the Asimov serial that was not listed in the letter. There were no Schneeman illustrations. But the cover was by Rogers, and the rest of the contents were identical: "Final Command" by A. E. Van Vogt;

"Gulf" by Robert A. Heinlein; "Over the Top" by Lester del Rey; "Finished" by L. Sprague de Camp; "What Dead Men Tell" by Theodore Sturgeon; and an article by R. S. Richardson.

Each author got an advance copy. And Richard A. Hoen got a special advance copy, autographed by everyone who appeared in the issue! Readers, it seemed, could still influence the course of the magazine, even at the end of the Golden Age.

CHAPTER 12

A Proliferation of Magazines

AT THE BEGINNING of 1938, *Amazing Stories* was doing so badly under the editorship of T. O'Conor Sloane that the magazine was sold to the Ziff-Davis Publishing Co., and the April issue appeared under their ownership. Being based in Chicago, they moved the editorial offices there from New York and set about finding a new editor.

Their choice was Raymond A. Palmer, a prominent fan who had been active in the major fan magazines. Somehow, Palmer managed to bring out a June issue without breaking the regular bimonthly schedule. This was no small accomplishment, since local artists had to be found and Palmer was not using the previous inventory of stories. (The first two covers under Palmer were photographic ones—an interesting but not very successful idea.)

In a fairly short time, *Amazing* collected one of the largest staffs of artists used by any science fiction magazine. Robert Fuqua, perhaps, showed the greatest understanding of the field, and a few of the machines on his covers were reminiscent of those of Paul. There were also Julian Krupa, Robert Gibson Jones, Malcolm Smith and Harold McCauley, as well as others who were used occasionally. All were highly competent, professional illustrators; if their work was seldom outstanding, it nearly always was effective in showing action and attracting interest, despite the handicap of having too much space filled with large and gaudy type that hailed the writers and contents.

Amazing also instituted a policy of devoting its back covers to paintings instead of advertisements, a practice which continued into the middle of 1948. These were often of genuine science-fiction interest. Frank R. Paul did several series of these, showing cities on the planets and life throughout the Solar System.

Inside the magazine, the stories were designed to attract a younger and less sophisticated audience than the one which read *Astounding*. Palmer wanted action and excitement. He seemed to care little about style, so long as the story moved. And all claims to scientific accuracy were abandoned.

Like Campbell, Palmer began collecting his own stable of writers, but he did this much more rapidly. Faced with the need to get out a magazine quickly with no stories he could use already at hand, he turned to friends from the area surrounding Chicago and to the high-production writers who could do a story quickly on order. While he was happy to get suitable stories by leading writers from other magazines (provided they suited his policy) and to feature their names on the cover, he did not depend on such submissions. He went out and got the stories he wanted. If necessary, he rewrote the results himself.

Robert Moore Williams gave up the slow process of laboring over stories that would suit Campbell and turned happily to quicker, less detailed work. (After all, Palmer paid one cent a word on acceptance—and sometimes more—just as Campbell did.) Eando Binder found a ready market for his work. And John Russell Fearn, who had turned out a tremendous quantity of stories without ever gaining a really high reputation, began selling rapidly under the names of Thornton Ayre and Polton Cross. There were also William P. McGivern and David Wright O'Brien, as well as a host of names that were really house pseudonyms. Palmer liked to use such names, and assigned them freely to the work of less-established writers in his magazine—thus making them familiar to the readers as "regulars"; he also used them for many of his regular contributors. William Blade, for instance, might be anyone, but stories under that name were common in the magazine. Palmer also used a number of pseudonyms for his own work, and these names might be placed on the work of other contributors.

Palmer's rule was simple: keep the story moving; if the action falters, drop an anvil from the sky and see what happens. Or at least that was what one writer told me he suggested.

The result was a plethora of stories that could be read and enjoyed briefly, but which could be forgotten even more quickly.

Robert Bloch, who had begun writing Lovecraftian horror stories, came to Palmer, his first science fiction being "Secret of the Observatory" in August 1938. Eando Binder developed a whole series of stories about a somewhat intelligent, superstrong robot named Adam Link, beginning in January 1939 with "I, Robot." In the same year, in August, the first story by Isaac Asimov, "Marooned off Vespa," was published. (Asimov had a second story in the magazine, but contributed very little once he was accepted by *Astounding*.) In October 1940, Don Wilcox—who was to become a prolific writer for Palmer—had "The Voyage That Lasted 600 Years," a very good story that foreshadowed Heinlein's "Universe" novelette. And Edmond Hamilton's *The Star Kings*, September 1947, was one of his better adventure novels, dealing with a modern man who switched identities with a ruler of a future kingdom of the stars.

Palmer also ran into difficulties because of the war. The restrictions on paper forced him to skip two issues in 1943 and then to go bimonthly. (Actually, only five issues appeared in 1944 and four in 1945. There were nine in 1946, but monthly publication was resumed with the May issue.) There seemed to be more issues on the stands, however, since Palmer began binding together three back issues from copies that had not sold and putting them out in bulky, impressive special issues.

Many of the writers were also called into the armed services. But in Palmer's case, this caused far less difficulty than it had done for Campbell. Palmer's writers tended to be interchangeable, with the stories influenced more by the editor than the men who produced them. New writers were found and assigned house names that were familiar to the readers, and the magazine seemed to continue with little change.

Then, with the March 1945 issue, Palmer began issuing a new type of story. These are referred to as the Shaver Mystery stories. The first of these was "I Remember Lemuria," by Richard S. Shaver. (Actually, this was preceded by a letter from Shaver which gave the "Shaver alphabet"—an attempt to use modern English to establish wild theories about the past by assigning meanings to each letter.)

There were a number of cultist features to these stories, all based to some extent on the idea that a great race from the stars had been on Earth in the past —from which we get legends of the cultist Lemuria of yore. But our sun gave off certain rays or produced an "ash" that fell to Earth. The great ones were debased by these. They had been immortal, growing all their lives to fantastic size; now they became shrunken trolls; they had been totally benevolent, but now they were malignant entities who sought to take over mankind by certain rays. These "deros" lived in great caverns under the Earth, and there were certain elevators which would go down to them when one knew the right code to press. These deros, of course, were the secret powers behind the Mafia, the creators of war, and all such. Before the series was finished, almost everything from the cults was added.

Palmer ran a special issue in January 1947 which recapped the whole legend and printed six stories about the Mystery. The whole affair got a buildup in the magazine that would have been an exaggeration if it had covered Armageddon. And for a time, even though most of the regular readers of science fiction fought it bitterly, it brought a host of new readers. Palmer claimed the highest circulation in the field. This may well have been true, though Palmer's tendency to magnify everything about the magazine cannot be discounted.

Palmer also produced a companion magazine. The first issue of *Fantastic Adventures* appeared in May 1939 in the large 8½ x 11 size. (It went back to the normal pulp size with the June 1940 issue.) It was a bimonthly at first, but became a monthly when it changed to the smaller size. This could not have been an imitation of Campbell's *Unknown*, despite many claims to that effect. It had obviously been planned some time before *Unknown* appeared on the stands. But it resembled the earlier magazine in about the same manner that *Amazing* resembled *Astounding*. It dealt with fantasy instead of science fiction, but the approach of the two Palmer magazines to fiction was the same. Perhaps the best stories were those by Robert Bloch, detailing the exploits of a Runyonesque Lefty Feep through a number of modern fairy-tale situations. Unlike *Unknown*, *Fantastic Adventures* continued publication throughout this period.

In the fall of 1949, Palmer announced that he was leaving *Amazing* to start his own magazine. This was *Other Worlds*, which published only one issue that year, in November. This was a digest-size magazine. Palmer had announced that he would be dropping the formula of action fiction he had used before and would now be publishing a higher quality of stories. But the first issue, while it seemed to promise an improvement over *Amazing*, did not set distinctive enough a pattern to indicate what it would be like. *Amazing* and *Fantastic* continued under the editorship of Howard Browne, who had been assistant editor previously.

Back in New York, *Thrilling Wonder Stories* continued with little change, except that it switched to a monthly schedule with the December 1939 issue; it continued such regular publication until April 1941, when it again became a bimonthly. After the August 1943 issue, it became a quarterly; it wasn't until 1946 that it was able to resume bimonthly publication.

The editorial control passed to Oscar J. Friend in August 1941, when Mort Weisinger left to take over the Superman line of comic books. Friend was hardly an inspired editor. He continued the general policy of Weisinger to publish stories for a younger group of readers, but there was little sparkle to them. The better stories of the early years appeared before Friend took over. These included the "Via" stories of the exploration of the planets which had begun with "Via Etherline" in October 1937; these were by Gordon A. Giles, who was really Eando Binder. Henry Kuttner also had a series of "Hollywood on the Moon" stories, named for the first one, which appeared in April 1938. Perhaps the best-remembered story during this period was "Dawn of Flame," a posthumous story by Stanley G. Weinbaum, June 1939. This tells of an America which has declined into small rural communities and a dictator who is trying to rebuild it. The dictator's sister, the Flame of the title, is a woman of strange fascination, capable of both sudden goodness and violent evil, and is a marvelous character.

Things improved with the Winter issue of 1945, when Sam Merwin took over from Friend. Merwin imposed much higher standards and began to move the departments from a very low level of juvenility into a sort of free-wheeling lack of formality that delighted the readers. For a long time after that, the letter column was one of the most interesting ones in any magazine. Merwin sought good adventure stories with the best writing he could find. Many of his stories were supplied by Murray Leinster, who was always a reliable writer. Merwin also attracted George O. Smith from *Astounding;* he was able to get adventuresome stories from many other writers who had made their reputations under Campbell. These stories were always entertaining, though many made no really lasting impression.

Wonder began to have a companion magazine, *Startling Stories,* starting in January 1939. This was intended to alternate with *Wonder,* and would feature a book-length novel, as well as shorter stories, leaving the novelettes for the other magazine. (Serials were frowned on by the Thrilling group of publications. And while some of the "book-length" novels were really only long novelettes, *Startling* did often feature stories that ran to 50,000 words, which could be made to fill a book.)

Both magazines tended to use cover art that followed a formula which included a girl in a brief costume against some science fiction background. Howard V. Brown supplied some of the covers for a time. But eventually, Earle K. Bergey became the most used artist. He was highly professional, capable of delivering exactly the type of art required. But the Thrilling Publications had an art department that imposed limitations which gave him little chance to win acclaim from the readers.

Startling got off to a fine start with its January 1939 issue, which featured *The Black Flame*, the longest story of Stanley G. Weinbaum yet published. This is really a sequel to "The Dawn of Flame" despite its earlier publication. It tells of a man of the present who goes into suspended animation and wakes after the dictator has re-established civilization. But he is found by rebels, who persuade him to help their rebellion. He meets the dictator's sister, the Black Flame—and thereafter, it's a story of conflicting loyalties and a hate that ripens into love.

Most later novels were not nearly so popular, until Merwin took over the magazine. Then there were a number of novels by George O. Smith, Henry Kuttner and Murray Leinster, as well as the early stories of Jack Vance. In September 1948, Fredric Brown satirized the dreams of a young science fiction fan in *What Mad Universe?*, where everything works as it might in primitive science fiction, and which yet provides an excellent story. In November of the same year, Arthur C. Clarke had *Against the Fall of Night*, telling of a strange closed city in which a young man begins to seek for sight of the stars. It contains some excellent writing and touches of the mystical insight which was to appear in several of his later novels.

There was a third magazine in this group, *Captain Future*, which began with the Spring 1940 issue. This was a quarterly which lasted until the Spring 1944 issue. It was another of the superhero type of magazines that had been popular in the thirties, complete with crime-solving spaceman hero and some odd companions. Most of the stories were done by Edmond Hamilton; and while none were excellent, they afforded pleasant reading for those who wanted simple adventure fiction.

In this period of science fiction remembered as the Golden Age, however, the original three magazines (together with their companion publications) were no longer alone. The magazine chains had seen science fiction succeed and now began to develop their own titles.

The first of these was *Marvel Science Stories*, published by Red Circle Magazines and edited by Robert O. Erisman, who also handled other magazines. This led a rather erratic, short life, changing its name to *Marvel Tales*, and then to *Marvel Stories*. It published nine issues, ceasing in April 1941. It also had a short-lived companion, *Dynamic Stories*, which only lasted for two issues in 1939.

Marvel got off on the wrong foot with readers by featuring a lead story by Henry Kuttner which was considered somewhat sexy in its time. The publishers had decided that sex should increase its interest, but they soon found that it turned the readers off—not to say the mothers of many of those readers. (It also hurt the reputation of Kuttner in science fiction for several years.) The magazine never quite lived down that feeling.

Actually, *Marvel* was not that bad, if the bits of titillation in that lead story could be overlooked. Two stories were remembered well for many years. Both were by Arthur J. Burks. The first was "Survival," a long novelette in the August 1938 issue, which deals with a group of people who are forced to hide underground, and who learn to survive and grow strong. "Exodus," in November 1938, deals with their eventual return to the surface. Together, they form a rather good novel. And in February 1939, Jack Williamson had a book-length novel, *After World's End*, a fine romantic story set in the distant future, filled with colorful characters—including a marvelous intelligent bird —which won enthusiastic response from the readers. But the magazine never proved as profitable as others in the chain, and the publishers dropped it.

The next chain to pick up science fiction was Blue

Ribbon Publications, a rather minor group of pulp magazines that paid low rates on publication. They began *Science Fiction* in March 1939 and added *Future Fiction* in November 1939. Finally, they brought out a third magazine, *Science Fiction Quarterly*, in Summer 1940. The first two magazines changed about rather wildly, dropping one title and combining it with another, then reviving it, changing names, and generally seeming totally uncertain about what they were doing. In one form or another, the two regular magazines published 29 issues, finally ceasing publication with the July 1943 issue. The *Quarterly* was more consistent, but it also ended with the Spring 1943 issue, after 10 had been produced.

These magazines were initially edited by Charles Hornig, who had once been editor of *Wonder* for Hugo Gernsback. In 1941, Hornig was replaced by Robert A. Lowndes, a well-known fan for many years. The magazines improved slightly after the change, but there were almost no memorable stories. The rate and slowness of payment were too discouraging to the writers who were still free to produce fiction.

The prestigious chain of Munsey Publications made the next try, and they were offering a different kind of science fiction magazine. *Famous Fantastic Mysteries* was a reprint magazine, drawing upon the wealth of all the stories that had appeared over the years in *Argosy* and other Munsey magazines. Since most of those stories were only glorious legends to the newer readers, no longer generally available, the idea seemed a surefire success. And it proved to be a good one. The magazine started with the September–October 1939 issue under the able editing of Mary Gnaedinger, and quickly became a monthly. However, it shifted to bimonthly with the May–June 1940 issue. Like most magazines in the category, it was somewhat irregular, becoming a monthly again in 1942, missing a few issues, and going back to a bimonthly schedule at the end of 1945. But it was apparently doing well, despite the changes in frequency.

In July 1940, a companion magazine was begun, to handle novels from the old magazines in complete form. This was *Fantastic Novels*, of course, and five issues appeared by March 1941. But when Munsey sold their magazines to Popular Publications in 1942, only *Famous Fantastic Mysteries* continued publication. However, in 1948, the March issue of *Fantastic Novels* started its reappearance, and both magazines continued on the stands thereafter.

These were handsome magazines with covers and interiors by Virgil Finlay. (The first five issues of *FFM* did not use cover art, but Finlay did the cover for number six.) When Finlay was caught up in the war, he was replaced by Lawrence Stevens, who signed only his first name to his art. Both artists were so well liked that portfolios of their work were printed and eagerly purchased by the fans. The lead stories were generally excellent, since all the back issues of the Munsey publications could be combed for good fiction. Later, novels were also reprinted from older science fiction and fantasy books and proved equally welcome.

Fiction House also came up with a somewhat different idea when they decided to try a science fiction magazine. This was *Planet Stories*, under the editorial direction of Malcolm Reiss. It was issued as a quarterly and somehow performed the miracle of appearing four times each year through the whole of this age of science fiction. (In a few cases, it used the names of months instead of seasons, but it remained effectively a quarterly.) This magazine was planned to use only stories of space, other worlds, and rousing adventures between the planets. It was the most specialized of all the science fiction magazines. It was frankly slanted toward pure adventure-type stories. Despite these restrictions, good editing made it a magazine much appreciated by younger readers; and even many of the more sophisticated fans found it good reading.

Some of the fiction was even excellent. It was in *Planet* that Ray Bradbury had "The Million-Year Picnic" in Summer 1946, the first of his *Martian Chronicles*. Many other Bradbury stories were later published by *Planet*. Leigh Brackett was one of the regular contributors. She quickly became the favorite writer of the magazine. Her fiction had an unusual combination of vigor and richness of atmosphere, and her picture of Mars and its ancient cities filled with the tinkling of the bells the women wore became part of the legend of science fiction. And the writers included Fredric Brown, Raymond Z. Gallun and many other favorites.

Before buying the Munsey magazines, Popular Publications had begun a science fiction magazine of its own, but felt so unsure of it, apparently, that *Astonishing Stories* appeared as a Fictioneers Publication. This was edited by Frederick Pohl, one of the leading fans among the Futurians, and the first issue appeared in February 1940. It was intended as a bimonthly, but began skipping issues in 1941 and finally ceased publication in 1943, after 16 issues.

Pohl's budget for the magazine was small and he could only offer half a cent a word. He filled the magazine with stories by his friends from the Futurians and writers who had been associated with the group, as well as some writers (such as Isaac Asimov) for whom he had acted as author's agent. Generally, the magazine was one of the better new ones, partly because of Pohl's work in rewriting much of what he bought.

Astonishing soon had a companion magazine, *Super Science Stories*, which began in March 1940. (From March 1941 to August 1941, the title became *Super Science Novels Magazine*, but was then changed back to the original.) This was also edited by Pohl. It published the first story by James Blish in March 1940—"Emergency Refueling." It also had two stories by

Lyle Monroe—actually Robert A. Heinlein—including *The Lost Legion* in November 1941; this is a novel about extrasensory powers that covers practically everything that can be done with them and was far ahead of its time in dealing with such abilities. The magazine continued until May 1943, when Pohl was forced to leave to join the army. It had published 16 issues by that time. It was revived under the editorship of Ejler Jakobsson in January 1949, and published five more issues by the end of this period.

There were also a few magazines not connected to any of the larger chains. F. Orlin Tremaine returned briefly to editing science fiction by bringing out a new magazine of his own, *Comet Stories*, beginning with the December 1940 issue. This continued for a total of five issues, ending in July 1941. Morey and Paul alternated on the covers. In the July 1941 issue, Edward E. Smith began a new series with "Vortex Blaster." Storm Cloud faces danger in wiping out vortices that threaten ships in space. Only this first was published by Tremaine, however, and two later stories about Storm Cloud appeared in *Astonishing Stories*. After the collapse of *Comet Stories*, Tremaine abandoned his career as a magazine editor.

Donald A. Wollheim, one of the leading fans of the day, brought out two short-lived magazines. The first of these was *Stirring Science Stories*, which was divided into two parts, with the second half carrying fantasy. This magazine published four issues, from February 1941 to March 1942. The companion was *Cosmic Stories*, which appeared only three times, from March to July 1941.

The trouble with these magazines was that Wollheim had almost no budget for art or fiction. He was forced to ask for stories from friends, promising that they would be paid if the magazines showed a profit. Cyril Kornbluth, under the pseudonym of Cecil Corwin, supplied two excellent fantasies, and the first

The Golden Age

issue of *Stirring* marked the debut of Damon Knight as a writer. But the promised profit never materialized.

Later, Wollheim became an editor for Avon Books, where he issued a reprint magazine, *Avon Fantasy Reader*, which published a number of excellent fantasy stories. This began in 1947 and lasted through this period, for a total of 11 issues (numbered but not dated.)

There was also a single issue of the *Magazine of Fantasy* in the fall of 1949. But this belongs to another age, where its evolution can be discussed properly.

Fantasy Book also numbered but did not date its issues. Issue No. 1 appeared in 1947 and carried the first Andre Norton story (under the name of Andrew North), "The People of the Crater." A total of five issues appeared during this period.

Altogether, there were about 20 science fiction titles published between 1938 and 1949, most of which were not successful. The peak year was 1941. That year, the U.S. stands carried a total of 100 issues, counting fantasy magazines (*Unknown, Fantastic Adventures, Uncanny Stories, Weird Tales* and *Strange Stories*) as well as science fiction. This sounds impressive, but it meant an average of just a little over eight magazines a month —not much compared to the number of paperback books now available each month.

There was also activity outside the United States. In Canada, *Uncanny Tales* published mostly reprints from American magazines, lasting from November 1940 until September 1943. In Sweden, *Jules Verne Magasinet* appeared weekly and had 330 issues from 1940 to 1947. Much of this was also reprint material.

In England, fans had been struggling to get their own magazine for several years. (In 1934 there was a weekly magazine called *Scoops*, which ran for twenty issues, but it was aimed at the juvenile audience.) Finally, Walter Gillings found a publisher to issue *Tales of Wonder*, which he edited. It had two undated issues in 1937 and lasted as a quarterly until Spring 1942, with a total of 16 issues.

One of the larger English chains brought out *Fantasy* in 1938, but this folded after three issues. Another magazine with the same title was brought out by Walter Gillings in 1946, but also lasted for only three issues.

After the war, in 1946, Edward ("Ted") Carnell, one of the most active British fans, became editor of *New Worlds*. There were only five issues by the end of 1949, but it endured far beyond this period, for a total of 201 issues.

For now, however, between the stresses of war and the difficulty of recovery, science fiction could not flourish in England.

CHAPTER 13

Science Fiction in Books

THE PERIOD from 1938 to 1949 is usually referred to by older readers as the Golden Age because of the development that took place in *Astounding* under Campbell's influence. But in the long run, this is only part of the significance of those years. This was also the time when science fiction was finally discovered by the publishers of books and made available in permanent form.

Of course, there had always been books of such material. Verne and Wells owed much of their reputation to book publication. And a trickle of other such books had persisted throughout the twentieth century. But usually, after the rise of the magazines, these were not of such nature that they could be classified as typical of the category. During the period covered here, C. S. Lewis had published a trilogy, beginning with *Out of the Silent Planet* (1939), which were essentially religious in nature, though two of them were laid on other planets. Olaf Stapleton had *Sirius* in 1944. And George Orwell's *1984* appeared in 1949; but, like most dystopias (or anti-utopias) this was more propaganda than science fiction.

In the early part of the Golden Age, fantasy seemed to do much better than science fiction. Henry Holt published *Lest Darkness Fall*, by L. Sprague de Camp, and *The Incomplete Enchanter*, by de Camp and Fletcher Pratt, in 1941. Both were from *Unknown*, as were a few other books published by Holt. And while the first was about time travel and could have been considered science fiction, it was apparently rendered safe by first appearing in a fantasy magazine.

Phil Stong edited a collection of 25 stories, *The Other Worlds*, for Garden City Press in 1942; this book contained five science fiction stories, but it was mostly devoted to fantasies.

It was Donald A. Wollheim who first convinced publishers to do books that were labeled science fiction. In 1943, he edited *The Pocket Book of Science Fiction* (for Pocket Books, of course). This used considerable "classic" material by Benét, Bierce, Collier and Wells; but it also contained stories by Weinbaum, Campbell, Sturgeon and Heinlein. He also edited *Portable Novels of Science Fiction* for Viking in 1945; but the four novels were not typical of the category.

The big breakthrough, judging by hindsight, came with two anthologies that appeared in 1946.

The first of these to appear was *The Best of Science Fiction*, edited by Groff Conklin and published by Crown Publishers. It contained 40 stories and ran to 785 pages, selling for $3.50—a good bargain, even in those days. There was some older material by such writers as Stockton, Poe, Doyle and Wells, but most was from the magazines; more than a third came from Campbell's *Astounding*. Four of Heinlein's novelettes were included, as an example. The reader who might have been introduced to science fiction by that book would derive a very fair impression of the field from reading it.

Conklin followed this in 1948 with *A Treasury of Science Fiction* for Crown, in which the proportion of stories from Campbell's magazine was very much higher. He went on to do a great many other anthologies for Crown and other publishers, indicating that this venture into publishing must have been successful.

The second anthology of 1946, however, was the really important one. This was *Adventures in Time and Space*, edited by Raymond J. Healy and J. Francis McComas and published by Random House. This ran to 997 pages, all tightly packed with type, and sold for the bargain-basement price of $2.95. As nearly as I can estimate, there were almost half a million words in the 35 stories in the volume.

Furthermore, they were very good words, indeed. McComas was an old devotee of science fiction who had sold a few stories under the name of Webb Marlowe. Healy was also a reader; he was employed by Random House and knew the market possibilities of the book. Together, they produced an anthology that would be considered the definitive volume for a quarter of a century—the best possible introduction to science fiction as it had evolved by this time. Most of the major *Astounding* writers were represented with some of their best fiction. (I was told by Campbell that Healy and McComas came to get permissions before Conklin did, even though their book was released somewhat later; thus they had first choice of all the stories that had been written for the magazines—a chance that could never happen again!)

The success of the book can be deduced from the fact that after it went off sale finally as a Random House book, it was issued as a Modern Library edition under the title *Famous Science Fiction Stories* and continued to sell for many years. A paperback offset edition of the original is currently selling well for Ballantine Books, thirty years after its initial publication.

Strangely, Random House was not sufficiently impressed by the sale of the book to consider publishing more science fiction. The idea of a giant anthology selected from the best of two decades was apparently a different thing from that of novels by writers unknown to the general public in an untried field.

The teenage market was more willing to take a risk. Heinlein sold Scribner's a series of so-called juvenile science fiction novels, beginning in 1947 with *Rocket Ship Galileo*, upon which the movie *Destination Moon* was loosely based. This was followed in 1948 by *Space Cadet* and in 1949 by *Red Planet*. In this last, Heinlein really began to hit his stride in writing for a younger market. His first two Scribner's books had been too consciously slanted toward youth; in the third, he either relaxed or convinced the publisher that young readers could accept real science fiction. His tale of revolution on Mars as seen by two boys and a Martian "flatcat" had all the realism Heinlein could bring to the future of man on other planets.

As a result of Heinlein's success, the teenage market became extremely active in science fiction during the next decade. Libraries began to find that younger readers wanted such fiction more than most other types; it was hard to keep the books on the shelves.

The only unfortunate aspect of this development was that Heinlein turned a major part of his efforts to writing such books, and the magazines found it hard to get stories from him. But since such books stay in print for years—there is a new audience every year or so—

Heinlein found the new market far more profitable. So did Andre Norton, Lester del Rey, and other writers who turned to it.

Publishers of adult books were much slower to accept science fiction as a worthwhile category. They crept into the field gradually. Simon and Schuster began publishing some science fiction in 1948. Doubleday followed in 1949—and for their initial experiment, they chose *The Big Eye,* by Max Ehrlich, who was hardly a writer with a reputation in the science fiction magazines, or a name that was well known to the fans.

Other publishers published science fiction, doing so somewhat as a youngster might thrust a tentative toe into a pool after the last snow has barely melted. Most —including Simon and Schuster—soon abandoned any plans to publish science fiction regularly, though Doubleday has continued to the present without a break.

It was left to a different type of publisher to enter the field earlier and continue until a measure of success could prove that there was a regular market for science fiction books. This was what I call the fan publisher—a longtime reader or group of readers who decided to start a publishing company to bring out the books that no general publishing company seemed to be doing. Readers had been complaining for years at the dearth of science fiction books, pointing out that nearly every other category was available. Now some of them decided to do something about the lack.

Thomas P. Hadley seems to have been the first to organize such a publishing firm. His Hadley Publishing Company chose one of the most famous classics of the field as a beginning, and Edward E. Smith's *Skylark of Space* came off the press in 1946. Campbell's heavy-science classic, *The Mightiest Machine,* was issued in 1947, and Hubbard's *Final Blackout* in 1948.

These were somewhat amateurish books. They were illustrated, but the quality of the illustrations added nothing to their appearance. There was no sign that the books had been designed; they seemed to have been produced by the simple process of handing the manuscript to the printer—one not used to books—and telling him to turn it into a finished product. *Mightiest Machine*, for instance, is printed in a heavy Bodoni typeface, which is hardly suitable for easy reading or for the somewhat heavy nature of the book. But the readers were delighted with any kind of a book and in no mood to be critical.

Fantasy Press, run by longtime fan and writer in the early magazines Lloyd Arthur Eshbach, did a much better job. The books were handsome and uniform. The same design and type seemed to be used for all of them. It was a good design for such a purpose; it might not have been perfect for any single book, but all were clean in appearance, easy to read, and well printed. The paper was of a higher quality than could be found in many regular publisher's products, and after a quarter-century is still in excellent condition. Good margins and generally good bindings make the books a pleasure to read.

Fantasy Press issued a long list of titles. Williamson's *The Legion of Space* appeared in 1947, as did E. E. Smith's *Space Hounds of IPC*—the latter being below Smith's usual level, but much sought by the readers. Heinlein's *Beyond This Horizon* was issued in 1948, as was Weinbaum's *The Black Flame*; subsequently, all the shorter fiction of Weinbaum was issued in two collections. In general, Eshbach exercised good taste in his selections; he rarely did a book merely because it was rare and could be sold, but only the ones that he might choose for himself as a reader.

Eventually, Fantasy Press issued nearly all the works of E. E. Smith. Smith even did a great deal of writing for the series, turning his *Triplanetary* into the first of the Lens series and writing a new book, *First Lensman*, to bridge the gap between *Triplanetary* and the other books about the Lens.

This was a labor of love on Smith's part. Eshbach treated his writers as well as he could. He offered as much as $300 in advance, and he paid royalties promptly. But at $3 per book in limited editions, the books offered small chance of making much money. However, Eshbach offered a bonus; he had two copies of each book bound in leather, one for himself and one for the author. The satisfaction from that was better than money then.

The only real fault with the books from Fantasy Press was in the art. Eshbach could not afford regular commercial artists, and in many of the books, the art might better have been omitted.

Prime Press was less successful than Eshbach's firm, though it started well. It was formed by four men: James Williams was a used-book dealer who specialized in science fiction; "Bud" Waldo was a longterm fan; Alfred Prime, who contributed the name and most of the money, was a more recent convert to science fiction; and Oswald Train was a collector of note, who had one of the largest collections of rare science fiction in the country.

The first book from Prime Press was *The Mislaid Charm*, by Alexander M. Phillips, issued in 1947. This was a short novel from *Unknown* about a shy young man who gets mixed up with a gnome celebration. This was followed shortly by *Venus Equilateral*, the complete series of George Smith's stories of interplanetary communication and high jinks. Smith did a sort of electronic blueprint to be used as the dust jacket, which made it outwardly a handsome volume. But this was printed in heavy Bodoni type—a fine display type, but hardly the best for reading.

Prime later did . . . *And Some Were Human*, a collection of stories by Lester del Rey, and another collection by Theodore Sturgeon, *Without Sorcery*. Prime also did *Lest Darkness Fall*, de Camp's humorous novel of a modern man transported back to Rome in the days of its decline, and other science fiction, as well as a couple of almost forgotten American utopian novels.

Shasta Publishers was organized by two prominent fans, Melvin Korshak and T. E. Dikty. Their first project was *The Checklist of Fantastic Literature*, which sold well to libraries and gave the company financial means to launch their full publishing program. They printed the stories of Don A. Stuart (under Campbell's own name) as *Who Goes There?* and *Cloak of Aesir*. They also began the *Future History* series by Robert A. Heinlein. Their program was ambitious, and they seemed to be doing well until bad feeling was aroused over a prize contest; Philip José Farmer was the winner, but the book was never published and the prize money —some contributed by Pocket Books, Inc.—was never paid to Farmer. (Much later, considerably revised, the novel formed the basis for Farmer's *Riverworld* series.)

The largest publishing venture was that of Gnome Press, run by Martin Greenberg with the partnership of a well-known fan, David A. Kyle. And for quite a while, this seemed the most likely to succeed of the fan presses.

Gnome published Asimov's Foundation stories in three books. (These were later purchased by Doubleday after Asimov became one of their leading authors.) They had *City*, by Clifford D. Simak, one of the most popular series from *Astounding*. There were novels by Leigh Brackett, A. E. Van Vogt, Arthur C. Clarke, Henry Kuttner, Jack Williamson, George O. Smith, L. Ron Hubbard, L. Sprague de Camp and Fletcher Pratt—many of the best names in the field. The list grew to be a long one, with new books appearing regularly.

Gnome managed to get the works of Robert E. Howard, the great sword-and-sorcery writer from *Weird Tales*, whose stories of Conan the barbarian were largely responsible (along with the stories of H. P. Lovecraft) for keeping that magazine from folding.

Howard had a devoted following, and his stories had long been unavailable. L. Sprague de Camp had discovered a number of new Howard stories that had never seen print; some of these needed considerable work and others were incomplete. With these new stories, rewritten and completed by de Camp, the program of books provided both the beloved older stories and new material.

There were also some major anthologies edited by Greenberg. These were ahead of their time in being issued on single themes, such as space travel or some other major division of science fiction.

For a time, all seemed to be going well with Gnome. But then there were signs of financial trouble. Authors complained that they were not paid, or that the royalty statements did not accurately reflect the sales that had been made. Kyle dropped out of any active part in the publishing venture, maintaining only the interest that his previous financial backing made necessary. And after some desperate efforts to save the sinking company—including a deal that gave readers fifty percent off on any book's price—Gnome folded, leaving the rights to many books in a tangle.

The trouble all these fan publishers faced was that they had no effective sales force and no firm relations with the regular book dealers and stores. At first, a few advertisements in the magazines sufficed to draw eager purchasers. But as the number of books increased, this was no longer enough. The fan publishers could not hope to compete with the publishing firms that had been established for years and knew how to sell books as well as how to issue them.

The writers initially greeted such firms with great enthusiasm. Most science fiction authors had long given up any hope of having their works published in permanent form. Even being included in an anthology among twenty or more other writers was an unexpected bonus. They eagerly accepted the advances that ranged from $100 to $300; the money meant far less than the chance for a writer to put a real book of his work on his shelf.

It turned out to be a very short-range bonanza to those writers who sold their major fiction to the fan publishers.

With a few exceptions—such as Doubleday's picking up the Asimov books from Gnome—the regular publishers did not want to do an edition of a hard-cover book that had already been exploited by some other publisher. True, the fan publishers seldom printed more than 3,000 copies of each title; but those 3,000 copies had already covered the surest group of buyers. The result was that most of the books issued by these fan publishers never saw later hard-cover publication when the major publishers began regular issuance of science fiction.

It was a pity, because a high percentage of the very best novels of science fiction were to be found among those that would not be given regular hard-cover publication.

However, the success of the fan publishers for a time proved beyond question that there was a market for science fiction books. Much of the acceptance of science fiction as a successful publishing category must be laid to the work of these early publishers.

CHAPTER 14

The Growth of Fandom

THE PERIOD FROM 1938 to 1949 was as much a golden age for the development of fandom as it was for fiction. During that period, fans even discovered conclusive evidence that they could not only influence professional circles, but that they could themselves become "pros."

Charles Hornig had already moved from fandom to a job as editor of a leading magazine, to be followed by Mort Weisinger. Now four other prominent fans made the transition—Lowndes, Palmer, Pohl and Wollheim. Another fan, Hannes Bok, became a much-admired illustrator for professional magazines.

There were also many who began as fans and then went on to successful writing careers. Among these were such names as James Blish, Lester del Rey, Isaac Asimov and Arthur C. Clarke. Many of the professional writers also made something of the opposite transition, becoming involved at various levels with fan activities. The separation between fan and pro was obviously much less a barrier than in many other fields. There was certainly a large area of common interest.

Even the war proved to be no great hindrance to fandom. Many of the fans managed to continue reading the magazines and writing letters to those publications and articles for some of the fan magazines. (It was during this period that the search for a convenient name for such magazines was finally rewarded.

From now on, the fan publications will be called fanzines—a simple and elegant solution that only seems obvious when looking backward; naturally, the professional magazines became prozines.) Remarkably, very few of the active fans were killed during that war. There was considerable speculation about that for a time, but no reason was ever discovered.

Incidentally, it was also during this time that an abbreviation for science fiction was finally agreed upon by most fans; it now became sf, usually pronounced esseff, and replaced the older stf (from scientifiction) which was pronounced steff, a bit too much like stuff!

The number and variety of fans also increased considerably. In the previous period, the best estimate suggested that no more than 200 active fans (ones visibly devoted to fandom by some activity, such as writing letters, publishing fanzines, or joining a club) existed. Almost all of those were male. But now the number swelled to at least 500, and a 1948 poll by Bob Tucker (a leading fan who later wrote fiction under his real name, Wilson Tucker) showed that eleven percent of those active fans were female. (They were femfans in the jargon of fandom.)

Campbell had also taken a sampling of readers, partly to satisfy his own curiosity and partly to give the advertising department help in securing the right type of ads. About 3,000 readers sent in their replies. The results did not at all agree with the impression most people had of a bunch of socially frustrated, very young and immature people. The average income for the readers was $5,400 a year—a rather good salary in those days. Forty percent had technical or scientific training, many with doctoral degrees. And the average age was nearly 30.

This sampling may have produced somewhat select results. It would almost certainly have given different answers if conducted by some other magazine. Yet it clearly indicated that the readers included a fair number of highly educated and successful people. It applied to readers in general, rather than merely to fans; but the fans grew out of such readership and were at least as intelligent and literate as the average.

The fanzines proved this. While some were crude efforts by very young fans, many were excellent examples of amateur publishing. Few of them were able to use letterpress printing, as the leading ones had done previously; but most moved away from the purple ink of the hektograph to the much more readable results of mimeography. Some of the mimeography by the end of this period was extremely good, with a considerable amount of artwork. (Damon Knight even produced a book on the technique of making full use of a mimeograph stencil—printed on a mimeograph.)

It is impossible here to list even a reasonable fraction of the fanzines that were circulated during this period. *Fanzine Index 1930–1952* lists 2,000 titles. Many of these had circulations running from 100 to 250 copies. Such circulation, incidentally, was made possible by a change in the method of distributing; at first, the fanzines were sold at some nominal per-copy or per-year subscription rate; but in time, the practice grew of exchanging subscriptions with other publications, or sending subscriptions to all contributors.

Some of these fanzines were quite ambitious. Harry Warner, who maintained a tremendous correspondence for decades with other fans, brought out *Spaceways*, filled with a large amount of material supplied by professional writers, some of which was fiction. A somewhat similar fanzine was *Stardust*, published by Mark Reinsberg and W. Laurence Hamling; Hamling later became an assistant editor of *Amazing* and eventually founded his own publishing company, which printed a few science fiction novels in the early sixties.

James V. Taurasi published *Fantasy News*, 1938–1948, a news magazine which listed major events in fandom, stories to appear in future prozines, and all other news of science fiction. Later he published *Science Fiction Times*, considered by many fans to be too professionally oriented.

Some fan clubs published magazines—clubzines. And there were highly specialized fanzines, such as *Fantasy Advertiser*, with a subscription list said to be 1,000 strong, printing mostly advertisements for books and magazines available for sale or wanted by dealers.

Fantasy Commentator devoted a great deal of attention to serious research about science fiction and fandom. The *Fanscient*, put out by Don Day, also gave much attention to professional writers and their works. It published bibliographies of the works of prominent writers during thirteen issues (September 1947 to Spring–Summer of 1951). Many of the bibliographies were later incorporated into serious research papers.

There were also less serious magazines. Bob Tucker's *LeZombie* concentrated heavily on humor and often satirized fannish activities. Damon Knight's *Snide*, which had only three issues in 1940–1941, lived up to its title. Its analyses of some science fiction writers and their stories were both clever and cutting—as exemplified by a particularly detailed examination of some of Van Vogt's plotting, as analyzed by Knight.

Fanzines also had their collectors, some of whom tried to get a copy of every fanzine ever issued. (This was probably impossible, since many early ones had so little circulation—and to such a narrow group—that they were hardly known to exist.) In the long run, this proved a wise and rewarding hobby. A good collection of fanzines today may sell for more than a similar collection of professional material.

The amateur-press-association idea remained very active during this period. FAPA had expanded to 50 members (51 for a time through a miscount) and had a long waiting list. As a result of this, there were several plans to set up other such APAs. One of these was the Vanguard Amateur Press Association, which was organized in 1945 by a number of the Futurians. This soon began to devote most of its space to music and other things far removed from science fiction; when fiction of any kind was discussed, it was usually centered around the works of Joyce and Pound, rather than Heinlein and Ley. And there were smaller organizations founded to exchange publications; most of these, however, had short lives with few submissions.

Fanzine publishing received quite a boost when the prozines began to notice such activity. *Startling Stories* began publishing reviews of the fanzines submitted to them in the forties, listing the price and address, so that readers could subscribe. And beginning May 1948, *Amazing* instituted a department called "The Clubhouse," where professional writer Rog Phillips (Roger Philip Graham) discussed and listed the fanzines submitted to him. Here a beginning fanzine publisher could be treated as seriously as if he were a major publishing house.

The number of science fiction clubs continued to increase. Whether the Futurians should be classed as a club or not is rather doubtful, since they were more like a group of friends (and sometimes enemies) who saw a great deal of each other and who were mostly intent on trying to write professionally; but the group was still very active in New York City. At times, members banded together to rent an apartment, one of which communal dwellings was known as the Ivory Tower. They were still often in a state of turmoil, and eventually broke up effectively, partly as a result of the war and partly because of feuding.

There was also a real club for fans, known as the Queens Science Fiction League. This was dominated by Will Sykora, James Taurasi and Sam Moskowitz, all important fans. The club lasted through most of the forties, and was claimed to be the largest of all the fan clubs. It held regular meetings and was able to get many of the professional writers and editors to make guest appearances.

The Newark Science Fiction League was organized in April 1940 by Sam Moskowitz, and boasted an attendance of 65 at its July meeting. This later became the Eastern Science Fiction Association, which met for years at Slovak Sokol Hall in a huge room above a bar. In 1948, it began a series of regular spring meetings, featuring major speakers from among the professionals. These guests were treated to a dinner at a local restaurant for their efforts.

Boston also managed to hold regional conventions, called Boskones (named for a villainous group in Smith's Lensman stories), from 1941 to 1945.

One of the oldest continuous clubs was the Philadelphia Science Fiction Society, which began in 1935 and continued to hold regular meetings through this period and beyond. Visitors to the PSFS were often surprised to see a huge sign in downtown Philadelphia with those letters glaring at them. It turned out, however, that this was a sign for a major company that had no relation to science fiction.

Other clubs were organized in Cincinnati, Minneapolis, Seattle, Portland—and in various parts of California, naturally.

Los Angeles fans originally began to organize as part of the old Gernsback Science Fiction League. But by 1940, they set up independently as the Los Angeles Science Fantasy Society, LASFS for short. They went through the usual internal struggles that beset so many clubs, but somehow managed to keep going, with Walter Daugherty as the director much of the time. They had their own clubroom and published their own clubzine. Despite frequent internal disagreement among members, they managed to survive far beyond the decade.

Fans in the San Francisco Bay Area also organized a

strong and lasting club toward the end of the decade. This one was distinguished by the name it chose for itself, derived from the comic strip *Barnaby:* The Elves, Gnomes and Little Men's Science Fiction Chowder and Marching Society. The Little Men, as they were commonly known, later awarded a prize to professionals they chose to honor; it showed a brass plate with two small footprints and was known as the Invisible Little Man Award.

For those who could not conveniently belong to any club, there was the NFFF—the National Fantasy Fan Federation. This was organized in 1941 to bring all fans together into a national organization. By 1949 it boasted 373 members. To a large extent, it failed in its original purpose. But it proved extremely helpful to many neofans (newcomers to fandom) through a welcoming committee which sent letters and offered introductions to each new member. Later it also reserved a room at major science fiction conventions; there fans who might not have a circle of friends were made welcome and given a chance to meet others.

There was also another club organized in New York City in 1947 by Frederik Pohl and Lester del Rey. It was named the Hydra Club, since nine people attended the organizing meeting, including Judith Merril, Philip Klass (William Tenn), David Kyle and Robert A. Lowndes. This was basically intended as a fan club for professionals and their close friends. It had an elaborate constitution, designed to prevent the feuds that had beset other New York clubs—and which seemed to work for several years. Membership reached about 50, and monthly meetings were held in an old apartment located in the meat-market area on Washington Street. It also held a big New Year's party each year. For several years, it was the effective center of much of the professional activity of science fiction.

Fan activities were not confined to the United States, however. There were active fan clubs in Montreal and

Toronto. In England the British Fantasy Society managed to last through all the dark days of the war. The Science Fantasy Society, as it was called in 1948, grew to include 150 members. There were even conventions, the Eastercon in 1944 and Loncon in 1949 being the major ones.

In Belfast, Walter Willis published one of the most literate and admired of all fanzines, *Slant*. In Australia, the Futurian Society of Sydney was organized in 1939 and became the Australian Futurian Association in 1941. Active fandom was really spread throughout the entire English-speaking world.

Probably the most important long-range activity of the fans, however, was the creation of "world science fiction conventions." (The quotes are proper for this period, though in time the rather grandiose appellation came to be justified.)

This activity was foreshadowed when a group of New York fans took a trip down to Philadelphia to meet with the fans there. The idea of different groups getting together was so attractive that it was suggested that a world convention should be held, and the New York fans returned, imbued with enthusiasm for the idea.

In time, this ripened into the determination to hold such a convention. New York City was the obvious place for this major convention; it was not only an area possessing many well-known fans but also was the center of science fiction publishing and the home of many of the professional writers.

The Nycon (as it was called) was held on July 4th weekend, 1939, at Caravan Hall in mid-Manhattan, and was a three-day affair. The Guest of Honor was Frank R. Paul. Most of the magazines had given considerable publicity to the affair, and fans came from across the country; this was literally true, since Chicago, Texas, Virginia and California were represented, as well as most other areas. Attendance was estimated at

200. The chairman was Sam Moskowitz, representing a group called New Fandom which had been organized to put on the convention. A fairly large number of writers attended, as did John W. Campbell and Leo Margulies, editorial director of Standard Magazines. An auction of art donated to the convention was held to help pay for it, and there was a banquet, but only 31 fans were able to afford the $1 cost of the banquet! Guests of Honor, auctions, speeches and banquets became regular affairs in future conventions, but the softball game played on the third day did not.

Perhaps the most famous—or infamous—part of the affair among fans was what came to be known as the Great Exclusion Act. Long before the convention, feuding had broken out between some of the Futurians and others working to hold the affair. When the convention opened, some of the Futurians who had been most active—Pohl, Wollheim and Lowndes, among others—appeared; after considerable hassling, they were denied admittance by Moskowitz. This was blown up into a major action by many of the partisan fans. Fortunately, it did not set a precedent.

The second world sf convention was the Chicon, held in Chicago in 1940. There was no struggle at the door this time, but there was a struggle among the fans putting on the convention which destroyed Chicago fandom for some time to come. The affair itself ran smoothly. Edward E. Smith was Guest of Honor. The banquet cost the unthinkable price of $2. And there was a costume masquerade, where fans and authors dressed up as characters from science fiction and vied for prizes for the best costume. (Unlike masquerades held much later, there were no costumes designed to reveal the maximum amount of the ladies' skin and other assets!) The affair had an attendance of about 125.

Denver hosted the Denvention in 1941, with Robert Heinlein as Guest of Honor. Only 70 fans managed to show up for this, but the reports I received made it seem an outstanding success.

The fourth worldcon (as they became known) was to be held in Los Angeles in 1942. But the war destroyed such plans, and it had to be postponed until 1946. To make up for it, the affair then lasted for four days, with about 120 people attending. In 1947, Philadelphia was host to the Philcon, this time held on Labor Day weekend. (Most United States worldcons have chosen that date since then.) This was attended by more than 200 people and was considered something of a record; indeed, it was the largest for several years.

For 1948, the fans made their first gesture toward fulfilling their claim of holding a world convention by voting that the convention be held outside the United States. Toronto was host to the Torcon.

The last convention of the decade (the seventh worldcon) was held in Cincinnati in 1949 and known as the Cinvention. This was distinguished by the fact that Ted Carnell was able to attend—the first British fan able to make the trip for a convention.

By then, the custom had been firmly established. It was taken for granted that there would be a worldcon every year, complete with auction, banquet, masquerade—and numerous speeches from both fans and professionals.

The conventions were to dominate future fan activities in many respects. A great deal of publicity about science fiction was generated through them. At the Cinvention, for instance, writers were invited to appear on a local radio station to discuss their activities, the convention, and the aims of science fiction. There were stories about the affair in all the local papers; some of these made overmuch of the sillier trimmings inevitable to any convention; but others discussed the affair fairly seriously.

The conventions acted as a central point around

which both fans and professionals could gather and find their common objectives. The magazines entered into the spirit of things willingly, contributing art for the auctions and a great deal of free publicity; the book publishers and dealers found the conventions an ideal place to hawk their wares; and the writers soon found the worldcons a fine place to meet some of their editors and to exchange shop talk with fellow writers —often with leading fans taking an active part.

More than any other activity, the worldcons gave a feeling of unity and common goal to all the elements of the world of science fiction.

CHAPTER 15

Reshaping the Future

To GET SOME IDEA of the importance of Campbell's first twelve years as editor, try thinking of what would be different without his influence. Let's begin by eliminating the writers he discovered and developed. There might be no Heinlein, Asimov, Sturgeon, Van Vogt, Clement, Piper, del Rey, G. O. Smith, de Camp or Poul Anderson! There would still be Clarke, Simak, Kuttner and Leiber, in all probability; but their work would certainly be different.

Science fiction might not be an accepted category for major publishers. The anthologies and many of the early novels which proved commercially successful came largely from the pages of *Astounding*. And after that supply was exhausted, many of the most successful books were produced by writers from Campbell's school.

Of course, some of the writers might have begun without Campbell. (I know positively that one would not.) Most of them, however, state that Campbell was the most important influence in their careers. Their work would have been different without him.

Campbell also infused his writers with a feeling of being part of a family of the elect. Competition was keen among them, but it was always friendly. Ideas passed freely among them, whether filtered through Campbell's enriching mind or not. And each writer was forced to stretch his limits to keep up with advances made by the others; that feeling of stretching was enormously stimulating.

Raymond Palmer created at least as large a stable of writers as did Campbell; and there was a great deal of goodwill among those who worked for him. But they were held together by Palmer's very considerable charm and a sort of predetermined idea of what their stories should be. Rather than stretching, they learned to fit the environment of Palmer's concepts. Had his ideas dominated the field, there would have been very little adult-type science fiction produced.

Perhaps Campbell's greatest contribution was the attitude he wanted from his writers. He wanted them to *live* in their futures. And he wanted those futures to be livable. The time to visit futures that were only stage fronts was over. We'd had enough of scenery with no backsides and creatures that seemed to have no life or history away from their machinery. It was time to go behind the scenes and discover the reality of those future worlds.

Campbell never put it quite that way. But looking back across the years, I can find no better way to express it. Campbell had grown up with science fiction, and the stage scenery of marvels was old to him; he had designed some of the best marvel stages of all. Now it was time to ring down the curtain and follow the actors outside, where marvels might exist in reality.

The writers he included in his stable were also largely men who had grown up with—and grown beyond—the routine of painted marvels used to stage petty melodramas. Most of them sensed much of what he felt. When they saw the beginning of something fresh in his magazine, they came flocking to join him. And those who were aware of the past deficiencies were also usually potentially better writers than most who had previously worked in the field.

Like Campbell, they had become future-oriented, with the sense that the present was not the permanent center of everything; to them, the future was a real place. It was three-dimensional.

Campbell insisted that anything in that future must have implications for other things—and for social patterns to fit. It was all well and good that writers had once predicted the motorcar and the traffic jams in the cities; but no one had predicted the changed social patterns that arose because of general mobility—or the huge network of roadways. That *should* have been predicted—inventions have social effects, as witness the cotton gin! Hence, all implications of any change must be considered. You can't have everyone owning compact helicopters without considering what all that noise and airblast does to a city—or whether there will be cities, when such easy and rapid transit makes it possible to locate a home in Vermont, a factory in New Jersey. . . . Well, *figure it out!*

Of all his writers, Heinlein probably was best able to give Campbell precisely what he wanted. Heinlein was a romantic realist. When Heinlein thought about replacing cars that moved on roads with roadways that moved, he rebuilt the society to go with them—even to what might happen when such roadways had union troubles!

Heinlein was also a master at taking the reader into the future without long descriptive lectures. His hero was usually a highly competent man who faced a difficult problem growing out of some aspect of that future. The reader was inserted directly into that man's mind to see and feel the future world as the hero did. It was all matter-of-fact, as a story of the present might be, and it seemed real and inevitable. By the time the reader had finished the story, he had lived in the world in which it was set.

In some contrast to Heinlein, Asimov was a realistic romantic. To him, the robot was one of the ultimate wonders, as it was to Simak or del Rey. But to accept it, he had to devise a set of rules for the robot—the so-called laws of robotics. Then he spent untold amounts of ingenuity examining every possible implication of those rules to show robots as the wonderful people he always knew they were.

For his Foundation series, he indulged his romanticism fully by having mankind master of all the galaxy. But he didn't do the obvious, which was to tell of marvelous wars between worlds, fought with fantastic future weapons. Instead, he turned to the past and used it as an analogue for the future. There had always been cycles, probably always would be. Empires rise and decay, giving place to new. So let's assume the ultimate—a Galactic Empire.

Asimov didn't invent this idea. Edmond Hamilton wrote about an empire of stars in the "Interstellar Patrol" series for *Weird Tales* in the twenties. But Asimov carried the idea further, by having a collapsed empire, once galaxy-wide. Reason said such an empire could not last forever, any more than the ancient and mighty empire of Rome could stand against the spread beyond the limits which it could govern speedily and firmly.

History showed that the fall of a great empire is followed by a long dark age. But Asimov wanted to eliminate most of that dark period. His method involved no great conquering hero, but merely a small set of events that would use the tides of history. The stories dealt with a great attempt at *social* engineering, rather than gadgetry. Thus Asimov invented "psychohistory."

Actually, Asimov's first story in *Astounding* had been based upon a social idea. The idea that men could build a ship to go to the Moon was ancient; but to that he added the further idea that there would be mass resistance to building such a ship, as there had been mass resistance to many other new ideas. It turned out to be wrong, but it was a legitimate extrapolation from many previous social patterns.

Campbell was always receptive to mixing the hard science—the physical, technological developments—in stories with as much social science as he could get. He pointed out that every major invention had changed society—with gunpowder as an example. Hence, to base a future on physical science and neglect the social developments was unrealistic.

A large number of his writers agreed. Heinlein's "Future History" contained extensive notes on social changes and the development of new tools for social science. Henry Kuttner based most of his better stories on some aspect of social change. And Fritz Leiber's first novel, *Gather Darkness*, dealt with a world in which science had become a religion—a fresh theme at the time, though often used—and often used badly—since then.

Despite what many older readers seem to remember, this was not a period of bright new ideas. Most of the basic ideas of science fiction were already in existence; the last may have been Wells' idea of using a machine to go through time, though time travel was itself already an old idea when he used it. Even Murray Leinster's idea of parallel branches of time in "Sidewise in Time" was not entirely new, though it was the first seminal use of this theme; there had been other stories of alternate time branches.

Still, if the ideas were not new, their treatment often was. Campbell tended to look on all obvious developments of an idea with suspicion. "Yes, but . . ." was one of his favorite openings to a discussion. Maybe Martians like it dry; maybe an enslaved race of intelligent quadrupeds need to be slaves; maybe it isn't power but weakness that corrupts. So far as he was able, he insisted that his writers approach every idea as if it had never been done before and question all the axioms of science fiction. The result was that a great many stories based upon old ideas suddenly became fresh and exciting.

As an example, T. L. Sherred wrote a story called "E for Effort," which immediately established him as a major writer. This was based on the old idea of a device that could see into the past. Sherred's hero used it to make spectacular movies of great moments in history, with lip readers to dub in the spoken part. Fine. Then the man decided to make a movie of the life of Christ! And all hell broke loose, because the reality didn't precisely agree with any sect's dogma! It was an inevitable development of human curiosity and human religious attitudes—but nobody had looked at more than the gadgetry before in using the idea.

This story exemplifies what Campbell wanted in another way; it is a very human story, told from the view of a man involved in the events, and detailing his emotions and reactions, rather than being a story of a gadget. The action in the story is dramatic—but it is made much more so by being shown from the reactions of the characters, with the action revealed only as they see and feel it.

From the beginning of his career as an editor, Campbell had been stressing this need for action's being subordinated to the reaction of the characters. A sun going nova and destroying its planets lacks emotional interest if no sentient beings are involved; on the other hand, a door opening slowly has no significance, unless the reader sees it through the emotions of a man fearful of what's on the other side. "I want reactions, not mere actions. Even if your character is a robot, human readers need human reactions from him," is the gist of Campbell's first listing of his requirements in the 1938 *Writers' Yearbook*.

Simak has stated that it was this type of personal, human reaction in the stories that made him resume writing science fiction after a long absence from the field. Certainly his stories usually involve men who care —care very deeply. Sturgeon had a great talent for making any idea one of odd but fascinating emotional appeal; in his hands, even a scientist fiddling around on a lonely island or a group of men spending an evening playing poker became instantly absorbing to the reader. In most of del Rey's fiction, the protagonist is essentially alone, against the world for some reason; and this fitted the emotional response of a majority of the readers. His stories tend to be close to here and now, where maximum identification is possible. De Camp also depended on emotional appeal—but his stories depend on the contrast of normal, rational human emotions and reactions against some unusual situation for their effect.

None of these changes in the magazine meant that the old sense of wonder was lacking. E. E. Smith continued to develop his *Lensman* series with greater and greater scope. George O. Smith went from engineering triumph to greater triumphs. Hal Clement began developing his alien creatures and backgrounds. And Van Vogt surpassed all limits previously set on wonders. One novel involves an immortal superman in a world divided between an all-powerful Empress and even more all-powerful shops that sold miraculous weapons. To complicate things, it turned out that the superman had created both conflicting powers in the first place. Now he was fighting for and against both of them. And that is only the background for wonders in *The Weapon Makers!*

Campbell wanted the marvels. But he wanted them

in stories that were at least as soundly plotted, motivated, characterized and developed as possible. And while he couldn't always get what he wanted, he managed to get a higher percentage of all the elements than anyone had succeeded in getting before.

He had no desire to "bring science fiction into the mainstream," as some writers now seem to wish. He had little use for the moribund mainstream, as he saw it. He claimed that the mainstream, limited mostly to here and now, was only a small sub-section of the area of science fiction, which encompassed all time, space and possibility. I have no idea how seriously he took this idea. But he was totally serious about the fact that science fiction was the only fiction which dealt fully with modern reality.

C. P. Snow had developed the thesis that there are two cultures, one of science and the other of the humanities, and that few people can exist firmly within both. Campbell agreed, according to the discussions I had with him. Most writers in the mainstream seemed almost unaware that there was a culture of science, even though most of modern civilization and society was based on that culture. Science fiction was one area where the two cultures could be fused, as they were being fused in the real world, whether people knew it or not.

Most early science fiction had neglected the humanities, of course. And that was just as bad as the fiction that neglected science.

Campbell was always something of a missionary. From the beginning of his tenure, he set about the happy business of proselyting at every opportunity, attempting to cross-breed the two cultures. To those who had some talent, he labored ceaselessly in trying to teach what he knew of the secrets of literature, as they had evolved over the centuries. He didn't expect great literature, but he wanted at least the measure of skill and literacy found in the better magazines devoted to other types of entertainment fiction. And for those who still confused the technology of early science fiction with real science, he began running editorials devoted to current developments, as well as articles. He also wrote innumerable letters to his writers speculating on the things he had learned from the scientists with whom he corresponded and whom he visited.

The result was that during almost all of this period and beyond, *Astounding* was generally recognized as the leading science fiction magazine, even by most of its competitors.

Of course, this doesn't mean that Campbell had cornered all the capable writers, or that all the best stories appeared in the pages of *Astounding*. There were excellent stories in even some of the transient, minor magazines. And for the taste of many readers, some of the better competitors were more satisfying. Quite a few readers complained that *Astounding* was too technical or that there wasn't enough out-and-out action in the stories.

Certainly after Sam Merwin took over *Startling* and *Thrilling Wonder*, the stories became much better written and had a much higher set of standards than before. And for those who wanted pure adventure beyond the limits of Earthly backgrounds, *Planet Stories* did an excellent job. Brackett, Kuttner, Leinster, Bradbury and quite a few other writers appeared fairly regularly in the pages of those magazines. The field as a whole was improving, and how much of that was due to the influence of Campbell is hard to say. A goodly share of the stories in other magazines were by writers who had been directly affected by Campbell. But there were other writers—Bradbury, for example—who had sold little or nothing to him. Edmond Hamilton deliberately did not submit to Campbell, feeling that there could be no meeting of minds between editor and writer, in his case.

Maybe the field would have evolved without Campbell. (Personally, I doubt it, which is why I've summarized this period through him and his writers.) If so, the evolution would have been much different. To some extent, Campbell built on what Tremaine had done. But Tremaine had gone as far as he could, and I can find no sign in the history of the time that anyone but Campbell was ready to carry science fiction in new directions. Rather, most who did become editors either copied or treated the field as no more than an area for good action stories.

Certainly, when the major publishers discovered science fiction as a successful category, they turned first to the works of writers who had appeared in the pages of *Astounding*.

And today, while there is considerable debate about the exact dates of the Golden Age of Science Fiction, almost all who refer to it do so in terms of what John W. Campbell was doing at the time in *Astounding*.

PART IV

The Age of Acceptance

(1950-1961)

CHAPTER 16

The Quest for Magic

THE PERIOD BEGINNING IN 1950 probably was as responsible for major changes in the nature of science fiction as that which had preceded it, though this was not immediately apparent. Hindsight suggests to me that one of the major factors in the further evolution was a tendency to put aside the previous dependence on technology and science, and to turn to other sources. One of these sources—perhaps the most influential—was what I can only call the quest for magic.

Ray Palmer had begun it with his Shaver Mystery stories about various ideas of mysticism and the occult. At the time, this was bitterly resented by most old-time science fiction readers; in fact, there were threats of boycotting his *Amazing Stories,* or passing stern resolutions against him. None of these came to pass. Yet the dissent of the fans apparently had some effect upon him, since he promised that his new magazine, *Other Worlds,* would not use the Shaver Mystery.

He kept his word on that, literally; but somehow, the spirit of his agreement was not in consonance with the obvious message. Within a short time, he turned to another wondrous mystery and began stirring up as much furor as ever.

His new hobbyhorse was the mystery of flying saucers. There had been some mention of such mysterious ships—or whatever—in the sky before; but it was Palmer who first began to exploit and promote the idea fully. He has since been called the father of flying saucers; perhaps he was only their godfather, but his part in developing the widespread interest in them is certainly a large one.

The mysterious objects he was interested in were not the present, rather staid UFOs, or Unidentified Flying Objects, which might be anything from ball lightning to things just outside our present knowledge. He was looking for real spaceships that contained alien creatures from some other world; and there was always a hint that these superior creatures were not too unlike some of the people of the old Shaver Mystery. Most of the accounts of little green men and god-like beings who brought great messages to save Earth were helped to full development by his contributions to saucerology. (After all, he had all the devices of science fiction in his memory, useful in enriching the stories of sightings that were often lacking in any real details.)

In 1951, he ran a two-part serial by "Captain A. V. G." entitled *I Flew in a Flying Saucer*. There is no proof, but many suspect that the story was written by Palmer himself. And while it was published as fiction, there was a strong editorial hint that it was not so fictional, after all. Eventually, *Other Worlds* stopped publishing avowed fiction altogether and became a new magazine, *Flying Saucers*.

To some extent, Palmer's proselyting for flying saucers spilled over into the other magazines. There was considerable discussion in many of the letter columns, and several magazines published articles on the subject, both pro and con. But the effect on the field as a whole was comparatively unimportant.

Dianetics, however, was another matter. This started in *Astounding*, the highly respected magazine that had always clung more rigidly to real science and technology than any other. It began with an article by L. Ron Hubbard in the May 1950 issue—"Dianetics, the Evolution of a Science." (Some of the details and terminology of this article differed considerably from those given in the book on the subject which was published soon afterward.) This was given a further jolt of publicity in January 1951, when *Astounding* published Hubbard's "Dianometry," supposedly a study of the measured results of the use of dianetics, but really a pretty strong bit of propaganda for the use of the new "science."

Furthermore, Campbell was thoroughly converted to dianetics and deeply involved with Hubbard and a few others in extending its use. The writers with whom Campbell corresponded or who visited him were bombarded with accounts of the miracle cures caused by dianetic "auditing."

This was not exactly something out of mysticism or the occult, of course—though it was very much something lacking in any proper relationship to science fiction publishing. But it had a few of the characteristics of magic. Cures were supposed to be so easy that anyone who learned the simple technique could achieve them; results close to the miraculous were supposedly produced. And the reaction to the critical reviews of experts were treated to the "closed minds" and "establishment vested interest" arguments brought against scientific facts by many of the cultists.

For a time, dianetics split science fiction readers into two sharply differing camps, and the arguments were hot and heavy. Among the writers and readers I knew, a majority seemed to accept dianetics, though those opposed—including myself—were more violent on the subject.

There was also a marked change in the nature of the stories in *Astounding* following this. More and more began to use the jargon of dianetics, and to be based—at least in part—on some aspect of Hubbard's teachings. This even spread to stories appearing in other magazines. Campbell swore he was not encouraging this; indeed, I know of cases where a story was rejected for being too much straight dianetics. But a number of factors influenced the writers: the false belief that this was what would sell to Campbell; the ease of finding new ideas in the subject; and the interest many of the writers had in the subject.

A. E. Van Vogt, at the height of his popularity, gave up writing entirely to devote himself to running a dianetics auditing service. For many years, he wrote no science fiction.

Eventually, some of the furor died down. Campbell came in time to question some things about dianetics, though he indicated that Hubbard's basic discovery was valuable. But a number of writers who had not been able to swallow dianetics tended to avoid *Astounding* from then on. Among them was Willy Ley, who had long been the source of countless excellent articles for the magazine. Others were afraid to submit to Campbell; they felt he would reject their stories because they had argued strongly against dianetics.

This was unfair; Campbell was still open to any good writer and story. (When it was reported to me that I would never again be able to sell Campbell because of articles I had written against dianetics, I immediately took him a story. He was as cordial as ever, bought the story, and suggested several more ideas to me.)

By the time the controversy had finally died down completely, Campbell had made another discovery. This was *psionics*—by which Campbell originally meant the use of science to create devices that would harness or augment the so-called psi powers—telepathy, levitation, clairvoyance, etc.

Campbell himself wrote the first article on psionics for the June 1956 issue of *Astounding*: "Psionic Machine—Type One." This dealt with what came to be known as the Hieronymous Machine. The device had an electronic circuit coupled to a flat plate of some nonconducting material. When various materials were placed at the proper spot on the device, a man was supposed to feel the plate suddenly get a tacky feeling (supposedly hard to describe), which could enable the skilled operator to sense the presence of just about whatever he was looking for. There was also an elaborate theory connected with the original machine, involving strange radiation to which only the human brain seemed to be sensitive.

Later on, Campbell revealed that the device would work just as well if one replaced all the electronics with nothing but a hastily drawn, penciled diagram. That obviously made it fully psionic, rather than semielectronic.

Campbell explained it all as being magic—his own word for it. And his fascination with all kinds of psi phenomena grew rapidly, far beyond the mere use of machines that augmented psi powers. Not surprisingly, more and more of the fiction in the magazine began to center around such things as telepathy, the ability to move things at a distance by mental power, etc.

Campbell did discover another psionic machine, however—a very ancient one, indeed. The first article on this was "Divining Rod, Standard Equipment," by Murray F. Yaco, in the October 1958 issue. According to this, the divining rod was being used to locate such things as underground pipes, rather than in dowsing for water. There was a big to-do in the magazine. Campbell even discovered that metal rods worked as well as the familiar willow or hickory dowsing rod. (They did, as a matter of fact—precisely as well.) Few stories used dowsing, however, probably because the applications didn't fit science fiction very well.

The next device was a means of getting a space drive without the use of rockets, and was first reported in an editorial in the December 1959 issue; later, in 1960, three articles were used on the subject, all written by Campbell. There was even a cover which showed a standard submarine being driven through space by use of this so-called Dean Drive.

The origin of the excitement was a device patented by Norman L. Dean for converting rotary motion into unidirectional motion, according to the patent application. It consisted of two eccentrically mounted, counter-rotating weights which produced an oscillation; at one point in the cycle, however, the oscillating part was coupled to a rod or the frame by a clutch; it was then supposed to transfer the energy to that rod or frame in one direction only. In fact, it did so, at least when operating against certain types of resistance that were hardly to be found in space. (There's still some controversy about just how it worked.)

In any event, there seemed to be little chance of deriving sufficient power-to-weight from it to operate any conceivable spaceship. But once again, it was used to prove that scientists won't look at any new ideas and that the establishment (whatever it is) is designed to preserve the status quo forever. And that helped spread further the idea of assorted magic just waiting for honest testing and exploitation.

In private discussions with writers and fans, Campbell showed an interest in numerous other wonders, many closely associated with cultism. He seemed to accept such things as a wonder-worker who could look at the photograph of a field of diseased wheat and cure it at a distance by treating the picture! But such things as these were never the subject for articles in the magazine, though some influence appeared in stories written by writers to whom Campbell had revealed these remarkable abilities and results.

Campbell and Palmer were not alone during this period. Under the editorship of Hans Stefan Santesson, *Fantastic Universe* published more articles about flying saucers and many other unaccepted mysteries than appeared in any other science fiction magazine. So far as I could determine, Santessen was skeptical about such things, but felt that all sides deserved a hearing and also that the controversies were good for circulation. Long before Erich von Däniken began writing books, the pages of *Fantastic Universe* were filled with accounts of ancient astronauts who were worshiped as gods, who led the Hebrews out of Egypt, and such things.

(Later, in 1963, when Campbell had just finished running a series of astrology "experiments" by Joseph F. Goodavage, Frederick Pohl began publicizing the search by R. C. W. Ettinger for a means of immortality —in this case, through freezing the body at death and trusting that science would someday find means of reviving the corpse and repairing the damage that had proved fatal. This evolved into a whole business of cryonics and some very sophisticated equipment that is still being used.)

Eventually, most of the excitement about any particular idea of Campbell (or Palmer) died down, and it has been a long time since any new miraculous discovery has appeared. But indirectly, the results and the attitudes are still affecting science fiction.

During the period under discussion, psi became one of the major sources of science fiction story ideas. It had been used previously, of course. It had served as a convenient trick for bridging the gap of language between humans and aliens, or as a means of coupling a man's mind to some complicated machine. Even before Campbell discovered psionics, the psi element in science fiction was increasing. Van Vogt gave telepathy to all his tendriled slans. Heinlein wrote a straight psi novel under the pen name of Lyle Monroe—*Lost Legion* in the November 1941 issue of *Super Science Stories*. But generally, psi had remained only a minor part of science fiction.

Now, however, encouraged by Campbell's fascination with the subject, more and more writers began using wild talents as the major source of their stories.

Some issues of *Astounding* had almost no other type of fiction.

The appeal to writers was obvious. Stories of future developments involving hard science required either knowledge of the subject or considerable research. The fictional use of psi required almost no effort by comparison. In many cases, psi even saved the trouble of hard plotting, since psi could be used as a happy means of solving any problem. That produced wish-dream stories, of course—stories which involved no real problem, but only success piled on success, until even the hardiest dreamer must grow bored. But many such stories were published. (*Jack of Eagles*, by James Blish, a 1952 expansion of his novelette "Let the Finder Beware," published by Greenberg, was an exception. In that, the psi powers constituted the problem facing the hero; and there was considerable effort to explain the psi factors by means of science. But this came before the real rush of psi stories.)

New writers, in particular, found psi irresistible, and editors were sometimes faced with a dearth of other types of stories. Many older readers began to stop reading the magazines. But in their place came new readers, more than willing to accept telepathy, telekinesis, and such things. Even the makeup of the science-fiction audience underwent considerable change.

The whole attitude toward science and scientists began to alter, also. Campbell's editorials on the closed-minded scientific establishment and the "conspiracy" against new ideas had considerable effect.

By now, psi is as much an accepted part of science fiction—whatever some readers may think—as space flight. Quite a few of the better writers in the field (such as Marion Zimmer Bradley, Frank Herbert and Anne McCaffrey) depend heavily upon it.

It seems strange that John W. Campbell, once the prophet of ultimate technological progress, should have become the source of what is essentially only fantasy. And I find it an unhappy fact that he—who had loved the hard sciences with deep devotion—should have instigated so much distrust of the methods that produced such science.

Yet, in a way, he may have been right in seeking such new types of fiction. Much of the material of the Golden Age had been growing stale from overuse. Some of the old excitement was gone. Something new was needed; and for good or bad, Campbell found new sources for his stories.

Certainly a field that does not evolve will eventually die of lethargy, as many other fields of entertainment fiction were dying. Campbell had led the field out of the doldrums when he first became an editor. Now, once more, he led it to other pastures. And if I'm not always happy with the results, at least science fiction is still lusty and alive!

CHAPTER 17

The Big Boom

THERE was a time when the devoted fan of science fiction bought every issue of every science fiction magazine and could remember exactly when and where almost every story had appeared. By 1950, that was becoming impossible. It was boom time for the field. During the year, some 25 different titles were issued, with a total of 110 separate magazine issues. (These figures must always be subject to some doubt, since they depend on what the compiler decides is true science fiction. I've tried to be accurate in my count—with the deliberate elimination of all-fantasy magazines; but researchers might find different numbers, or even discover some obscure magazine which has been omitted. These figures serve as close approximations, however, and indicate relative relationships rather closely.)

Many of the magazines offered little competition to the pre-eminence of *Astounding*. But there were two important exceptions.

Late in 1949, Anthony Boucher and J. Francis McComas had edited one issue of *The Magazine of Fantasy*. In 1950, this became *The Magazine of Fantasy and Science Fiction*, henceforth referred to as *F&SF*, the name by which most readers came to know it. Only four issues were published in 1950, but by the end of 1952 it was a regular monthly publication and has continued so to the present.

This magazine set standards different from those of *Astounding*, but certainly not lower ones. The editors wanted science fiction of high literary quality. They didn't cater to the "hardware" type of reader, but rather to a reader who normally did not seek his reading material in the popular magazines. The rate of payment was equal to that of *Astounding*—now two cents a word on acceptance; and Boucher soon established himself as an editor with whom writers enjoyed working. The new magazine rapidly became the prestige one of the field.

Then, beginning in October 1950, *Galaxy Science Fiction* appeared, edited by H. L. Gold. Gold came to his editorship with an extensive background. He had written a number of stories in the past and had served as editor for comics and for crime magazines. (The magazine was initially published by an Italian publishing firm, seeking to break into the American market. Soon after its beginning, however, with the November 1952 issue, it was sold to the Guinn Publishing Company, where Robert M. Guinn gave Gold a very free hand in shaping the magazine.)

Gold was determined to give Campbell strong competition. He offered his writers higher rates, beginning at three cents a word. (Campbell was soon forced to equal these rates.) The magazine appeared monthly, and offered a major new market to writers. He went after writers with vigor and enthusiasm, and they came to him. Many of the serials and stories that normally would have gone to Campbell began appearing in *Galaxy*.

Basically, Gold seemed to want a slicker and perhaps in some ways more superficial story than Campbell preferred. Plotting to him was less important than the impact of the story on the readers' senses. But the difference between *Galaxy* and *Astounding* was not so great that many stories could not have been at home in either magazine. Gold also instituted a regular book-review column by the well-known anthologist, Groff Conklin, who continued from October 1950 through October 1955. Willy Ley also began a monthly science column, which lasted until his death in 1969.

Gold had a mixed reaction from writers. Many flocked to him with enthusiasm, and his weekly poker session was always jammed. (Gold was suffering from agoraphobia and did not leave his home, so writers came to him.) Others swore bitterly at his acerbic comments and his tendency to do major rewriting on stories he had bought. (I found that this problem seemed to arise from the unwillingness of writers to warn him on this; in my case, he agreed to make no changes without my consent and kept his word scrupulously.)

The chief coup for *Galaxy* in 1950 was the securing of Clifford Simak's novel *Time Quarry* (later published by Simon and Schuster as *Time and Again*). This is a complex story of time travel and a struggle between man and robot.

Astounding was unaffected by the new magazines in 1950. March saw the beginning of L. Ron Hubbard's serial *To the Stars*, later published by Ace Books as

Return to Tomorrow. This was Hubbard's last major story and was at the top of his form. It deals with men who trade between stars, traveling at nearly the speed of light; for them, time is greatly slowed so that a month for their ship may be a century for Earth. They can never return to friends they knew. And behind it all lies a strange mission. This is a grim novel that somehow manages to retain a feeling of hope and romance. The science is hardly accurate, but the writing makes up for that.

In April, *Astounding* published "Okie," a story by James Blish in which New York City is lifted as a whole and flown to other stars, in search of profit; this was followed by a series of related stories and made Blish a major writer. Cyril Kornbluth appeared in July with "The Little Black Bag," laid in a world where total welfare has encouraged mediocrity and overburdened the few truly capable men. And in August, H. Beam Piper had a Paratime story, "Last Enemy," in which a world gains positive proof that any man can be reincarnated. It is one of Piper's best stories.

In *Startling Stories*, Edmond Hamilton had a complete novel in the January issue. *City at World's End* is one of his most successful works. In it, a small city is suddenly shifted to a time when Earth is old; the inhabitants must somehow prevail against a whole galactic civilization to survive as themselves.

1950 also marked the first appearance of a number of writers: Gordon R. Dickson collaborated with Poul Anderson; Randall Garrett appeared under the pen name of David Gordon; other new writers were John Jakes, J. T. M'Intosh, Chad Oliver, and Richard Matheson, whose "Born of Man and Woman" in the Summer issue of *F&SF* was instantly acclaimed a major story. Perhaps the least heralded was Cordwainer Smith (Paul Linebarger), whose "Scanners Live in Vain" appeared in *Fantasy Book #6*, where few read it. But in time, its reputation grew to outrank almost any other story of the year. Smith's strange outlook and society are unique contributions to the field.

Fantasy Book #6 also used the first cover by Jack Gaughan, who later became one of the most popular artists in the field. And H. R. Van Dongen made his first appearance on the September 1950 cover of *Super Science Stories*. During most of the period covered in this section, he was one of the regular cover artists for *Astounding*.

In 1951, *Galaxy* reached its full stride. In January, Isaac Asimov appeared with a three-part serial, *Tyrann*, later published by Doubleday as *The Stars Like Dust*. This takes place in the same universe as his *Foundation* series, but much earlier, before the Galactic Empire is established. Then in September, Robert A. Heinlein began *The Puppet Masters*. Getting this was a triumph for Gold, since Heinlein seldom appeared in the magazines at this time. It is based on the old theme of parasitic creatures invading Earth and taking over the minds of men—hardly the best of Heinlein's novels, but still a well-handled story.

Among the shorter lengths, Ray Bradbury's "The Fireman" appeared in February 1951. This was later expanded to *Fahrenheit 451* for Ballantine. Lester del Rey appeared in March with "Wind Between the Worlds," a suspense story in which a matter transmitter suddenly begins to pump all Earth's atmosphere off into space. And in April, Cyril Kornbluth expanded his social ideas of the rising tide of mediocrity in "The Marching Morons."

By comparison, *Astounding* came in second in major stories, though the average level was still high. Hal Clement's *Iceworld* began in October, with a splendid cover by Van Dongen. Here Clement revealed his talent for handling truly alien worlds and their strange life forms. These aliens live at the temperature of gaseous sulfur—and to them, Earth is an impossibly frigid planet.

In September 1951, Sam Merwin left *Thrilling Wonder* (and *Startling* one month later) to be replaced by Samuel Mines. Merwin had done a great deal for the two magazines and a great many writers and readers regretted his decision to quit. In October, P. Schuyler Miller began *The Reference Library*, a regular monthly book-review column in *Astounding*. He continued this until his death in 1974.

Among the new writers appearing in 1951 were Wyman Guin, Zenna Henderson, Harry Harrison and Edgar Pangborn. Pangborn's June *Galaxy* novelette, "Angel's Egg," remains a fresh and moving story.

Galaxy continued to dominate in the serials during 1952. January saw the beginning of Alfred Bester's *The Demolished Man*, the story of a supercriminal in a world where no successful crime is supposed to be possible, written with superb inventiveness and detail. It remains one of the great novels of science fiction, and many of its inventions have been adopted by other writers. It was followed in June by *Gravy Planet* (published by Ballantine as *The Space Merchants*), a serial by Frederik Pohl and C. M. Kornbluth. This is a satirical extrapolation of a future where advertising controls everything and where the project of colonizing Venus is only a sales gimmick. It won wide acclaim and was imitated extensively by other writers. In a sense, it helped to establish much of the later spirit of *Galaxy*. In December came Simak's *Ring Around the Sun*, a story of a complex struggle for the use of alternate Earths. Among the major shorter stories was Theodore Sturgeon's "Baby Is Three." This later became the basis for his tour-de-force novel, *More Than Human*, in which he explored the possibility of what he called "homo gestalt"—a strange superman type of story in which a group of social rejects pool their peculiar abilities to gain superman effects.

Ward Moore appeared in November 1952 *F&SF* with "Bring the Jubilee," which he later expanded into an excellent novel. This is an alternate-present story in which the South has won the war. Lester del Rey had "Stacked Deck" in the November 1952 *Amazing*—a minor story, at best, but one which first suggested a serious race between the U.S. and Russia for the Moon. And in *Startling Stories* for August 1952, Philip José Farmer made his debut with the then-shocking "The Lovers," a story of love between a human and an alien female of peculiar biological nature. It was probably the most discussed story of the year.

Other new writers were Algis Budrys, Mark Clifton, Theodore R. Cogswell, Philip K. Dick, James Gunn, Theodore L. Thomas, Frank Herbert, and Robert Scheckley, who soon became one of the most popular writers for *Galaxy*.

The major serial for 1953 was Hal Clement's *Mission of Gravity*, beginning in the April *Astounding*. Many consider this to be the finest "hard-science" novel of science fiction. It tells of a world that rotates so rapidly it has become a thin disc, with gravity that varies from three times Earth normal at the equator to hundreds of times at the poles. The strange natives face enormous difficulty in performing a mission for Earth—and for themselves, as it turns out. Also popular was Isaac Asimov's *The Caves of Steel*, beginning in *Galaxy*, October 1953. Men have emigrated to the stars with robots as their companions. On Earth, men shun robots and live below the surface, turning into agoraphobes. But an Earthman is forced to work with a robot to solve a crime. It's a good mystery as well as good science fiction.

In the September *If*, James Blish had *A Case of Conscience* (later made into an award-winning novel). This is a deeply philosophical treatment of religion, in which a priest must face and accept a world of ultimate heresy—where Satan proves to be capable of creation.

Marion Zimmer Bradley, Anne McCaffrey and James White broke into print in 1953, and Kurt Vonnegut, Jr., made his first appearance in a science fiction magazine with "Unready to Wear" in the April *Galaxy*. Damon Knight began a regular book-review column in the short-lived *Science Fiction Adventures*.

Outstanding stories were infrequent in 1954. Among those best remembered is Tom Godwin's short "The Cold Equations," in the August 1954 *Astounding*. This is a seemingly simple story of a girl who stows away on a spaceship that has barely enough fuel to make a landing without her added mass. The ending is the only possible one. Frederik Pohl had "The Midas Plague" in *Galaxy* for April. This story reverses the usual fear of overpopulation leading to starvation; here, overproduction forces everyone to consume to his utter limit—or beyond. Evan Hunter's novelette in the January *If*, "Malice in Wonderland," is one of the first stories of a world of drugs to appear in science fiction. It was later expanded and published as *Tomorrow's World* by Pyramid Books. Heinlein's *Star Lummox*, published as *The Star Beast* by Scribner's, began in the May *F&SF*. This is one of Heinlein's supposed "juveniles," but an excellent story on any level. It tells of a beast from the stars that has lived for generations with an Earth family—until its people come for it.

New writers for 1954 included Brian Aldiss, Avram Davidson, Thomas N. Scortia, and Robert Silverberg.

Frank Herbert appeared with a major novel in 1955, beginning in the November *Astounding*. *Under Pressure* deals with men who must go into enemy territory in a submarine to mine the sea of needed oil. They are beset by psychological breakdowns and mysterious crimes, as well as by the risk of enemy action. George O. Smith began *Highways in Hiding* in the March *Imagination*; this is a story of mind reading and an esper who must save himself from a crime he did not commit. It is a much more serious and carefully done novel than previous work by him. The serial which won most acclaim, however, was Walter M. Miller's *A Canticle for Leibowitz*, beginning in the April *F&SF*. This has the Catholic Church in the far future facing a strange Armageddon. And Cordwainer Smith finally returned with "The Game of Rat and Dragon" in the October *Galaxy*; after this, he continued to appear with fair regularity.

The listing of stories seems to taper off from 1950 to 1955. I think this accurately reflects what was happening in the field. There were many good stories published, even in some of the lesser magazines, but there was a decline in the number of really excellent ones. During this period, there simply were too many magazines, and the book market was also becoming active. It was a time when any fair story (and some far less than fair) could be sold and when established writers were being assiduously wooed for stories. For most writers, there was no time to ripen ideas or to devote the proper care to each story. It seems to me that the quality suffered as a result.

This period was known as the "big boom" in science fiction. Without question, the term was justified. In 1953, by the best count I can make, about 36 titles were published, with a total of 174 issues. This was the largest number ever reached. And it does not include fantasy magazines that used little science fiction, nor does it count the British magazines which could be found on some American stands.

Certainly, in the U.S., 1953 was the high-water mark for science fiction magazines. In Britain, however, 1954 topped 1953, probably because *New Worlds* only published three issues during 1953.

And yet, all was not well. *Famous Fantastic Mysteries*, which had reprinted so many classic stories, ceased publication in 1953. *Weird Tales* ceased in 1954; this was a fantasy-horror magazine, but it had once used the work of many science fiction writers, and its loss was keenly felt by many old-time fans. And in 1955, three of the best adventure science fiction magazines folded: *Planet Stories, Startling Stories,* and *Thrilling Wonder Stories,* the final version of a magazine that had been one of the original three.

I haven't room to cover the complete history of all the magazines for the period from 1950 to 1961. And many unfortunately deserve little more than a listing. For more extensive coverage, giving changing names, date of issue, and stories contained, see the *Index to the S-F Magazines, 1951–1965,* published by the MIT Science Fiction Society.

A number of the entries below published mostly (and in a few instances entirely) fantasy stories; but since almost all fantasy magazines published some borderline material, I have included them.

The coding is fairly simple. If the magazine both started and ceased publication between 1950 and 1961, two dates are given. A single date indicates that both events happened the same year. No date indicates that the magazine began before 1950 and continued after 1961. Otherwise, *ceased* indicates when the magazine ceased publication, having begun before 1950. Many magazines changed titles, and I have used the most common title. In a few cases, a title might lapse and be picked up by another publisher. This is noted; though it may have been essentially a different magazine, it is listed by title.

AMERICAN SCIENCE FICTION (AND FANTASY) MAGAZINES, 1950–1961

Amazing Stories Annual: 1950, 1 issue.
Amazing Stories: 127 issues.
Astounding Science Fiction (Analog): 144 issues.
Avon Fantasy Reader: ceased 1952, 7 issues; *Avon Science Fiction Reader*: 1951–1952, 3 issues. Magazines combined 1952, 2 issues.

Avon Science Fiction & Fantasy Reader: 1953, 2 issues.
Beyond Fantasy Fiction: 1953–1955, 10 issues.
Cosmos Science Fiction & Fantasy: 1953–1954, 4 issues.
Dynamic Science Fiction: 1952–1954, 6 issues.
Famous Fantastic Mysteries: ceased 1953, 20 issues.
Fantastic Adventures: ceased 1953, 39 issues.
Fantastic: 1952–1953, 9 issues. Combined with *Fantastic Adventures,* 1953.
Fantastic Novels: ceased 1951, 9 issues.
Fantastic Science Fiction: 1952, 2 issues.
Fantastic Story Magazine: ceased 1955, 23 issues.
Fantastic Universe: 1953–1960, 69 issues.
Fantasy Book: ceased 1951, 3 issues.
Fantasy Fiction Magazine: 1953, 4 issues.
Fantasy Fiction Stories: 1950, 2 issues.
Future (Science Fiction): ceased 1960, 48 issues.
Galaxy Science Fiction: began 1950, 117 issues.
Galaxy Science Fiction Novels: 1950–1958, 31 issues.
If (Worlds of): began 1952, 65 issues. (Purchased 1959 by Guinn Publishing Company as a companion to *Galaxy.*)
Imagination Science Fiction: 1950–1958, 63 issues.
Imaginative Tales: 1954–1958, 23 issues.
Infinity Science Fiction: 1955–1958, 20 issues.
Magazine of Fantasy and Science Fiction: 126 issues.
Marvel Science Stories: revived 1950, ceased 1952, 6 issues.
A. Merritt Fantasy: ceased 1950, 4 issues.
New Worlds Science Fiction: (American reprint) 1960, 5 issues.
Orbit Science Fiction: 1953–1954, 5 issues.
Other Worlds Science Stories: ceased 1953, replaced by *Universe Science Fiction* (q.v.); resumed 1955, ceased 1957, 42 issues.
Out of This World Adventures: 1950, 2 issues.

Planet Stories: ceased 1955, 30 issues.
Rocket Stories: 1953, 3 issues.
Satellite Science Fiction: 1956–1959, 18 issues.
Saturn, Magazine of Fantasy & Science Fiction: 1957–1958, 5 issues.
Science Fiction Adventures: 1952–1954, 9 issues; under new publisher, 1956–1958, 12 issues.
Science Fiction Digest: 1954, 2 issues.
Science Fiction Plus: 1953, 7 issues.
Science Fiction Quarterly: resumed 1951, ceased 1958, 28 issues.
(Original) Science Fiction Stories: 1953–1960, 38 issues.
Science Stories: 1953–1954, 4 issues.
Space Science Fiction: 1952–1953, 8 issues. New Publisher 1957, 2 issues.
Space Stories: 1952–1953, 5 issues.
Spaceway: 1953–1955, 8 issues; sporadic appearances much later.
Star Science Fiction: 1958, 1 issue.
Startling Stories: ceased 1955, 40 issues.
Super-Science Fiction: 1956–1959, 18 issues.
Super-Science Stories: ceased 1951, 10 issues.
Ten Story Fantasy: 1951, 1 issue.
Thrilling Wonder Stories: ceased 1955, 28 issues.
Toby Press Novels: 1953, 1 issue.
Two Complete Science Adventure Books: 1950–1954, 11 issues.
Universe Science Fiction: 1953–1955, 10 issues. (See *Other Worlds.*)
Vanguard Science Fiction: 1958, 1 issue.
Venture Science Fiction: 1957–1958, 10 issues.
Vortex Science Fiction: 1953, 2 issues.
Wonder Story Annual: 1950–1953, 4 issues.
Wonder Stories: 1957, 1 issue. (Extension of *Thrilling Wonder.*)
Worlds Beyond: 1950–1951, 3 issues.

BRITISH SCIENCE FICTION (AND FANTASY) MAGAZINES, 1950–1961

Authentic Science Fiction: 1951–1957, 85 issues.
Futuristic Science Stories: 1950–1954, 15 issues.
Nebula Science Fiction: 1952–1959, 41 issues.
New Worlds (Science Fiction): 108 issues.
Nova Science Fiction Novels: 1953–1954, 7 issues.
Science Fantasy: began 1950, 50 issues.
Science Fiction Adventures: began 1958, 23 issues. (Originally a British reprint, but lasted beyond original U.S. magazine.)
Tales of Tomorrow: 1951–1954, 11 issues.
Vargo Statten Science Fiction: (Also *British Science Fiction* or *British Space Fiction*) 1954–1956, 19 issues.
Wonders of the Spaceways: 1951–1954, 10 issues.
Worlds of Fantasy: 1950–1954, 14 issues.

Obviously, there was no dearth of science fiction to read on either side of the Atlantic during the boom period.

CHAPTER 18

And the Collapse

A SUPERFICIAL INTERPRETATION of the number of magazines and issues beyond 1955 might indicate that the boom continued for several more years. In fact, it wasn't until 1959 that the total number of issues published fell below that of 1950. Nevertheless, I have placed the sub-period of collapse between 1956 and 1961. When three of the leading science fiction adventure magazines—*Planet, Startling,* and *Thrilling Wonder*—ceased publication in 1955, the signs of trouble for most of the magazines became evident.

The enthusiasm for publishing science fiction magazines certainly waned. Five new titles were started after 1955, but none did very well. Four others were either revived or picked up by other publishers—two of them apparently only to retain the right to the titles. As against that, ten of the previous titles were abandoned.

There was also a general feeling on the part of the readers that magazine science fiction, at least, was dying. Oh, there had always been some who claimed that the good old days were dead; that had been the cry of some when John Campbell began changing *Astounding*. But this was different. Now, whenever I went to almost any gathering of science fiction readers or writers, there was a general attitude of pessimism. One of the most common topics for speakers or panels was the death of science fiction. And when editors made guest appearances, most of them no longer discussed the great things they would be doing in future issues, but rather spent their time explaining the difficulties of getting good stories or some problem with getting the magazines to the readers. It wasn't a healthy atmosphere for a tiny field of literature that had always depended on a stubborn enthusiasm to spread the good word.

I have already mentioned the fact that from 1950 to 1955 there seemed to be a gradual falling off of the number of excellent stories published. This tendency continued through the years, unfortunately. Here and there, some really outstanding stories still appeared, but they were relatively infrequent. (And the tendency toward the fall from excellence was much more pronounced in the shorter works than in the serials.) Also, in the first half of this "age," there had been a great many writers appearing in print for the first time who then went on to establish themselves as worthy regulars. Far fewer appeared in the second half, though the ones who did were generally very good.

Three who first appeared in 1956 were: Christopher Anvil, who became one of the frequent contributors to *Astounding* for many years; Kate Wilhelm, whose works are now always contenders for the top honors in the field; and Harlan Ellison, probably the most controversial writer ever to hit science fiction, and the leader of a whole subcategory of science fiction.

Frederik Pohl had a long novelette, "The Man Who Ate the World," in November 1956 *Galaxy*, a story which is still regarded as one of his best. The other major stories were all serials. In October 1956, *Galaxy* began Alfred Bester's *The Stars My Destination*, later published by Signet as *Tiger, Tiger!* This is an extremely complicated story of a man who can "jape"—that is, teleport himself—caught up in an interplanetary war; his talents are immense, but he has no idea of how they work. Isaac Asimov's *The Naked Sun* began in *Astounding*, October 1956. It is a sequel to *The Caves of Steel*; in this case, the agoraphobic detective is called upon—with the help of his robot friend—to solve an impossible crime on a world of wide-open spaces, where people choose to live apart, separated by huge distances.

The real star of the year, however, was Robert A. Heinlein, who suddenly returned to doing adult novels after devoting most of his efforts for several years to the so-called juveniles. His *The Door into Summer*, beginning in October 1956 *F&SF*—October again!—is a wonderful romp of inventions and time travel, splendidly worked out. And his *Double Star*, in February 1956 *Astounding*, is Heinlein at his very best. It's the story of a not-too-good actor called upon to play the double of the most important man on all the planets; when the political leader is fully incapacitated, the actor has to take over for an indefinite period.

In 1957, the situation was reversed; most of the major stories were novelettes. *Astounding* had three of these. H. Beam Piper's "Omnilingual" appeared in February; this is the story of a team trying to trace the ancient culture of the dead Martians, and the discovery of the most logical Rosetta stone—books of science containing such things as the Periodic Table, which must be truly omnilingual. Kate Wilhelm's first major story, "The Mile-Long Spaceship," appeared in April 1957. And in the same issue was Poul Anderson's "Call Me Joe," which tells of a man's mind put into the brain of a centauroid creature on Jupiter—and the growing identification between alien and human.

Venture published Tom Godwin's "Too Soon to Die," in March 1957. This was later expanded into a novel and published by Pyramid as *Space Prison*. It is the story of a group of people marooned on a terrifying planet and how they learn to cope and eventually to avenge themselves on the enemy that has stranded them. And Philip José Farmer had "Night of Light" in June 1957 *F&SF*. Farmer had been running a series of stories about Father Carmody, a priest on strange worlds; this time, it is a world where a periodic disturbance upsets mental stability—and Carmody is forced to face both the good and evil in himself and others. It became a particularly powerful story when expanded to novel length and published by Berkley under the same title. (Title changes seemed to be the particular love of book publishers; quite a few novels have had at least three titles. This adds to the confusion of the field and contributes nothing, so far as I can see; usually the original title is as good as or better than the others.)

Among the serials, Pohl and Kornbluth's *Wolfbane*, beginning in the October *Galaxy*, stands out. In this, the two authors abandoned their usual formula for extrapolating some current trend into a satire. They took the problem of humanity enslaved by an alien race and dealt with it as honestly as possible. Their aliens are truly alien—one of the few times this can be said. It is a book to be taken seriously today, when readers seem more willing to examine heavier science fiction than was once true.

The other serial of importance was John Christopher's *No Blade of Grass*. This is a fine example of what might be called the British school of disaster stories. In it a plague is developed that destroys all grass—including all our cereal foods. It is perhaps more interesting, however, for the fact that it appeared in *The Saturday Evening Post*, a magazine that had sworn never to use science fiction at that time. (Over the years, the *SEP* published a great many fine science fiction stories, from Lord Dunsany's "Our Distant Cousins" to Heinlein's "The Green Hills of Earth." Apparently, they liked the stories, so long as nobody told them they were science fiction.)

In some ways, 1958 was a rather sad year, and events seemed more important than the stories. Henry Kuttner and Cyril Kornbluth died. Both were comparatively young men, at the height of their power and going on to even better things. The loss of two such writers so unexpectedly came as a shock to the world of science fiction. Lloyd Arthur Eshbach, one of the pioneers in publishing science fiction books, closed down his Fantasy Press and sold out his remaining stock. And Anthony Boucher resigned as editor of *F&SF*, after having acted as sole editor for several years. The magazine continued under several editors, but Boucher had a special touch that could not be replaced, and his relations with his writers were unique.

Astounding took the lead with major stories. In the October 1958 issue, it carried Clifford D. Simak's "The Big Front Yard," a novelette of a simple man who opens a shrewd trading business with strange aliens. And there were two excellent serials. In February 1958, Poul Anderson's *The Man Who Counts* began; this was published by Ace as *War of the Wing Men*. It was the first of a series of stories about Nicholas van Rijn and others associated with him. In this, van Rijn gets stranded on a world of primitive flying men where he cannot eat native food; to save himself, he has to force the natives to break all their customs and to change the course of their history. In May 1958, Hal Clement's *Close to Critical* began—a story of a robot from Earth who brings up a brood of native children according to Earth culture; but when the robot has to rescue a human child who has crashed on the inimical planet, he discovers that the other natives, with their own culture, may know more about their world than he can learn with his superior science.

Gordon Dickson's *Dorsai!* began in May 1959 *Astounding*; this was published by Ace as *The Genetic General*. It is the first of several novels by Dickson which deal with the political development of worlds and their interrelationship in the future. This is the tale of a man from a world which rents mercenary soldiers to maintain itself, and the technique of the man in rising to power.

Joanna Russ and Keith Laumer made their first appearances in 1959.

In 1960, the Columbia chain of magazines gave up its long struggle and folded. The magazines had been guilty of numerous name changes, but *Future* and *(Original) Science Fiction* were ones that had long been wide-open markets for the younger writer. And John Campbell began changing the name of *Astounding Science Fiction* to *Analog Science Fact/Science Fiction*. He was tired of the "lurid" name of the magazine and apparently wanted to improve its image. (I doubt that he succeeded in that; by now the new name —with "Fact" and "Fiction" reversed—is accepted; but the new name never quite evokes the tone of affection that the old one did.) He did this rather sneakily, gradually fading *Astounding* out and bringing in *Analog* over it. So, henceforth the magazine must be called *Analog*.

Ben Bova and R. A. Lafferty made their first science fiction appearances in 1960.

Harry Harrison established himself as a major writer with his serial beginning in January 1960 *Astounding/Analog*. This was *Deathworld*, to which there were two sequels later. It is the story of a man sent to help fight an impossible war against the deadliest planet man has tried to conquer. The harder the men fight against the complex of wild native life forms—plant and animal—the stronger that life becomes against them. It is a hopeless battle, grimly told and well resolved. And in July 1960 *Analog* Poul Anderson began *High Crusade*, a tour de force of cleverly twisted logic and subtle humor. When a small medieval town is getting set to go on the Crusades, an alien spaceship comes down, all set to conquer Earth. The leading Crusader manages a surprise that overcomes the aliens, and decides to take this easy conveyance to the Holy Land; but he is tricked and taken back to an alien world. His only hope is to take over the whole world—and then the whole Galactic Empire. And in December 1960 *F&SF*, Algis Budrys had a short novel, *Rogue Moon*—later expanded to full-novel length; this deals with a strange device on the Moon and a man with a death wish who is sent there to test it.

In 1961, Fred Saberhagen made his debut. Anne McCaffrey had "The Ship Who Sang" in the April 1961 *F&SF*—the first of several stories about a woman's brain in the body of a spaceship; these were later collected into a book. And Mack Reynolds had a short serial beginning in December 1961 *Analog*, *Black Man's Burden*. This is part of a considerable body of Reynolds' stories about the emerging nations of the world.

Also in 1961, H. L. Gold gave up his editorship of *Galaxy*. He had been increasingly ill and found the job too demanding. He was replaced by Frederik Pohl, who edited *Galaxy* and *If*—as well as a couple of other magazines put out by Guinn Publishing Company—for most of the next "age" of science fiction.

In a way, Gold's resignation marked the end of this age with a certain finality. Boucher was already gone. Howard Browne, who had long been associated with *Amazing* and *Fantastic*, first under Palmer and then as successor in editing the magazines, had gone to Hollywood to write. Cele Goldsmith had taken over, and was doing a remarkable job of trying to rebuild the magazines, but was faced with impossible difficulties; she lacked the full authority needed, for one thing. Robert A. W. Lowndes was gone with the passing of Columbia Publications. Sam Merwin had left. Of all the editors who had imposed their own personalities on the magazines of this age of science fiction, only John W. Campbell remained.

By 1961, the collapse was no longer questionable. In 1956, there were 18 titles with 114 issues; in 1957—which strangely showed a promise of a return to boom times—there were 22 titles with 146 issues; things fell off only slightly in 1958, with 21 titles and 131 issues. But 1959 proved that the collapse was not a temporary affair; there were only 13 titles with 88 issues. This worsened in 1960—9 titles with 67 issues.

And in 1961, the collapse was complete. Only six science-fiction titles remained, with a total of 60 issues! Contrast this with the figures for 1953, when 36 titles were published. England also had joined in the collapse. Only *New Worlds* and *Science-Fantasy* were still being published, with a total of 18 issues. Science fiction had regressed almost to where it stood at the end of the Golden Age.

There were a lot of causes for the collapse, as there were for the preceding boom. And in some ways, the cause of the collapse was an outcome of the cause of the boom.

But this complicated subject, which involves a great many things that affected all magazine publishing, deserves another chapter.

CHAPTER 19

The Magazine Business

AT THE TIME of the events, the boom was explained by the fact that science fiction had finally been accepted as more than "that kid stuff." The atom bomb was partly responsible for this; science fiction had accepted and written about atomic power when there was total ignorance of the subject elsewhere—partly caused by an imposed government secrecy, of course. As a result, a sort of grudging respect entered into mention of the field in newspapers and other magazines. For the first time, being a writer or reader of science fiction carried a measure of respectability. As for the bust that followed, that was usually blamed on a breakdown of distribution.

Both explanations are much too simplistic. The growing acceptance was real enough, but I doubt that it brought many new readers into the field. Certainly *Astounding*, the best source of information on atomic developments during the war years, did not receive any sudden increase in readership. And the breakdown in distribution was merely a symptom.

By 1950, the entertainment magazines were already in serious trouble. Television was taking up much of the "escape" audience for Westerns, mysteries and love stories, and the paperback books were competing on the same stands and at the same prices as the magazines.

There were also difficulties arising out of an old decision by many magazines. Back during the depression, a couple of magazines dropped all serials and featured only complete stories; they did very well at the time, and most other specialized pulps (outside of the science fiction field) rushed to climb aboard the bandwagon. But without serials, there was no way to insure that a reader would pick up the next issue of a particular magazine in any given field. The serials had guaranteed reader loyalty—and had also given the needed length for major stories. I think their loss was a great mistake; but once the mistake was made, the publishers blamed everything but their own judgment and clung to that policy.

The real troubles, however, came from greed and cheapness on the part of some publishers. They existed by robbing the readers from the better magazines; anytime a good magazine succeeded, they rushed in with a horde of inferior imitations. They paid bottom rates and exercised almost no editorial judgment—in fact, many of the editors of those magazines knew nothing of the field and cared even less. Stories were accepted as long as they filled a stock plot formula for the field and could be read without too much pain.

Such exploitive magazines drew off readers from the reputable publications, which needed higher sales to justify the rates they paid and the editorial experience they required. The imitators could get by on smaller circulation. And when readers realized that the magazines were bad, the titles were changed for new ones, to continue the exploitation.

The resulting decrease in the circulation of the better magazines had another serious effect. The distributors could no longer afford to devote much attention to magazines that might have a national sale of far less than 100,000 copies per month. (There were some distributors that seemed to specialize in handling the shoddier pulps, but they did so by paying less to the publisher per copy; and such distribution tended to be mechanical and rather slipshod.)

Hence, by 1950, many of the better chain publishers faced the fact that they could not continue. Street and Smith began to concentrate on their slicks, such as *Mademoiselle*, killing off their pulps. Campbell told me that *Astounding* was kept only because he convinced the publisher that it was not a real pulp, but a "specialized slick." (It was no such thing, but the term was adopted by many of the fans of the field.) At that time, science fiction also had less competition than most categories, and hence was still profitable. Popular Publications began converting to the semislick male-adventure field. And Standard Magazines began moving toward the paperback book field with their Popular Library. Fiction House found no place to go, and simply gave up, dropping *Planet Stories*, along with their other pulps.

Strangely, this general sickness of the magazine field was at least partly responsible for the boom of the science fiction magazines!

Television covered most fields of entertainment fiction. For sports fiction, it could substitute broadcasts of real games. And the detective-mystery, Western and romance types of stories became staples of television. But television found it difficult to handle science fiction to any great extent. So the science fiction magazines had fairly little competition from television. Also, in 1950, they had no real paperback competition. In a sense, they were still in an enviable position.

To the smaller publisher or the remaining chains, faced with a loss of sales in other fields, science fiction must have looked remarkably good. *Astounding* was doing very well, and its sales were actually increasing. (None of the putative science fiction publishers seemed to know why, or care. They probably didn't read *As-*

tounding to see what was wanted; certainly they made no analysis of its readership and the special requirements that had grown up for the field.)

Publishers who had once issued a science fiction magazine hastily revived it, no matter how poorly it had done before. Those who had no such magazine immediately planned to issue new ones. And in this, they were encouraged by the distributors.

Distributors couldn't bother with any magazine that sold in small quantities; but when there was a rapid decline of the whole pulp field, they began to discover that their profits were declining. They also spotted the fact that science fiction still did rather well, and they went to many of their marginal publishers with instructions to rush one of them-there-science-things out. (If I show contempt for some—not all—distributors, it is purely intentional.)

Such smaller publishing firms were often totally at the mercy of the distributors. They worked with almost no capital. When the distributor okayed a magazine—a necessary step in these cases—an agreement was drawn up whereby the distributor advanced the publisher a certain amount for each issue upon its coming from the press. This paid for the editorial and printing costs, usually. In return, such a distributor would make a smaller return to the publisher on each copy sold. (At the time, the magazines sold for 35¢, as a rule. By funding himself and dealing shrewdly, a publisher might get 23¢ per copy; but one chained to a lesser distributor would get only 19¢ per copy—a considerable difference, which was often taken from the editorial expenses, so that rates for fiction became minimal.)

Some of the boom between 1950 and 1955—or perhaps even later—was real. There was certainly room for quality competition to *Astounding*, and both *Galaxy* and *F&SF* were logical additions to the field.

But a lot of such an increase in the magazines was a symptom of the sickness of the general pulp field. It was, in many ways, a phony boom, and it could not last. Also, while it lasted, it probably tended to abort the normal development that science fiction might have experienced in the magazine field. There was room for at least three quality magazines and perhaps four or five others that were wisely chosen to find individual places in the general (and less sophisticated) adventure-science fiction market. There was no room for 36 magazines, even good ones—which many of these were not. Opportunistic publishers had learned nothing from the collapse of their other markets; they used the same technique in printing science fiction that had destroyed other magazines.

I was editing three science fiction magazines and one fantasy during this boom time. The distributor had practically ordered the publisher—who had previously published "art" (read "girlie") magazines—to bring out science fiction. When I first went in with a story at the suggestion of my agent, I found total confusion. Nobody knew a thing about what science fiction was. And when I suggested some elementary facts, I was immediately hired, with no question about my qualifications. Payment to writers was only after publication—and as I discovered much later, often not made at all. The magazines might have succeeded—they were generally well received. But a lot of factors dictated by lack of any idea about fiction publishing made them fail, though I had resigned before the last issues appeared.

There were two bad results of this artificial boom. The first was obvious. The same thing was happening that had ruined the other pulp magazines. There were too many on the stands. Very few readers were able or willing to buy up to twenty magazines in any month. But the new magazines did attract a fair number of the readers who might otherwise have purchased a better magazine; there was always the hope for some fine new magazine, and curiosity to see what each new title was like. This cut seriously into the sales of even the best of the others—less in the case of *Astounding*, with its long-established hard core of readers, but to some extent even there.

The other result was that many who might have become readers of science fiction were sadly discouraged. A potential new reader, perhaps grown curious from some comment about science fiction's so-called prophecies, had no clue as to which magazine was the best. Hence, the odds were pretty high against his choosing one of the better ones. If he had any taste at all, he read with mounting disgust at the shoddy stories too many magazines contained; then he resolved never to bother with that stuff again.

What happened to science fiction was an inevitable repetition of what had happened to the rest of the magazine field. There simply were not enough good writers to supply such a boom market. Some writers took advantage of things by palming off all the stories they had in their reject file or mass-producing hasty new ones. Other writers moved from their dying markets with no knowledge of the new field. And editors took what they could get. Even in the top markets, it became harder and harder to get first-class stories. Too many of the writers were trying to turn out too many stories and not giving sufficient attention to quality. The exploiters began to hurt the pace-setters—and were finding the science fiction field no different from the other fields they had exploited to death. The surprising thing is that science fiction proved sufficiently tough to survive at all.

The magazines that did survive after 1955 usually had at least one of two assets: an experienced science fiction editor; or other, bigger national circulation magazines in the same company to secure them better treatment on the stands. Having both was ideal, of course. *Astounding* was published by a company that now had several leading slick magazines and the top editor; *Amazing* and *Fantastic* could depend on the sales force Ziff-Davis needed to promote its successful technical hobby magazines; and while only *Ellery Queen's Mystery Magazine* helped greatly with the sale of *F&SF*, that magazine had an editor who inspired fierce loyalty from readers and writers. Those magazines not only survived, but maintained monthly schedules of publication. *Galaxy* was sometimes in more trouble than H. L. Gold knew, but it had a publisher who was genuinely devoted to the magazine and willing to fight to keep it going. And the Columbia Publications (*Future* and *Original Science Fiction*) had Robert Lowndes for editor—a man who was used to facing difficulties with magazines of lesser stature and somehow making them work.

The magazines declined through 1956. Then in 1957 there was a sudden upsurge—before the launching of Sputnik, and hence unrelated to that. This is almost impossible to explain. I can only guess that, as the weaker magazines collapsed, the market seemed more promising to publishers. At any rate, it was the last, dying gasp of the boom.

Then, in June 1957, American News Company ceased operations. This was the largest magazine-distributing company, and the one that had most of the outlets in such places as railway stations, subway stops, etc., where people with an hour or so to pass were most likely to pick up a magazine. It created a great turmoil in the field when this giant operation ceased. Publishers who had depended on it scrambled desperately to find new distributors and outlets.

One result for many of the marginal publishers was that they suddenly had no capital. They had depended on final returns of magazines long since printed; now these were tied up in the folded company—and a new distributor would mean a long wait for more money.

Actually, this was less of an immediate disaster for the science-fiction magazine publishers than was claimed at the time. Many of their magazines were already handled by smaller distributors. Their loss came from the inability to get their magazines onto many of the stands that had been controlled by American News and shared according to complicated arrangements.

Anyhow, the collapse of American News was only a symptom of the previously mentioned sickness of magazine publishing as a whole. There were other reasons for their ceasing operations.

The effects were not felt immediately in the appearance of the magazines, of course. An issue of a magazine is sent to the printer long before it can be put on the newsstands. The collapse began to accelerate many months after the end of American News.

In my opinion, it was made worse by another mistake made by many publishers.

Sputnik went into orbit in October 1957—man's first definite step into space. And again, the visions of science fiction were confirmed. Obviously, if the atom bomb had led—at least partially—to the acceptance of science fiction, real space flight should increase that acceptance.

(There is some question as to whether the bomb really helped science fiction very much. True, it made the former "silly" stuff seem a lot less silly. But the rise in readership was not that remarkable for the magazines. And any reader who turned to the magazines for help in trying to understand the bomb and overcome the fear of it was doomed to disappointment. The writers were thrown by the real results of atomic power almost as much as any other laymen. During the period following Hiroshima, there were numerous stories of doom and despair in the science fiction outlets. Radiation would produce mutations that would destroy the germ plasm of mankind and result in all kinds of horrible futures; war might come devastatingly in countless ways. This was a period when many stories of our barbarous descendants were in print, showing the deculturation of humanity after a holocaust.)

Anyhow, space became very much the thing, and numerous covers appeared that featured things like the various orbiters Russia and we (tardily) sent up, as well as spaceships galore.

It was a grave misreading of the public's reaction. People were suddenly interested in space, to be sure; but now it fell into the news or current-events category. It was no longer science fiction. The fiction magazines couldn't hope to compete with the newspapers that might bring developments before they were covered in fiction!

The marginal publishers had exhausted themselves finally, and began to drop away, unable to understand this last viable field of pulp literature. Most of the other pulp categories were already dead, with a very few lingering representatives of the Western and mystery fields continuing to exist on marginal circulation.

Pulp fiction had been murdered—or had committed suicide, if you like; one interpretation of the events is as good as the other, depending on whether you consider the exploiters to be a true part of the business.

Six magazines remained in the science fiction field—and somehow, to the amazement of most of the prophets, continued to survive through the next age. The oddball relation of the pulp ménage had proved stronger than all the rest of the family.

Strangely, despite the decline in titles and issues of the magazines, the real boom continued—but that was in another part of the publishing world.

CHAPTER 20

Wider Horizons

AT BEST, magazines in the "pulp" categories had a bad reputation among readers who considered themselves people of good taste. They were considered to be only marginally better than the comic magazines and were still associated with the "penny-dreadful" publications of another century. In many cases, this bad reputation was probably deserved, despite several polls which indicated that the better pulps were read by people of higher intellectual attainments than was generally the case for the so-called slicks.

One trouble with the pulps was that they looked cheap and usually garish. Since they had to be printed cheaply to get by without much advertising, they showed little polish or slickness. And even those which used tasteful and subdued cover illustrations were buried among a host that appealed for readership by sensationalism in their art. The science fiction magazines were naturally to be found among other pulps—even after some had changed to the digest size and made considerable effort to appear respectable.

As a result, many readers who might have been attracted by the stories never discovered science fiction; they simply never looked for reading material where such magazines were to be found. And when young, more experimental readers brought home such magazines, they often met with opposition for wasting their time on "trash."

More than one fan who left home for any length of

time returned to find his prized collection of magazines had been thrown out by a wife or mother who objected to such garbage in the house. This was a common experience among young veterans returning from World War II. (Some guilty of such acts lived to regret it; by the seventies, the value of the destroyed collections often became thousands of dollars!)

A certain grudging acceptance was given to science fiction as being prophetic. The dropping of the atom bomb and the destruction caused by V-2 rockets proved that some of the wild ideas of science fiction were no longer laughable. But the low repute science fiction enjoyed as literature remained essentially unchanged.

The real acceptance of science fiction came with the general issuance of the stories in book format. Books are somehow respectable. Books are literature—whatever that is. *The Three Musketeers* may be as wild as any science fiction and certainly as irresponsible in the casuistic morality it glorifies; but the works of Dumas were regarded as perfectly respectable reading.

The beginning of the regular publishing of science fiction books had begun a few years before this period, of course, mostly by fan publishers. And while most such publishers soon dropped out, a few continued. Gnome Press was the most active over the years, continuing to publish a great many excellent science fiction titles throughout the entire age of acceptance. Fantasy Press also lasted until 1958, when Eshbach sold his remaining stock to Martin Greenberg, to be sold with other Gnome titles; and even then, Eshbach continued some limited publishing as late as 1962.

These were well-produced books, unlike some of the earlier editions by fan publishers. On the whole, their appearance was better than some books by established publishers. They were obviously respectable. Nevertheless, it's doubtful that they were able to contribute much to the acceptance of science fiction. The publishers lacked either the reputation or the sales force that was needed to place them widely in the regular bookstores. They were necessarily sold primarily to readers who were already devoted to science fiction, chiefly through advertisements in the magazines.

Nevertheless, they demonstrated that science fiction was a salable commodity in book form, and the major publishers soon began experimenting with it. There was soon a long list of publishers who featured science fiction.

Grosset & Dunlap began a series in 1950, publishing Henry Kuttner's *Fury* among other books. Greenberg Publishers issued James Blish's *Jack of Eagles* (an expanded version of "Let the Finder Beware") in 1952. Frederick Fell published several titles and also featured a series by E. F. Bleiler and T. E. Dikty that anthologized the *Best Science Fiction Stories* of the year from 1949 to 1956. This was the first such series, to be followed by many others which collected the "best" stories from the magazines into single volumes, and which brought those stories to many who would not otherwise have seen them. Pellegrini & Cudahy issued Fritz Leiber's *Gather Darkness* in 1950. Simon & Schuster began an ambitious program of science fiction, though it soon dropped out of any really active interest in the market.

Houghton Mifflin published Arthur C. Clarke's *Childhood's End* in 1953. Later books by Clarke were published by Harcourt Brace, beginning with *The City and the Stars* in 1956. Harper & Row published Fred Hoyle's *The Black Cloud* in 1957. (Hoyle, one of the world's leading astrophysicists, proved to be an excellent writer of fiction and one quite conversant with science fiction, as he proved with several later novels.) E. P. Dutton began publishing the science fiction novels of Fredric Brown, following their success with his excellent mystery stories. And Putnam published the *Okie* stories of James Blish.

Putnam secured the works of Heinlein from 1959 on. (They also obtained all of his "Future History" stories, which had been begun by Shasta Publishers; these were issued in a huge, omnibus volume as *The Past Through Tomorrow* in 1967.) In getting Heinlein, they also obtained the science fiction publishing coup of the period. In 1961, they published his *Stranger in a Strange Land*, which drew an audience far beyond that of any other book of science fiction. It is the story of a boy raised on Mars by Martians. He learns Martian attitudes, and finds conditions on Earth all wrong when he is brought back. But he has also learned the Martian secret of surviving after death in a conscious and even visible form when he wishes. After his death, he sets out to establish a following to bring the Martian philosophy of free sex, universal love, and various other things to humanity. The book rapidly became must reading for many of the cults and still continues to sell well.

But it was Doubleday that went into science fiction most wholeheartedly. Doubleday had been one of the leading publishers of category books of all kinds—Western, mystery, romance, etc. They were equipped to turn out such books economically and their sales force knew how to market them. They also had an arrangement with many of the libraries to handle their category books. To them, apparently, science fiction was nothing unusual; it was just another category, to be issued on a regular schedule.

They were fortunate, however, in having an editor who could understand such fiction. Walter Bradbury liked and respected science fiction. (At a time when most book editors were wondering what the stuff was, I was on a radio program with him in which he outlined the virtues and appeal of science fiction so well that I wish I had a tape of it now for inclusion in a later chapter.) Doubleday's science fiction publishing program began on a regular schedule in 1950. Among the books then was one by Heinlein, *Waldo and*

Magic, Inc. This seemed to violate good publishing sense; it used two stories, rather than a single novel, and one of those was an out-and-out fantasy from the pages of *Unknown*.

By 1951, the program was well established, and Doubleday had a clear lead over other major publishers. Among the books issued that year were: *Rogue Queen* by L. Sprague de Camp (an extremely well-done novel of aliens with a hive culture, one of my favorite de Camp books); *The Puppet Masters* by Robert A. Heinlein, perhaps the best novel of alien creatures who can take over the bodies of humans; *Tomorrow the Stars*, edited by Robert A. Heinlein, one of the best anthologies of its time; *The Day of the Triffids* by John Wyndam (John W. Beynon Harris), a superb example of the quiet British type of disaster novel, which was first serialized in *Colliers*; and *The Martian Chronicles*, by Ray Bradbury, a collection of related short stories (many from *Planet Stories*) which clearly established Bradbury as a major writer.

That stands up today as an excellent list of books. But there was more. In 1954, Doubleday published Hal Clement's *Mission of Gravity* and an original novel by Leigh Brackett, entitled *The Long Tomorrow*. This is unlike Brackett's usual swashbuckling and was one of her finest stories. It deals with a world where technology is taboo; but two young men find evidence that it is still being carried on somewhere in secret; they eventually find the place—but not quite what they've dreamed about. In 1956 and 1957, Doubleday published Heinlein's *Double Star* and *The Door into Summer*, two of his finest novels.

Doubleday also found a marketing system, one that had previously worked well for their mysteries. In 1953, they set up the Science Fiction Book Club, whereby readers could receive selected science fiction books at a discount (unless they returned a card saying they didn't want the books). While they carried selections from other publishers, a good many of the selections were (justifiably then, certainly) from Doubleday. This club has continued since, with a large group of members.

Walter Bradbury was responsible for getting Isaac Asimov to begin writing books. (Previously, all of his fiction had been written for the magazine market only.) In 1950, his *Pebble in the Sky* appeared—the story of an old Jewish tailor who is transported to the future where the Galactic Empire is still thriving. There, on a ghettoized Earth, he is caught in a struggle between Earth and the rest of the galaxy; happily, good old Earth does not overcome all the other worlds!

This led eventually to Asimov's decision to abandon teaching biochemistry and devote his time to writing. The association with Doubleday has lasted for more than a quarter of a century. From 1950 on, Doubleday has published all Asimov's serials and numerous collections, as well as an original novel, *The End of Eternity*, which deals with a group that controls time; it is a complex but excellent novel. Eventually, Doubleday also obtained from Gnome Press the right to Asimov's Foundation and robot stories. He did a series of juvenile novels (under the by-line of Paul French) about Lucky Starr in space.

This was a true boom period for science fiction juveniles. (The term is not entirely accurate, despite the fact that the books were primarily published for school libraries. Many of the novels were serialized in adult magazines or paperback books without complaint.) Heinlein began a series for Scribners in 1947 and did a dozen books for them before he left for Putnam in 1959. These are undoubtedly the top examples of how good such so-called juveniles can be.

Winston began a series in 1952, issuing six titles at a time, many by well-known science fiction writers. Lester del Rey (under his own name and three pen names) did nine novels and one fact book on rockets before Winston was incorporated into Holt, Rinehart and Winston and the line began to fade out. (Originally, del Rey was supposed to supply plot outlines for all Winston books, and did for several series. That may explain why he did so many of the books.)

Andre Norton (Alice Mary Norton) was perhaps the most prolific of the juvenile science fiction novelists. Her books seemed to appear from Ace Books with amazing frequency; many of them were series, such as those about a Star Guard and Indians in space. She also had a highly popular fantasy series about a Witch World. The books were read with equal enthusiasm by both the juvenile and adult audiences.

Heinlein, del Rey and Norton seem to have started a whole generation toward becoming science fiction fans. People still come up to me to declare that one of my juveniles was the first science fiction they ever read. Most of those books were still in print twenty years after they were first published. Certainly, over the years, those books must have had a strong effect toward increasing the acceptance of science fiction among many who might not otherwise have discovered it.

Yet there were limits to the effect of hard-cover books. Even at the price of books in 1950, few people wanted to buy many of them. A magazine may be an impulse purchase; but usually a reader stops and thinks before he invests in a book. Also, such books were available only in bookstores and from libraries, where most readers were a lot less likely to encounter them than would have been the case if they had been spread to every newsstand, like the paperback books that were available for other categories.

In 1952, however, science fiction made the final leap toward wide acceptance. Two companies suddenly decided to bring out a regular line of science fiction in paperback form—and at prices no higher than those of the magazines.

Donald Wollheim had pioneered in getting the very

first science fiction paperback—*The Pocket Book of Science Fiction*, which he edited in 1943. Now, in 1952, he became an editor at Ace Books. He immediately began planning regular publication of science fiction to match the other categories at Ace.

Ace began with a clever idea—the publication of two novels in one book, arranged back to back so that the book could be turned over to show two separate covers, one for each novel. Thus the reader would get two books for the price of one—or at least, that was the selling feature. In actual fact, there were not two full-length novels; sometimes there was one novel and a long novelette, and at other times there were two rather short novels. But the reader was still getting a bargain, since the wordage ran to a total of about fifty percent more than that of the average book. The Ace Doubles did well, as did the regular single novels when Wollheim issued them.

The Doubles, in the long run, produced another advantage. With a strong novel by a major writer for one half, it was only sensible to include a second novel by a less famous writer for the second half. Wollheim made excellent use of this fact. During his tenure at Ace, he discovered or published first novels by more writers who later became famous than any other editor. Among such authors were John Brunner, Samuel R. Delany, Philip K. Dick, Ursula K. Le Guin and Roger Zelazny.

Ballantine Books began, also in 1952, when Ian Ballantine left Bantam Books to found his own company. A pioneer in paperback publishing, Ballantine was now looking for new fields with which to establish his line. He chose science fiction as one such field.

His original plan was to publish simultaneously in hard cover and paperback formats and to offer advances of $5,000 for a novel. His funding proved inadequate for this, however. But while the scheme was working, he collected a prestigious group of writers—Anderson,

Clarke, Kuttner, Tenn, Sturgeon, Kornbluth and Pohl —many of whom stayed with him after he was forced to reduce his advances to the usual level.

Many other paperback houses began putting more emphasis on science fiction. Signet issued books by several top writers. Bantam, Pocket Books and Dell used science fiction sporadically. And Pyramid developed an excellent line, particularly after Donald Bensen became their editor in 1957. But Ace and Ballantine were the leaders in the number of titles and regularity of scheduling.

To the writers, the active book market more than compensated for the loss of magazine markets during the collapse. Most novels were now written on contract to a book publisher, with the chance of magazine sale a bonus, rather than a necessity. For the first time, a good writer had a fairly decent chance to make an adequate living without having to hold down some other job.

To some extent, this proved detrimental to the magazines. The shorter fiction soon began to be neglected by established writers. There were still anthologies—a great many of them, both in cloth and paper; but getting included in them for the extra money such recognition would bring was much more of a gamble than selling a novel under contract, and usually less rewarding in terms of time spent at the typewriter. In general, there was a marked decrease in the number of really good shorter stories submitted to the magazine editors.

Nevertheless, the total amount of published material in 1960 was not far below (and may have been above) that of the peak boom year of 1953; and the rate of payment averaged a good deal higher.

The field was also beginning to interest readers who had never bought a science fiction magazine. Science fiction was no longer a category reserved for those who enjoyed browsing through garish magazines. Books could be taken anywhere without eliciting mocking remarks from others. Science fiction was now at least as accepted as most other entertainment forms of literature.

CHAPTER 21

FIAWOL or FIJAGH?

MOST OF THE ACCEPTED JARGON of fandom is useful in conveying an idea without long roundaboutation. The above acronyms are examples. Fiawol (Fandom Is a Way of Life) expresses the attitude of the devoted fan who seems to eat, breathe and sleep for nothing but the one subject. Fijagh (Fandom Is Just A Goddamned Hobby) is the moderate stand of one who can enjoy without making a career of his hobby. Both attitudes in such capsule form are described somewhat tongue-in-cheek, but there's a good deal of serious intent behind them.

Another sharp distinction is made between what is sercon and what is faanish. Sercon (serious, constructive) attitudes are those of the devoted fan of the literature, while faanish attitudes indicate more interest in the activities of fandom and other fans than in science fiction itself. Either term can be pejorative; sercon may imply a lack of humor or sense of proportion; faanish can be used to describe someone who is frivolous or insincere.

By 1950, there were few cries of "Fiawol" from most of the fans I met; they seemed inclined to accept fandom as something to be enjoyed now and then. And most of the fanzines I received leaned toward the faanish. This seemed to be a period of moderation that lasted throughout the decade. The turmoil that had often upset fandom as a result of feuds had decreased markedly, and the general attitude seemed to be one of consolidation of gains, rather than any form of crusading. Sometimes it seemed that fandom had even accepted a sort of quiet desperation; toward the end of the decade, there were a good many discussions about the supposed death of science fiction, reflecting the feeling that the literature was no longer as exciting as it had been.

Fandom was growing mature. There were still very young fans, but their boisterousness was tempered by the many older fans who had been through it all before. Many had gone through World War II and were now enduring the Korean fracas. Many others had quietly gafiated—from the acronym gafia, Get Away From It All—though some of these returned eventually.

It seemed that the pioneering work of fandom had been accomplished. Fan clubs still sprang up, and some older ones (such as LASFS, PSFS and ESFA) were still active. But most clubs tended to be social groups with an interest in science fiction and not hotbeds for activists. The APAs were continuing, but the mailings tended to be desultory. More fanzines were being published than before, and many were excellent. But they no longer generated the excitement that had once been stirred by some of them.

The most demanding activity of fandom seemed to be the holding of the annual worldcons. Those still generated considerable friction among the groups putting them on, but most of that was kept fairly well within the limits of those groups.

There was a brief flurry of excitement in 1950 when ESFA and the Hydra Club pooled their talents to put on a July Fourth weekend regional conference at the Henry Hudson Hotel in New York City. This was structured like a major worldcon—hardly an original idea, though such affairs did not become common for several years. That year's worldcon was to be in Portland, Oregon, over Labor Day weekend, and we wanted something for those who could not make the trip to the West Coast.

Will Sykora and a few others decided that our affair was meant to steal attendance from the worldcon. (Actually, New York and Portland remained in friendly touch throughout.) Sykora began a furious letter campaign to have us boycotted. The result was that more people heard about it from him than from our limited mailing. At least 200 came to the Henry Hudson, including a group Don Ford brought from Ohio. There was a highly successful banquet where Isaac Asimov made his debut as toastmaster.

Sykora showed up and was allowed to attend on the condition that he should cause no trouble. But he soon began circulating a petition against us. The hotel, alerted to possible trouble, had him quietly removed. And that ended the excitement. (Well, outwardly. The conference was soon blamed for causing broken marriages and much reshuffling among half the pros on the East Coast. Its reputation was exaggerated—somewhat.)

The Portland worldcon, with Anthony Boucher as Guest of Honor, set a new record for attendance. According to careful estimates, some 250 fans showed up for it.

I shall not list all the worldcons hereafter. But a few deserve special mention.

Chicon II, in 1952 at Chicago, was the one that went far beyond the most optimistic dreams of anyone guessing at possible attendance. By the best estimate, 870 people attended to honor Hugo Gernsback. This record stood until 1967.

This was also the scene of considerable contention and hassling over the selection of the next year's site. The Little Men had sent a group from San Francisco with the expectation that they would be chosen as hosts almost automatically. They had put in a bid the year before, and had been unofficially assured that they would be the next choice. But a few of the East Coast fans decided that the Little Men were being too arrogant about it all, and began contriving to steal the bid away from them.

In this, the Easterners were successful, through some rather complicated trickery that was planned out in an all-night session before the bidding. The plan involved setting up a number of bids for various cities, such as New York and Pittsburgh, with the idea that all of these would collapse on signal and throw their support to Philadelphia. (Getting a fan to put in such a false bid for Pittsburgh proved difficult for a while.) By the time the arguments had gone on for what seemed hours, the fans who were not aware of the trick were more than willing to go along with anything that offered a reasonable hope of compromise.

Looking back on it, I regret that. The Little Men took their unexpected defeat like gentlemen, proving that they had been nice guys all along. And the whole rigging of the bidding was hardly to the credit of those fans (including myself) who were part of it. But at the time, it seemed a splendid victory.

One result of this was the establishment of rules for all future bidding. From then on, the convention was supposed to rotate from West Coast through Central Zone to East Coast and then return to the West Coast. This made for more orderly bidding and also prevented any one section from keeping control because of the preponderance of fans from that area. With minor modifications, the plan has been continued since then.

The Philcon II, at Philadelphia in 1953, established a new tradition in fandom. As one of the features of the convention, it was decided to give awards, voted on by the members, for the best novel, artist, magazine and several other categories. These were called the

Hugo awards, named for Hugo Gernsback, just as the Mystery Writers gave their Edgars in memory of Edgar Allan Poe. The physical awards were in the form of stylized rockets mounted on wooden bases. Alfred Bester's *The Demolished Man* was the winning novel.

The Hugos were not given in 1954 at the SFCon in San Francisco. But the idea had proved popular, and it was reinstated at the 1955 Clevention in Cleveland, with considerable changes in some of the categories. From then on, it has been a regular feature of all world conventions. The categories eventually were largely fixed, except for a couple of options for each convention, and voting was kept open to all convention members, either attending or supporting.

Over the course of years, these awards have become generally accepted as the highest awards in the field. For a novel to be a Hugo winner now often results in a considerable boost in sales, and many far outside the world of science fiction are aware of the importance of a Hugo. There were rumors that some of the early awards were "fixed," but certainly for most of their existence they have been handled with scrupulous honesty. Perhaps not all winners proved to be quite the best of the year, but the average of the selections has been very high.

The 1956 NewYorCon in New York City (usually called Nycon II) almost equaled the attendance of Chicon II. Despite that, it was distinguished by losing money somehow, so that the fans had to take up a subscription at the end to bail the committee out and to preserve the excellent reputation the worldcons had previously achieved.

In 1957, the worldcon finally moved off the North American Continent and became genuinely entitled to its claim of being a World Science Fiction Convention. Loncon I was held in London, with John W. Campbell as Guest of Honor for the third time—the first man thus honored more than twice. 268 fans attended, many of them from the United States. This interrupted the system of rotation, but provision was made in the rules that such conventions outside of North America would be special, and the rotation would resume in regular order afterward.

1961 saw the convention in Seattle (Seacon), where Robert A. Heinlein was Guest of Honor for the second time. This was the smallest American convention since 1951, with only 300 attending. But those who went to it insisted it was one of the best of all conventions.

Another and unofficial addition was made to the traditions of worldcons in 1953. This was the organization of TAFF—the Transatlantic Fan Fund, designed to bring a British fan to America or an American to Britain for the conventions. (Forrest J. Ackerman had previously tried to establish a Big Pond Fund for the same purpose, but without adequate support.) TAFF was organized by Don Ford and Walter A. Willis, and first became operational in 1955 when Ken Bulmer was brought over for the convention in Cleveland.

This is still in operation. It works by selling the right to vote for the person to be selected, each vote to be accompanied by a donation of at least one dollar. It represents another good example of the hard—and often unnoticed—work fans are willing to do to promote their interests.

Seemingly, fandom had settled into an acceptance of itself as simply pursuing a pleasant hobby. Fijagh. (Except for those fans who devoted a year or more of their lives in hard work to put on a convention for other fans.)

Nevertheless, there were still fans who were making the activities of fandom a way of life. They were doing it quietly, without the previous amount of excitement and turmoil, but they were perhaps working harder at it than ever. And out of their work, some very real contributions were made to the world of science fiction.

One such fan was Donald B. Day, who had been

chairman of the 1950 Norwescon in Portland, Oregon, and was also the publisher of *Fanscient,* an excellent and informative fanzine. He was a collector of most of the magazines published to date (except for some fantasy magazines), and he had begun keeping a voluminous cross-indexed list of stories and authors on card files.

In 1952, he organized Perri Press to bring out all the material from his index in book form. This was the *Index to the Science Fiction Magazines, 1926–1950.* It listed all the stories separately by author and title, all alphabetized; and there were further listings of the magazines and cover artists, as well as a list of back covers when used. The book was offset from typed copy, giving the magazine, page number and date for each story, and was bound in sturdy cloth. There was also considerable information about pseudonyms, editors, artists, etc.

It was a monumental piece of work, considering that there was no help from computer indexing. It sold for $5.00 before publication, $6.50 after, and was printed in a limited edition of less than 2,000 copies. There could be no hope of profit from the venture.

But it proved to be invaluable. Most of the professional anthologists depended heavily on it—and still do, in many cases. It also set the standard for future work of similar nature. This was a major piece of genuine fan scholarly research into the field, fortunately made generally available in permanent form. It seems a shame that no special Hugo was ever awarded for the work.

Sam Moskowitz is another fan whose real work in life has been devoted to fandom. He has one of the most complete collections of science fiction (including very old and rare material) and art in existence, accumulated over many years of patient search. And his ambition has been to become the complete historian of science fiction. This started with a series of articles in *Fantasy Commentator*, where he began tracing the history of fandom during its early years in the New York area.

These were revised and collected in 1954, when a group of other fans set up a publishing company to issue them in permanent form. *The Immortal Storm* was published by the Atlanta Science Fiction Organization Press, with the text set on Varitype and offset, together with photographs of many of the prominent fans and authors. Since Moskowitz was one of the fans most involved in some of the feuds of the time, it presents a view somewhat biased toward things as he saw them, but is probably as fair an account as can be given by any one person. The book treats the turmoil among fans as having slightly more importance than World War II—but that is surely an accurate reflection of the feeling among those involved. It is invaluable as an account of the early days of fandom.

Down in Australia, Donald H. Tuck was devoting almost all his available time to collecting everything he could find in print of a science fiction nature; and his ability to do so at such a remote location, away from most of the sources, was surprising. He also began preparing bibliographic records of what he collected. Some of this material was mimeographed in 1954 as *The Handbook of Science Fiction and Fantasy*; this was revised and expanded into two volumes in 1959, and he began planning a still larger edition in encyclopedic form, which is currently being issued by Advent: Publishers.

Advent was another fan press, but was devoted to issuing books of serious nature which no regular publisher would have found of sufficient immediate profit. It was organized by Earl Kemp in 1956 in Chicago, with the assistance of Edward Wood, Sidney Coleman, John Stopa and Robert E. Briney. It first published a collection of the critical columns by Damon Knight that had appeared in various magazines. *In Search of*

Wonder was a success and has been continuously in print; it is now available in an enlarged and revised edition.

A Frank Kelly Freas art portfolio was issued next, with opposition from Wood, Stopa and Briney, and was not successful. After a number of further plans which did not reach publication, Advent issued *The Science Fiction Novel*, a symposium of the lectures of Robert A. Heinlein, C. M. Kornbluth, Alfred Bester and Robert Bloch that had been held at the University of Chicago under the direction of T. E. Dikty. This was a further contribution to the criticism of science fiction, and is still in print. Robert Bloch's collection of articles from fan magazines, *The Eighth Stage of Fandom*, was less successful. This was followed by the *Proceedings* of the 1962 and 1963 worldcons and a reissue of *Of Worlds Beyond*, originally edited by Lloyd Arthur Eshbach for Fantasy Press—the first book to consider the technique of writing science fiction seriously.

By this time, Kemp's original four partners had left Chicago, and James O'Meara and George W. Price, Jr., were added. Then Kemp left for California, and Price took over the Chicago operations, with long-distance help from Edward Wood and his wife.

To a large extent, Advent became what might be considered the University Press of science fiction. It has taken on the mission of making the best works of historical and critical scholarship about science fiction available to libraries and researchers. It has published two books of reviews by James Blish, a nostalgic history of *Astounding* by Alva Rogers, Harry Warner's history of fandom in the forties, Alexei Panshin's critical examination of the fiction of Heinlein, and a number of other important books.

These books represent true contributions, in most cases. It is significant that most such scholarship began—and continues—as the work of serious fans, with very little contribution from scholars from outside the circle of science fiction enthusiasts.

In most cases, the rewards to the writers don't begin to pay for the effort involved, either in money or in academic prestige—of which there is rarely any. And the publishers of such works can expect little return on their investment of time and money beyond the satisfaction of contributing to the field.

After 1950, most of the boisterous ebullience that led to the shouts of "Fiawol" began to fade. The leading fans matured and could examine their literature and their fan activities with a far better sense of values. But fandom as a way of life did not end. Fan devotion to the field might have become more critical, but it was no less real. And a large part of the real acceptance of science fiction as a form of literature is due to such devotion.

CHAPTER 22

Watershed

IN MANY WAYS, the period from 1950 to 1961 represented a time of transition from the previous pattern of science fiction to a complex of patterns that would appear more strongly in the next age. Perhaps this was inevitable. After a quarter of a century, some of the early habits and ways must have grown somewhat stale, and new attitudes and ways of looking at the field had to be found.

Previously, the field had been dominated by one editor during any given period. Gernsback set his mark upon science fiction as a sort of worship service for technology and science. Harry Bates modified this by introducing more conventional pulp standards, but it was not until F. Orlin Tremaine became editor of *Astounding* that the real influence of Gernsback began to fade. Tremaine was in turn displaced by Campbell, who set his personal standards so firmly onto what was accepted as good science fiction that his magazine clearly dominated the field—in influence, if not always in circulation.

But after 1950, even Campbell began to lose his control—and there was nobody to replace him. H. L. Gold and Anthony Boucher were also strongly influential; each attracted and influenced a group of writers and became the focal point for a segment of the more knowledgeable readers.

By the end of 1961, both Gold and Boucher were gone, and Campbell was still in control of his magazine. But a number of factors prevented his ever exerting the dominance that had once been his. For one thing, the emergence of books as an outlet for original science fiction had weakened the influence the magazines could exert. For another, Campbell had seemingly lost the driving will that had been his originally.

This should not have been surprising, after all. Campbell had built his stable of writers and seen them disappear into the war. He had shrugged his massive shoulders and rebuilt it. And then, when things were getting back to normal, Gold and Boucher appeared on the scene, to funnel many of the stories intended for *Astounding* to their new markets. Unlike most other competition, they could meet Campbell's rate of payment and sometimes even exceed it. (Gold was the first to offer 3¢ a word. And when Campbell matched it, Gold began offering 4¢ a word to the writers who appeared frequently in his magazine. This didn't last, but it helped Gold attract some of Campbell's best writers.) Furthermore, their magazines were meant to be "quality" publications, unlike the action-centered competition Campbell had faced before.

Also, many of the leading writers were now beginning to think in terms of sales to the books. Unlike magazines, books offered an advance payment to an established writer on the basis of a simple outline. If an author could secure the sale of his novel to a book publisher, he could make at least as much as he could in selling it as a serial—and probably be able to sell serial rights to one of the magazines, as well. Hence, many of the writers were now directing their primary attention to book publication.

Campbell was growing tired. There must be a limit to the amount of energy any man can keep expending continuously; and there are also limits to the frontiers of any one man's vision. He had given science fiction most of what he had to give. Now other interests occupied much of his attention.

He had become an advocate of parapsychology and psionics. When many of his scientist friends refused to entertain these subjects as even worthy of serious attention, he became disenchanted with the sciences he had previously extolled. His editorials began to reflect the idea that scientists were establishment figures, banded together to preserve the status quo, all having closed minds and myopic vision.

Strangely, despite what many believed, Campbell did not become bitter. When some of his oldest friends, such as Willy Ley and Isaac Asimov, drifted away from him because of his new beliefs, he remained as fond of them as ever.

He still had enough influence to make one final change in the field, however, and that change was a major one. Previously extrasensory-perception stories had been rare, except for the use of telepathy to make communication possible with aliens. Now *Astounding* began to feature stories dealing with the so-called psi phenomena. And this rapidly spread to other magazines.

Obviously, it was an attractive subject to many writers who had never mastered the fields of science that had been the sources of much previous fiction. Old writers picked up the subject and many new ones came in who wrote about little else. The result was that psi quickly became an accepted basis for science fiction, and remains so today.

This produced a considerable change in the readership of the magazines—and the books, since the rise of psi spread almost at once through the whole field. Some of the older readers, particularly those with technical training or interests, stopped reading science fiction, finding too little of what interested them. But a larger number of new readers were attracted by the new subjects. Much of the original unity of interest was disappearing.

At best, the readers of the magazines probably never had more than a small influence on what those magazines published; but they did exert some influence. Now that began to wane. The new readers and the old ones were in such strong disagreement about their preferences that there could be no consensus to exert even a tiny pressure on an editor.

Besides, another change had come about after 1950. Before then, almost all the magazines had carried extensive letter columns where the readers could sound off. Many of those letters were obviously written for egoboo (fan jargon for ego boost, and a truly lovely term). But even many of the most contrived letters also carried the writer's evaluation of the stories. Whenever some story was particularly liked or disliked by most letterhacks, the editor was inclined to give that story some consideration, good or bad.

But with the coming of the digest-sized magazines, space became more limited, and most letter columns disappeared. *Astounding* (and later, *Analog*) continued to run several pages of letters, but few of the ones published dealt with the fiction; most discussed the editorial or the science article.

As a result, the fans found little incentive to write. The hope of seeing a letter published was probably not the only reason for most of the letters, but it was the strongest. Once that hope was gone, comparatively few letters were received by the editors, and those few were not sufficient to exert any influence. The communication link between editor and reader disappeared.

With it also went the chance for communication—or feedback—between reader and writer. Most of the writers I knew in the previous period turned to the letter column first, to see how their stories—and those of their fellow writers—were rated. I know that I read the letters before the stories. And once in a while, those letters taught me things I needed to know. Other writers reported gaining valuable help in the same way. Anyhow, having some reaction—even a limited one—to one's stories always seemed to be important. It made science fiction a more personal field of writing. Now this disappeared, and many of the writers missed it. We could still get some reaction from the fans we might meet at conventions, but that was necessarily suspect; a reader would find it harder to be completely critical when discussing a story in person with the man who wrote it.

There were book reviews, of course. The anthologist Groff Conklin had a column from October 1950 until October 1955 in *Galaxy*; P. Schuyler Miller had one in *Analog* until his death in 1973; and there were others. But these were not the same as the readers' comments. For one thing, they only covered the novels that were published in book form, offering no help to the writers of shorts and novelettes; for another, they were professional reviews, usually tempered and moderate, lacking the candor of the comments in the letters.

To decrease the feedback still further, most writers

with reasonably high output were acquiring agents. During this period, both Scott Meredith and Frederik Pohl (under the firm name of Dirk Wylie) were very receptive to science fiction writers and together they represented most of the major writers. Pohl gave up his agency early in the period, but by then other agents were interested, and quickly took on most of his list.

Generally, editors return stories (or accept them) with much less comment when an agent is involved; and in many cases, these comments never reach the writer. Hence, despite the services an agent can perform for a writer, he does act as a screen between writer and editor, cutting off even the feedback that might be obtained by a writer working directly with that editor.

As a result of the breakdown of most of the communication links, writers were generally left with very little guidance of any kind, other than what might occasionally be provided by an editor or an agent. And during the boom period, when almost any vaguely readable story could be sold, even this meant nothing.

Writers were undergoing a major change in their whole manner of thinking about science fiction at this time. Previously, the writing of science fiction had been little more than a hobby, with very few who had any idea of making a living from their stories. With limited markets and low rates, science fiction had to be a labor of love.

During this period, all that changed. With magazine rates up to triple what they had been and with the possibility of book sales (and anthology sales for shorter works), a reasonably good writer had an opportunity to make at least a large part of his income from the sale of science fiction. This was the first time, for instance, that several young writers never found it necessary to take up any other occupation. Even after the boom collapsed, the better writers found science fiction an attractive market.

Suddenly writers found they were in the writing *business!* The bull sessions among writers, which previously had been mostly a mixture of idea exchanges and almost fannish discussion of the stories in the magazines, suddenly were filled with rates of payment, how to slant for some particular editor, and other commercial aspects of writing.

There was even an attempt to organize. A number of writers met in New York to discuss setting up something like the organization the mystery writers already had. They drew up and ratified a constitution and elected officers for the Fantasy Writers' Guild. There was even stationery printed. Then, for reasons known only to one of the elected officers, no meetings were ever called. By the time some of the members could get together, it seemed too late to attempt to salvage things, and nothing more came of it.

Another attempt by writers to get together was more successful. Judith Merril, Damon Knight and James Blish decided to hold a conference for professionals in Milford, Pennsylvania—where they all were living at the time. Word of this was spread during the 1956 worldcon (held in New York City that year), and the Milford Conference followed the end of the worldcon by a day or so; thus many of the writers who had come to New York for the worldcon were available to make the short extra trip to Milford.

About thirty writers attended, including old-timers like Theodore Sturgeon and Lester del Rey, as well as Robert Silverberg and Harlan Ellison, who were just beginning their careers. The conference lasted for several days, culminating in a final party. During that time, most of the sessions were free exchanges of opinion on every subject from writers' slumps (the liveliest discussion) to religion in science fiction.

This proved to be so successful that it became a yearly event. In time, Damon Knight became the one who masterminded these Milford conferences, and the nature of the meetings changed. Discussions were still held, but the emphasis began to be on workshop sessions.

(A "workshop" is a meeting where everyone who has submitted a manuscript gets together to discuss all the manuscripts that have been submitted. The manuscripts for the day are read in advance by all. Then all take turns criticizing. Writers seem to regard these as very productive—or at least, beginning writers do. My own reaction is that the idea of everyone being competent to criticize is false, and that a consensus is soon reached where the chief product is egoboo. Nevertheless, workshop sessions have become the main feature of many writers' conferences, both in science fiction and other fields.)

In time, the Milford conferences became so well established that the tradition and name persisted, even when Damon Knight—many years later—moved to Florida and then to Oregon. There came to be a regular group of attendees, composed of both established professionals and writers who had sold only one story —or very few stories. Traditions and a strong feeling of togetherness (as well as considerable consensus of taste) were developed until the group was referred to as the "Milford Mafia" by both themselves and those who disagreed with them strongly.

There was another short-lived result of the first conference. Damon Knight and Lester del Rey took on the job, in 1957, of putting out a fan-type magazine for writers, called the *Science Fiction Forum*. About 60 writers subscribed, and the first issue was well received; it was intended to carry both articles on writing and a story-by-story review of all the stories in the major magazines—to supply some of the feedback that had been missing.

Response was so good that the second issue ran to 68 mimeographed pages, with 20 of those pages made up of letters and replies.

There was no third issue. Knight had an eye infection and del Rey was bothered by cataracts; further work became so difficult it was postponed. Then the second issue drew almost no response, and articles that had been promised were never delivered. This lack of reaction convinced the editors to abandon the project.

Usually, academic interest in science fiction is dated after this period, but such dating is inaccurate. The first college course on science fiction that I can discover was given as a night course at City College of New York Extension School; this began in 1953 and was conducted by Sam Moskowitz for three years. (It was then continued for several years by Hans Stefan Santesson.) Certainly this was the oldest continuing course on science fiction. At that time, Moskowitz had no difficulty in securing such writers as Heinlein and Asimov as guest lecturers. Another science fiction course was given by T. E. Dikty at University College, University of Chicago, in 1957.

Science fiction art also changed during this period. At the beginning, each magazine depended on a principal artist or a small staff, and most of the artists were men who had become familiar with the traditions of science fiction. Then, as new magazines began springing up, new artists appeared—among them such men as Frank Kelly Freas, H. R. Van Dongen and Ed Emshwiller, who came before the height of the boom.

During the peak magazine period, however, there was no hope of using only experienced science fiction artists. Most of those hastily drafted did the same work as was done for other magazines and what seemed the easiest course for an artist—they abandoned the alien scenes and technology for stereotyped faces. This unfortunate development—from the view of the older readers—spread rapidly and became the dominant magazine art form.

At the same time, Ballantine Books was creating another departure from traditional science fiction cover illustrating. Ian Ballantine wanted something new and distinctive to identify his books. For this, he turned to the largely non-representational work of Powers. A majority of the paperback publishers quickly followed Ballantine's lead. Many are still doing so.

"Art" was also becoming a matter of concern among some of the writers—but they were interested in what they conceived as the art of science fiction writing. They were apparently ashamed of the old pulp tradition of the field and wanted science fiction to be treated as a serious art form. Most of the early advocates of this avowed art were not among the highly successful writers, though Damon Knight and James Blish were leaders in the movement. Perhaps the reason for this concern with art among many of the less successful writers lies in the fact that far more writers can handle style well than can plot skillfully—and editors tend to favor good plots. Somehow, style is usually believed to be akin to art, while plotting is considered only a mechanical skill. And, naturally, every man considers his own product to be the right and proper one. The topic led to many long and serious discussions.

But the full development of that concern with writing as art had to wait for the next period.

PART V

The Age of Rebellion

(1962-1973)

CHAPTER 23

The Survivors

IN THE THREE PREVIOUS AGES of science fiction, the magazines had dominated the field. Readers were forced to develop their tastes from magazine stories and writers necessarily tailored their fiction to suit the requirements of magazine editors. To a large extent, this tradition continued for a few years after publishers began to issue science fiction books regularly.

By the beginning of the fourth age, the magazines were having hard times. Although a faint statistical boom can be shown for 1965, involving a few extra issues, there was never a real recovery from the great bust following the boom of the third age.

Only five science fiction magazines were able to publish through all the years of the fourth age: *Amazing, Analog, Galaxy, If* and *F&SF*. There was also *Fantastic Stories*, but that used more fantasy than science fiction; and listing *F&SF* as science fiction is somewhat doubtful, since it depended increasingly on its stories of fantasy. Most of these magazines were in trouble. Circulation figures—with the exception of those for *Analog*—declined sharply until few could achieve even the modest per-issue figure of 40,000 sales.

Only *Analog* and *F&SF* were able to continue regular monthly publication throughout the period from 1962 to 1973. *Galaxy* and *If*, edited by Frederik Pohl, began the period as bimonthlies. *If*, which won three Hugo awards during Pohl's editorship, switched to a monthly schedule in October 1964 and *Galaxy* did so with the June 1968 issue. Pohl also started a new magazine, *Worlds of Tomorrow*, in 1963; this had a somewhat erratic schedule, though it was supposedly bimonthly. It merged with *If* in 1967. Pohl also edited *International Science Fiction*, using stories from other countries and translations; only two issues appeared, one in 1967 and one in 1968.

Then in 1969, Robert Guinn sold his magazines to Universal Publishing and Distributing Company. Ejler Jakobsson replaced Pohl as editor. Printing difficulties and other troubles from the changeover resulted in a few skipped issues. In 1970, both *Galaxy* and *If* became bimonthlies, though *Galaxy* went monthly again in September 1973. *Worlds of Tomorrow* was revived briefly for two issues in 1970 and one in 1971, but then died.

Ziff-Davis continued *Amazing* and *Fantastic Stories* on monthly schedules until 1965, when the magazines were sold to Sol Cohen, who had previously worked for Robert Guinn. Cohen turned them into bimonthlies, on which schedule they continued. He also changed the policy to one of using reprints from the huge inventory the magazines had acquired during their years of publication, with only a token of new material. He soon began issuing numerous other magazines (many of them one-shots) that were filled with reprints from back issues. Many of these had titles which were suggestive of the leading magazines of the previous years.

Cohen hired Ted White to edit the magazines in 1969, and White began gradually switching back to the use of original stories, until he was finally able to discontinue the reprints.

Venture was revived briefly in 1969. There were three issues that year and three in 1970, before the magazine again died.

There were several attempts to start new science fiction magazines, the longest enduring of which was a string of magazines put out by Health Knowledge, Inc., edited by Robert A. W. Lowndes. These were small, cheaply produced magazines with erratic schedules, using mostly reprint material. *Magazine of Horror* ran from 1963 to 1971 for a total of 36 issues; *Startling Mystery* ran from Summer 1966 to March 1971 for 18 issues; and *Famous Science Fiction* printed nine issues between 1966 and 1969. These magazines used occasional new science fiction stories.

A much more promising magazine began publishing on the West Coast in 1973. This was *Vertex*, a large-size slick-paper magazine with copious illustrations, edited by Donald J. Pfeil. The price per issue was a startling $1.50, but the five issues printed during the year seemed to do well.

In England, the situation was worse than in the United States. *Vision of Tomorrow*, a joint Anglo-Australian effort, had three issues in 1969 and nine in 1970, but then ceased. *Science Fiction Adventures* managed to publish six issues in 1962 and three in 1963, but then it also ended.

This left only E. J. "Ted" Carnell with two magazines, which he was forced to give up in 1964. *Science Fantasy* was then continued under the editing of Kyril Bonfiglioli, and it changed from bimonthly to monthly in 1965. Then the name was changed to *Impulse* in August 1966. It ended in 1967, after publishing only two more issues.

New Worlds, which had maintained a monthly schedule in 1962 and 1963, went temporarily bimonthly after the editorship passed from Carnell to Michael Moorcock, but a monthly schedule was kept between 1965 and 1967. Thereafter, publication was erratic. The magazine ran into trouble in 1967 and was saved by a grant from the Arts Council. It lasted until April 1970. (There was also a slim issue sent to subscribers in 1971, containing an index and a single short story, making the total number of issues for *New Worlds* 201.) Then it metamorphosed into a paperback book.

Its career from 1964 on was a stormy one, since Moorcock made it a center for what was to be known as the New Wave of fiction; that, however, is the subject for another chapter. After the magazine ceased publication, there was nothing left of science fiction in the British magazine field.

Generally, there seemed to be a decline in quality as well as in quantity during this period. There were still excellent novels; but since the good ones were due in book form shortly after their magazine appearance, they were a less compelling reason to buy the periodicals than previously. The magazines needed strong short fiction to compete—and while a few first-class shorter works appeared, the average level was falling. The older, regular writers were turning their attention to books where the payment was better, and few were doing more than an occasional short story. The new writers often displayed considerable stylistic competence, but they seemed too willing to rework familiar material.

Readers complained that the magazines were no longer exciting, and I met many who hardly read the magazines, though they bought some, mostly out of habit. (This lack of excitement was probably the real reason for the declining circulation, though editors and publishers blamed distributors for not doing an adequate job—which was true, but only part of the story.) Editors complained that they found it harder and harder to get the type of material they wanted—and obviously, no magazine could publish better than it received. My own experience as assistant editor on the *Galaxy* magazines in 1968 and 1969 confirmed the fact that very little good short fiction was being submitted. Generally, the submissions from new writers I saw in 1953 were better than those of this period, and the same was true for many professionals. Pohl tried to stimulate more interest with his "*If Firsts*"—featuring a first sale and giving a biography of the writer—but it was only a partial success.

Of course, there is some difficulty in judging what stories are good from the limited hindsight of a few years. It's easy to make some reasonable judgment across fifty years to the beginning of the field. Time helps to weed out all but the better examples. Ten years gives less perspective. Hence, as I approach the present, I tend to list fewer stories and be less specific in evaluating them. Still, some selection seems necessary to do justice to the period.

One outstanding novelette in 1962 was Theodore L. Thomas' "The Weatherman" in the June *Analog*. This involves a remarkably plausible method for controlling the sun to regulate the weather on Earth so that an old man can have his idea of a perfect day. *Analog* also began H. Beam Piper's four-part serial, *Space Viking*, in November. This novel (published by Ace, 1963) is one of my favorite high-adventure science fiction stories. It not only shows an empire that has fallen and the men who now begin looting it, but deals in depth with the reason for such a fall and the nature of civilization. *Analog* also got into astrology with a series beginning in September by Joseph Goodavage, attempting to predict the weather. Campbell and Goodavage felt it was significant; the rest of us who checked the predictions against the facts found little reason to agree.

First appearances in 1962 were Roger Zelazny, Ursula K. Le Guin and Thomas M. Disch; for 1963 there were Piers Anthony and Norman Spinrad.

Dune World, by Frank Herbert, began in the December 1963 *Analog*. This is the first part of what was published as *Dune*, a book that has gained a following far beyond the usual science fiction circles. In it, we are shown the ecology of an arid, forbidding planet and the life of those who struggle there; it also deals with complexities of power in the future and the problems of a prophetic gift. Clifford D. Simak's *Here Gather the Stars* began in the July 1963 *Galaxy*. (*Way Station* is the Doubleday book version.) This is one of Simak's best novels, dealing with a man who keeps a crossroads station for those aliens who travel between the stars. His friends are all aliens, and he seems detached from Earth—until his mission proves more valuable to Earth than any other. Roger Zelazny's "A Rose for Ecclesiastes" appeared in the November *F&SF*—a story which helped to establish him as a major writer. This deals with an Earthman who is translating our poetry into Martian, a flower, and a Martian girl who is the last hope for the red planet.

Larry Niven first appeared in *If*, December 1964, with a short story entitled "The Coldest Place." He quickly established himself as the leading new writer of the "hard-science" type of fiction.

1965 was a better year in the quality of leading stories. Frank Herbert's *Prophet of Dune* (the second part of *Dune*) began in the January *Analog*, running for five installments. In October, *F&SF* began Roger Zelazny's . . . *And Call Me Conrad* (Ace paperback, *This Immortal*). This tells of an immortal man who must lead a group desiring to take over the ruins of Earth for aliens. There is a strong background of mythological history in the story, confused and yet significant to the plot. Robert A. Heinlein's *The Moon Is a Harsh Mistress* began in the December *If*. This tells of the struggle for freedom by the Moon against the oppression of Earth. The fight is led by a marvelous sentient computer, and there is a wealth of detailed material on what life may be in a lunar colony.

Harlan Ellison's "Repent Harlequin Said the Ticktockman" appeared in the December *Galaxy*, representing the writer's predilection for long titles and demonstrating a new power to his writing. Originally, Ellison had begun by writing fairly routine stories, apparently trying for quantity rather than quality. Now his whole attack changed. He gave up conventional plotting and began doing nightmare visions with a fury of style that sometimes seemed to be a continuous scream against the injustices he saw in life.

1965 also witnessed the return of E. E. Smith's greatest and most beloved villain, "Blacky" DuQuesne. *Skylark DuQuesne* began in the June *Galaxy*. Smith had apparently gotten rid of DuQuesne back in 1934. But the readers had never been content. Now, 31 years later, Smith brought him back. This time, without changing his basic philosophy, DuQuesne becomes the real hero—as he had been all along to the old-time readers.

In 1967, Ed Ferman, the son of the publisher, took over the editing of *F&SF*, a position he has held since. Under him, the magazine turned more toward fantasy for its shorter works, though it still published some science fiction.

Anne McCaffrey's "Weyr Search" appeared as a novelette in the October 1967 *Analog*, to be followed by *Dragonrider*, a two-part serial beginning in December. The two stories were combined as the Ballantine paperback *Dragonflight*, a book which became extremely popular. This tells of Pern, a world beset by dangerous "threads" that fall through space from another world. Men have trained great "dragons" to carry them and to burn the threads as they fall. The number of trained men and dragons is too few, but the heroine learns to send her dragon through time to recruit help from the past.

New Worlds started a controversy in 1967 by publishing Norman Spinrad's *Bug Jack Baron*, a six-part serial beginning in December. This is the story of a radio personality who gains tremendous power from his program and of his compulsions and chance to win or lose immortality. The novel has a good deal of power. But the controversy centered around the fact that the magazine published it complete with four-letter words and graphic descriptions of oral sex. The British distributor refused to handle the issues in which the story appeared, and the matter was finally debated in Parliament.

In 1968, the March *Analog* carried "Birth of a Salesman," the first story by James Tiptree, Jr. This seems strange now, since Tiptree became identified with Pohl's magazines and *F&SF* as one of the new writers most capable of departing in mood and treatment from Campbell's type of fiction. (Tiptree recently turned out to be named Alice Sheldon.)

The April *Galaxy* began Clifford D. Simak's *Goblin Reservation*. In this, Simak blends science fiction and fantasy. It has an alien invasion, time travel—and the ghost of William Shakespeare. Despite this odd mixture, it won the $1,000 prize offered by *Galaxy* that year as reader's choice for best novel of the year. It is the first of several novels in which Simak blends science and magic.

In September, *Galaxy* ran "Nightwings," by Robert Silverberg. Silverberg had been considered a "hack" writer who churned out routine stories to order. Now he was trying to change his image by doing more mature work. In this story of a strange future where aliens have taken over Earth, he succeeded in creating a strong feeling and atmosphere, with the color that had previously been missing from his work. (It was not the first of his serious efforts, but this story finally won him recognition as a serious writer.) This and two later novelettes—unfortunately not up to the high level of the first—were combined into the Avon paperback *Nightwings*.

The July 1969 *Galaxy* began Frank Herbert's *Dune Messiah*, carrying the career of the "prophet" of *Dune* through the bitterness and turmoil of the successful transformation of the planet and the conquest of an empire, culminating in what seemed to be an act of self-immolation. 1969 also saw the first stories by Joe Haldeman, David Gerrold and Barry Malzberg.

In 1970, Robert A. Heinlein's *I Will Fear No Evil* began in the July *Galaxy*. This story is far from the type that had established his original reputation, though probably fine for those who made a cult of the last part of *Stranger in a Strange Land*. It deals with having an old man's brain transplanted into the body of a young woman. Somehow, he finds the woman's mind now sharing the body with him, and then goes on to argue sexual attitudes and discoveries with her. Straight science fiction fans usually regard it as Heinlein's worst novel, though some "liberated" readers disagree. I have no reports on what happened when someone turned to it from one of Heinlein's juveniles.

On July 11, 1971, John W. Campbell died. He died quietly in his home of an aneurism. He had been suffering from a combination of gout and high blood pressure for years—a combination that made the treatment of either difficult. *Locus*, the fanzine that served as the newsmagazine of the field, published a special two-part issue of tributes to him. As the magazine's editor, Charles Brown, said in making the announcement, "An era of science fiction came to an end on July 11 when John W. Campbell died."

There were now none of the editors who had done so much to shape the course of science fiction left active in the field.

Condé Nast, the publishers of *Analog*, took applications for the job and spent several months considering them. Finally, in November, Ben Bova was selected as the new editor.

Strangely, next year in 1972, Frederik Pohl had his first sale to *Analog*—"The Gold at the Starbow's End," which ran in the March issue. This was never seen by Campbell, though I believe it would have pleased him. The story is a complete departure from the satire for which Pohl had become famous. It deals with a test of human ability by sending a crew to a star to find a planet which those sending the crew know does not exist. The solution is one of those sweeping ideas Campbell usually loved.

When Isaac Asimov wrote his first novel in sixteen years, *The Gods Themselves*, it was published in both *Galaxy* and *If* in 1972—March *Galaxy*, April *If*, and May *Galaxy!* This is a departure from Asimov's usual novel—no Galactic Empire, no robots, and a middle section about some truly nonhuman aliens. It won him both the Nebula award and the Hugo award as best novel of the year.

Galaxy also scored something of a triumph in 1973 by publishing Arthur C. Clarke's first serial. *Rendezvous with Rama* ran in the September and October issues. This is the story of a great spaceship that enters the Solar System from far outside—one obviously built by a race greatly in advance of mankind. The fascination of the novel lies in the wonderful details Clarke has worked out for his ship and what it contains.

In 1973, J. R. R. Tolkien died, and his death was announced suddenly at the banquet of the worldcon held in Toronto. While Tolkien had never written science fiction, his *Lord of the Rings* trilogy was well known and loved by a majority of science fiction readers.

During the period from 1962 to 1973, the magazines discovered a large number of new writers. A few of these developed into valuable additions to the field. But most did not, either because they appeared too rarely or because their work did not arouse sufficient interest.

Generally, the fourth age wasn't exactly a bad one for the magazine readers—but it certainly wasn't a good one. Perhaps the best word to describe the period, despite some outstanding exceptions, was lackluster. The sparkle was gone, most of the ideas used were simple derivations of earlier ones, and sometimes it was hard to see why even the few survivors among the magazines still continued.

CHAPTER 24

The Torch Passes

IN PREVIOUS AGES of science fiction, the magazines dominated and largely determined the field. There were always some books of science fiction being published, but their circulation was limited and their cost prohibitive to younger readers, while libraries rarely stocked them. The advent of paperback books, which could compete directly with the magazines, changed this situation; but it wasn't until late in this period that their full influence was felt.

By the end of the period, however, there could be no doubt that writers and readers were looking first to the books. *Locus* reported that there were 346 original and 315 reprint books published in 1973. These figures cover fantasy and some marginal books, but the editors, Charles and Dena Brown, knew the category much better than most who compiled statistics of this kind, insuring reasonable accuracy.

By contrast, counting original science fiction and fantasy magazines published in the United States, there were only about 74 issues in 1965—the year of maximum number for this period. Also, in the past the books had frequently been magazine serial reprints; but now many of the magazines were using novels that had originally been commissioned for book publication.

Many of the science fiction readers were not reading

the magazines at all by the end of this period; a few did not even know that such magazines existed. This is confirmed by James Gunn, who questioned a class of 150; he found that his students read about five times as many books as they read issues of magazines.

Most of the influence was due to the paperback books, of course. Hard-cover publishing by major publishers had suffered something of the fate of the magazines in the previous age. Simon and Schuster, for instance, had let its early ambitious program fade away to a few scattered books. In most cases, publishers failed to find the returns they had expected, and dropped the category. (Part of the reason may have been that their sales forces simply didn't know how to market science fiction.) Even the publication of so-called juveniles declined. By the beginning of this period, the major push of hard-cover publishing was over.

The exception to all this was Doubleday, who continued to publish science fiction regularly. They had established numerous library outlets, and these were enough to assure almost any science fiction book an adequate sale. They also had their Science Fiction Book Club. For readers removed from convenient bookstores, this was a boon. The Club offered its selections at bargain prices—often no more than a quarter of the original list price. Naturally, a fair number of the titles had been published by Doubleday. (This changed somewhat; by the end of the period, the Club was frequently offering novels originally bought by paperback houses—at prices little higher than the later paperbacks would cost.)

As time went on, the Doubleday science fiction novels tended to become rather routine, with a large number picked up from minor English publications by writers of less than major stature. But many authors remained loyal to the company from the days when Doubleday had first given them book publication.

Asimov was the star of Doubleday. Except for a few

collections, his science fiction had already been published, but they continued to sell. (Doubleday seldom kept older science fiction books in print, but they made an exception for Asimov.) In 1972, they issued *The Early Asimov*, a large book containing over twenty of his early stories, along with a running account of how the stories were written, and details of the world of science fiction, as he had seen it.

This was an excellent idea for a book, of value to both the reader and historian. It was followed by a similar volume, *Early del Rey*. Unfortunately, the size of the book needed to do justice to the idea made it expensive, which apparently caused difficulties with some libraries that had standing orders with the firm. As a result, later volumes for Jack Williamson, Frank Belknap Long and Frederik Pohl were severely shortened. Then the series was dropped, which seems a pity.

Doubleday also published a number of other huge collections of stories. Harlan Ellison edited *Dangerous Visions* in 1967. Ellison asked the major writers in the field to contribute the stories they felt were unpublishable elsewhere because of a daring or unusual theme. At the time, the book created considerable controversy. It was followed by *Again, Dangerous Visions* in 1972.

In 1970, *Science Fiction Hall of Fame* was edited by Robert Silverberg, with stories chosen by members of the Science Fiction Writers of America as the best stories of the past. The selections were excellent, and the chronological arrangement made them serve as a running history of progress in the field. In 1973, a similar collection of longer stories was issued in two volumes, edited by Ben Bova.

Doubleday also published Harry Harrison's *Make Room, Make Room!* in 1966—a bitter but believable vision of a future ruined by overpopulation; the movie *Soylent Green* was derived from the book, but did little justice to Harrison's story. John Brunner's *Stand on Zanzibar* was published in 1968. This is an ambitious attempt to present the future and its problems of overpopulation, politics, etc., in a kaleidoscopic style hitherto used only in the mainstream. And finally, after sixteen years of waiting, Doubleday was able to print a new novel by Asimov in 1972—*The Gods Themselves.* This broke all records for science fiction by selling paperback rights for $60,000.

Probably the second most important hard-cover publisher during this period was Putnam, who seemed to have a policy of publishing authors, rather than individual books. They acquired Heinlein in 1959. In 1967, they obtained all Heinlein's "Future History" stories, many previously published by Shasta, and combined them in a huge volume entitled *The Past Through Tomorrow*. They issued his *The Moon Is a Harsh Mistress* in 1966 and his *I Will Fear No Evil* in 1971. Then in 1973, Heinlein finally completed *Time Enough for Love*, the long-awaited sequel to *Methuselah's Children*, giving the further exploits of the near-immortal Lazarus Long, 32 years after the earlier novel.

In 1968, Putnam began publishing the novels of Clifford D. Simak, beginning with his *Goblin Reservation*. In 1969, they published Frank Herbert's *Dune Messiah*, the sequel to his now-famous *Dune*, originally issued by Chilton in 1965; Putnam eventually secured the rights to this, also.

In 1971, Putnam published Philip José Farmer's *To Your Scattered Bodies Go*, an extensive rewriting of the novel which had won the Shasta prize contest in the mid-fifties, but never been published. In this, there is a huge world laid out along a winding river where everyone who has ever lived suddenly finds himself resurrected. The main character is Sir Richard Burton, translator of the *Arabian Nights*. There are hints that it is all some devious scheme by mysterious beings responsible for creating the world. This novel was followed in the same year by Farmer's *The Fabu-*

lous Riverboat, in which Mark Twain builds a steamboat to explore the river.

Throughout the period, other publishers brought out books, though on a less determined basis. W. W. Norton published Anthony Burgess' *A Clockwork Orange* in 1962—an extrapolation of a world where youth gangs are completely out of hand. Farrar, Straus published J. G. Ballard's *The Crystal World* in 1966; this tells of a cosmic event that results in all life becoming crystallized, and was much admired by those devoted to the New Wave—a movement to be covered later. And there were many others, including the popular books by Kurt Vonnegut, Jr.—which I have not included because Vonnegut insists they should not be called science fiction, a decision in which I concur.

Toward the end of this period, many more hardcover publishers began active programs of science fiction; among these were Harper and Row, Scribners and some of the other more prestigious publishers.

The greatest activity took place in the paperback field, however. A sampling of firms actively engaged in publishing science fiction through most or all of this period would include: Ace, Ballantine, Berkley, Avon, Lancer, Pyramid, Signet, Dell, Belmont, Pocket Books, Paperback Library, Bantam, Award and Macfadden-Bartell. Most British paperback publishers were also active.

Ace and Ballantine, both of which began using science fiction heavily back in 1952, were probably the leaders. Ace, under the direction of Donald A. Wollheim, published a strong line which included a wide range of material, from hoary reprints and crude action stories to some of the finest novels being done. Many of the best new writers began here, such as Zelazny and Le Guin.

Roger Zelazny's *F&SF* serial . . . *And Call Me Conrad* was retitled *This Immortal* in 1966; in the same year, Ace did his *The Dream Master*, a story of the ability to control dreams. Four of his novelettes were collected in *Four for Tomorrow* in 1967. And in 1969, Ace published *Isle of the Dead,* dealing with a man whose job was the literal building of worlds.

Ursula K. Le Guin began in the Ace Doubles in 1966 with *Rocannon's World* and *Planet of Exile*—the latter dealing with Earthmen on an alien planet learning to cope with a tough environment and with another sentient race. Her 1967 *City of Illusion* is another novel in her related series, this one dealing with aliens who have taken over and changed the Earth. But it was in 1969 that Le Guin gained full recognition with her *The Left Hand of Darkness,* which I consider one of the finest science fiction novels ever written. It is set on a frozen world where the otherwise-human people carry both male and female attributes, swinging randomly with each cycle. It deals with man against nature, man against man and alien attitudes—and is a penetrating study of human love.

Many of the writers first published by Ace went on to major hard-cover publication. But it was Ace that gave them the early showcase needed to display their talents. The same might be said of Philip K. Dick and John Brunner. Unfortunately, while Ace published the works of H. Beam Piper, his tragic death in 1964 made it impossible for him to go on to better markets.

Ace was also responsible for two very well-received series.

Marion Zimmer Bradley's Darkover series seems not to have been planned for continuing books. It began in 1962 with two short novels—*The Planet Savers* and *The Sword of Aldones.* (By internal evidence, the latter seems to have been written first, since it varies from the background of later novels.) In these, Bradley describes a world lying under a dim, red sun—a rugged, cold world. People from a long-lost colony ship have been forgotten and have evolved a culture seemingly simple but capable of using certain crystals to give them strange psi powers. Now Earth's Empire has discovered Darkover, and there is a conflict between the two cultures. All this has been enriched in later novels, of which there were four more from Ace. The books have developed almost a cult following. They form no typical series. Bradley made no effort at consistency, writing each without too much regard for previous details. They were also not written in order. Each may be read independently.

The Dumarest series, by E. C. Tubb, is another matter, and it has become eighteen books long at this writing. The novels appear in order, starting with the 1967 *The Winds of Gath,* and Ace published the first eight. In these, men have settled the galaxy and Earth is forgotten, except for vague myths. But Dumarest was born on Earth, before he drifted away. Now he moves from world to world trying to find clues to Earth's location, pursued by a savage cult that needs a secret he has stolen from them. The fascination of the series lies with the strange worlds. Dumarest is one of the few strong-man heroes who is intelligent and cares for others.

In 1971, Donald Wollheim left Ace to found his own publishing company, DAW Books, devoted to publishing nothing but science fiction. Since then, he has issued four or five books per month, including the later books in the series by Bradley and Tubb. Of all the Bradley series, I find the 1975 *Heritage of Hastur* one of the richest in its picture of the culture of Darkover.

Frederik Pohl followed Wollheim briefly as editor of Ace, but he soon left. After that, Ace published little new fiction, except for their monthly issue of two or three Perry Rhodan juvenile novels translated from the German.

Ballantine Books also published many novels by beginning writers, some of whom gained high reputations. But Ballantine, which had begun with top payment to authors, ran into a series of difficulties with its distributors; by 1962, they were forced to cut back severely. Many authors remained loyal to them, however, since they offered writers treatment which seemed to compensate. (It's interesting that both Ace and Ballantine paid near-bottom advances yet remained the leading influences in paperback science fiction.)

Anne McCaffrey came to Ballantine in 1967 with *Restoree*, which seems an adaptation of what is called woman's fiction to science fiction. Then Ballentine did her *Dragonflight* in 1968; this is the novel version of her *Analog* stories about the dragons of Pern and their riders. It was followed by a sequel, *Dragonquest*, in 1971. These books have remained steady favorites with readers.

Another favorite Ballantine author is Larry Niven. In 1966 Ballantine published his *The World of Ptavvs*, in which one man discovers strange aliens among us. Niven's *Ringworld* (1970) became a favorite novel of hard science. It features a giant world, constructed as a ring around its sun, with a surface so vast that thousands of Earth surfaces would be lost on it. Other books by Niven are usually laid in a consistent universe and based on extrapolations of real science.

Frederik Pohl was one of Ballantine's top authors from the beginning. In addition to his own novels and collections, he collaborated frequently with Cyril Kornbluth and did several series with Jack Williamson. Robert Silverberg brought many of his more serious books to Ballantine, such as his bitter *Dying Inside* (1972), a grim story of a telepath who is losing his power.

Both Ace and Ballantine also became involved with books which were peripherally related to science fiction. The first case of this was involved with the estate of Edgar Rice Burroughs. For several years, the estate had refused to discuss paperback publication (though Dell had published two Burroughs' novels in the late forties). Some of the books were no longer under copyright, and Ace decided to go ahead with publication of these. A new manager of the estate, Robert M. Hodes, quickly got in touch with Ballantine, who had been trying to buy rights to the works. After considerable hassling, Ballantine gained the rights to all the Tarzan and Martian novels (certainly the most popular of the books) and Ace agreed to do the Pellucidar, Venus and other books under contract.

Something of the same situation occurred with the Tolkien fantasies. J. R. R. Tolkien's *Lord of the Rings* had gained a high reputation, and both Ace and Ballantine tried to buy rights. But no response was made to their offers. Then Ace discovered that the books had not been properly protected under U.S. copyright law and brought out the trilogy without authorization. The hard-cover publisher turned to Ballantine, where the books were quickly issued in slightly revised form as authorized editions. Tolkien's appeal to readers to buy only the Ballantine editions proved so successful that Ace withdrew.

These two properties were extremely valuable to Ballantine. Perhaps as a result of Tolkien's success, Ballantine also tried a line of "Adult Fantasy" books, edited by Lin Carter. Most of these were reissues of classic fantasy (though Katherine Kurtz' series about the Deryni was not; this deals with an alternate medieval Wales where a race of telepaths vie for power with normal humans). The devoted fantasy readers loved the books, but other readers did not buy enough to make the venture profitable.

By the end of 1972, Ballantine was in serious trouble because of actions by the company controlling them. Then Random House, a large publishing firm with no mass-market paperback affiliate, bought Ballantine. By the beginning of 1973, Ballantine—which had struggled for years without adequate financing—became part of a major publishing "empire."

As a result, Betty Ballantine, who had handled science fiction, felt it necessary to turn this over to an assistant and hired Judy-Lynn del Rey and gave her authority to act on her own. From then on, Mrs. del Rey handled all science fiction for Ballantine. She came to the job with a background of magazine publishing, having been managing editor of the *Galaxy* line of magazines for several years. This gave her many friends among writers and readers, whom she soon began using to strengthen and extend the Ballantine line.

One of the last acts of Betty Ballantine was the purchase of paperback rights to Arthur C. Clarke's *Rendezvous with Rama* for the sum of $150,000—a figure previously undreamed in science fiction.

Other paperback publishers released many good books. Signet did well with selected authors, such as Heinlein and Clarke. Berkley brought out many of the Putnam books in paper. (They frequently issued a joint contract for both hard-cover and paperback, an advantage to the author, who did not then have to split his paper rights with the original publisher.) They also issued the first novel of Thomas M. Disch, *The Genocides*, in 1965—one of the first New Wave books by an American author. Lancer Books had an extensive line of science fiction and the novels about Conan the Barbarian—Robert E. Howard's original (and to me, best) sword-and-sorcery series. And Pyramid continued to issue a number of classics, including the works of Edward E. Smith. But after Donald Bensen left, the line did little new publishing of science fiction.

But no publisher was as strongly oriented to science fiction as Ace or Ballantine, where Wollheim and Betty Ballantine established strong personal contacts with the writers and where science fiction was considered the most important part of their efforts. The field would have been much poorer without the other publishers—but Ace and Ballantine really set the pattern for original paperbacks.

Anthologies and collections, in hard and soft covers,

flourished during all this period. Most of the major writers had their shorter works collected, thus preserving some of their best fiction. And anthologies—either on a theme or not—seemed to do well. The anthology of original stories—begun by Ballantine in the *Star* series back in 1953—was slow to catch on. Ted Carnell began a successful series in 1964 with his *New Writings in Science Fiction*; and Damon Knight persuaded Putnam to let him edit a series to be called *Orbit*, beginning in 1966. Knight's emphasis was more on what he considered style than on other story values, but his series won many awards for the stories used, and *Orbit* has lasted until the present day.

Then Roger Elwood began mass-producing such original anthologies. Generally, he devised an idea for a theme, gave it a title, and sold the idea to some publisher. After that, he selected writers to fill the book. The books began appearing in 1973, usually each with one or two stories by major writers and the rest by lesser names. By the end of the year, he had contracts for over thirty books. And the flood of his anthologies was just beginning.

CHAPTER 25

Rebellion: The New Wave and Art

By 1962, science fiction had evolved greatly in matters of style and characterization. But it was still not—and not really intended to be—a "literary" form of fiction.

In the beginning, it had been what might be called Tinker Toy fiction. The ideas with which it tinkered were the toys of scientific speculation; its characters were not unlike stick men in too many cases; and its style and plot devices often seemed to be assembled by fitting together certain standard spools. But by the beginning of the age of rebellion, it had become a fairly respectable literature, though one with a personality that required special interest or considerable acquaintance for acceptance.

The change had come about through a process of evolution and growth. Despite a great deal of talk from some of the newer writers and readers, and a number of signs that some kind of ferment was going on under the surface, no radical change had occurred. The older readers often complained that it had lost its enchantment, but the chief gripe seemed to be that science had caught up with fiction and that there were no new ideas.

Of course, science had always been ahead of fiction in its speculation and wilder ideas, and there was now a whole new body of biochemical knowledge to be used. But science fiction seemed content to neglect new possibilities and go on mining the old ones.

This comfortable nirvana came to an end in the sixties with an influx of new writers who were generally totally disenchanted with science or the idea that there was a bright future of endless progress ahead. Many of them had grown up in the aftermath of World War II and atomic bombs; they saw the growing ugliness of the cities, the beginning of man's destruction of the environment, the apparent shrinkage of the dignity of the average citizen, and the total failure of politics to deal with technological problems logically.

Furthermore, the background they brought to science fiction was unlike that of earlier writers. Few of the previous authors had originally intended to be writers; their writing was a by-product of their fascination with the future, gained from science courses, some profession, or a background of reading the science fiction magazines.

By contrast, the new writers were *primarily* interested in writing as a thing in itself. Many came out of college literature and creative writing courses. They did not turn to Heinlein or Asimov for their background, but to Faulkner, Joyce, Kafka and other authors deemed worthy of study by professors, rather than "mere" entertainment reading. (Somehow, literature courses seem to overlook the fact that Faulkner and the others wrote excellent entertainment.)

In the previous ages of science fiction, there had been no market for such writing. The magazines were generally edited by men who knew the traditions of science fiction or by editors who came from some background of pulp writing where plotting dominated style. The same could be said for most of the leading book editors.

Now this changed, at least in the book market. Many of the editors were ones who had gained their ideas from general courses in college or who had previously known nothing of science fiction. To some of them, science fiction was a peculiar form of fantasy where anything could happen and the normal standards of writing were forgotten. The stranger the material looked, the surer they were that it was what the field demanded. (Some of them didn't last long at the job —but they were usually followed by others with the same ideas.)

In one case, the new writers also found a welcome market in a magazine. This was the British *New Worlds*, long edited by E. J. "Ted" Carnell. Under his direction, it had become the most successful of the magazines published in England, and its contents were well within the traditions of the field, since Carnell was a longtime reader and fan.

In 1964, however, Carnell resigned from the magazine. In the summer of that year, the editorship was taken over by Michael Moorcock. At the time, Moorcock's reputation was founded on his writing of fantasy stories—the so-called "sword-and-sorcery" type, in which brawling heroes fight with primitive weapons across strange worlds in which magic and wizardry dominate. Moorcock's Elric stories were generally liked by the readers of that type of fiction, but they were hardly innovative.

As an editor, his intention seemed totally unrelated to his earlier writing. He set out deliberately to make radical changes in the magazine, both as to format and contents. Instead of the usual pulp approach, he began experimenting with different formats, slick paper, new forms of art, and fiction unlike what had been carried in the magazine previously. He began collecting a stable of the new writers, mostly British at first, though some of the new American writers soon moved into his orbit.

The magazine had a stormy career under his control. As mentioned previously, the magazine was saved from financial disaster in 1967 by a grant from the Arts Council. But despite being banned by the distributor for the publication of Norman Spinrad's *Bug Jack Baron*, it managed to last until April 1970. Thereafter, it was changed to paperback book form.

Moorcock claimed that what he wanted was fiction with ideas; but he never seemed to define what he meant by that. In practice, his magazine seemed to be devoted to stories that were controversial, either by the breaking of the reputed magazine taboos or in treatment and style.

These stories came to be known as the New Wave of science fiction (sometimes later called the New Thing). And for several years, the subject of the New Wave became the hottest topic for debate in the field, particularly among American science fiction readers.

When Judith Merril moved to England, she discovered the New Wave; some say she gave it the name, though I've never been able to verify this. In any event, she immediately became an ardent convert and began preaching the new gospel vigorously as the ultimate form of science fiction. In 1968, she published a collection entitled *England Swings SF*. And when she returned to America, she began an ardent campaign of proselyting.

Nobody ever managed to define exactly what this New Wave was. But judging by the stories usually accepted as New Wave by the writers and readers, it was a strong shift away from most of the traditions of science fiction and toward some of the traditions that had shaped the little literary magazines for at least forty years. (It was still called avant-garde and experimental, despite its long existence.)

It seemed to be based upon the idea that the primary element of fiction lay in the handling of style and attitude, rather than in story development, plotting or ideas. What was said was assumed to be less important than how it was said. Symbolism—sometimes with little evidence of real referents for the symbols—became a virtue, and the more intricate and abstruse the structure of a story, the better it was considered to be.

The philosophy behind New Wave writing was a general distrust of both science and mankind. Science and technology were usually treated as evils which could only make conditions worse in the long run. And mankind was essentially contemptible, or at least of no importance. There was an underlying theme of failure throughout. Against the universe, the significance of mankind was no greater than that of bedbugs—if as great.

This was not true of all the fiction, of course; some stories simply used the older themes and disguised them under new tricks of handling. But generally, the feeling of gloom and despair ran through most of the New Wave. Futility was a strong keynote. The old heroes were gone, and antiheroes and blank-faced and blank-feeling characters pervaded the fiction. Many of the stories were laid in backgrounds where our culture had failed or was about to fail. (There had been such stories in classic science fiction, of course—but there the emphasis was on recovery; here it all went downhill from start to finish.)

Some advocates of the New Wave defended all this on the ground that it was realistic, as opposed to the neverland romanticism that had filled science fiction too long. But the New Wave exaggerated at least in one direction as much as romanticism had exaggerated in the opposite. (Anyhow, I question how real this can be, in the light of history. Mankind has often stumbled; but the long history of our kind tends to indicate some progress, rather than a steady regression.)

Somehow, the leading writer of this type of fiction was usually said to be J. G. Ballard. His early work hardly suggested such a place of pre-eminence. He began doing rather undistinguished books of the "British disaster" school of science fiction, which went back to H. G. Wells' *War of the Worlds*, at least. This type of fiction dealt with some sudden disaster that hit the Earth and threatened to destroy all mankind. Initially, most of such stories had happy endings, but the need for this had disappeared by the time Ballard came on the scene. Other examples might be John Wyndham's *Day of the Triffids* (1951) or John Christopher's *No Blade of Grass* (1956). Ballard used such things as a flood that drowned all the world or a great drought that parched all the surface. The scientific foundation for the novels was weak, but some of the scenes of the effect of the disasters on the people were quite effective. The books did well enough but created no great excitement.

His writing tended to become more involuted and his characters and their actions further removed from the normal development of such stories. In *The Crystal World* (1966), however, he achieved what many New Wave followers considered his finest novel; this involved a strange process of crystallization for all living things, full of chase scenes that got nowhere and a slow disintegration of character. Apparently it was designed to create an impression of total confusion, and in that it succeeded—at least for most readers.

He also did a number of shorter works, and it was from these that much of his leading reputation derived. According to him, in his pronunciamentos about his writing, he was getting away from "linear fiction" and developing "condensed novels." Just what those terms mean is hard to determine, but certainly he was tossing out all the normal rules for crafting stories.

Another writer closely associated with the New Wave was the American Thomas M. Disch, whose first novel was *The Genocides* (1965), a story of the last human survivors wandering around after an alien invasion; eventually, mankind fails. In some ways, his work has been the most consistently cynical of all the writers of this group. Charles Platt became a leading figure in the New Wave and carried on *New Worlds* for a time after Moorcock left in 1970. And there were a number of others, mostly British, whose work appeared within the pages of that magazine before it ceased publication.

Like most proselyting movements, the New Wave claimed a number of people who achieved success, but who did not properly belong to it. Probably the foremost of these was Brian Aldiss, who vigorously denied being part of that clique. Since he had been doing his own thing long before the New Wave began, his denial was certainly justified, but he was frequently listed as a New Wave writer. Keith Roberts was also listed at times, and some hailed his *Pavane* (1968) as outstanding New Wave writing. How he felt about this is not on record; but this collection of stories woven into a novel hardly has any of the normal characteristics of the movement. It is an excellently written and developed story of an alternate world in which the Spanish Armada defeated England.

In America, it was hard to find any writer (other than Disch, perhaps) who would admit to being a New Wave author, though some of the younger or more "experimental" writers hotly defended many of the ideas behind the movement.

Harlan Ellison was often referred to as the leader of the American New Wave. But his writing showed little direct relation to the English movement. Ellison made no claim to being avant-garde in his style; instead, he depended mostly on an extremely impassioned use of words that struck repeatedly at the emotions of the reader, mixed with a certain "with-it" jargon from the younger and more revolutionary groups outside the writing field.

His mission seemed to be to make science fiction relevant to the events going on around him at the time. He used most of the current fads and ideas. And his writing took the form of nightmares in which he could protest the things in both fate and human nature which he saw around him.

Perhaps Damon Knight came closest to sharing some of his ideas about writing with the New Wave, as exemplified in the long series of *Orbit* anthologies he edited, beginning in 1966. He avoided much of the flagrantly obvious controversy of *New Worlds*, but he did seem to put more emphasis on style than story content in many of the works he accepted, and he seemed to be devoted to bringing the techniques of the literary magazines into science fiction.

Ellison, Merril, and a number of other writers and editors also carried on a crusade against the term "science fiction," feeling that it was too limited and, perhaps, unworthy of their interests. They tried to adopt the term "speculative fiction"—a term Heinlein had suggested back in 1947.

For several years, the New Wave was a source of much argument in science fiction. The subject was debated at many of the conventions. Generally, the college-oriented readers seemed to be in favor of that type of writing, while the older fans regarded it as a betrayal of the whole spirit of science fiction.

I took a stand against the New Wave, since I objected strongly to the missionary zeal with which such writing was being pushed as the *only* worthy form of science fiction, the only true possibility of future development. I also objected to the rather low average level of writing (despite claims to the contrary), characterization, motivation and idea development. There should be room enough under the heading of science fiction for many types of writing—but surely that writing should at least live up to the basic rules of all good fiction, if it is to deserve praise. Much of the New Wave seemed to be an effort to peddle the work of one group of writers by propaganda, rather than by merit.

Anyhow, the New Wave fervor soon died down in America, at least partly because of the poor sales such literature enjoyed here. By 1972, it was hardly ever mentioned. Most of the readers went back to reading and voting awards to regular science fiction.

In England, the effects of the movement were less transient. Many of the writers and readers there still show evidence of having developed some of their taste under its influence, and that influence from the New Wave is still evident in much English critical writing on science fiction.

Meantime, other forms of rebellion against the established traditions were appearing among writers—though with much less interest from the readers.

Many of the newer writers—and a few of the established ones—were now making writing their primary goal in life; the old idea of writing science fiction as a somewhat lucrative hobby was not acceptable to them. Normally, they might have turned to general fiction or to the literary magazines. But most such markets were gone and those that remained required perhaps more development than many could bring to them. They also paid rather poorly on the average. Hence, writers turned to science fiction as the chief outlet for their work.

Some of these writers decided that they were no mere craftsmen, but should be considered artists. Now an artist would normally be defined as someone who had produced art—a definition which requires a body of outstanding work. But these writers found a definition which justified their claim: an artist was anyone whose *intent* was to produce art; if the results were less than good, he might be an inferior artist, but he was still by God an artist!

Some of this reaction probably came from the lingering lack of prestige enjoyed by science fiction among most critics of literature. Just as fans at one time had compensated for the ordinary disregard for their chosen literature by insisting that all readers of science fiction were intellectually superior, so now the writers began assuring each other in forums and by correspondence that science fiction was really *the* significant area of modern literature and that those writing it were the unappreciated artists of the day.

Then having assured themselves of the superiority of the field and their place in it, they proceeded to borrow heavily from the mainstream (or some parts of it) and to write as if the closer science fiction came to that mainstream the better it must be. The pulp and adventure backgrounds of science fiction were largely rejected. So-called experimental writing—derived, of course, from the avant-garde experiments of forty years before—was regarded as somehow superior, and social consciousness of a sort was more important than extrapolation. (There had been an earlier interest in social consciousness, but that had largely involved adapting large hunks of anthropology into the backgrounds of stories. This time, there was the self-conscious social consciousness of the writing of the twenties and thirties, with its dedication to showing the ugliness of society, the sad plight of the helpless and lost people who became such fiction's leading characters, etc.) In many ways, the themes of the New Wave were the themes of this development among writers, though I believe most of them were shaping their course independently of the somewhat organized New Wave.

Curiously, many of these writers seemed preoccupied with the limited goal of "breaking taboos"—and somehow, this rather mechanical trick became identified as an artistic achievement.

Naturally, when science fiction was basically a magazine form of fiction, with the magazines devoted to pleasing everyone from adolescent to grandmother, there had been limits on certain types of material. Indeed, many of these limits were long accepted in most of the literature published during the first half of this century. Thus overt sex in any graphic detail was out, as were certain terms. Incest and cannibalism were to be avoided. And the elimination of bodily wastes was not mentioned.

Of course, the more skillful writers had always been able to find ways of saying what they felt necessary to the story. And in some ways, science fiction had been less limited than much of general fiction. Large variations from the accepted norm of family practice had been used as background material in a number of stories. And even incest had been necessary to certain tales of limited planetary colonization. Periodically an editor would get a story which he could bill as one that broke all taboos, as was the case when Philip José Farmer's "The Lovers" was published.

Also, by this time most of the so-called taboos no longer applied to the general literature in books. The most daring Anglo-Saxon words had all been printed, and sex had been dealt with in detail since before World War II.

But science fiction books were still somewhat influenced by the magazine fiction from which they had been derived. And now the writers began making a virtue out of violating these taboos in their stories. (It turned out that most of the book editors didn't consider them taboos, and were quite willing to see them broken; but the ease of the conquest was never mentioned by those who felt they were achieving something by breaking what were mere habits.)

Hence, there was a rash of sex in science fiction, along with a "daring" use of four-letter words. Unfortunately, most of the sex scenes were dragged in to get sex into the stories, rather than being essential elements, and many of those scenes were routine or badly imagined. As someone asked me, "Why do they have to make sex seem so damned unpleasant?"

Eventually, the limited shock value of such writing wore off, and most science fiction settled down to the calm acceptance that good fiction dealt with people and what people did, without the necessity of trying to be shocking about it.

Another minor wave on the science fiction pool was the result of the interest in various so-called psychedelic drugs. There was nothing too new in the coverage of drug-taking in science fiction. Evan Hunter's "Malice in Wonderland" had used this as a theme in 1954; and Aldous Huxley had used drugs in Brave New World (1932). But now there began to appear stories resting heavily on drugs in the future, many of which seemed to extol the use of such drugs as ways to open up wider vistas for the mind, or to unlock psychic powers.

This was part of a somewhat broader demand for the "exploration of inner space." The cry was that too much concern had been placed on outer space and gadgetry; now it was time to explore inner space—the space within the mind.

That, of course, had always been one of the interests of serious literature, and there was no reason to believe that science fiction writers were better equipped to understand and reveal the mind than others. (True, they could expose men to stress of a kind not possible otherwise; but since no men had been through such experience, there was no guide beyond uncontrolled imagination as to what could logically be expected.) In practice, much of this inner-space exploration consisted of little more than the assumption of those psi powers already used in much routine science fiction. Certainly no science fiction story explored inner space more effectively than Joyce did with Molly Bloom. But somehow the idea of inner-space exploration is still being given a respect—all out of keeping with its results—by some critics and writers who are only partly familiar with the field.

Some—though by no means all—of the ferment in science fiction centered around a new association of writers. This was the Science Fiction Writers of America, founded in 1965 by Damon Knight. There had been a previous and unsuccessful attempt to organize science fiction writers, and there had long been the expressed need of such an organization. Nothing seemed about to come of it until Knight simply created the organization and its rules and wrote letters to most of the writers asking them to join.

The rules for joining were extremely liberal. Anyone who had a story accepted by a science fiction publication or sold a book of science fiction could become a full member, for the year of acceptance and also of publication. (There was a possibility of belonging for several years on the basis of one short story, if the publication were held off.)

In 1966, a banquet was held to award the Nebula prizes—those voted for best stories of various lengths—to the 1965 entries. And similar banquets have been held annually since. These have also been lengthened to include sessions and discussions for a couple of days before the banquets, and regional meetings are also recognized.

Such meetings certainly offered an opportunity for an exchange of views and aspirations. And the liberal entrance requirements made it almost inevitable that those writers who were not yet successful enough to be content with established ways should find mutual support in whatever rebellions might be current. By 1971, there were more than 440 members—a number that obviously had to encompass far more than would have been considered professional by most standards.

Much of the rebelliousness soon began to die down, of course. And probably the results of it did serve to broaden the field. Certainly many of the books published in 1972 would hardly have been recognized as science fiction twenty years before. Whether this is a good thing or not is still largely a matter of individual opinion.

One major change in the field, however, was more than welcome. This was the emergence of many new women as writers of science fiction.

There had always been a few women who wrote science fiction, from its very beginnings in the magazines —or before. Leigh Brackett and Catherine Moore had been among the most popular writers. But science fiction had generally been the province of the male writer, like most forms of adventure fiction.

Suddenly, in this period, a great many women began writing and achieving success in science fiction. To pick only a few of many names, there were Marion Zimmer Bradley, Ursula K. Le Guin, Anne McCaffrey, Vonda N. McIntyre, Joanna Russ, Pamela Sargent and Kate Wilhelm.

Of all the changes going on in the field, this evolution was probably the healthiest and most promising for the future.

CHAPTER 26

Enter: Academe

UP UNTIL THIS TIME, the schools had chosen to disregard science fiction. It was held on something of a par with comic books by most academics. Certainly it could not be considered a serious part of literature. Creative writing courses might cover the mystery and the Western—though usually without great pleasure—but science fiction was alien.

There were a couple of exceptions. Moskowitz held a night extension course for City College of New York in 1953, 1954 and 1955. And Dikty gave a course at the University of Chicago in 1957. Professor J. O. Bailey did an academic study of the subject, *Pilgrims Through Space and Time*, which was published as a book in 1947. And some courses dealt briefly with the works of H. G. Wells.

Nevertheless, it was not only possible but probably desirable to go through high school and college without ever hearing of science fiction. And if a student brought the subject up, it was not considered worth classroom discussion. (There were some teachers—though not many—who were more than willing to discuss it with students outside the classroom, as I discovered.)

This attitude began to change strongly after 1962, and suddenly there was a rush to adopt this strange literature and fit it into the curriculum.

A number of factors may have entered into this altered attitude. Probably the leading one was the availability now of science fiction in book form. The magazines had hardly lent themselves to adoption by the schools. They were rather garish, on the average. The pulp paper, the fact that many had rather messy gray ink and poorly reproduced illustrations, and the whole feeling made them lacking in serious respectability. Furthermore, good stories and obviously inferior ones often came jumbled together, while the novels were strung out over several issues.

Books, on the other hand, were sometimes quite respectable in appearance. True, some of them were at least as garish and badly printed as any magazine; but there were at least many which could hardly have been told from accepted literature. And with books, it was possible to cull out the less worthy and develop a library of quite acceptable reading material.

A few of the better anthologies even offered a fairly concise library of acceptable science fiction which could be used for classroom study. Such books could be ordered through the college bookstores for use by the student, without the professor either having to hunt out copies himself or find ways to arrange for many to read the copy he might own.

The collapse of the general fiction market for shorter works also contributed to the need for some place to which aspiring young creative writing students could turn for possible sales.

And probably the furor over the beginning of the space age gave some measure of respectability to what had hitherto been regarded as the silly dreams of teenagers and a few wild engineers. There was a big drive to train enough scientists for the demands of this space age, and suddenly science had academic glamour. (It didn't last, of course.) Science fiction managed to be noticed in the rush.

Much of the credit for the change, however, must be given to a number of people in the teaching profession who had long been fans of the literature and who recognized that at least some of science fiction was well written, thoughtful, and deserving of its place with the other forms of literature. Certainly among these should be listed Jack Williamson of the University of New Mexico and James Gunn of the University of Kansas. They were both established writers of science fiction as well as teachers. Others, such as H. Bruce Franklin of Stanford University and Thomas Clareson of the College of Wooster, were fans of science fiction who were willing to devote great energy to pushing its merits.

Once the initial few courses were tried, the subject developed its own momentum. Students thronged the classes, often with far more wanting to register than could be accepted. Gunn reported a class of 150! Most were far smaller than this, of course, but there was no question about the popularity among students. By the end of this period, Williamson estimated that there were at least 200 college courses in science fiction being given.

There were also a large number of such courses being given at the high-school level. I have been able to find no estimate for this, but I know that there were many; from nearby schools, I received numerous queries from teachers on such things as a suitable syllabus, while other classes asked me to speak before them.

Some of these courses were taught by knowledgeable people who were well versed in science fiction from long reading in the field, particularly at the beginning. At first, probably most courses were organized by teachers who really wanted to give them. Obviously, such men as Gunn, Williamson and Philip Klass of Penn State (who was a recognized writer under the name of William Tenn) were well qualified to discuss the subject with their students. There were probably many more capable of organizing good courses. Professor Low of NYU, to my knowledge, was a longtime reader of science fiction, and his syllabus was excellent.

Unfortunately, such excellence soon was not the

rule. As the popularity of science fiction in colleges spread, courses were handed out with little regard to which instructors might or might not be qualified by familiarity with the field—if any such should be found on the faculty. It was often assumed that anyone capable of teaching courses in *real* literature must surely be more than skillful enough for science fiction. (No, indeed, the feeling that science fiction was inferior literature did not vanish at once—certainly not from department heads!)

My sister-in-law registered for a science fiction course, only to discover that the teacher was someone whose interest lay in the literature of children's fairy tales! Obviously, to that school, this was a suitable choice—and the teacher felt that it did indeed qualify her! She apparently saw little difference, except perhaps in the history behind fairy tales, between the two forms of literature. Usually, it seemed to be felt that the person to teach such a course was whatever instructor happened to be free from too great a load of other courses.

Oddly, some of the better courses were not given in the English departments. Sociology teachers and those teaching history and even economics sometimes used science fiction to illuminate their subjects, and they discovered that this could arouse fresh interest on the part of students. Obviously, of course, science fiction was almost designed for the new futurology courses, and some of the stories applied very well to such subjects as ecology. (Some time before, M.I.T. had used science fiction in a course of industrial design to promote new ways of looking at problems.)

Inevitably, there soon came to be booklets with suggestions for teaching such courses and lists of recommended study books. These were supposed to enable the teacher unfamiliar with the subject to guide the students properly. From comments I have heard from students who obviously wanted to know more about science fiction—but who already knew something by reading—this expedient left much to be desired. A teacher who knows less than some of the students will always have difficulties, no matter how sincere and dedicated.

Science fiction also invaded the creative writing courses, and here was certainly one place where it belonged. For the hopeful writer who was not yet willing to devote the time and effort needed to turning out novels, science fiction was undoubtedly the best market available, and one of the few where promising efforts would be encouraged.

Unfortunately, very few creative writing teachers in the regular institutions had themselves learned to write science fiction—or in most cases, even tried to. And too many of them assumed that the regular methods they taught, and the regular suggestions they made, would be good enough for this pulp field of literature.

Quite possibly, some of the ferment covered in the last chapter—though by no means all—was the result of students of such early courses who came out and tried to apply what they had learned to the real market.

There remains some question as to whether science fiction can be learned by any process except that of reading a great deal of the literature. There are attitudes that are at least as important as the basic writing skills. The experience of writers from other fields who tried to break into science fiction during one of the boom periods suggests that this market is far more difficult for the outsider than is the mystery, Western or general adventure market. And the equating of science fiction stories (at least the category ones) with the fiction in the literary magazines may be considered by the professors to be flattering, but really doesn't help.

Undoubtedly, a few such courses offered some help to those who wished to write science fiction, but others may have produced more confusion than benefit.

One of the most successful attempts to teach the writing of science fiction was organized by Robin Scott Wilson at Clarion College in 1968. Wilson had written and sold science fiction, and his purpose was to concentrate directly on the teaching of that category. The course was a summer extension one, with the students discussing science fiction—somewhat in the style of the very successful Breadloaf system. A series of science fiction writers were brought in to conduct classes and run workshop sessions, each writer usually spending a week on this. Among the lecturers were Damon Knight, his wife Kate Wilhelm, and others who had already gained experience at the Milford Conference sessions.

This proved quite successful with students. When Clarion College gave up the program, it was moved to another college; at a later period, there were two branches at different colleges, both operating under the same system and calling themselves Clarion, despite the changed locations.

I never attended these sessions, but I heard glowing reports from both the students and the lecturers. Unfortunately, the accomplishments there always seemed to be surrounded with a haze of glory, of the sort that might accompany an unusually successful religious retreat. I was assured that the program was filled with intensive work, but I heard more about letting down all inhibitions between people, developing sort of a unified soul—not the words used—and generally things not much different from an Esalen meeting!

Certainly Clarion produced selling writers, and a few very promising stories were written during the conferences. Several writers made their first sales as a result and got a start on their careers. The degree of such success was greater than for any other science fiction teaching method I know.

Yet the results were somewhat puzzling. Three paperback books of stories written by Clarion students were published, supposedly as examples of what could be learned there. (There were also various tributes included from the lecturers.) In going through these, I was surprised by how little of the fiction could be considered science fiction by even the loosest standards I could use. A few of the stories were science fiction in theme—and a few others were obvious fantasies. But the majority were everything else, with a preponderance of the type of fiction that represents a young writer simply sounding off with passion.

Obviously, while Clarion may have taught something about writing—and have been particularly good at getting the students to sit down and write—it either made too little effort to teach the nature and practice of science fiction—or tried and failed.

Science fiction proved to be a fresh and welcome field for the subjects of monographs for degrees, or opportunities to beat the publish-or-perish rule for college teachers. Papers and books began pouring out. H. Bruce Franklin examined some of the science fiction prior to the twentieth century in *Future Perfect* (1966). Mark Hillegas surveyed the dystopias in *Future as Nightmare* (1967). Unlike these two examples, many of the others were superficial. Some seem to be designed to pin on the field a single label which would be academically more suitable (or impressive) than science fiction. (Variations frequently seemed to relate to some equivalent of disaster, as if science fiction dealt solely with assorted dooms to mankind; certainly some stories do, but over the years the fiction has been generally more concerned with an optimistic victory of man over the universe.) One book spent a lot of effort trying to tie science fiction down to a narrow religious view. Another examined the writing of Isaac Asimov, both fiction and nonfiction, by counting the average number of words in his sentences! Far too many have indicated a quick study of the field designed to establish a point for a paper, rather than to examine even one aspect of science fiction carefully.

There is a fertile field to be exploited for scholarly research, and it probably will be given serious attention eventually. But from the books which I have seen so far, the most worthwhile research in science fiction is still being done by the fans.

There is also a scholarly fan magazine—or learned journal, take your pick. This is *Extrapolation and Science Fiction Studies*, edited by Thomas Clareson. This is open for articles by both academics and other practitioners in the field of science fiction.

During this period, there was also a great interest in the collecting of material on science fiction by a number of the colleges. Authors were persuaded to donate original manuscripts and papers—initially reaping considerable income-tax write-offs for their contributions, though the IRS put an end to that by declaring that such papers would be valued at no more than their value as stationery. Many of the libraries are also collecting the magazines and books; unfortunately, this activity didn't begin until many of the items were rare and expensive. Harvard, Syracuse, Stanford, Mississippi State University and the University of Kansas all have excellent collections, and many other universities are beginning to acquire the works of writers. There is also a Science Fiction Research Association designed to coordinate collections, keep track of available material, and handle many of the problems that come up in this growing area.

By the end of 1972, there could be no doubt that science fiction had been accepted as a regular part of academic activity. If not before, this should have been demonstrated at the 1969 meeting of the Modern Language Association in New York City. There, a whole afternoon session was devoted to the subject. The meeting was chaired by H. Bruce Franklin, but the panel for discussion included several science fiction writers with no pretension to academic standing. And it was very well attended.

CHAPTER 27

The Big Con Game

By 1962, it would seem that fandom had explored almost every activity conceivable; and during this period, there was very little really new to be tried. What remained, apparently, was an increase in quantity.

Some increase in the size of active fandom was inevitable. The success of books for the young teenager had brought many into science fiction in their early high-school years—or at earlier ages. (The estimated circulation of some of these books through the school libraries ran to several times as many readers as the most successful magazines could boast, and more than even the most popular paperback books.) The boom of the mid-fifties had probably created some new readers who were now beginning to awaken to more active fandom. And the spread of paperback books had carried science fiction to many readers who would not have read the magazines.

Yet the rapid increase in visible activity was surprising, at least as shown at the local conventions and worldcons.

At the beginning of this period, there were several well-established regional conventions, but whole areas of the country had no such activity. It was quite possible for a fan to get to all of them without too much careful planning. And those who did attend any specific regional were pretty sure of most of the people they would find when they got there.

By 1973, there were several dozen such cons, with almost no fan beyond the reach of one or more. The East Coast was well covered, from Boston through New York, Philadelphia and Washington, D.C., to Baltimore, with a small side trip to Pittsburgh. No fan could hope to make all of them. There were even conflicts for time; the Minnicon in Minneapolis tended to occur at about the same time as the Lunacon in New York City.

Perhaps the Lunacon typifies the rapid development of many cons. It was begun in the late fifties by a group of fans who called themselves the Lunarians. The event then took place in a single large room, either a hall or some not-too-expensive hotel. There was usually a local Guest of Honor who gave a speech and got a plaque as his reward for coming; and there might also be one or two other speeches or panels to entertain the audience. It all ended before dinner, and those who wanted to might go out together to eat. About seventy fans might show up, counting the members of the Lunarians.

This was a typical local con of the time; a few were larger or lasted longer, but there were smaller and simpler affairs. It was fun to attend for an afternoon, and most people who did attend were pretty well known to each other. (It might be remembered that this drew on the largest metropolitan area in the country, the seat of the science fiction publishing business and the home of a large number of the professionals in the field.)

A few years later, in 1971, John W. Campbell was the Guest of Honor. This was shortly before his death and was the last time I saw him, so my memory of the event is fairly clear.

The event bore almost no similarity to the earlier cons from which it had evolved. Only the name was the same. This time it was a weekend affair, and the facilities of a large hotel had been engaged. There were rooms for an art show and for huckster tables where dealers could display their wares. There was a regular auditorium-sized room provided for the main activities, complete with seats set up in advance and public address facilities.

Beforehand, there had been an efficient group who served as officers for the event, with one man responsible for providing the speakers. There was a printed program, and the timetable of events was generally followed closely. There were numerous panels during the daytime and activities well into the night. And there was a banquet the next day, with a good attendance and the major speech from the Guest of Honor.

Many of the attendees had come from all over the East Coast, and a fair number were stopping at the hotel, where room parties could be heard after all formal affairs were over. Campbell had been provided with a suite by the convention, and his other expenses were being paid. (He told me that in all his experience—including being three times Guest of Honor at worldcons—this was the first time that any convention had paid his expenses. By that time, it had become customary, both at worldcons and regionals. But the practice as a regular custom was still fairly new.)

I never learned the exact attendance, but it was at least 700!

This wasn't quite typical of other local cons in registration—most did not run to that number. But attendance in the hundreds—300 and up—was not uncommon.

In other words, by the end of the period, the local cons were essentially equal to what the worldcons had been 10 years or so before. Most of the regionals were now weekend affairs, rather than one-day meetings. Most included fairly elaborate entertainment by panels and speakers, and sometimes there were other amusements. Many of the cons were using banquets to help defray the cost of holding the meetings at regular hotels.

Rusty Hevelin, an old-time fan now retired from his regular activities, spent most of his time touring from one con to another through a major part of the year. He defrayed his expenses by huckstering books and older magazines.

The worldcons were also growing. In 1962, the Chicon III attracted 550 by accepted estimate, as now given in the record of past cons published in the annual program booklet. (These numbers are probably on the low side, but close enough to give a fair idea.) Things continued at about this level until the Tricon at Cleveland in 1966, when 850 were registered. (The 1965 worldcon went to London, out of the country. There, as was expected, the attendance dropped to 350.) So far, no convention had exceeded the attendance of the 1952 worldcon in Chicago—a record of at least 870 that remained apparently unbeatable.

That record fell in 1967 when Nycon III in New York City reached 1,500! This, incidentally, was a location for the worldcon that everyone knew could never win the bid. After the last previous New York worldcon, the fans had vowed that they were through with that city for such events. And there were two other strong bids for the convention when it came to a vote for the site in 1966. When Ted White approached me to be Guest of Honor at New York, I appreciated the honor, but considered it an unlikely event. But White began going to almost every regional, drumming up support for his bid. Then the other bidders began feuding, hurting each other. White won the bid, and found himself with the biggest convention ever on his hands. (My most notable achievement as Guest of Honor was to give the shortest speech on record; other speakers at the banquet used up most of my time.)

Attendance then stayed pretty much at the 1,500 level for several years, except for 1970, when the worldcon finally went to a country where English was not the native language. This took place in Heidelberg, Germany, and the convention was called the Heicon '70 International. There were three Guests of Honor: Robert Silverberg from the United States; E. C. Tubb from England; and Herbert W. Franke from Germany. (I was to be toastmaster, but had to cancel, due to a personal tragedy. I understand John Brunner substituted with great wit.) Attendance was 620, a very good number for a convention outside the United States.

The 1971 worldcon was called the Noreascon, held in Boston. The official attendance was up slightly, to 1,600. As might have been expected, since the solidly established New England Science Fiction Club was behind it, it was the best organized and run convention to date; the Sheraton Hotel contributed to this by considerable prior preparation.

The 1972 L.A. Con in Los Angeles lifted the attendance to just over 2,000, and was considered immense. By this time, finding an adequate hotel for such a large group had become a problem for the bidders. Some cities were rendered ineligible, apparently, because of the facilities needed. And because the bigger convention hotels were booked up long in advance, bidding on the next site had to move ahead an extra year; thus the 1974 site had to be chosen at the 1972 convention.

Then in 1973, twenty-five years after it first held a worldcon, Toronto became the worldcon site. I'd been actively interested in seeing the Torcon bid win (which it did without opposition), and I was delighted to see that the convention lived up to all the promises I had made for it. Despite having an attendance of about 3,000—2,900 officially—it managed to be an unusually pleasant one, thanks to the hospitality and management of the convention committee and to the Royal York Hotel, which justified its reputation as one of the best in North America.

Three thousand fans at one convention! And obviously more to come in the future.

There have been a lot of reasons advanced for this enormous increase. In my opinion, one of the most important factors was a convention calendar Frederik Pohl began running in *If* soon after he became editor. There, for the first time, the readers who were not on the fan mailing lists or subscribers to fanzines had a chance to see when some convention might be held near them. Many of them were curious enough to go. Obviously, most of them liked such conventions and went back; many went on to others, including the worldcons.

There had always been some announcement of the worldcon for the year in the magazines. But that was usually not convenient, and fans who were not well known probably felt they might be overlooked at worldcons. When they saw a local event, it was both easier to go and more likely to yield new friends from nearby with shared interests. So they came, they saw—and were hooked.

Otherwise, the fans' activities were most noticeable for a number of excellent publications for which they were responsible.

Fan-magazine activities were extremely wide-ranging. But a few during this period made eventual impressions beyond the normal range of fanzines. Andrew Porter started *Algol* in 1963, and it quickly became better in format and more general in interest. As the period went on, it began to become a professional-appearing magazine concerned with science fiction, with some of its articles of importance to the field. Richard E. Geiss was busy. He had dropped his former *Psychotic*, and thereafter his fan publication went through a number of changes in title. (It eventually ended up after this period as *Science Fiction Review*.) This was a personal magazine (a term usually shortened to 'zine), filled with chattings with himself, defense of pornography as a legitimate form of literature, and almost everything else. But it had a definite personality and was liked by a considerable number of other fans.

And in 1968, Charles Brown and his wife began *Locus*, which quickly became *the* newspaper of the field. It attempted to cover all news of forthcoming books, magazine events, people, places and things in science fiction—and to a large extent, it did what it tried. The circulation soon exceeded 1,000 and went on rising. It was as eagerly read by many publishers and editors as by writers and fans.

In the field of book publications, the major achievement was the production of *The MIT Science Fiction Society's Index to the SF Magazines, 1951–1965*, compiled by Erwin S. Strauss. (All that goes on the cover!) This was published in 1966, and filled a long-existing need to continue the work that had been begun by Donald B. Day in his *Index*, which had only gone through 1950.

The MIT Science Fiction Society was very active at this point and they had the advantage of being able to gain access to computer time. This made a seemingly impossible job merely difficult. All the entries were put onto cards. These were then sorted, cross-indexed according to which list they were to be in, and finally the entire book was set in type by computer!

There were the usual entries by author's name and by story title, as well as a listing by magazine. Every effort was made to secure every issue of every magazine —and for this, the library of the Society supplied most issues.

This index was thereafter supplemented by annual volumes for each year, but the further work was done by NESFA—The New England Science Fiction Society. They still used the computer to maintain uniformity in later issues. (NESFA is a large, active fan club with the unusual characteristic of having members who are always willing to work, and it is somehow always being well funded for whatever activities—such as the Boskone regional cons they put on—the club may choose to undertake.) With the various Indexes, it has become possible to locate any story from the beginning of magazine publication, with no more than a few months' lag.

Whether Sam Moskowitz should be entered as a fan or as a pro becomes somewhat difficult during this period. But however professional the publications he authors, the spirit behind them is still that of a fan, so I include him here. It was during this period that he began establishing himself as one of the leading writers about science fiction. In 1963, his *Explorers of the Infinite* was published by World Publishing Company. This was a collection of profiles he'd written for the magazines covering early writers, from Cyrano de Bergerac to A. Merritt. This was followed in 1966 by *Seekers of Tomorrow*, similar profiles giving the lives and work (as well as considerable opinion) about some of the leading writers from the science fiction magazine period.

And in 1969, Advent published Harry Warner, Jr.'s *All Our Yesterdays*. This was the history of science fiction fandom through 1949. Warner showed remarkably little bias in telling of the people and events, and his knowledge of all the activities of the time proved remarkable. It remains the best history of fandom—so far as it goes—to be done.

By the end of the fourth age, fandom was still going strong and still an important part of the field.

CHAPTER 28

The Fifth Age (1974–   )

In 1976, science fiction celebrated its fiftieth year as a separate category of fiction. *Amazing Stories*, the magazine that started the whole thing and had somehow kept publishing under the same title all those years, planned a big anniversary issue. In due time, it appeared on the stands. It was a little late, since the April 1976 issue appeared as the June number, and it wasn't quite as big or gala as had been planned. But the fact that it did appear was quite an event, both for science fiction and for the history of pulp magazines.

All of the other category fiction (or pulp) magazines that had been on the stands in 1926 were gone. In fact, many of the categories had vanished. But this peculiar magazine that had once seemed obviously doomed to failure had outlasted them all.

And that was one of the few things that could be said with satisfaction about the science fiction magazines at this beginning of the fifth age. Only *Analog* and *F&SF* were still reasonably healthy. Both of them were still operating on a monthly schedule and seemed reasonably sure to continue, particularly *Analog* with its high proportion of subscriptions and steady sales. Others were not doing well.

If continued its bimonthly publication through December 1974 and announced that was the last; henceforth, it would be "combined with *Galaxy*"—or it would be gone, with *Galaxy* taking over its subscriptions, to translate the expression into its real meaning. This was a surprise. Ejler Jakobsson had resigned as editor of *If* and James Baen had taken over, giving the magazine a livelier format and new features. It seemed to be doing better and subscriptions were up. But apparently management decided to concentrate all efforts on *Galaxy*. That magazine continued, but by the end of 1976 it seemed to be in trouble. Writers reported that getting payment for stories was even more difficult than usual, and Baen was forced to fill the issues with new names and to exist on a sort of issue-by-issue basis. Most people who knew the situation expected the magazine to fold. But despite a few missed issues later on, it continued. When Baen left to become editor for Ace Books, John J. Pierce, a well-known fan, took over as editor.

Amazing and *Fantastic* continued under the editorship of Ted White, but the circulation was so low that it seemed impossible to continue them. Circulation was barely over 20,000 copies for each issue. Eventually, the magazines became quarterlies.

In 1975, *Vertex*, the large-format West Coast magazine, shifted to a tabloid style on cheap paper. It managed only a few more issues before folding. A new magazine, *Odyssey Science Fiction*, edited by Roger Elwood, lasted for only two issues. In September 1976, another new magazine appeared; *Galileo* was large in format, but seemed only semiprofessional and had a limited circulation. Its mixture of features, articles and fiction seemed to please readers, however, and by issue No. 7 (undated) it seemed to have established itself as a regular bimonthly. But despite the new titles, the number of issues of all science-fiction magazines appearing on the stands in 1976 was smaller than it had been since the very early days when the magazines were just beginning.

Among books, the situation was entirely different. The total number had been increasing each year for some time, and this continued. According to the figures published by Charles and Dena Brown in *Locus*, there was a total of 954 science fiction books published in 1976, of which 470 were original titles and 608 were paperbacks—proving that paperbacks were leading the field.

A number of these books were quite specialized editions. During this period, several companies began bringing out reprints of classics and books not easily available in hard covers. These were meant for sale to libraries, principally; they were specially bound and printed on acid-free paper meant to endure for centuries. Hyperion Press began this in 1973 with 23 volumes, plus seven of the books by Sam Moskowitz on the history of science fiction. Garland Press brought out 45 volumes in 1975. Several other companies entered this field, including Arno and Gregg.

If these special editions are set aside, Doubleday was the largest hardbound publisher of science fiction, with 26 original titles, followed by Harper and Putnam/Berkley. Among the paperback publishers, Ace published 79, a majority of which were reissues from their backlist or the juvenile Perry Rhodan series; Ballantine had 70; DAW and Berkley, 62 each; Laser, 36; and Pyramid, 35.

The price of books had increased steeply, and this was particularly noticeable in the case of paperbacks. At one time, science-fiction paperbacks had been almost uniformly priced at 35¢ per book—the same as the price of a magazine then. Now most were priced at $1.50, and quite a few went for $1.95. There was some grumbling among readers; but there seemed to be no slackening of sales.

By 1976, however, anthologies were not generally selling well. Apparently the market for such books had been too heavily saturated by the stream of anthologies edited by Roger Elwood. The various "best of the year" anthologies and a few by well-known editors, such as Terry Carr, continued. But the market for such books was no longer healthy.

In 1975, Harlequin Books entered the science fiction paperback business with a heavy schedule. Harlequin had made a success of selling romance novels through chain stores and supermarkets, and they saw science fiction as their next field. The books were edited by Roger Elwood with covers by well-known artist Kelly Freas; all were priced at 95¢ and ran the same number of pages. They were supposed to apply a sort of adventure formula to science fiction—not too complex, suitable for the unsophisticated reader.

The formula didn't work, apparently. The books were issued regularly, three each month, through 1976. Then there were rumors that they would soon fold. And shortly after, they suspended publication.

Ace, which had been in financial doldrums, was purchased in 1976 by Grosset and Dunlap and began to come back strongly, though they still depended heavily on reissuing books from their large backlist.

DAW Books continued to flourish under the direction of Donald A. Wollheim. He quickly developed a number of series, some of which ran through many volumes, such as those by Alan Burt Akers about an Earthman fighting for his princess against all sorts of monsters and villains on worlds around an alien star. The Darkover series continued, with Marion Zimmer Bradley now permitted to develop her novels to greater length and in greater detail. And E. C. Tubb carried on his series about Dumarest's quest for legendary Earth.

Wollheim still offered a welcome to beginning writers. Two of his most promising discoveries were women, Tanith Lee and C. J. Cherryh. Cherryh's second book, *Brothers of Earth* (1976) was one of the best novels of the year, and she later was chosen for an award as best new writer for that year.

Betty and Ian Ballantine left Ballantine Books in 1974, and Judy-Lynn del Rey was now in full control of the science fiction line there. She persuaded Leigh Brackett to return to the field with a series about her old hero, Eric John Stark. She also began a series of "The Best of ———" books, the first with the works of Stanley G. Weinbaum. Others in the series covered Frederik Pohl, John W. Campbell, C. L. Moore, Henry Kuttner and Fritz Leiber. These were intended to present the best short works of major writers who had contributed to the greatness of the field. She also exerted a strong influence on the art used on covers, insisting on illustrations of strong, representational nature; many of the artists she used were new to the field, though well established as commercial artists.

She was accused of trying to set the field back twenty years, and she took this as a compliment. To some extent, she and Wollheim were moving the field back toward the more strongly plotted and adventuresome type of fiction that had been popular earlier. But the readers seemed pleased, and both DAW and Ballantine enjoyed excellent sales during this period.

Frederik Pohl was hired by Bantam Books to edit their science fiction. Among his selections was Samuel R. Delaney's *Dhalgren*, a huge book about events in a city ruined by a mysterious disaster. Many science fiction readers disliked the book, but it proved very popular among many who normally did not read science fiction.

Arthur C. Clarke received $200,000 from Ballantine for the paperback rights to *Imperial Earth*, his 1976 novel about the celebration of America's five-hundredth anniversary. The next highest advance was for *Mindbridge* (1976) by Joe Haldeman, whose *The Forever War* (1974) won both Hugo and Nebula awards as best novel of the year. These prices were exceptional, but generally the advances to writers tended sharply upward.

Berkley brought out Frank Herbert's *Children of Dune* in a hard-cover edition in 1976, with a strong advertising campaign. It quickly reached the best-seller lists. Within a few weeks, the publisher had filled over 100,000 orders and was still going back to press. This had previously occurred only for *The Andromeda Strain*, which was marketed as a thriller, with no reference to its being science fiction.

In most other ways, the field continued to thrive. The academic interest showed no signs of slacking off. By 1976, there was no good way to estimate the number of college courses being given in science fiction, but four hundred was probably a conservative figure, with untold other courses given in high schools.

In fact, the subject became so popular that James Gunn organized a summer session for the purpose of teaching the teachers how to give courses in science fiction. The number of books carrying explanations and selections designed for classroom use continued to increase. Ballantine Books even compiled a list of books to be kept in stock, together with a teacher's guide prepared by L. David Allen, in an attempt to meet the rising need for a handy source of science fiction for teachers.

Donald H. Tuck's *Encyclopedia of Science Fiction and Fantasy* was issued by Advent in 1974—or rather, Volume I, A–L, was issued. Purchasers had to wait four more years to complete the alphabet with the second volume. Such problems of scheduling tend to beset fan publishers. A book such as this must take an immense amount of work to prepare for the printer, and Advent had to depend mostly on the spare-time efforts of George Price and Edward Wood. On the other hand, few regular publishers would have considered such a project, valuable though the reference books are.

The attendance at the 1974 Discon II, held in Washington, D.C., set a new record for worldcons, exceeding 4,000. A good many fans began to worry about the need to keep attendance from going higher in the future; even that figure would make it difficult to put on the kind of affair the fans wanted.

There was a grace period, however, since the 1975 worldcon took place in Melbourne, Australia, where attendance ran to just over 600. But the 1976 Mid-AmeriCon was to be held in Kansas City, Missouri, with Robert A. Heinlein as Guest of Honor for the third time. The combination of Heinlein and such a central location suggested huge crowds.

The convention committee made every effort to discourage "fringe fans." They offered no inducements to comic-book fans who had begun flocking to worldcons to huckster their wares, or to the many *Star Trek* followers who were not also regular science fiction fans. The feeling was that such people had their own conventions. The membership fee was also raised, and last-minute registration was discouraged by an at-the-door price of $50.

Perhaps the committee tried too hard. The best estimate I have seen for attendance ran to no more than 3,000. And it now appears that the Discon II record may stand for a long time.

Finally, what seems to lie in the farther future for science fiction?

Obviously, there is no way to be sure. Like all long-term estimates, this must be mostly guesswork. Still, science fiction has proved to be a very hardy form of literature, and it has managed to overcome almost all opposition, intellectual or commercial. With the readership it now has, particularly among young people, it should survive through the rest of the century—and perhaps may become a permanent part of the publishing business.

For the immediate future, at least, things look extremely bright at first analysis. More and more publishers are entering the market, and many of them are planning to issue a larger number of science fiction books.

DAW Books is issuing five books a month, and there are rumors that this will be increased to six. Ace Books plans to issue six or more a month, and Berkley is planning another six per month. Ballantine began publishing six each month at the end of 1976. And early in 1977, their science fiction and fantasy line was set up as a quasi-independent organization under the parent company to permit greater freedom and opportunity to deal with its market. This division was named Del Rey Books, after the husband-and-wife team of Judy-Lynn and Lester del Rey. (Lester del Rey was hired to edit the line of fantasy, starting in 1975.) Several of the books issued by Del Rey during the year reached high positions on the best-seller lists, something unheard of a few years previously.

Bookstores seem to be gearing up for larger sales. The big chains have established sections to handle science fiction, and many of the smaller stores now prominently display shelves devoted to the category. The specialist bookstores, dealing only with science fiction (pioneered by the Science Fiction Shop in New York City in 1973), have become a widespread phenomenon.

Many of these stores handle a few specialized magazines which have developed out of fan-magazine activities. Among these are Richard E. Geis's *Science Fiction Review*, Charles and Dena Brown's *Locus*, and Andrew Porter's slickly produced *Algol*. These magazines even show some profit, and have sometimes been denied the right to compete for fanzine awards as a result.

The professional magazines have not shown the increase in circulation that might be expected. But several new ones have appeared, with 1977 very active in such endeavors. *Unearth* publishes only the work of hitherto-unknown writers. *Cosmos* existed briefly as a slick, large-format magazine. *Galileo* also appears in large format, with a mixture of articles, features and fiction; its circulation was small at first, but it now seems to be catching on. And most successful is *Isaac Asimov's Science Fiction Magazine*, published by Joel Davis, who also publishes *Ellery Queen's Magazine*, and hence has both the experience and magazine outlets needed. This, despite Asimov's name, is really edited by George Scithers, longtime fan and writer. It began as a quarterly, but is now appearing six times a year, with some prospects of going monthly. If it succeeds, it will be the first new science fiction magazine to do so in a quarter of a century.

Well, according to the cycle that science fiction seems to have followed up until now, 1977 should have been a boom year—and it was such. After that, if things run true to form, there should be a bust. And there is some evidence that such may be the case.

Advances on books of science fiction have begun to climb beyond all sensible limits. A young writer's first novel recently drew a paperback advance of $30,000. And it's not at all uncommon now to hear of a book that went for $20,000 or more.

Such advances sound fine for the writer, and would seem to indicate progress in the field. That would be true—if most of these books had a chance of earning back such advances out of sales. But the sales I can project rationally for many of these books on the basis of experience are less than needed to pay back such advances. If we assume a price of $1.95 per book—justified only for long or very special books—at the maximum royalty of 10 percent, each sale returns less than 20¢ royalty; a sale of two-thirds of the total printing is considered quite good. For a $30,000 advance, this would require a printing of almost a quarter million copies. (And let's not talk about an advance of $100,000!) In most cases, the price and royalty rate are lower, requiring even greater numbers of copies to be printed to pay back the advance. And few works by any but the major writers can justify such printings. Of course, a book *may* show a profit before the advance is repaid—but large advances are still questionable.

If the publisher prints heavily, there is a good chance that his percentage of copies returned will be so high that he will take a loss, even without considering the advance. If he doesn't print enough copies, he's most certainly wasted his advance.

That means a fair number of publishers are going to be quite unhappy about their science fiction. Then what happens? Does the publisher blame his bad judgment? Not by past experience. He decides that the science fiction bubble has burst, that it was all a flash-in-the-pan affair. And word gets out through him to other publishers and through his salesmen to booksellers. Presto—everyone begins to be scared. And then, to some extent, the bubble does burst. Such things have happened before in other fields.

Also, there has to be a limit somewhere to the number of such books the market can absorb. As more and more books get published, the space on the shelves for display will not be enough; and even the most ardent readers are going to have to be far more selective in their buying.

That doesn't mean any total collapse of the science fiction market. (Remember that the total amount of science fiction printed in any bust period seems to exceed that of the boom in the preceding age.) Those publishers who have long experience and whose editors are familiar with the science fiction readers' tastes—as all too few seem to be—will probably not suffer greatly, particularly if they keep their advances and expectations at a reasonable level. (So far, the experienced ones seem to be doing just that.) For them, the bust period may even be a fine opportunity, as other publishers desert the field.

Science fiction will survive, as it has done before.

But there's at least some reason to expect that the old boom-and-bust cycle may go on operating.

PART VI

Parallels and Perspectives

CHAPTER 29

Fantasy

FANTASY is almost certainly the oldest and most widespread fiction of mankind. The tales of spirits and gods might have been religion to early peoples, but they were also filled with wonders. And inevitably, some reciters discovered that it was the wonder that caught the listeners, and elaborated on that wonder—and soon learned to tell of wonder that had nothing to do with religion. Thus, while the *Iliad* deals with the gods of Ilium, the *Odyssey* has little to do with gods, but much to do with wonders met on a fantastic voyage.

And in time, even religions became fantasy. Ancient grim gods became witches and warlocks—or sometimes fairies and pucks; spirits became werewolves, or kobolds. (Recently, we even created new "little people" and began telling of gremlins.) Ancient demigods became myth stories, and eventually fairy tales for children. Somehow, humanity preserves its wonders, and myths die very slowly.

In a way, fantasy is the mother of science fiction, with the new myth being the godlike nature of science. Obviously, the relationship is close. Both require Coleridge's "willing suspension of disbelief," since both science fiction and fantasy begin with some assumption not accepted here and now.

But the two literatures diverge quickly. Science fiction, explicitly or implicitly, is based on possibilities of science and tends to be future-oriented. Fantasy implicitly denies science and looks to something from the past—beliefs, myths, or worlds of barbaric or medieval nature from a glorified past. Both must use logic in handling their assumptions, but science fiction claims a degree of rationality for the assumptions, while fantasy must be irrational in its basic concepts.

Many of the same tricks can work. Men can fly—in metal planes of science or on carpets of magic; men can see across oceans—by scientific television or magic crystal balls. Magic accepts what cannot be disproved; science accepts only what can be proved. But the body of theory behind one is no less rich and requires no less rigor than that of the other—at least in good fantasy. Fantasy is illogical in assuming there are wondrous worlds or histories beyond our own; but science fiction uses logic to establish the possibility of worlds around other stars with other races and other histories.

Yet behind both fictions there lies a human need, and that is the need for myth and wonder. Science fiction has spent half a century inventing myths and giving visions that may suit the future—and that is no small achievement. But fantasy has a whole body of myths that tap deeply into our heritage from the past —and we need those, somehow, as well as any other myth we can accept.

The whole past is a testament to this need for myth and wonder. The rather dull story of Charlemagne was turned into the *Chanson de Roland*, the song of the wonderful events and deeds that generated a whole cycle of wonderful tales. There was the *Roman de la Rose*, with marvelous allegory for the thoughtful and wonders for all others—the majority. What fantasy could be richer than Ludovico Ariosto's early-sixteenth-century *Orlando Furioso*—though hardly less probable? There were literally hundreds of tales spun out about marvelous places, things, deeds and heroes. And to those who have only discovered such medieval fantasy through the rather artificial and very late *Faerie Queene* of Spenser, I recommend an examination of the riches that lay behind it. The tales of Arthur and Merlin are also late in the form we have them, and depend on vast amounts of fantasy of earlier times. See how rich is the fantasy developed about the so-called Fisher King (le Roi Pêcheur, which really meant the Sinner King).

By the time of well-developed civilization, when men stopped lopping off heads with broadswords and began spitting each other with rapiers, they were already getting scientific about phlogiston, and leaving most fantasy to the large masses of uneducated. But it never really died out. And eventually, the highly educated turned to it again. William Morris has been called the inventor of fantasy—which is arrant nonsense, of course, unless you narrow that down pretty fine with qualifying adjectives. But certainly his 1896 *The Well at the World's End* brought a certain type of fantasy to popularity. He is supposed to have invented the idea of a created world apart from ours for his fantasy. (Forgetting the world of Asgard, as distinct from our Mitgard and a dozen other worlds beyond ours where many wonders occurred.) Certainly he invented it in rough form as a literary device, and he also invested it with a medievalism that seems to be an almost inevitable part of the idea. In 1922 E. R. Eddison created another knightly world in *The Worm Ouroboros*. But perhaps the richest use of other worlds of fantasy was that of Edward Plunkett, Lord Dunsany. His events in *The King of Elfland's Daughter* (1924) specifically take place beyond the edge of the world. His shorter works give us still other worlds. Fletcher Pratt (as George U. Fletcher) took a few hints about one of these worlds as the basis for his *The Well of the Unicorn* (1948), which I consider one of the best examples before 1950.

(Oddly, H. Rider Haggard never thought of a world other than ours, or a history wildly different. He depended on the very old trick of putting his "pocket universe" cultures in little lost spots on Earth. Yet he used more way-out fantasy than any other popular writer of his time, and his *She* is certainly one of the great characters of fantasy, though She-Who-Must-Be-Obeyed was introduced to the public in 1887.)

The most popular of all such invented worlds was, of course, the Middle-Earth of J. R. R. Tolkien's *Lord of the Rings* (1954–1955). (This was preceded by his *The Hobbit*, but in this children's book Middle-Earth was much less fully developed.) Here, for the first time, the act of what he called sub-creation was fully realized. His secondary Earth was more than a local habitation and a name. It was a world like ours, but with different laws, a different nature, its own history going back in detail for thousands of years, and even its own detailed genesis. With him, finally, the acceptance of such secondary universes came to full fruition. (Yet it preserved a great deal of medievalism in its weapons, fighting means, courtly conduct, social structures and everything else. Fantasy draws on the past.)

Tolkien wrote in one of what seem to me to be the five great categories of fantasy. His was the *epic* fantasy. It is fantasy which deals with some epic struggle of Good and Evil, both personified, and it often involves a quest. (Such stories existed long before Tolkien in legends. Merritt used such a general idea in his *The Face in the Abyss*.) But the essential for such a story is what Tolkien called the sub-creation of a full, related but different world, a secondary one to our primary one, but equally acceptable to the reader. Without that, most of the wonder and potential grandeur of the epic will not come about fully.

Somewhat related, but totally different in mood and effect, is what should be called the heroic fantasy, often called *sword-and-sorcery*. Stories of this type usually look toward a period of savagery in the past. Most derive from Robert E. Howard's tales of Conan, the barbarian who looted his way to the throne of ancient Aquilonia, most civilized of all post-Atlantean kingdoms. Few have the gripping power that underlies Howard's writing, for all its crudity, or the ability to make nevertime into a period of seemingly real history. A few even neglect the essential element of magic (sorcery) and become little more than constant action (sword). In general, the rule is to take a barbarian world and put a more savage warrior up against all the forces of men and sorcery, then let him win by strength of determination and arms—getting one or more willing females in between bouts.

There is the *weird* story—a classic form in which some dark force or creature threatens: a malign ghost, evil witch, demon, etc. Such stories are written to send cold chills down susceptible spines. Following Ira Levin's *Rosemary's Baby*, there have been a lot of these novels tried on the general reader.

There is *whimsy*—the only description I can find for a certain type of fantasy humor, which doesn't work well with funny writing or comedic tricks, but requires a highly cockeyed viewpoint toward the whole business of magic and the supernatural. Thorne Smith did it well for the period of Prohibition. There must always be something that is inappropriate to the stock use of fantasy: a ghost who's scared of people, a modern vampire who does well as night watchman in a blood bank, or a demon who has no knowledge of souls but simply wants to eat his summoner. There has always been a certain amount of such fiction published, but John Campbell gave it a home in his short-lived *Unknown*, where it became perhaps the best-liked type of fantasy.

The fifth type is what I call the *fantastic conceit*. This is a type of story which really has no honest fantasy element at all. It depends on something fantastic being or happening—something that is clearly out of the ordinary, but does not involve magic or the supernatural. A man sees a beautiful girl three times in his life, each at a crucial moment, and never gets to know her or what her connection with him is; two children stray into some valley that is summertime, though they live in winter, spend a day there, and never can find it again; or there's a book that always opens to the right page—but only in emergencies. (The last, at least, borders on real fantasy.) Often these stories are much admired by editors who don't like real fantasy, and too frequently they are "too beautiful to print." They also tend to contain "wonderful" philosophical bits, usually banal. But once in a while, a good example gets written and deserves the praise it subsequently gets.

Most magazines used some fantasy—aside from the rigid category magazines. But the first magazine to make some success of presenting nothing but fantasy was *Weird Tales*. This began in 1923, edited by Edward Baird. After a little more than a year of less than success, Farnsworth Wright became editor, and he showed a much surer grasp of what readers wanted. He continued until the magazine was sold in 1938, after which Dorothy McIlwraith carried on. The magazine lasted until 1954, when it finally gave up the struggle.

This was the magazine that introduced H. P. Lovecraft to the national audience.

Lovecraft became best known for his Cthulhu Mythos and the mythical book that went with it—the *Necronomicon* by the mad Arab Abdul Alhazred; those who try to read it usually also go mad or die in some horrible way. (Surprisingly many not only believe in the existence of this fictional book but claim to have seen it.) According to the mythos, Earth was taken over in the primordial past by evil creatures from the stars, such as Cthulhu. Eventually driven out, they still try to regain their ancient power. And all other myths are probably just dim reflections of their evil. This is best exemplified in Lovecraft's long novelette, *The Shadow Out of Time*, which appeared in *Astounding Stories*, June 1936, not in *Weird Tales*.

After Lovecraft died in 1937, two writer friends named August Derleth and Donald Wandrei formed

Arkham House to publish his work in book form. Derleth also finished many of Lovecraft's incomplete stories and wrote others about the Mythos himself. Through their efforts, Lovecraft's work continued to grow in popularity.

Today, many critics consider Lovecraft one of our major writers. A bust of him, executed by Gahan Wilson, is the award presented each year to outstanding work by the World Fantasy Convention. It seems a little ironic that recognition came too late to help him or the magazine where so much of his work appeared.

Robert E. Howard was nothing like Lovecraft, but shared the honor of being largely responsible for the success of the magazine. He tried several swashbuckling, sorcery-fighting heroes, but finally settled on Conan of Cimmeria, with the epic of Conan told in random order through numerous stories. There was a vigor that swept the reader along in every line he wrote. His one full-length novel was *The Hour of the Dragon*, perhaps his best Conan story, which was later published by Gnome Press (1950) as *Conan the Conqueror*.

Howard committed suicide in 1936, and there was no publishing house set up to keep his works alive. But L. Sprague de Camp discovered that Howard's agent had unsold and incomplete drafts of Howard's work. De Camp began polishing and rewriting, and persuaded Gnome Press to begin issuing the books; they met only fair success. Then, perhaps 15 years later, de Camp talked Lancer Books into issuing them in paperback form—and this time they were very successful. Björn Nyberg wrote a sequel to *Conan the Conqueror*; de Camp completed and rewrote Howard's stories, as well as writing new stories to fill gaps in the history of the barbarian. And eventually, Lin Carter began collaborating with him. The books kept coming out.

When Lancer folded, other publishers began bidding fantastic amounts for the rights, which were still tied up in legal hassles. This took far too much time to set straight. But now both Ace Books and Berkley Books are publishing the Howard and post-Howard material in some complicated arrangement, and Conan is still flourishing—as he has also been doing in comic books.

The death of its two leading writers within a year was a sad blow to *Weird Tales*. But there were at least a great many writers who remained loyal to the magazine. Clark Ashton Smith wrote his exotic tales of ensorcelled lands in equally exotic prose. Edmond Hamilton had always done some of his best work for the magazine. And Ray Bradbury established his ability with a series of splendid fantasies. Among artists, Virgil Finlay and Hannes Bok were major discoveries. In its own way, *Weird Tales* was a great magazine and an important one.

The Clayton magazines had brought out a competitor in 1931, entitled *Strange Tales*. It lasted for 7 issues, until the magazine chain failed in 1933, and was not a bad magazine, though it emphasized action far more than did *Weird Tales*. Howard and other established writers contributed to it, and some of its own discoveries were promising. I've always felt that Street & Smith made a mistake in not buying it when they purchased *Astounding Stories*; it might have grown into the leading fantasy magazine under Tremaine's editorship.

1939 was a major year in fantasy publishing. Three magazines began during that year. Standard Magazines brought out *Strange Stories* as a companion to their science fiction magazines. However, it was not too well received, and it seemed to depend too much on formula material. It lasted until 1941, but left no real regrets when it ceased publication.

Both John Campbell and Ray Palmer also decided to bring out fantasy magazines, apparently with the same general idea in mind. (Their ideas were independent, however; Palmer's magazine was already at the printers when Campbell's came out.)

Campbell's *Unknown* (later *Unknown Worlds*) began with the March 1939 issue, as a monthly. Later, as paper became hard to get, it became bimonthly. It was finally discontinued in October 1943, after publishing 39 issues. Again, paper shortages during the war killed it; Street & Smith were putting more paper into magazines like *Love Story* and dropping their smaller-circulation magazines, even though those still were making a profit. After the war, an attempt was made to revive it with an initial all-reprint issue. They printed 300,000 copies of that, despite Campbell's advice; and while it outsold any prewar issue of *Unknown*, the unsold returns were large because of the excess number printed. So the idea was dropped.

Many, even today, consider it the best of all fantasy magazines. Campbell demanded stories for modern readers without nameless horrors and other clichés, and the same examination of ideas he wanted for science fiction. When Harold Shea sent himself to the land of the Norse gods, he found himself subject to the laws of that universe, where all iron rusted, stainless steel or not, and where lighters couldn't light because the principles didn't exist for such action. And when his professor friend joined him in the Faerie Queene universe, said friend could make magic, but not get quantitative control of it, so he might ask for a dragon and get a thousand dragons—or .001 dragon. (*The Roaring Trumpet* and *The Mathematics of Magic*, by L. Sprague de Camp and Fletcher Pratt, are now included with a third novel in the Ballantine/Del Rey *The Compleat Enchanter*.) The logic of the assumptions had to be followed completely. For the first time, the hard-won skills of science fiction were being carried back to fantasy, very much to the benefit of that fiction.

Palmer's *Fantastic Adventures* appeared later, dated May 1939. It followed a course opposite to *Unknown* for a time, beginning as a bimonthly and then becoming a monthly. (It also went through periods of being a bimonthly again, then a quarterly, monthly, bimonthly and eventually a quarterly. It also went through assorted name changes. When Ziff-Davis tried to develop a "quality" fantasy magazine called *Fantastic*, that lasted for just five issues; then it was "Combined with Fantastic Adventures" for a time; then it was *Fantastic Science Fiction Stories, Fantastic Stories of the Imagination,* and finally *Fantastic Stories* in 1965 and thereafter.)

Palmer's idea was similar to that of Campbell. He wanted fantasy fiction for modern readers, in modern style and settings; no hoary castles or clanking ghosts —stories should be fun to read. His execution of the idea, however, was different. He used stories like those often found in *Amazing*; they were too obviously hastily plotted and superficial in many instances. Some were better, of course; Robert Bloch wrote a series about Lefty Feep in Runyonesque style—which was clever then but is out of date now, or the stories would be well worth reprinting. I still remember Bloch's tale of a union organizer who went to Hell—and immediately began organizing the downtrodden there. But all too soon the Shaver Mystery began to fill *Fantastic* as it filled *Amazing*.

When Palmer left, Howard Browne and William Hamling tried to make the magazine more like *Unknown*, but the effort failed, as did later efforts by Browne and others. By then, few writers considered fantasy a market worth considering, and getting stories was difficult.

Still, *Fantastic* has managed to exist until the present time, and is still appearing as a quarterly. That would seem to make it the most successful fantasy magazine ever published.

Famous Fantastic Mysteries and *Fantastic Novels* reprinted quite a bit of classic fantasy as well as science fiction. And Donald Wollheim brought out the *Avon Fantasy Reader* (which used little original fiction, as

I remember) in 1947. This lasted through 18 numbered but not dated issues.

And in 1953, two new magazines appeared. I edited *Fantasy (Fiction) Magazine*, which began with the March 1953 issue (February on contents page) and was supposed to be bimonthly. Despite those who assured me fantasy wouldn't sell, it outsold the three science fiction magazines I also edited. But part of the credit for this must go to Hannes Bok, who did all the covers; he won the first cover art Hugo for his work. Then, after only four issues, I quit because of a disagreement with the publisher about payments and other conditions. Nobody else was willing to accept such conditions, it seemed, and the magazine was dropped.

H. L. Gold brought out *Beyond Fantasy Fiction* to go with *Galaxy* in July 1953. It ran through 1954 and ended in 1955 after only ten issues. I suspect that the trouble lay in the fact that the covers may have been beautiful, but they didn't offer a clue to the real nature of the magazine. Fantasy readers looked at the title and cover and decided it must be something strange—and that they wanted fantasy, not something "beyond" fantasy fiction.

Naturally, the end of the two magazines proved that fantasy wouldn't sell. And that fact was communicated to the paperback publishers at once. Publishers wouldn't look at fantasy. "Turn this into science fiction and we'll buy it," I was told. "Fantasy doesn't sell."

In 1965, Ballantine Books issued a paperback edition of J. R. R. Tolkien's *Lord of the Rings* trilogy. The Ballantine editions hit the best-seller lists and sold millions of copies.

Did that mean fantasy sold? No, indeed. Booksellers solved that by making a new ruling: Fantasy didn't sell; Tolkien sold.

But the Ballantines were determined to try to publish fantasy. They adopted a unicorn head as a symbol and decided to bring out books as "Adult Fantasy." To help find the books, they called in Lin Carter, who has read and loved and remembered more fantasy than anyone else I know. He was to locate classics for republication.

It seemed a good idea. By publishing such works, there could be no question about the quality of the line. But it didn't quite work. The most ardent fantasy lovers admired the books—but too often already had copies. Many others found the style too often unnatural in its affectations, or the stories old-fashioned. Again, I suspect that the covers were not right; many were beautiful—as art—but they didn't reflect the nature of the books.

The sales were meager, on the average, and the line was abandoned, though some books were kept in print. Among these were the books of Katherine Kurtz about the Deryni, Welsh mental mutants of an alternate tenth century, and Evangeline Walton's reconstruction of the events of the *Mabinogian*.

In 1975, Ballantine Books decided to try fantasy again, this time concentrating on original stories. Lester del Rey was hired as editor. The unicorn head was reluctantly dropped in favor of a shield-enclosed basilisk; and with no reluctance, the word "Adult" was dropped; that word had too many unfortunate connotations, none of them indicating real maturity. Illustrative covers were planned.

By singular serendipity, a long novel by an unknown writer came in just when this was being discussed; the novel was *The Sword of Shannara*, by Terry Brooks, and was precisely what del Rey felt was needed to establish the fantasy line. This was the first long epic fantasy adventure which had any chance of meeting the demands of Tolkien readers for similar pleasures.

To help interest potential readers, the book was printed with eight black-and-white illustrations, a map, and a two-page color centerspread, and was given simultaneous hard-cover and trade paperback publication—that is, publication in a large-format soft-cover edition the size of the hard-cover book, and with a price much higher than most mass-market paperbacks. It sold to a leading book club and received unprecedented prices from foreign publishers throughout the world. It was the first fiction ever to reach the top of the *New York Times'* trade paperback best-seller list, where it remained for five months. And after that record, it was no longer easy to believe that fantasy would not sell, provided it was properly slanted to the readers. (The extraordinary sale of the later *Silmarillion* was also noteworthy; but, of course, that was Tolkien, who was already established.)

Further experience with other fantasy novels has helped to confirm the fact that there is indeed a very active buying public for real fantasy. In many cases, fantasy can even outsell most science fiction. By now, booksellers seem happy to add such novels to their racks (though fantasy is still placed in with the science fiction—which is perhaps just as well). And other publishers are now beginning to feature fantasy.

This should really be no surprise to anyone. For the last fifteen years, science fiction has been including more and more elements of fantasy, and few readers have objected. There will always be a need for science fiction that precludes anything but the most rigorous attention to scientific plausibility; and it seems that there has long been a need in our myth-craving dreams to find an outlet of pure fantasy. That leaves a large area between the extremes to be filled.

I do not believe that rigid boundaries ever improved any field of literature, though some books are better for setting limits within their own territory. And I suspect that science fiction and fantasy still have much to learn from each other.

CHAPTER 30

Buck Rogers and Mr. Spock

FOR A GREAT MANY YEARS, science fiction had to put up with being called "that Buck Rogers stuff." When that description was finally forgotten, a new phrase came into use: "Oh, like Mr. Spock." And since explanations were useless to people who thought in such absolute symbols, all we could do was sigh and turn away. The unfortunate truth was that there *was* an element of truth in the associations, though most people had the cart before the horse.

Anthony Rogers first appeared in public in the August 1928 issue of *Amazing Stories*. This was in a novelette by Philip Francis Nowlan, "Armageddon—2419." In the novelette, Rogers slept in suspended animation from 1927 to 2419, and emerged to find America vanquished by a scientifically advanced but savage conqueror. With the help of a small band, he began to fight to free his country. And in this story and its sequel ("The Airlords of Han," *Amazing Stories*, March 1929) he succeeded.

It was better told than most stories of its time, despite the rather chauvinistic acceptance of the fear of a "yellow horde" and the eventual manifest destiny of America. But it was a science fiction story appearing in a science fiction magazine before it ever became a comic strip.

Perhaps this was too early for science fiction to have been classified as trash, but apparently someone in the

John Dille feature syndicate read it and saw possibilities. Nowlan was called in and asked to write it up into continuity for a comic strip, and Dick Calkins was hired to illustrate it. The strip ran as *Buck Rogers 2429*, beginning January 7, 1929. (His name was changed to Buck because Anthony was obviously too high-toned for comic readers, I assume.) For a time, the title was changed to keep it always five hundred years ahead; but eventually it was changed to *Buck Rogers in the Twenty-Fifth Century* and left that way until the daily strip finally ended July 8, 1967.

Phil Nowlan died in 1940, and the strip was carried on by others. But Nowlan, shortly before his death, returned to his first love, the writing of science fiction, which he had never really abandoned, having written a few stories between 1927 and 1939. Obviously, he had kept up with it and was familiar with its advances, since John Campbell bought the first story in what was to be a new series and was genuinely pleased with it.

1933 saw the beginning of another science fiction comic strip: *Brick Bradford* dealt with a hero who could go into the past or future for excitement by means of a time machine. Continuity was by William Ritt, and it was drawn by Clarence Grey. (The time traveling was later used a bit more amusingly in *Alley Oop*, written and drawn by Vince Hamlin, who once told me that he was an ardent science-fiction reader.)

In January 1934, Alex Raymond began *Flash Gordon* and his adventures on the planet Mongo, trying to overcome the dastardly plots of Emperor Ming the Merciless—who also had a touch of the Yellow Peril about him. Raymond's comic art was so outstanding that his somewhat routine adventure continuity didn't seem to matter.

All of these were fairly close to the general spirit of science fiction stories being used in the magazines; perhaps Raymond's was a bit ahead of its time, since the use of strange planets for plots that might have been better called sword-and-sorcery became more common later on.

Then the comic books, which had been using reprints of comic strips from newspapers, began seeking new material. And in June 1938, *Action Comics* introduced *Superman*. This was the creation of Jerome Siegel and Joseph Shuster, who had once been active science fiction fans; in fact, the real birth of the character had taken place rather crudely in Siegel's limited fan magazine. Superman himself had some touches of purported science fiction in his background, having come from another planet; and once in a while, he used something that might be called a science fiction gadget. But his ability to jump enormous distances and even change directions was a bit too wildly in defiance of Newton's laws of motion without any justification. Anyhow, he was really one of the crime-solving, vigilante heroes so popular in the crime series–character magazines. There were soon lots of variations of the pseudo-science-fiction-hero comics, and some were scripted by leading science fiction writers.

A much more genuinely science fiction strip began in the *New York Daily News*, in 1952. This was *Beyond Mars*, drawn by Lee Elias and adapted from his own stories by Jack Williamson. Under the pseudonym of Will Stewart, Williamson had written a number of stories about a group of men struggling with the problem of learning how to use contra-terrene (c.t.) matter. This is matter where the particles have the opposite charge from those of normal matter; in contact, the two forms explode into pure energy. When Williamson's *Seetee Shock* appeared, the *News* decided to turn it into a comic strip. But while it pleased science fiction readers more than most such strips, it never gained the desired general popularity and it was dropped in 1955.

Meantime, science fiction had completely invaded the comic books during their boom period around 1950.

A great deal of science fiction was used, and some of the stories were obviously lifted (or more or less adapted) from the science fiction magazines. Most of the continuity writers and artists then were fans, and quite familiar with the field; they often made quite good adaptations. But the practice became less common when writers discovered what was going on and began suing.

Nevertheless, science fiction and fantasy continued to be popular in the comic books. Today, vague derivations of science fiction are common; and they are vague to the real fan, since they bear fairly little relationship to what is being published elsewhere as science fiction or fantasy, even when Conan is the hero. Most of those that I've seen manage to use the science fiction or fantasy to set up grim, barbarian worlds (before history—or post-holocaust) in which some brutal and largely naked hero runs about being strong and dominant, usually with a partially dressed woman who helps him and another who is trying to seduce him to evil. By and large, they don't please me. However, if I were trying to run a school on how to become a young militant fascist, I might change my mind.

If the comics are derivative of the science fiction magazines, the cinema certainly is not. Science fiction began there long before the first all-science-fiction magazine was published.

Georges Méliès produced a short film called *A Trip to the Moon* in 1902 (and continued to make fantasy and science fiction films for many years). *Frankenstein* was first brought to the screen in 1910 by J. Searle Dawley. The less said of that, the better. But *The Cabinet of Dr. Caligari* (1919) may deserve more serious attention; I don't know, never having seen it, but some people regard it as worth seeing, even today. The 1925 version of *The Lost World* was the first science fiction film I ever saw; if my memory is right, it was pretty crude in its effects, but better than some made in a similar vein much later. And Fritz Lang's *Metropolis* is a powerful film in some ways, and is still being shown at science fiction conventions. The dark mood of the film remains, though some of the action is more funny than impressive.

Fritz Lang also produced *Die Frau im Mond* (The Woman in the Moon) in 1928. The film could hardly seem good to audiences that have seen the real trip to the moon. But Lang went to considerable trouble to make it realistic according to what was then known. He made a deal with the German Rocket Society to act as advisors in return for funding them in their early experiments.

1931 was an important year for the development of a certain type of film. It was in this year that Universal turned out *Dracula* with Bela Lugosi and *Frankenstein* with Boris Karloff—films still being shown on television. Paramount also produced *Dr. Jekyll and Mr. Hyde,* starring Fredric March, with Rouben Mamoulian directing. These were highly successful films, and they really started the "monster" trend which remained Hollywood's conception of science fiction for decades. The stories had nothing to do with science fiction, of course; they were all classic horror stories (though Mary Shelley's story is considered the beginning of science fiction by some).

The advantages film makers could gain from monster films were instantly apparent. The audiences were not looking for great stories or fine acting, as experience showed. They wanted gruesome monsters to shock them. And monsters were not that difficult to get from the makeup departments. Grade-Z quickies about monsters might not become classics, but they were cheap and easy to produce and they made money. Stories could be found in public domain which enjoyed some acceptance as classics.

It seems surprising that some real attempts at science fiction films were made—and at least one of them ambitious: *Things to Come* was an expensive film to produce, using excellent actors and a script adapted by H. G. Wells from his book. For 1936, the special effects were extremely lavish and good, too. The film continued to be featured in theaters for perhaps thirty years after it first came out.

The other films from the period that are best remembered by science fiction readers are *Flash Gordon* (1936) and *Buck Rogers* (1939). Both starred Buster Crabbe, both were adaptations from comic strips, and both were designed as serials—meaning that they were made in short segments, each ending with a cliffhanger, intended to keep the audience coming back next week to find out what happened. They were about as crude as films could be, but somehow they came closer to catching the feeling of much real science fiction than more serious attempts; and television has been showing both films, patched together from the segments to make a feature film from each.

1950 began a period of blessings for the science fiction filmgoer. That year *Destination Moon* appeared, adapted freely from Robert Heinlein's *Rocket Ship Galileo*, and presenting a quite fair picture of the scientific principles of spaceflight. In 1951, we had *The Day the Earth Stood Still*, freely adapted from Harry Bates' *Farewell to the Master*, and the Balmer and Wylie *When Worlds Collide*, with quite remarkable special effects. John W. Campbell's superb novelette, *Who Goes There?*, was turned into the monster movie *The Thing from Another World—* which was pretty good science fiction until they began showing the rather unbelievable monster. And in 1953, H. G. Wells' *War of the Worlds* was a triumph of really beautiful special effects that followed the original story fairly closely.

Forbidden Planet (1956) was something of a surprise. This was an original screenplay, not an adaptation of some classic science fiction story; yet in many ways, it might have come straight from the pages of *Startling Stories* or *Planet Stories*. It was pretty much pure and unadulterated adventure science fiction, with the most effective monster ever shown—and a true science fiction monster, at that. I loved every minute of it.

Hence, the answer to the science fiction reader's constant question as to why the movies couldn't make science fiction was: They could—and they did! The trouble was that they also made some pretty dreadful quickies and monster films, most of which were also classed as science fiction by the filmmakers. It wasn't the absence of science fiction, but rather the dilution, that seemed to make Hollywood oblivious to the category. I've skipped over a fair number of films that could be classed as true science fiction, too; and there were some excellent fantasy films that achieved considerable popularity—*Death Takes a Holiday* and *Lost Horizon*, to mention only two.

In 1968, *2001: A Space Odyssey* became a tremendously successful science fiction movie—one that deeply impressed even those who couldn't stand science fiction before. Stanley Kubrick approached Arthur C. Clarke to collaborate on the film, and no expense was spared. Douglas Trumbull's special effects were the most lavish ever seen, and most of them were completely convincing. I was in the minority in liking little beyond the splendid hominid section; to most people, the mysticism of the ending in which mankind seems to need transformation into alienness or to require extrahuman help was satisfying. (Just what the ending meant was something I never could learn from Clarke; his later novelization, however, was an improvement over the movie in several respects.) Anyhow, the film was a financial success.

Unfortunately, Hollywood seemed most impressed by the special effects; later films seemed unaware of the need for any logic or story value. *Silent Running*

(1971) had a splendid robot, but was ruined by the idea that the men who could devise a great spaceship to save the plant life on Earth were unaware that plants need sunlight to stay healthy. And *Logan's Run* (1976) was a blinding revelation of nothing except that the future was horrible and fools were superior to intelligent men.

Star Wars is another matter, but it really comes after the first fifty years of science fiction as a category. I'll get to that in the last chapter.

Radio and television are entirely separate media, so far as their connection with science fiction is concerned. Radio did some of the finest fantasy ever presented to a nationwide audience. Little of it was derivative. And its ability to deal with even the wildest fantasy or most futuristic science fiction was probably due to the fact that no visual effects were possible, leaving all such things to the imagination, with a few clues in the stories. Arch Obeler presented a great deal of fantasy and science fiction; and the old *CBS Playhouse* did a little of everything, including some very fine fantasy.

The best-remembered radio drama of a science fiction nature, of course, was the Orson Welles production of *The War of the Worlds* (1938). Actually, most of the accounts of the public's wildly fleeing in fear from the vicinity of the purported landing site were grossly exaggerated. Still, despite the obvious and repeated statements that it was all fiction, many people apparently did believe it, though I doubt their number included even one regular science fiction reader. The script was both effective and rather obvious; and I remember many broadcasts of fantasy and science fiction that struck me as better fiction.

Television did little of the genuinely original work that had filled the radio broadcasts. There was one short series presented by Channel 7 in New York—in the summer of 1950, as I remember—which showed promise. Among other interesting productions was one —with a single actor and almost no staging beyond the use of light—which showed a man on trial for exceeding his legal murder permits—by his own suicide, it turned out. But generally, television seemed to regard science fiction as something for a very young audience.

Captain Video began in 1949, produced by Olga Druse with a minimum budget and considerable ingenuity, including the use of old films to fill out the time. It appeared five evenings a week on the old DuMont network, and it was broadcast live. Captain Video was kept busy in his spaceship, saving the Earth from all kinds of space pirates, aliens, and whatnots— much in the manner of Edmond Hamilton's Captain Future novels. Each episode ran for several weeks. Many were written by science fiction writers. Within the limits possible, Olga Druse wanted the real feeling of science fiction. And considerable ingenuity was used in stretching the budget to cover interesting effects. (For a time, I acted as a sort of science advisor to the show.)

In 1950, the interest generated by *Captain Video* apparently aroused a major network to try some of the same. The result was *Tom Corbett: Space Cadet*, a fifteen-minute show—which just happened to go on at the same time as *Captain Video*. The budget permitted far more elaborate special effects and considerable experimentation, however. Willy Ley was advisor for the series.

Rod Serling's *Twilight Zone* began in 1959 as a weekly program of half-hour dramas. This was an anthology of separate stories, not a series, and it was more or less adult in its appeal. It is one of the few television shows to be mentioned fondly by science fiction fans. I'm not entirely sure why this is so. Monsters were used fairly frequently, and such monsters were usually automatically evil in intent. I thought science fiction had long since abandoned the concept that looks proved intent. Nevertheless, there were some shows that had both force and subtlety.

In 1964, Irwin Allen gave us *Voyage to the Bottom of the Sea*, which added nothing to the luster of TV science fiction. And he followed this in 1967 with *Time Tunnel*. This time the idea was not bad—a tunnel through which men could go back to the past to observe and perhaps avert ancient disasters. The special effects were fantastic. The scripts were routine, to say the least. Before *Time Tunnel* premiered, a number of science fiction writers and editors were brought in for a special showing to give their honest opinion, supposedly. Some of us did say what we thought, but I'm sure our remarks were carefully filed in a shredding machine. The attitude toward any criticism seemed to be: What could mere science fiction writers know about science fiction?

Gene Roddenberry's *Star Trek*, which premiered in 1966, was another matter. Roddenberry was a reader of science fiction and he seemed honestly interested in bringing as much of its real spirit to the TV medium as possible. He also held a preview of his first show for a science fiction audience; it may not have done any good, but he listened with interest. Furthermore, he went out of his way to try to get science fiction writers to provide him with scripts. (Not always easy, since most of those writers had no clear idea of the limits of television or the cost of new sets.) A number, including Harlan Ellison, did sell scripts to him.

The show was a series involving certain fixed characters, but it was loose enough in structure for considerable variety in the nature of the individual shows. And during the first year, some of the individual shows were very good. Roddenberry apparently was unusually insistent on maintaining a level of quality. But the network was not too pleased. At the end of the first year, there was a threat to drop the series. When word of this got out, the network was flooded with indignant letters. As a result, the show was continued, but with somewhat less control in Roddenberry's hands—and some decline in the level of many of the shows, in my opinion.

The third year was a repetition of the second. Threats to drop the show produced another avalanche of letters—this time partly as a result of an organized campaign to save *Star Trek*. But while the show was allowed to go for another year (thereby accumulating enough scripts to make it eligible for syndication afterward and the obvious financial rewards from continuing to appear), Roddenberry had even less control over the scripts. Many of these were produced by the regular, non-science-fiction writers available at a moment's notice in Hollywood. A few good shows were done, but some were pretty far from Roddenberry's original intent.

This didn't seem to matter. *Star Trek* had become something of a cult. This was because of one character, played by Leonard Nimoy—an alien "Vulcan" with big ears and, supposedly, a totally logical mind. Mr. Spock simply took over *Star Trek* and made any script fine, so long as he appeared in the show.

For the next few years, the masquerades at the World Science Fiction Conventions were dominated by people with rubber ears playing Mr. Spock. Eventually the fans of the show organized their own conventions—ones often far bigger than the largest science fiction convention on record. James Blish began writing up the episodes from the show into a series of books. The replays of the show were soon commanding bigger audiences than had been true during its prime-time seasons. Then an animated series was made for the younger audience—and that immediately drew all the *Star Trek* followers—the trekkies. Alan Dean Foster wrote these episodes up into further books, all of which sold well. Ballantine published the plans for the Star Ship *Enterprise*, where Mr. Spock was an officer, as well as a manual on everything relating to the ship—both of which enjoyed high sales.

None of this either helped or harmed science fiction much. The trekkies seemed to believe that all science fiction began and ended with *Star Trek*, though a few probably did try other science fiction—particularly the other stories by Foster. But despite its faults (particularly in the third year), *Star Trek* was essentially honest science fiction, if a bit primitive. There were monsters and enemy aliens—but the aliens had reasonable motivations and many of the monsters were actually good guys. A fair number of real science fiction themes were done quite well. A sophisticated reader of science fiction might not always find the series totally engrossing —but there was nothing in it to make him turn away in displeasure.

Unfortunately, that wasn't true for the 1975 *Space 1999*, which was supposed to be for the older viewer what *Star Trek* had been for the younger one. It repeated every mistake that had ever been made in science fiction films and television. The Moon was somehow propelled away from Earth by an explosion of atomic wastes—which was bad enough science. But then it managed to develop speeds far greater than the velocity of light but at the same time linger around some world or other for days while the characters made the same mistakes over and over again. And, of course, there were evil monsters—many disguised to look like human beings, but still really monsters.

Probably the best that can be said about television's use of science fiction is that it once produced an almost forgotten anthology show, *Outer Limits*—and *Star Trek*. Beyond that, the less said the better.

CHAPTER 31

Glossary

LIKE EVERY OTHER specialized human activity, science fiction has a vocabulary and set of accepted conventions that vary at least somewhat from standard usage. Until these are mastered, the reading of the more sophisticated stories can prove somewhat difficult at times.

Science fiction fandom has also developed words necessary to the activities of fans. Even the word "fan" is not quite what it may be in other fields. A fan is not just someone who reads the fiction—indeed, some fans seem to avoid reading science fiction, yet remain accepted as science fiction fans; the word conveys a sense of active participation in some manner that relates to science fiction, with attendance at conventions, writing to other fans, or publishing fanzines as examples.

In the following glossary, those words preceded by an asterisk (*) are part of fanspeak, or the vocabulary developed by fans. Many are neologisms, but they save a lot of time and trouble. Actually, the list is smaller than it might once have been; many expressions were less useful than supposed, and were quietly dropped. Few fans today make any great effort to speak in jargon, fortunately.

Certainly the following glossary should be generally adequate:

*Actifan: a fan still involved in fan activity; active fan.

Alternate World: a world separated from ours (by some time or dimensional barrier) in which the development and history are not precisely like ours.

Android: now used for a synthetic humanlike servant or worker, grown or created. Androids are of flesh-and-blood, though often denied full human rights. The 'droids in *Star Wars* were really robots.

Anti-gravity: an artificial force designed so that it repulses matter, opposite to the effect of gravity. Probably completely unscientific. Artificial gravity is also sometimes used; it acts as a substitute for real gravity on spaceships, for example.

Anti-matter: sometimes called contra-terrene matter, or c.t. This is matter in which the subatomic particles have charges that are the opposite of normal matter. In contact, the two forms of matter explode into pure energy.

Aristotelian Logic: a type of thinking based on two-value logic, where *good* and *bad*, or *go* and *no-go* have no conditions shading between. Non-Aristotelian logic recognizes all shades of meaning.

Asteroid: little worlds or chunks of matter, usually found between the orbits of Mars and Jupiter. A few are hundreds of miles in diameter. One theory is that these are the wreck of a planet that broke apart. Many may have valuable minerals, and numerous stories deal with the rough miners who exploit the asteroid belt. Probably less dangerous to spaceships than most stories indicate.

*BEM: bug-eyed monster; this refers to any alien creature, monstrous in form, used in science-fiction art. It need not have the faceted eyes of insects—and rarely does. The prevalence of BEMs is sometimes indicative of fiction which overemphasizes action.

Big Bang: the theory that the universe started with

a huge explosion which led to the expanding universe and created most matter as we know it. Sometimes it is assumed that all matter will eventually be pulled back to a central clump by gravity, with another explosion to start it all over again.

Blaster: nowadays, almost any type of energy weapon; a gun which produces such intense heat that it can volatilize matter.

Black Hole: in theory, matter which has condensed so radically that there is almost no empty space between particles, millions of times more dense than normal matter. Surface gravity becomes so great that light is bent inward and cannot escape, hence the object is black and appears like a hole in space, into which energy can fall but never get out. Usually considered to be the ultimate destiny of a star that has burned up its energy, except for gravity, but sometimes theorized to be possible for very small objects. Science fiction has used black holes for travel through time, between the stars, and in numerous other ways, probably all impossible.

*****BNF:** big-name fan. A fan whose activity has made him well known to most other fans, and who exerts considerable influence in all matters pertaining to fans, and occasionally to professionals.

Bussard Ram-jet: a method of gathering fuel for star travel from space itself. In this, magnetic fields spread out before the ship and direct all particles in space into the "throat" of the jet, where matter is converted to energy to drive the ship. It will only work after considerable velocity is attained.

Clone: in science fiction, almost always a duplicate of a human being made by inducing cells from the body to grow a new individual. A clone would be a biologically identical copy of its "parent," rather than a mixture of genes from two parents.

*****COA:** change of address—one of the plagues of publishing fan magazines and keeping the mailings going to the subscribers.

*Con: any convention, whether local, regional or worldcon.

*Crudzine: a poorly done fan magazine, filled with bad or pointless copy.

Cryogenics: a process of freezing the body (now usually after death) at very low temperatures to preserve it until science may learn to repair whatever caused death and revive the person.

Dean Drive: a device which is supposed to convert rotary motion into a drive in one direction. The device is real and patented, but the hope that it might lead to a way of driving spaceships now seems impossible.

Dirac Drive: named for P. A. M. Dirac, a great scientist. He theorized that matter might extend throughout all space, each particle being infinite, but "focused" at one point. Writers have suggested various tricks for moving the point of focus, thus moving the ship. Dirac was also responsible for other theories, but few have been used in science fiction.

Disintegrater: a weapon or device which can either turn matter directly into energy or so loosen the atomic bonds that an object will fly apart. Nowadays, seldom found in science fiction.

*DUFF: Down Under Fan Fund, a voluntary system of collecting donations to bring Australian fans to the U.S. (or vice versa), with the contributors voting on their choice of fan to be selected.

Dyson Sphere: a method whereby an advanced race can collect all the energy from a sun by using the matter of planets and other bodies to form a gigantic sphere completely around the sun. Proposed by Freeman Dyson as a serious possibility.

*Egoboo: boost to the ego, any activity or conduct that leads to an expanded self-image. Almost self-explanatory, and perhaps the most valuable word invented by fans.

Entropy: The most misused word in science fiction. Entropy is the degree of randomness in the distribution of energy. The increase of entropy should eventually lead to the "heat death" of the universe, where all energy has become heat and that is uniformly distributed, or without any ordering. In an isolated system, the entropy of all bodies contained in the system increases during every irreversible process—such as light striking a body and becoming heat. Entropy never decreases. This is part of the second law of thermodynamics. It has been stated rather loosely as the principle that "in the long run, you can't win."

E.T.: extraterrestrial. Any being (usually intelligent) from any world except Earth.

E-Type World: a world generally similar to Earth, having an atmosphere containing oxygen, sufficient water, a similar gravity, and a temperature not too different.

Exogenesis: the process of obtaining offspring outside the mother's body. Very popular in early Utopian and dystopian science fiction.

*****Faan:** usually, a fan who is more interested in fandom than in science fiction. A faanish fan is considered lacking in serious interest by some other fans, whom he regards as humorless and stuffy. Once a prejorative, though now accepted by the ones so labeled.

*****Fanac:** fan activity.

*****Femfan:** female fan. When there were few females in fandom, the distinction between sexes was stronger than now, and the term is gradually disappearing from serious use. (The plural of fan as "fen" is also vanishing.)

*****FIAWOL:** Fandom Is A Way Of Life—a somewhat exaggerated statement used by those who take fandom very seriously.

*****FIJAGH:** Fandom Is Just A Goddamned Hobby. The obvious answer to Fiawol.

*****First Fandom:** an organization of fans actively interested in science fiction in 1938 or before. They give an award annually to someone deemed to have added luster to the field in early days.

Force Field: a force around some center, as magnetism around a magnet. In science fiction, any protective force surrounding a spaceship; protection against hostile rays.

Fourth Dimension: a mathematical way of looking at time along with the normal three dimensions for location of events. In fiction, mostly considered some physical dimension at "right angles" to our world through which other worlds may be reached. Most fictional explanations and achievements are nonsense, but sometimes fun.

*****Fringe Fan:** someone barely acceptable as a fan because his interests lie outside the field proper.

FTL: faster-than-light travel. (Also called super-c, since c symbolizes the velocity of light.) Impossible by current knowledge, but necessary for many stories. An accepted convention.

*****Fugghead:** someone who is stupid or hopelessly confused. Like entropy, fuggheadedness tends to increase.

*****Gafiate:** from gafia—get away from it all—meaning to give up science fiction activities. Most who leave degafiate later.

Gas Giant: a massive world like Jupiter (J-type world) with an immense and unbreathable atmosphere.

Gene Pool: the variety of genetic material available to any group such as a colony; too small a gene pool may lead to genetic drift.

General Semantics: a system intended to promote clear thinking proposed by Alfred Korzybski and explained in *Science and Sanity* (1933). Korzybski emphasized that the symbol must not be treated as the thing, the map as the territory. Some aspects were covered in fiction by Robert A. Heinlein and A. E. Van Vogt.

Generation Ship: a ship operating at reasonable velocities to reach another star. Hundreds of years may pass on the voyage before the descendants of the original voyagers reach their goal. In a closed world, all resources except energy can be used over and over again, making the duration of the trip over centuries possible.

*****Ghu:** a bit of fan mythology, a sort of god (or ghod) of space, used for oaths. Not taken seriously.

GOH: abbreviation for Guest of Honor at a con.

Hieronymous Machine: the first psionic device discovered by John Campbell, supposedly capable of analyzing samples by the tackiness of a plate on which the fingers lay. Campbell claimed it worked as well with a schematic drawing in place of real electronics; I assume it did indeed.

Hive Culture: alien life organized like ants or bees, where the individuals are subject at all times (often by telepathic contact) to the total hive mentality.

Hyperspace: a science fiction convention, used to permit travel between stars in short periods of time. Supposedly another space in which either distances are less or the limiting velocity is greater. Usually ships travel in it by "jumps." Also sub-space.

Inertialess Drive: a method of faster-than-light travel proposed by E. E. Smith. Without inertia—resistance to change in velocity or direction—the limits against such velocities should be removed.

Ion Drive: a real spaceship drive, though not yet applied to real flight. Ions are charged particles of atoms which can be accelerated to high velocity by magnetic fields; the ion drive could replace chemical rockets more efficiently, at least in theory.

L-5: a proposal by Gerard K. O'Neill to build colonies in space, rather than on planets. Named for a stable point in the orbit of the Moon where such a colony might be developed.

*****Letterhack:** a fan who writes many letters to the editor. Not meant as a put-down.

Light-year: a measure of distance (not time); the distance light travels in one year—about six million million miles.

*****LOC:** letter of comment, usually to a fanzine about a previous issue.

Mass: matter; equivalent to weight when affected by gravity; mass possesses inertia even when no gravity field affects it.

Matter Duplicator: a device capable of creating many copies of an original—exact copies. Sometimes can duplicate humans.

Matter Transmitter: sort of a means of sending solid objects by radio transmission—or even instantaneously across space. Supposedly, an object is scanned and re-created elsewhere. Some stories deal with transmission errors, which can cause terrible messes.

*****Mundane:** not part of the science fiction world. Mundania is the world of those who haven't discovered science fiction.

Mutant: a creature (usually human) whose hereditary pattern has been messed up by radiation, chemicals, etc. Most real mutations are small and seldom beneficial. But science fiction uses mutation to provide supermen with great mental powers as well as deformed monsters.

*****Neofan:** a newcomer to fandom.

Neutronium: supposedly, matter collapsed to high density or composed mostly of neutrons, used as a shield on spaceships against radiation. Sometimes called collapsium.

Neutron Star: a star which has collapsed into very high density, but not so great as in a black hole. Light can still escape.

Parallel Evolution: a theory that certain factors will make evolution proceed similarly on all worlds. Used to justify having human beings on other planets—even cross-fertile ones.

Parallel Universe: a universe in some other dimension, close to ours, which may have a somewhat different history. People might have duplicates there, but ones living slightly different lives.

Paratime: H. Beam Piper's universe in which time extends not only forward and backward, but crosswise, with many earths lying side by side, like pages in a book. Each earth differs slightly from the others; thus a panorama of histories is available for exploiting by those who can travel through paratime.

Parsec: an astronomical unit, a second of parallax. It is equal to 3.26 light-years and is always a measure of distance, not time.

Parthenogenesis: the process of conceiving a child without the need of male sperm. Necessary to the postulate that only women exist on some future worlds.

*Pro: one who sells material to professional publishers. Often referred to as dirty or filthy, but usually affectionately.

Psi: any form of extrasensory phenomena—from telepathy to telekinesis. Too often used to find easy solutions to story problems. Psionics originally applied to mechanical or electrical means of handling psi powers, but now is often confused with simple psi.

Psychohistory: as used by Isaac Asimov in *Foundation*, a science of mass psychology which could predict future historical trends; not directly related to the real discipline by the same name.

Ray: a beam of radiation, usually used as a weapon, as in a ray gun. Pressor rays thrust things away, tractor beams draw them, pincer rays can cut off other rays, etc. Most had rich colors and visual effects in early stories, and were clearly outside our known energy spectrum.

Relativity: in science fiction, this is usually confined to some aspects of Einstein's Special Relativity. As a body approaches the speed of light, its mass approaches infinity. (Its rest mass is divided by the square root of one-minus-v²-over-c², where v is the body's velocity and c is the velocity of light. Obviously, when $v = c$, mass is divided by zero—which yields infinity, and hence is not attainable by any amount of energy for acceleration.) Time slows with the reciprocal of mass increase.

Robot: a more or less sentient construct of mechanical parts, usually given manlike form. Some robots are more intelligent than men.

Sci-Fi: a term that is anathema to science fiction people, used in ignorance by those outside the field. When used by fans, the term indicates only scorn. The correct abbreviation is sf or rarely, S.F. The older stf (scientifiction) is no longer used.

*Sercon: originally, applied to fans who were serious and constructive; now often a term indicating that the fan lacks a sense of proportion or humor. Someone more interested in science fiction than in fannish activities; the opposite of faanish.

Shield: some kind of protective force field around a ship.

*SMOF: secret masters of fandom. Smofing is the getting together to plan some scheme for behind-the-scenes maneuvering, either seriously or for fun.

Sophont: creature (usually alien) having intelligence.

Space Opera: almost any story involving space, though it properly deals with those in which action takes precedence over other writing details. Analogous to horse opera for Westerns.

Space Warp: somewhat like hyperspace. By "bending" or warping space, the distance to another star is supposedly reduced.

Star Gate: a strange portal through which one can step instantly to the surface of another world. Most seem to have been designed by some ancient race. Extremely popular recently.

Steady State: the theory that the universe is being constantly created, with atoms of hydrogen appearing spontaneously throughout space. This had the support of several leading scientists at one time, but now seems not to fit the evidence.

Subjective Time: a misnomer to describe the time aboard a ship with a velocity near the speed of light. Actually, the shorter time there is just as real and objective as that on Earth. Also sometimes referred to as tau time.

Suspended Animation: a means of reaching the future or enduring long passages to other stars by having the body frozen so that the vital processes are slowed almost to a stop. Hibernation has also been suggested, requiring no freezing.

Tachyon: a theoretical particle proposed during the examination of some aspects of relativity. Tachyons would exist only at velocities greater than that of light, and would gain mass as they slowed toward light speed. No real evidence for them exists, but science fiction writers have used them for space drives and as a means of communication between stars.

*TAFF: Transatlantic Fan Fund. Voluntary contributions to bring European fans to American cons and Americans to European cons. Contributors vote upon the fan to be brought.

Terraforming: a process of changing other worlds to make them suitable for human habitation.

Terran: a human from Earth, or an adjective referring to Earthly things. The preferred form, as is Venusan for Venus, Martian for Mars, or Jovian for Jupiter.

Totipotency: a process for stimulating regrowth of a lost or damaged limb or organ. Based on the ability of some lower life forms to regrow parts.

*Trufan: originally, one who does good work as a fan; now usually equivalent to faan.

Uncertainty: a principle stated by Werner Heisenberg; the impossibility to locate a particle exactly for both a given time and given place; hence, the advisability of dealing with such particles in terms of observable phenomena. This indeterminancy principle is important in quantum mechanics. In science fiction, the term has been used improperly to justify the idea that nothing is sure and that anything can be made to happen.

Worm Holes: tunnels through space, proposed by scientists, which are assumed to be produced by black holes. Some fiction has used them as a means of star travel.

Xeno-: a prefix used in science fiction to indicate alien or nonhuman life, as xenanthropology and xenobiology. Xenophobia is a term describing a neurotic fear of strangers; in science fiction, it is used to mean fear of alien beings.

CHAPTER 32

Themes and Variations

DURING MORE THAN FIFTY YEARS, science fiction writers spent a lot of time seeking for new ideas. Indeed, science fiction has often been called a literature of ideas. And to a large extent, that has been true for the overall picture. Particularly in the shorter fiction, it is probably difficult to begin a catalogue of all the ideas that have been used.

But there have been certain themes that have always dominated the field. Often the problem of the writers seemed not to be that of finding new themes, but rather finding some acceptable variation on an old one. Most of these basic themes can be found in stories that antedated the beginning of the category magazines.

Still, considering both themes and major variations, science fiction has acquired and developed a far larger stock of story situations than any other field.

Since the beginning, the single most important theme has been that of getting out into space. From Lucian's *True History* to a majority of the current books, man apparently has dreamed of leaving Earth.

At the beginning of the magazine period, these trips were fairly simple. A trip to the Moon was enough to justify a whole novel—particularly if it turned out that there was life on the Moon. Everything from anti-gravity to astral projection was used as a means of reaching our satellite. But the favorite means was logically by rocket. Many of the stories were at least acceptable in the scientific basis for the trip. Almost all failed to consider the economics or the amount of labor in developing such a ship; too many were ships that were cobbled together quickly by a few men, perhaps with the help of some rich man who could fund them.

Mars and Venus beckoned, of course. And many were the trips made to those planets. (Mars was still as Lowell imagined it, and Venus a wet and usually savage world where dinosaurs still roamed.) In most cases, both planets seemed to teem with life, often including human beings who were mysteriously capable of mating with Earthmen. But there were some honest attempts in the light of the knowledge of the time to show realistic explorations. A few pioneering writers even took their ships out to the moons of Jupiter.

Piracy was rife in many of the old stories—a plot device now seldom used. Trade flourished between worlds, often in goods that would have been cheap enough to produce on Earth. Accidents happened so often in the stories that it was hard to see why any ship went out. And there was always the danger of being hit by a "meteorite"—which should have been a meteoroid, of course. The asteroid belt between Mars and Jupiter was a constant danger, and ships might be hit numerous times by small objects. (Few stopped to figure the average distances between objects, which rendered such a hit highly unlikely.) And interplanetary warfare was always good for a new story, often between Earth and the inhabitants of other worlds who also had spaceships—apparently inventing them just when we did.

Then Edward E. Smith opened up a larger frontier with his *Skylark of Space* and its sequels. Soon trips were being taken to other stars and all around the galaxy. And that is a basic theme that has endured to the present with no sign of wearing out. The variations, major and minor, seem to be without end.

Except for Smith, who paid no attention to relativity (after he provided atomic power for his ship), most writers were aware that getting to the stars was going to take years, no matter how much power they had. Hence, many of the early stories about star travel were filled with attempts to explain how they overcame the difficulty. Usually, it was by the same method in vogue today—the use of "space warp," or "hyperspace"; if the ship couldn't go through normal space fast enough, provide a space without the limitation—or a shortcut through some other space. Now it has been explained so often that writers simply accept the existence of such a drive, in most cases. Sometimes that seems a pity, since some of the more interesting parts of older stories deal with the problem and its solution.

The logical solution was to accept the limits and use a ship that could travel at reasonable speeds for generations to reach the other star. In the magazines, Murray Leinster popularized this concept, and it was amplified later by Don Wilcox and Robert A. Heinlein. But it never became too popular, probably because you couldn't get the hero from Earth to Centaurus that way—it was his descendant who arrived. In most cases where such a trip was used, some element of mutiny on board or displacement between generations was the basis of the plot.

Trading, warfare, accidents and even piracy moved from the planets to the stars. But as time went on, more attention was spent on the problem of colonizing worlds around other stars—worlds that had their own ecologies and environments, where small bands of men and women were forced to start again under wildly new conditions.

In many cases, these colonies became lost. Either they were forced somehow to land without trace on some planet other than their goal, or communication broke down. Then, when rediscovered millennia later, they had created their own wildly different cultures, of course. The best known such "lost colony" is probably Marion Zimmer Bradley's Darkover; and this is one of the few where we can see how and when the loss occurred and also see the results long after.

Of course, there was war between some of the native races and Earth. But this quickly faded into a very minor theme. Usually, when an alien race was discovered (a very common occurrence), there was difficulty, but Earthmen and autochthons frequently had a basic misunderstanding that was set right before the story ended; the evil aliens in science fiction had become less acceptable by the end of the first period. Earthmen were sometimes pictured as the bad guys—but not usually; many stories even assumed that Earth had set up a strong code to prevent human beings from destroying or even changing other cultures.

First contact between Earthman and alien was and remains a good theme for a story, despite Murray Leinster's classic "First Contact." The possibilities for conflict remain largely open to any writer. This contact can occur on Earth when aliens find us, in the middle of space between two ships, or on any planet where man may go. And each has its own variations.

In the fourth period of science fiction, a number

of new ideas from the speculations of scientists gave even more fictional possibilities for stories. Black holes could do almost anything, fictionally, from providing unlimited power to serving as shortcuts to the stars. Tachyons—the purely theoretical particles that can only travel faster than light—were the latest justification for instant communication and star travel. The Bussard ram-jet, by taking the needed fuel directly from space, could not exceed the velocity of light—but it made a very close approach at least possible; and at such speeds, the rate of time within the ship would be slowed to the point where a man could make the trip between stars without dying of old age on the way. The Dyson sphere—a huge world built around its sun like a shell in the orbit of Earth—offered a new kind of world to explore.

Politics entered into the future where star travel was common, of course. With a number of worlds dealing together, the problems of governing and policing all of them became important. The idea of an empire of stars —later a Galactic Empire of all the stars in our galaxy— grew quickly. Isaac Asimov took that as his starting point to show the results of the breakup of such an empire, along the lines of the breakup of the Roman Empire.

Sociological stories were very much in vogue during the fifties—and many of those deserved the name only by charity; too often, they involved some other world in which some small culture from Earth's history (sometimes with minor variations) was planetwide. There have been some serious attempts, fortunately still appearing, to examine what an alien culture might really be like, however.

And space travel gave an opportunity for all kinds of "cosmic" theorizing. Every new idea of science about the origin or death of the universe tended to get stories written about it. Few of them are still read, though some were good fun at the time.

Almost as popular as space travel was the idea of traveling through time. It was done in every possible way, from suspended animation—which could only go to the future—to the machine that could go everywhen. One of the advantages of time, for the writer, was that nobody really seems to know anything about it. Einstein had treated it as *a* fourth dimension; as a result, every bit of nonsense about *the* Fourth Dimension (supposedly at right angles to the other three) was tossed off as if it were scientifically valid.

In the early days, many of these stories used many ingenious ways to get someone into the future or the past. (It took quite a while before the idea of a story simply laid in such times could be accepted by all writers, just as it took time for writers to realize that a hero could exist on another world, without having to be carried there somehow.) Some stories were interested in the seeming paradoxes of time travel. (If you know what caused your death, you should be able to avoid it. Or suppose you accidentally kill yourself in the past—what happens? Usually, it's your grandfather you kill—but that has too many possibilities for cheating on someone's part.)

Then, in "Sidewise in Time," Murray Leinster introduced (at least to the magazines) the idea that there might be other directions than straight back or straight ahead. There might be other Earths where time is somewhat different. Each event in the past that had more than one possible outcome caused time to divide to follow both, and all such worlds might now lie across time from each other. This branching of time led to other stories. (If you go back and show Newton how to use a slit instead of a hole to study light, he'll discover the elements by their patterns. Science gets a huge jump, and the world changes. You go with that world; but the old world stays—though you can't get back to it. Now go back and take the slit away before he discovers Fraunhofer lines—and you're in a third world.) William Sell did an excellent example—"Other Tracks"—for his single science-fiction story.

H. Beam Piper built a series of stories around his "paratime," which essentially dealt with branched time. In his stories, however, all these worlds shaded gradually across infinite possibilities, those close together being almost alike, those farther apart being vastly different. And he had one race that was exploiting all the worlds. His stories remain some of the best and most complicated examples of the idea of many time tracks together.

At one time, also, the idea of "the Fourth Dimension"—or Fifth, or Sixth—was used for numerous adventure stories. The device was really just trimmings to get the hero onto some other world where he could get involved in all kinds of strange incidents. This seems to have pretty much vanished from the scene.

There were also a few other forms of travel used by science fiction writers. In a few stories, men managed to travel out into the greater macrocosm—to burst this universe which is only an atom in a larger one and venture beyond. (Most writers in the early days seemed to believe that an atom looked somewhat like a planetary system.) Other stories dealt with the microcosm. A few shrank their heroes small enough to enter into other human bodies—as was done in a fairly successful movie or so—or even to such tiny size that they could land on a world within the atom. Ray Cummings' early *The Girl in the Golden Atom* remains the classic example of this plotting device. But most readers today are too sophisticated for such ideas.

Dooms of various sorts were always fairly common in science fiction stories. Unlike most category fiction, this field did not demand a happy ending every time, so the doom could be averted or not, according to the wish of the writer and his ability to make his ending somehow interesting.

The amount of suffering undergone by humanity and

the Earth in science fiction makes history look like a study for Pollyanna. The human race has been wiped out—or threatened and nearly wiped out until the end—by plagues that have no cure, by invasions of giant insects (though more often in the movies than in the magazines), by being destroyed by the machines, by mutated plants, by the return of the ice age, and by monsters from the laboratories. Now it is subject to doom from the use of microwaves and from radiation—either by melt-downs in atomic plants or the slow accumulation of wastes from those plants.

After World War II, the atom became the chief source of doom. When it didn't wipe out the race directly in war, as in Nevil Shute's *On the Beach* (which made far too light of the atmospheric barrier between the Northern and Southern hemispheres), it produced mutations in the human germ plasm, so that all children were born as monsters. In a few bad stories, grown humans somehow mutated, despite the fact that that's scientifically ridiculous.

Many others placed this doom somewhere in the background, and the stories dealt with Our Barbarous Descendants—a type of story so common as to justify its own classification. This showed humanity pretty much going back to primitive life, often with only a few people left eking out a precarious living in a world turned horrible. In a more subtle form, this post-catastrophe story continues to be written. The idea of man knocked loose from his civilization and forced to begin again seems to prove interesting. One of the better novels of this type is Leigh Brackett's *The Long Tomorrow*.

Earth itself was endangered often. The sun went out—or it went nova, burning the fuel of millennia in 24 hours. Comets also jostled it from its orbit or broke it in half. There was even a novel in which a hole in the ocean drained off all the water, leaving none to fall as rain. (Where the water went when it ran through the hole in the ocean wasn't told.) Other planets came hurtling out of space to take up our orbit. Men used up the material from the planet over the ages to power their rockets, until almost nothing was left. Anything could happen. In a few stories, the entire universe collapsed.

There was also war as a source of doom. We were constantly being invaded—and often taken over—by aliens. Our colonies on the planets or around other stars grew too big for us and rebelled when we would not grant their freedom. Dictatorships gained a hold over all Earth, and bitter revolutions had to be fought. A final war left no victors. And even our machines either stopped working or actually began attacking us.

Some of the doom stories are still quite popular. A few writers have taken science fiction ideas and managed to sell them to the mainstream audience, such as *Lucifer's Hammer*, by Larry Niven and Jerry Pournelle, both established science fiction writers. This proves that the old menace of cometary collision hasn't yet been exhausted or made impossible by science.

More happily, immortality is offered to humanity in a few stories. It never became a common theme, but fiction dealing with the subject appeared now and then through the years. Occasionally, some other race that has gained it is mentioned in a story that does not basically deal with it. Most stories that deal directly with the subject limit themselves in their view of a world which has such a gift—probably because simple immortality may be a strong wish, but it makes for a rather dull piece of fiction.

The problem of a man attempting to gain it, either from someone selling it at a hopelessly high price, or from a society which confers it only on some merit, has been done several times. Other possibilities are suggested by stories that deal with someone who finds himself losing his supposed immortality, or problems connected with the means of achieving it. R. DeWitt Miller's "The Master Shall Not Die" tells of one man given (relative) immortality at the cost of killing another man each time he must renew himself—and the ethical problems he must confront; this remains one of my favorite short stories of science fiction.

Longevity is fairly common as an assumption in science fiction, though usually not the central idea of the story in which it appears. An exception is Robert A. Heinlein's *Methuselah's Children*, in which extreme longevity is gained by having the right ancestors and careful breeding for it; but there must have been something more, since the hero, Lazarus Long, came early in the experiment and has far outlived anyone else. In other stories, longevity is renewed by some mechanical device or drug which periodically restores youth, with greater or lesser success.

Superman is another theme which does not occur too frequently in stories. But it remains one of the strongest themes in its interest for many readers. The difficulty with a story of a truly superior being is that any attempt to describe his way of thinking must be limited by the non-super ability of the writer. A. E. Van Vogt overcame this in *Slan*—or in the early part of the novel, at least—by making his superman an immature boy who had not yet attained full powers. Norvell W. Page, in *But Without Horns*, never showed his superman; instead, his superior but still purely human detective is constantly foiled, until in the end he goes into a room where the superman sits—and we see the effects on him afterward.

Strangely, most supermen in science fiction turn out to be failures. Odd John, in Olaf Stapledon's novel, is more believable than most supermen, but he first is forced to retreat to a private place and then gives up. Stanley G. Weinbaum's hero in *The New Adam* is a rather helpless failure. It would seem that a true superman, if such there might be, should at least be able to cope with the world a bit better than normal man and have some survival value; but that too rarely happens.

Other stories have approached the superman idea somewhat at an angle, attempting to show an increase in mental power by having several brains coupled together, or by adding some type of auxiliary mechanical device to a human being. A few temporary "supermen" have appeared as the result of some wonder drug. But these devices do not fascinate the reader nearly as much as any story dealing with a being who has supposedly made the next jump in evolution beyond man.

Biology is obviously a rich source for science fiction ideas—or at least should be. Evolution has often been the basis for a story—usually some forced evolution, since fiction has no time for generations. H. G. Wells' *Island of Dr. Moreau* is an early example of biological tinkering. Several stories have dealt with adapting man to live in the ocean as a water breather, or reshaping him to live on worlds normally uninhabitable. A few stories have even found ways for women to reproduce and create societies without men.

Recently, the transplanting of organs has led to a number of stories in which spare parts are "banked," and Larry Niven has dealt with the black market in such repair parts. Cybernetics has been added to the mix, producing cyborgs that have many organs replaced with nonliving parts. And cloning has enjoyed a rash of popularity in a number of books and shorter works. An outstanding novelette was Ursula K. Le Guin's "Nine Lives," which explored what it might mean to be one of many clones, all with the identical genetic makeup.

Curiously, very little has been done in science fiction with the possibilities made available through an understanding of DNA and recombinant cell manipulation. Lester del Rey covered some options in his *The Eleventh Commandment*, back in 1962. Since then, aside from the use of cloning, few have made use of the new knowledge as a source for stories.

Robots (and, to a lesser extent, androids) have always been popular in science fiction and each year brings out new stories about them. Originally, the robot was conceived of as a sort of clumsy helper to man. Often in the very early days, the robot was a danger to humanity. But by the end of the first period, this began to change. Clifford D. Simak and Lester del Rey treated their robots as loyal friends of humanity—rather better in some ways, in fact, than man; Isaac Asimov propounded his three laws of robotics, guaranteed to save man from harm. And through most of the magazine period, robots have been objects of affection, rather than fearful creatures. A robot growing old and incapable of functioning can arouse pity in the reader as quickly as a human could. And in a number of stories, mankind perishes to leave the robots behind as his true children—with no feeling of loss.

A few writers have tried to show the robots as being the equivalent of slaves or the objects of discrimination; but such transparent attempts to adapt mainstream themes to science fiction seldom succeed well. This type of story somehow does succeed better when androids replace robots; the fact that androids are created of flesh and blood—grown in breeding vats, perhaps—apparently makes them more suitable for human prejudice.

Teleportation or matter transmission is another theme that has provided a fair number of stories. Some of the possibilities seem obvious. If a man is sent from Earth to Mars by matter transmittal but fails to arrive —well, the insurance companies and his heirs are going to have considerable legal hassle. If he arrives on both the stations at Mars and Venus—that's worse; what do you do with two of him, both correctly claiming his wife, house, kids and job? You can't kill one of him— because that's still murder. Probably such teleportation was originally simply a device to get the man somewhere faster than a spaceship might carry him, but its possibilities invite many other stories, and have been used for quite a few. Matter duplication also has another possibility. A man who is fortunate enough to have a bottle of 1961 Mouton Rothschild in the year 2000 might find it hard to get others; but put it through the right hookup on a duplicator, and he can have cases of the wine. (This is assuming, as such stories do, that the energy required isn't impossible.) Pretty soon, everything is duplicated, from food to cars. And what happens to the economy? A number of stories have had fun with that idea.

Recently, there has been a sudden spate of novels based on a variation on the matter transmitter. This is something called, more or less, a star gate. Usually, star gates are simply found on various worlds (with hints or statements that they were built by some previous race). They offer instant passage to other worlds. Sometimes they take you where they're set; others have no known key, but send you to an unknown destination. C. J. Cherryh's *The Gates of Ivrel*, her first novel, offers a complex situation based on such a star gate.

The appearance of the device frankly puzzles me. It suddenly popped up in several novels whose galleys I read for review, apparently independently in each case. The idea wasn't new, but the sudden rash of books on that theme was surprising. Apparently, when it's star-gate time, you star gate. Anyhow, it's a good idea for stories, and its possibilities haven't begun to be exhausted, so more writers will probably use it.

Nothing is impossible as a theme for science fiction, so far as I can determine, although some ideas must be handled more carefully than others. (This was true for sex for a long time, when overt sex was usually not wanted. Yet science fiction often used such ideas as concubinage, group marriage, short-term marriages, colonies where one man must fertilize several women, etc.) Most of the taboos of the normal pulps could be transcended safely, if carefully.

But religion would seem to be the roughest subject to adapt to science fiction. Yet a number of stories not only involved religion and God directly, but some were published in the magazines with considerable success. The best known is probably *A Case of Conscience*, by James Blish, dealing with a situation where a priest must accept the heresy that Satan is creative. Clifford D. Simak had "The Creator" in a small magazine in the early thirties. And Lester del Rey's "For I Am a Jealous People" deals with the God of the Old Testament who has betrayed mankind's ancient covenant and is leading a war against Earth—with man about to defeat Him. This was not in a magazine, but its appearance in *Star Short Novels* brought no outpouring of indignation against the writer.

A fairly large number of early stories used myths as the basis for showing that the former gods and devils were simply spacemen or time travelers. Later, pseudo-religions based on science became common in stories. It is also often assumed that the Christian religion will disappear sometime in the future to be replaced by some other belief, though that isn't the basic theme of such stories. In fact, about the only novel I can remember which uses a future Christianity little changed from the present is Walter M. Miller, Jr.'s *A Canticle for Leibowitz*—which perhaps makes up with its success for the lack of others.

Currently, however, the interest in using religion in any form as a basis for science fiction seems to have abated.

In fact, in the present science fiction market, the chief subject seems to be psi—or usually, some form of telepathy with perhaps other extrasensory powers. This began to be a major theme shortly after the end of World War II and its place in science fiction has been increasing steadily since. I haven't kept accurate count, but my guess is that nearly half of the novels of science fiction I read today have at least some aspect of psi woven into their basic structure. To a great many writers, it has replaced all the science and gadgetry of the older stories, and often at considerable savings in study and thought. (There are exceptions, like Marion Zimmer Bradley, who work out their psi mechanism with as much detail as any writer ever worked out his means of getting to the stars, but they are all too few.)

Certainly adventures on some other planet and the possibilities of psi dominate the field today, often combined.

CHAPTER 33

Utopias and Dystopias

I'M NOT CONVINCED that the books to be covered briefly here have any place in science fiction, other than perhaps historically. Yet they have so often been classed with science fiction that it would be hard not to give some attention to them.

Utopia (which comes from Greek roots, meaning "far country") was the title of a tract written by Sir Thomas More in Latin in 1516, and later translated into English in 1551. It became sufficiently popular that the name was later given to all books of somewhat similar nature. (Perhaps there was some confusion with the roots that would have resulted in Eutopia—"beautiful or good country.")

More began with a diatribe (in dialogue form) against the ways of the culture around him; and since there were more than enough grievances to be found against sixteenth-century England, it was probably appreciated by many at the time. But it is the second section that has insured a measure of lasting appeal for the work. In this, More described a country where everything was just as he thought a reasonable paradise on Earth should be. It seems pretty naïve today, of course. I doubt that any modern man would find it at all to his liking, were he to try living thus; probably even More's contemporaries would have hated it. But on paper, it was attractive.

It wasn't by any means the first utopian writing. Probably Plato's *Republic* would qualify for that honor, at least out of what has survived. (It was, of course, a perfect model for a fascist state. But like most "model" cultures, Plato was setting it up to overcome what was wrong with his own society, not seeing the pitfalls of his creation. It was meant as an ideal, at least.)

After More, there were many other attempts to show how men might live in some ideal society. In America, the first was probably the anonymous *Equality; or a History of Lithconia* (1802), which has its moments of humor for modern readers. Next was a much better example, Mary Griffith's *Three Hundred Years Hence* (1836), which is still of historical interest in terms of the development of later real movements. In it, the machines are supposed to bring about the end of slavery, to put an end to the drinking of alcohol and to free women from their subservient roles. (Both of these books were republished by Prime Press in the late forties.)

The best known of the American utopias is *Looking Backward, 2000–1887*, by Edward Bellamy (1888). This also presents a world where the machine is supposed to have ended all evils. A visitor to the year 2000 is shown all the wonders (many fairly good predictions of technical developments) and is lectured in long diatribes on the wonderful virtues of the socialist state that has now reached perfection. The book was reissued in paperback form a few years ago and seemed to enjoy a fair sale; I can't quite see why, having been bored by it when I was still young and willing to read almost anything.

The closest thing to a true science fiction utopia is perhaps Hugo Gernsback's *Ralph 124C41+*, which is about a world where the machines seem themselves to constitute the utopia. Since Gernsback's idea of utopia was that of a technological-minded hobbyist, it wasn't surprising that his hobbyist readers loved it and that it was considered a landmark in science fiction; as prediction, it may well have justified their admiration, since it has never been equaled, despite the incredibly clumsy writing.

H. G. Wells has often been referred to as a writer of scientific utopias, but that is hardly valid on careful analysis. He did have a vision of a desirable socialist-type state, but in almost all his novels this is clouded by his pessimism about mankind's ability to make anything but a mess of its future. In the one pure utopia Wells tried, he was perhaps more successful than most in maintaining interest, however, probably because he worked hard to avoid having a totally static culture. This book, *A Modern Utopia* (1905), deals with a small group who are transported to a world purportedly far in space (but to be taken as in the future, surely) in which man has largely learned to control himself, destroy disease and pests, stabilize population, and achieve happy moderation. But even here, Wells' pessimism comes through in the end. It is discovered that the "tourists," unable to adapt to such perfection, are poisoning the ideal world, and the hero is sent back to his own world finally, albeit freed from most of his ills. It is the easiest of utopias to read; Wells was, after all, an excellent craftsman, and he was aware of the difficulties he faced in trying to make such a world interesting.

The chief difficulty with most such accounts is that they deal with totally static societies. Perfection has been achieved; hence, change is not needed. As it is now, so it will ever be. That makes for darned little plot; at best, we usually get a conducted tour for diversion.

Another difficulty is the dreadful preachiness all too common.

Utopias are not meant for entertainment. They are works of propaganda. The writer is saying to the reader: "See, I know how things should be. I've got it all figured out. Now just relax and I'll show you how great things would be if you just had enough brains to leave things up to me and become disciples." It never seems to occur to most of the planners that the great schemes of the past usually turn out to be the snares that gum up the future by catching the very men who believe in their perfection.

And of course this idea of achieving perfection by building a state which will never change is totally antithetical to the basic drive of science fiction—the acceptance that change is the one constant.

Perhaps fortunately, utopias are becoming less frequent in our literature.

Dystopias are the opposite of utopias in spirit— though there is considerable similarity in motivation and inner form. (It's from the Greek roots for "bad country.") A first-class dystopia is as barren of possibility for real change as is the usual utopia, simply because the evil that afflicts it has gone too far for human power to remedy.

On the other hand, a dystopia can have considerable conflict and plot development; the few characters who are not completely cowed into abject submission to things as they are can struggle through episode after episode, up to their eyebrows in trouble. But, of course, they haven't a chance. The ending is written out before the first struggle begins.

In a way, Jeremiah may have been responsible for this type of denunciation, though it probably preceded him. He didn't exactly set up a future or distant country to show how bad things could be. Instead, he told his listeners directly that all this evil was going to get them personally if they didn't mend their ways and return to the virtues of their fathers. But the intent was the same.

H. G. Wells' *The Time Machine* (1895) is something of a dystopia of the far future. "If this goes on, we're going to wind up with our workers shut off from all that is good and turned into ugly Morlocks; and our leisure class will become Eloi—and then watch out!" But the vision of the farther future, despite its gloom, rather removes it from the realm of standard dystopia; in the end, none of it is going to matter as the sun cools.

E. M. Forster's *The Machine Stops* is a better example from a few years later (1909). Its vision of life crowded into subterranean cells with each human isolated from others—except by television—and the machines that do everything is a grim forecast of certain trends extended into the future. Unlike most, it isn't just unrelieved gloom, however; the machines stop working, producing a far worse fate than the life shown before.

Probably the dystopia most closely associated with science fiction is Aldous Huxley's *Brave New World* (1932). This presents a rigid society of the future, with every human categorized into one of five classes from which he cannot escape, babies removed from their parents by being raised in state incubators and creches, and the only relief coming from mind-numbing euphoric drugs—except that each has the final release of euthanasia.

Strangely, most of the science fiction readers apparently misread the message. To many of them, this was a vision of some of the *wonders* of the future—

babies born without pain, drugs to ease all worries, gadgets and machines to take care of most needs.

George Orwell's *1984* cannot be misread as to intent. Orwell's future is a world where an absolute dictator controls everything through his brutal agents, with absolutely no regard for the good of the people. Even thoughts are controlled, and language is designed to misinform. This is an almost purely political dystopia, with little gadgetry added to what we had at the time of its writing. Probably that helped make it available to most readers, who were willing to accept it in the light of what they had read about the methods of Hitler and Stalin.

Of course, the trouble with Orwell's forecast was that most of it had already happened, and the future might well hold slightly less of such fate than had the immediate past. At most, it was a simple exaggeration of techniques used previously. Still, many seemed to find it frightening and prophetic.

One of the few dystopias produced by a science fiction writer with science fiction techniques is *Make Room! Make Room!*, by Harry Harrison. This 1966 novel deals with a world at the turn of the next century where overpopulation has destroyed all real civilization. Men kill for a little food, shelter is a rare value, and the streets teem with hordes of hopeless, desperate people. Harrison plays on every possibility to produce about the grimmest world of all future visions. It remains an unusually effective novel, despite what the movie *Soylent Green* did to it.

Then there are the more satirical novels of Stanton A. Coblentz, Frederik Pohl and C. M. Kornbluth, and Kurt Vonnegut, Jr. These are sometimes classed as dystopias. (And perhaps Vonnegut's *Player Piano* of 1952 merits the category.) But most of such books begin to blend back into more general literature or science fiction.

The motive that shows through from dystopias is

not greatly different from that of the writers of utopias. The books carry the message from the writer: "Look, you stupid idiots. I'm warning you! Unlike you, I can see where all the wrong things you are doing will lead you—and here is where! Listen to me and beware. Maybe I don't have any answers for what you should do, unlike the boys who write utopias—but you'd better stop what you are doing."

Sometimes, of course, the things that should be done to prevent the doom are obvious, as in the case of overpopulation. But nobody knows how to apply them. The dystopian writer can't be bothered figuring that out, but simply delivers his jeremiad. The true science fiction writer would be trying out methods fictionally, instead of ranting.

Again, the dystopia hasn't much to do with science fiction, usually. It's propaganda, not really fiction, meant to frighten into making changes, not to entertain. When it is fiction, it can be more entertaining than utopias—but with only the obvious ending. And it is essentially denying of the continued change that science fiction considers basic.

In most critical circles, both utopias and dystopias are considered far more worthy of respect as literature than is science fiction. Having read a fair amount of them, I can only wonder why.

CHAPTER 34

But What Good Is It?

FOR MANY YEARS, whenever my interest in science fiction was made obvious to someone engaged in teaching or pursuing "serious" literature, there was a fair chance that I would be asked, "But what good is that stuff, after all?" And the smile that went with the question indicated there was no point to be gained by any answer. (In a surprising number of other cases, however, I discovered a fellow reader.)

I tried asking what good regular fiction was, and usually was told that it taught us about real life. I've never been convinced that Thomas Hardy, Franz Kafka or many others studied in school had much to teach about life as we know it. I'm not sure enough that most of the thoughts in the minds of the characters I read show any reality—particularly when I find that the writers have never experienced similar events. But those points are not taken well by many in the humanities.

What disturbs me more is the whole concept of purpose as applied to any literature. To the Marxists, intent upon subordinating everything to the good of the state, the arts must serve a direct purpose in life—usually propaganda, I'm afraid. But why people in this country accept such Marxist ideas is a puzzle. (Ursula K. Le Guin objected to my reference to such "Marxist" ideas, once, stating that Marx was never responsible for such an idea of purpose in the arts. But, of course, that has no bearing; Marx was not a Marxist, any more than Christ was a Christian—it was their followers who became Marxists and Christians. And the followers of Marx did propound the theory of necessary social purpose to the arts very seriously.)

If fiction has any major function, that function is to entertain the reader. All other functions are better served by nonfiction, or sometimes by poetry, which can present beauty of expression and, ideally, lucidity at more than one level of meaning. For understanding of life—meaning always people, since the humanities rarely consider animals other than man—there are excellent case histories, memoirs, letters, etc., of real people, both humble and great. The insights that can be gained into other people must surely be the better for not being filtered through the view of a writer who has not experienced their lives. For instruction, there can be no comparison.

Certainly the purpose of science fiction has always been to entertain, and while it can only entertain a certain portion of the public, that is true of most other fiction. It is true that a few writers recently claim they intend some purpose in writing fiction other than entertainment; but their publishers, seeking a profit, still try to sell those books to entertain, and a vast majority of readers buy books and magazines for that purpose.

Why "mere" entertainment value in fiction should be denigrated is something I cannot understand. Chess is respected, though it certainly serves no purpose beyond the intellectual—perhaps—entertainment of the players and spectators. Sports are accepted in most major colleges—yet they are hardly more than entertainment. (And when the injuries are counted against the dubious physical benefits, better health is hardly the purpose. Nor is the development of sportsmanship, from what I have seen of the anything-to-win spirit of college and professional sports.)

The most priceless off-time occupation for the intellectual is discussion. But try to prove that most of that is more than "mere" entertainment. Usually nothing is accomplished, other than the pleasure—entertainment—derived from such talking; it really isn't much different in purpose from the chattering of Kipling's Bandar-log.

However, as has gradually become evident, science fiction does serve a number of purposes, beyond that of entertainment, some of them quite well. Probably more than 90 percent of the readers get little benefit from such service—but again, that is true of most things in life.

For one thing, science fiction seems to win more youngsters and young adults to the ease and enjoyment of reading than any other form of literature. This has been my own considerable experience from giving away books and from talking with youngsters in various schools at which I appeared. I've heard the same thing from teachers and from librarians when I've attended their meetings. And I've received numerous letters from younger people who claim rarely to have opened a book voluntarily until they discovered science fiction, but who now read whenever they can—"even some of those good books!"

Certainly, at a time when the teachers are finding it harder and harder to interest youngsters in reading and when remedial-reading courses seem to be taking over the school system, this is no small service.

For several decades, science fiction also served to turn many young men and women toward science. A number of my friends went into the sciences because of interest aroused by reading science fiction. A far larger number of working scientists whom I met later told me that science fiction had stimulated them to work for a science or engineering degree, even though that had not been their first intent. At a time when the sciences are becoming more crucial to the success of our nation and culture, this must be counted on the plus side of the ledger.

However, this is somewhat less true today than it used to be. Science fiction is less technological in its orientation; fewer stories try to show real science. But somehow, the stimulus is still there to a large degree.

Of course, much of the science in science fiction was hokum; some was totally wrong. Somehow, that didn't seem to matter. Once interest was aroused, the readers usually went on to discover the facts for themselves. And beneath all the surface trickery of science fiction, there was a general respect for science and some appreciation of its methodology, which is probably more important than the facts that can be found in a handbook.

Certainly there is more correlation between science fiction and real science than might at first be supposed. The evidence for this comes from the high percentage of real scientists who either read science fiction or have read it extensively in the past. I was once placed on a panel of fairly well-known scientists to deal with questions from a technically trained audience. When the moderator asked for my qualifications and learned I wrote science fiction, he winked at me. Only one man on the panel turned to stare. And not one member of the audience made any disparaging remark at my presence, though I probably took more than my part in the ensuing arguments.

Science fiction has also served in a number of classes as a teaching aid. These were usually not literature classes, but courses in economics, history, various technologies, social sciences, etc. The teachers find that introducing examples for discussion from such an outside source is highly stimulating toward a fresh insight. The students learn more and do more thinking for themselves, according to what teachers have told me.

In one respect, science fiction serves a unique function.

C. P. Snow, the British scientist and novelist, has proposed that our culture really consists of two cultures. One of these deals with the humanities and some social sciences, as well as the arts. The other deals with the science and technology of our civilization. And to a very large degree, the two cultures do not converse, cannot comprehend each other's world, and are out of touch with values outside their own spheres.

Most literature is directed to the humanities culture. In book after book, aside from the mention of a gadget such as television now and then, the modern world of science and the scientific insights do not exist. Such literature might also have been written back a hundred years ago, except for slight changes in the moral values and jargon. A whole half of the modern world never impinges upon the reader.

On the other hand, the science culture reader finds such books so out of step with the world he sees and the way he thinks about it that he finds little interest in them. He tends more and more to restrict his reading to his own field. And hence we have two cultures, neither more than half aware of life—the subject supposedly revealed in fiction.

Science fiction, for those who can enjoy it, serves as a link between cultures. The scientist may snort at a story dealing with his own field—or write a letter correcting it. But he finds the *Weltanschauung* sufficiently familiar to his own that he can enjoy many of the stories, even when their basic development owes more to the humanities than to science. The humanities man may be somewhat put off at first by the outlook, but the elements are mostly familiar; people involved in difficulties and working out interpersonal problems are still things he can understand, even when he finds them a bit less developed than he might like; and bit by bit, he learns to accept the outlook that seems more natural to the scientist. The younger reader of science fiction, not yet firmly fixed in either culture, absorbs both from his reading; thereafter, neither culture can be quite so strange to him, unless later college training teaches him carefully to disregard one of them.

Within the past decade, a further and perhaps more important purpose to science fiction has appeared. (Obviously, this purpose was not in the minds of the writers before that. It was not the purpose intended, but merely one that had been operating all along unbeknownst to them. It is somewhat like wire, which was never designed back in history to carry electricity; the wire-drawing technique was designed for another purpose. Nevertheless, certainly one of the valid purposes of some wire is the carrying of electricity.)

Alvin Toffler brought the situation to public attention in his book *Future Shock* (1970). The basis of the book was the idea that we not only face change from decade to decade now—where once any degree of change took centuries to be obvious—but that this change is itself accelerating. Thus after the invention of the vacuum tube, an engineer could keep up easily with advances between 1925 until about 1950. Tubes did everything electronic for twenty-five years, and the use of the tube manual and load line was dependable. Then came transistors, requiring a radical change in his thinking. (Some men found the change difficult to make, indeed.) Transistors didn't operate in the same manner, though they accomplished approximately the same thing.

But once he learned to use transistors, he should have been good for another 25 years, at least, shouldn't he? Didn't work that way. By 1965—only 15 years later—the integrated circuit chip began replacing simple transistors. That was made up of from half a dozen to several hundred transistors, all in a transistor-sized device. And these were specialized devices. Even the simple operational amp type of IC required special understanding. Well, after 40 years, he has probably retired before his inflexibility hits another problem. But his son may be working on computers. And those IC devices are already changing every five years or less.

At one time, a man who had learned his profession could depend upon it throughout his life. Now he may have to relearn his job a dozen times before his career is over. And things promise to become worse. Each new development speeds up the process of speeding up new developments to speed up . . .

The old stability is rapidly vanishing. And men who cannot change are going to be in trouble. It's already creating psychological havoc in many areas, and will reach far more in the future.

The future is no longer even roughly fixed. A new future may arrive tomorrow—and the next day may be still different.

Here, apparently, science fiction serves as a sort of play model for reality. The reader of science fiction learns to cope with a new environment, a new future —even a new way of looking at reality in many cases— every time he turns to a new story; every story tends to develop its own future and world outlook.

Of course such vicarious experience of what are really make-believe situations cannot overcome the problems of facing a real changing future. But it seems that many of the mental attitudes needed to adapt to change are not unlike those in adapting to new stories. The principle is similar to children playing grown-up roles to learn to be grown up, or kittens staging mock hunts to get ready for real hunting.

It seems to work. At least, among science fiction fans, the discussion of new challenges seems to involve more enthusiasm than dread, while the contrary is often true in other groups. This is particularly noticeable among older readers of science fiction, where the tendency to become set in a pattern should be greater. (Of course it could be that science fiction appeals to readers who have more flexible minds to begin with. I cannot rule out that possibility. But I've known men who seem to be extremely flexible in their attitudes toward their own jobs, indicating that they can adapt, but who are as set about the future as most others and just as subject to shock when it deviates from their expectations.)

Science fiction has always been future-oriented, and that habit of thinking beyond today cannot but help in a world which is itself becoming more future-centered. The field is unique in literature in that respect, too. Almost all other fiction is at least partly past-oriented, as well as being chiefly concerned with the vanishing present.

To some extent, science fiction has helped to prepare the world at large for some of the coming events. Science fiction readers were looking forward to space long before we got there. Some of the best early writings on the subject were found in the factual articles in the science fiction magazines. Even a small, vocal minority, if it is as vocal as many science fiction readers, can help to change attitudes. When that minority is also by far the best informed from its regular reading, its influence can be quite large.

While no proof exists, I believe science fiction helped to combat some of the prejudice that existed when the magazines first began. The stories, during the first few years, were probably as prejudiced as most other popular fiction. But as the writers began expanding to other worlds and other races, many of these prejudices disappeared; small differences in form—black or white, male or female—began to seem less important when writing about truly alien beings.

There was some prejudice shown by a few fans and writers, but far less than normal by 1950. And long before general literature accepted the notion of true equality, the better science fiction writers were quietly taking it for granted—or at least trying to. Some of that acceptance of human beings without asking what form must have been communicated to the younger readers.

Certainly Heinlein and some other writers wanted to communicate it in their teenage books.

Some of these claims of value are less strong than might be needed to demonstrate any true good from science fiction. Some are less capable of proof than I'd like, though they seem valid to me and to many others who read science fiction.

But if even some of these values of science fiction are genuine, I think it is the rest of fiction that must prove its purpose—because most other fiction has far less justification. (That one about learning about life isn't an advantage against science fiction; somehow, a lot of readers seem able to learn more about life from science fiction than they do from the books they read only with reluctance in school. Any reading helps somewhat, and more is better, up to quite a heavy schedule.)

Nevertheless, the essential purpose of science fiction remains that of providing entertainment for readers who are unable to find it in equal measure in other literature.

Science fiction can present almost any type of story in almost any sort of environment. It's the last bastion of real adventure, one of the few challenges to the dreams of young readers, and a source of food for imagination, which is usually considered a good thing. It's also one of the few places where many of the old, traditional values tend to be preserved. In science fiction—on the average, though certainly not in all stories—it's better to be competent than not, better to try than to give up, better to be of goodwill than otherwise. Rewards still tend to go to those who earn them. And respect for all intelligent beings is held up as a virtue. These values certainly cannot harm either the young or old; and to the surprise of some, the younger readers seem happy to find them.

Try that on most other literature being produced today!

And then, if you want to find the purpose of science

fiction for yourself, try a few books: skim those that give no pleasure, and enjoy the others.

Or accept the fact—which is easily proved—that science fiction is read by a large segment of that part of our population that reads by choice; and that a good percentage of those readers are respected members of most professions, many with quite high degrees. Surely there has to be some good reason for them to make such a choice.

But all this is simply justification, of course. And during more than fifty years of vigorous growth and survival, science fiction has justified itself.

CHAPTER 35

Mene, Mene, Tekel . . .

I KNOW OF NO FIELD of literature which is now given as much discussion in print as science fiction. And certainly few fields have been so carelessly treated. Reviews of the books abound at all levels. For a long time, there was little true criticism, but recently that has changed radically, if not entirely for the good.

Let me separate reviewing and criticism at once. Reviewing is the process of providing a potential reader with some information to guide him about the nature of a book and an evaluation by the reviewer as to whether the book is worth buying. Criticism is the careful examination of a work to determine its value within its intents (so far as is apparent), to try to find why it succeeds or fails, and to further evaluate it within the body of the type of literature it represents. Good criticism seeks further insights. It is essentially designed to reach those who have already read the work.

Reviews of science fiction now appear in all sorts of publications. Most newspapers carry some reviews of such books, though few seem to demand any familiarity with this field of literature from their reviewers. Too often, I see reviews that are little more than summaries of material on the dust-jacket or back cover of the book.

The magazines in the field have long carried reviews, usually by regular reviewers who are established writers in the field, such as P. Schuyler Miller, Damon Knight, A. J. Budrys, Groff Conklin (an anthologist, not a writer), Lester del Rey, and Anthony Boucher. The chief trouble with such reviews, aside from some tendency on the part of many reviewers to like everything, has been that publication schedules keep them from appearing until most of the books are off sale—which rather ruins the value of reviews.

Several journals review the books primarily for the guidance of libraries. In these, the quality of the review depends upon the person selected to do the reviewing —and I find little system in most such choices. There is also *Publishers Weekly*, where the short reviews are often done quite well; but there the guidance is mostly for booksellers, rather than book buyers.

Then there is a host of reviews which appear in uncounted fan magazines. A few of those who review in these journals are highly knowledgeable and capable reviewers; at their best, the fan reviews can be very good. But in most cases, youthful enthusiasm is no substitute for knowledge. Books get judged by current fads, according to what may impress other fans, by the personal and unstated hobbies of the readers, and even according to which publishing house issues the work. Frequently they seem to be evaluated from misunderstanding. Yet at their worst, fan reviews probably average about as good as those in newspapers and some professional journals, perhaps because the fans do at least read before they review.

Criticism is much rarer. For a long time, there was almost none to be found. Only rarely would some magazine like *Harper's* or the *Atlantic* run a short article attempting to make some broad criticism of the field. It was almost always done from limited knowledge and on the apparent assumption that if science fiction wasn't like some other type of fiction the "critic" liked, it was not worth bothering with. Even such a generally admirable and thoughtful man as Bernard DeVoto demonstrated that he was writing about a field without taking the time to learn about it—something he would never have done in the case of most other literature.

In a few instances, individual books were given a measure of thoughtful attention. The result of the criticism itself might be good; but usually, the conclusion seemed to be that this book was not science fiction *because* it was worth reading.

This situation began changing in the mid-fifties, though I'm not sure it was much for the better. More attention was paid to science fiction books, but usually without more than a superficial acquaintance with the body of work in the field. (Can one really evaluate the work of any single story by a Russian writer without some knowledge of what was common to most of them? Or could a mystery story be given adequate criticism without an understanding of the conventions of the mystery story?)

Kingsley Amis wrote a book on science fiction entitled *New Maps of Hell* (1960), which received some attention. It was a survey of the field with some critical pretensions. Amis was an accepted writer of other types of fiction, and quite surely must have known his own field well. But his thesis seemed to be that science fiction dealt properly only with doom and nightmares. (This was an idea to be picked up later by a number of others.) The rather limited research and choice of examples used to prove the thesis would have been amusing, except that the book was eagerly accepted by many in the field because it was a genuine book about science fiction—and by those outside the field through careless ignorance.

Recently new books analyzing science fiction have been appearing fairly frequently, and articles on the field in general and on specific works have been published in many journals, including some scholarly journals. Thomas Clareson edits a regular magazine, *Extrapolation*, which attempts to secure critical articles from both academic and nonacademic sources.

Some of those books and articles make honest contributions toward founding a criticism of science fiction. Few are as filled with complacent ignorance as what little appeared in print prior to 1950. But all too many are apparently done with more interest in getting into print than in what is printed.

Too many books have seized upon some attractive (to the writer) theme and then wantonly juggled a limited set of facts to fit. Thus one book was based upon the theory that science fiction was really derived from the religious drive of the writers and readers. (It could hardly have found a worse field for evidence, despite the stories that have dealt directly with religion of some kind.) Perhaps this might have been partially justified by examining the myth-making quality of science fiction and equating that to the inner source of religion; but nothing that thoughtful was done. Another book sought simply to change the name of the category, apparently by proving that science fiction stories all were related to catastrophes.

There have been several other attempts to find some comfortable slot into which to classify science fiction and get it classified as one of the recognized forms of literature. But at best, such efforts are simply attempts to manipulate the thing by controlling its label—which is both bad semantics and bad scholarship. The label is not the thing. Science fiction may be a misnomer for the diverse field as it now exists, but we've managed to live with it without serious misunderstanding for fifty years. And it is far less restrictive than any suggested new label. After all, oxygen means "acid former"—which it is not, really; but this hasn't kept the chemists from understanding what the word means.

Unfortunately, deep under the supposed acceptance granted to science fiction, I suspect that there is still the vague mental shadow out of former years—the shadow that shows the field really isn't quite respectable as a source of scholarly studies. When many of these writers gaze at SCIENCE FICTION emblazoned on the wall, they still hear the ancient cry: *Mene, mene, tekel, upharsin.* Mentally, as the minas and shekel are added to one pan of the scale weighing science fiction, it falls. "Weighed in the balance and found wanting."

Criticism of any work demands multiple skills. It must begin with a genuine and passionate love of what the work or the field can be, or the criticism will lack spirit. But in contrast, it requires an almost cold-blooded hunt for the evidence that can be turned by insight—trained insight—into further understanding. When judging a whole field, probably even harder standards are needed. And those standards must be derived from knowledge.

So far, we haven't yet been blessed with scholarship or critical ability at that high a level. The top level of scholarship has probably already found its life work in other areas. We have been able to win full attention from only the second level—and too often, the hungry third level, where the need for an area of seeming competence really exceeds the limits of that competence. Probably more time is needed for those of the necessary potential to find their interests in science fiction, or for those who are already interested to develop fully.

At that, we may be better off with the efforts of those who are discovering us from academic circles than we are from many who consider themselves critics within our field. Some of the dicta from them could be followed only along the path to hopeless sterility. Consider one often-quoted and admired criterion for good fiction: "Science fiction, like all fiction, can only be good when it illuminates the tragedy of man."

Certainly that is the lowest cry of pessimism, as well as a rather shoddy piece of logic. There is no more tragedy inherent in being a man, certainly, than in being a mouse—or not being at all. And throughout the duration of literature, many of our greatest works have hardly fitted that formula. Historically, the statement is sheer bunk; man may not have gone to the heights he should, but his progress in a brief million years looks like a triumph to me.

(I haven't named the writers supposedly responsible for the dictum because I have yet to hear this statement directly from the lips of either. I can only hope that neither man, whom I like, really said it. But others are trying to use the catch-phrase seriously in evaluating our fiction.)

Far too often, also, the work is being judged by prejudice against the writer—an *ex hominem* judgment. Some writers are good or great; therefore each book they write is to be praised. Others are believed to be hacks—therefore the reviewer is expected to hack the work to pieces. This is unfortunately the lowest form of criticism—and the most common. Robert Silverberg suffered from such treatment for several years, largely because he had publicly admitted he wrote to make money; hence no one noticed the good parts of his stories, but only the bad. Then, by a great deal of effort, he convinced the critics that he was now serious about doing artistic books. Behold, all his faults vanished, and his books were suddenly in contention for prizes.

Certainly science fiction is in desperate need of some firm guidelines by which it can be assessed. At present it is a sprawling category, covering a large number of types of fiction (genres, except that too many are using that word for the whole field). It seems to be going off busily in all directions, with neither its storytelling nor its way of writing receiving any consistent evaluation. There must be something behind all the various forms and attempts that has made it so popular. But so far, I have not seen any credible analysis being done.

In the end, I am left with my own rules, for what they are worth. Perhaps they will be of some help to others who are seeking to formulate their own guidelines:

Every book deserves to be read as a thing in itself, and that includes science fiction. But when it is specialized, as many of the categories are, some recognition must be given to the type of fiction. Thus no book should be either praised or condemned because it is science fiction (or Regency romance, or anything else). But when reading science fiction, the reader cannot expect the attention to small details of daily living that he may find in a contemporary novel; there isn't room to put in the details of such things and still present a detailed picture of the changes that make the time, culture or world of interest. Science fiction deals with change, not the eternal present; the mating habits, work habits, or most cultural manifestations do not remain fixed forever, and science fiction should not be put down because something seems wrong at first; if it is justified in the work, it is valid.

Basic assumptions must not be violated, though some modification can be made. Thus, if it is stated that the world is decivilizing for want of energy, the hero can't get from New York to Alaska in one day; he wouldn't have the airplane available, except for some striking reason. This is obvious—but less obvious deviations can be just as symptomatic of bad science fiction. That same hero cannot be casual about his clothes, food, or anything else—because such things require energy, unless the author has indicated some source of the products that is not too expensive of energy.

When science is used, explicity or implicitly, as the basis for the story—as it must be for any interstellar civilization, for instance—that science must not violate basic science as we know it, unless the violation is covered by some other use of science. Thus, a ship in space is subject to the laws of motion proposed by Sir Isaac Newton (and not repealed by Einstein!). It cannot do sharp turns in space from high speeds; it can only turn by the use of fuel to introduce a vector into its course. However, if the writer has satisfactorily postulated some means of overcoming inertia, this objection no longer applies.

The leading character of science fiction may well not be a human being—and his actions can only be judged by what the author develops of his character, not by purely human character behavior. Robots and aliens are frequent characters. But sometimes the real character in a novel is the world itself on which events occur, or the culture in which things develop. Furthermore, even the human characters may not react as contemporary standards dictate. Many habits—even mating habits—are shaped by the culture. Don't condemn a novel for unbelievable characters because they aren't today's characters until discovering whether they are acting in a way that makes sense for their culture.

In most other ways, science fiction stories should be judged as would be any other fiction. There should be a recognizable beginning, middle and end to the story —it's a story, after all, not some true-life event which must be taken as it comes. These three elements, however, need not appear in their natural order; in some cases, science fiction has found ways to scramble them logically. If it works for the reader, who cares?

Don't expect to find deathless prose and exquisite,

elegant style in most science fiction. Wise science fiction writers are not writing for the ages—there is a measure of transiency to any work attempting to deal with the future and possible developments of science. And most of the writers are hardly paid or expected to spend years in polishing their prose. The standard of writing to be expected should simply be that of a good adventure story. If the writing has enough vividness and maintains sufficient interest to carry the reader along without noticing clumsiness, that is about as it should be; better style may be desirable, and worse may be found, of course, but let's be realistic, at least in our expectations.

But most certainly the writing should be clear enough to be followed easily, and the background should not be confused or muddled. (Sometimes some facts are withheld for a valid reason until later; that is acceptable, if enough is given to maintain interest.) There is currently a vogue of turgidity, as if being unclear were a virtue. This is perhaps acceptable in certain types of contemporary fiction, where the reader has come to accept it. But science fiction is inherently a story of something that is different from the ordinary fiction; it is enough to ask the reader to accept a new culture, world or mode of behavior; it is then the writer's job to make that accessible to the reader. Science fiction should be read, not studied.

Symbols in writing probably have their place, and the writer of contemporary fiction who is attempting to do a penetrating study of some contemporary human being may need to use symbols to convey all his meaning. But science fiction cannot possibly do an equivalent study; the humans in the story are automatically removed a bit by the changes introduced in setting up a science fiction situation. The symbols—other than normal metaphor—would be wasted on most readers, and should be; this is merely an attempt to transport one of the techniques of a specialized type of contemporary fiction to a field where it has no relevance.

The use of such devices as the cavalry coming over the hill at the last moment or any deus ex machina is just as bad in science fiction as in any other fiction. This includes the use of psi powers, unless those powers have previously been well established and can logically be made to save the situation.

Present tense has been substituted for past as a narrative method in some science fiction and has been promoted as a more artistic way of writing. It has no virtue beyond novelty—which isn't needed in science fiction, where the novelty is built into the basic concept. Typographical tricks have also been used in an effort to enhance some stories. These should be regarded with suspicion as more trickery; occasionally there is a use for some, but good writers rarely need to resort to them. On the other hand, the use of italic type to indicate thoughts (as when transmitting words telepathically) is an accepted convention.

Some things in most science fiction stories are not explained, such as the "jump" the ship uses to get from one star to another in less than the time light requires. These should not be condemned out of hand, since many are conventional devices so long established in science fiction that they are taken for granted by the readers. But aside from such conventions, the writer should think out and show the steps he uses in establishing any new principle after the story is well started.

Consistency is perhaps the greatest overall need of good science fiction. It covers character handling and the use of background, as in regular fiction; but it must apply to every new concept developed in the story, with particular strength. If you have a boy, born on a generation ship, step out onto a planet and simply walk around, you're dealing with inconsistency; his whole development would make the sight of an open sky seem unbelievable; he has either spent his life learning to live in low gravity or allowing for coriolis force from the spinning of the ship (unless the ship has some form of artificial gravity). And the smell of the planet, as well as the horizon's disappearance, are going to shock him. It is consistency that establishes believability, and the small details frequently achieve the effect even more forcefully than major ones.

Perhaps relatedness is a word to describe another need of science fiction. The writer should think out his background and history to the fullest possible extent. If he tells you that everyone commutes to his office by helicopter, he hasn't thought very hard about how cities could be designed to stand all that drumming of air during rush hours, and he hasn't considered where all those helicopters are going to land and stay. One helicopter takes up a lot of room—more by far than a car. And the cities are already in trouble with traffic. (If the writer can describe a city where such commuting would work, he's a genius—forget the story and write a review of praise for his idea.) If he has some means of doing the commuting by teleportation, begin to wonder why offices and manufacturing plants are located in cities when such easy, instant transportation is available. In a story of a changed world, one idea must relate to another, one development influence many details of other behavior. The better writers spend a lot of effort to cover this; the poorer ones usually seem to feel it's up to the reader to figure all such things out.

The science fiction reader's responsibility traditionally ends when he buys and opens the book. As I must insist again, science fiction is sold as entertainment, so it should entertain. If it doesn't, there are no further demands on the reader. It's up to the author to find ways to keep him reading. Thus, while implicit plotting may get by in books that are bought by a small group of readers who are accustomed to such tricks, the reader of science fiction expects the writer to finish the job he started.

No book should ever be judged for review without considering who will want to read it and why.

Finally, it's not up to the reader to judge the author; he must judge the book as a thing in itself. It doesn't matter what the intent of the author was in writing the book; the important thing is what the reader gets out of reading it. And while there is obviously good reason to buy books by an author who has previously pleased rather than one who has disappointed, that applies only to the purchase. Once the reading begins, the book should be considered on its own terms. One of the worst writers of fiction, according to my opinion at the time, wrote a story I have read with pleasure several times and remember still. (This was R. DeWitt Miller's "The Master Shall Not Die," which I previously recommended.) And more than one of my favorite authors have done books that did not please me at all.

Relevancy is a word that should never have been attached as a desideratum to science fiction. The word is usually used to mean the making of science fiction relevant to a burning issue (at least to some) of today, or to current fads and ideas. But science fiction must deal with what the author hopes will be relevant to the time of his story—and, of course, to whatever human values will always remain relevant. Even such issues as the women's movement for equality should not normally be an issue in a story taking place in the year 2250; by that time, the matter will have been resolved, one way or another. (It is possible, of course, to have the struggle lost and resumed then; but it will seem like an artificial trick by the writer to be "with it.") Of course, there's nothing wrong with assuming that women do gain equality and trying to show a future society where that is taken for granted. But no great point should be made of that—because readers ten years from now, particularly younger ones, may also take it for granted and wonder what all the fuss is about.

The use of sex is neither a virtue nor a sin in science fiction. As in any other fiction, it should be used when it has some real significance in the story and not otherwise. The general rule of reasonable parsimony in means to achieve effect still applies.

And, of course, if reviews and criticism of science fiction are to be more than superficial, it's desirable to gain as much acquaintance with the field as possible. This includes an awareness and sampling of material from the past, as well as the current output of books.

Judging science fiction is not particularly difficult for one who can judge other fiction and will approach the field honestly. It does take thought, as does the writing and reading of it. And it should include a reasonable freedom from any one clique which attempts to mold it into a single type or form. There is too much that is both good and very bad in all types of science fiction, and the field is too constantly in flux, for narrow limits.

Given honesty in judgment, science fiction should be able to stand up as itself, not as some strange outgrowth of another branch of fiction.

CHAPTER 36

After *Star Wars*

In 1977, too late to be properly part of the first fifty years of science fiction as a category, a science fiction movie was released which grossed more than $200,000,-

000 within about one year. This was George Lucas' *Star Wars*, to date the most successful film ever shown.

As a book made from the movie script, *Star Wars* was equally successful in its paperback appearance. Millions of copies were sold, and it rapidly climbed onto the best-seller lists all over the country.

The story is essentially simple. Luke Skywalker, a young man on a backwater planet, becomes involved in a war between a rebel band, led by a princess and some robots, and a monstrous and evil empire which is seeking to control all the galaxy. Luke is accompanied by an old man, a hero predating the conquest by the evil forces. From him, Luke learns to use the Force, apparently a psi power. They rescue the princess from the giant artificial world which is used to destroy planets. Then in the final battle, Luke and his friends manage to blow up the monstrous attacker, saving the princess and the good guys.

It's obviously an example of what has been called "space opera," long one of the favorite forms of adventure science fiction. And it does well by that type of fiction, using a host of interesting aliens and robots, while the evil leader is truly made to seem monstrous. The special effects were right out of the best of the old illustrations, and very convincingly done.

I enjoyed it thoroughly, as did most of the science fiction readers and writers I knew. Some few demurred or spoke strongly against the movie as having no significance. (I wonder what significance many of the real operas have?) But mostly, the reaction was one of strong approval, and a sense that this could do nothing but help science fiction in general.

Several writers have since pointed out that the movie may have lacked any obvious message of significance, but that it did have positive moral values. In that, too, it was akin to many of the true "space operas" of the magazines.

Certainly the effect on many viewers was intense. When the screen credits were shown in the theater where I saw the film, the audience broke into applause. (And some of my group who were not science fiction readers were among the first to applaud.) I've since heard of people who have seen the movie more than twenty times, and a lot of my friends have seen it more than once. A movie that can inspire such enthusiasm should have some effect on the field.

Yet I remember that *Star Trek* was supposed to have some vast effect on the circulation of science fiction. Probably it had some—but not much. And when Sputnik went up, everyone was convinced that the age of science fiction had begun—after which the circulation of the magazines continued to fall slightly.

Obviously, only time will provide the answers. But in my opinion, *Star Wars* is going to have a very strong effect on the continued success of science fiction.

I discount the results of *Star Trek* from my experience with the followers of that television program. By and large, the audience that watched those programs did not become fans of science fiction, though there was considerable science fiction used. They became primarily fans of Mr. Spock, the long-eared Vulcan member of the crew, as played by Leonard Nimoy— and to a lesser extent of the rest of the crew. It was much more like other fandoms than like the fandom of science fiction. Many, in fact, acted as if they believed in the literal truth of what they saw, and most seemed to take the program far too seriously to dabble around with anything else in science fiction.

Sputnik simply convinced John Campbell that he'd better watch his covers and begin cutting back on space scenes. (He never did, but the art director of the magazine and others were involved in that decision.) We agreed in our first conversation after the satellite went up that people were going to react by deciding science had caught up with science fiction, and with a measure of initial fear. They did. Rather than helping science fiction, Sputnik made it seem outmoded.

But *Star Wars* has a different impact. To begin with, of course, it *is* science fiction from start to finish. It takes its robots, its alien, its star travel and everything else very much for granted, just as science fiction learned to do. (George Lucas, unlike most directors in Hollywood, seems to have an excellent familiarity with science fiction.) The characters are not the basic center of interest—rather, the whole movie is.

Furthermore, there is a much stronger and wider tie-in with paperback science fiction. Ballantine/Del Rey Books is bringing out a series of "spin-off" novels, each dealing with some of the characters of the movie. These will be by established science fiction authors. It is hoped that readers who buy such books will be led to other works by those same authors, thus moving them from *Star Wars* to general science fiction. The first of these books, *Splinter of the Mind's Eye,* by Alan Dean Foster, has already been released, and preliminary reports following a healthy sale indicate that Foster's other books are beginning to sell more rapidly.

In the case of *Star Trek,* the original novelizations were done by James Blish, a highly regarded writer; but when the young fans of the series tried his other books, they must have found them totally beyond their age level. There was little cross-movement into science fiction as a result.

Actually, the one single element that I am convinced was most responsible for the rapid growth of science fiction was the appearance in the school libraries of the "juveniles" by Robert A. Heinlein and others. I know that a great many current readers were first turned on to science fiction through those books. And from what I can see, the most devoted followers of *Star Wars* are of about the same age level as those who discovered the books in their libraries.

It seems to me that the effects of the movie will take some time to be felt. But then there should be a marked increase in new readers; this will continue to grow for several years, just as it did from the appearance of the juveniles. The new readers may even negate the "bust" which it seemed to me might soon be coming. It may be hard to believe that science fiction can go on increasing from its present sales—but that's what I expect.

The effect on Hollywood will probably be less, though they are expecting great results. But almost certainly the success of Lucas' movie will be followed by a hasty set of imitations which will negate much of the business faith in science fiction that now exists. (Some of those attempts to cash in are already in production. Other than the uncertain feature film of another *Star Trek*, most seem to be done with almost none of the quality of story that made *Star Wars* succeed. Rather than even trying to imitate Lucas, they seem bent on imitating the ideas that were humdrum before.) However, Lucas is already busy on a second science fiction film to follow his first successful "space opera" on film, and the fact that he chose the late Leigh Brackett to write the script seems to indicate that he is still very much attuned to science fiction.

If there is a reasonable carryover from the movie to the paperbacks, the influx of new readers should be assurance that science fiction will remain healthy and prosperous throughout this century. Most of those new readers are in their teens. They will be no more than forty at the turn of the century. This will ensure that a large number will continue reading until that date, from what we know of previous reading patterns.

What kind of science fiction will there be?

Now we get into fairly sure short-range predictions, but the picture grows uncertain in the further future. If anyone had asked in 1955 what kind of science fiction would do well in 1958, the answer would have been fairly simple. But for 1970, any guess would have been wrong, since the brief reign of the New Wave did leave lasting effects; mostly, it achieved a fractionation of the field, in which no one type clearly dominated.

It seems obvious that for a time the adventure type of science fiction will be very much in demand. This will be fiction with strong story lines, a clear (though not necessarily fully happy) resolution, and considerable action between beginning and end. It need not involve the type of action to be found in the worst dramatic writing for television or suspense books. But there should be definite problems with complications throughout. The protagonists or heroes will probably tend toward people with positive abilities—ones who pitch in and aren't afraid to take the consequences. They need not be very young. (Han Solo, the pilot of the ship that carried Luke Skywalker, was far older than Luke, but to many he was the real hero of the story.) Rich backgrounds will be wanted, and good aliens will always add to the story. Judging by the willingness to accept considerable technical background in the movie, the new readers will welcome a fair level of honest science added to the story.

Hmm. That's pretty much the type of science fiction that has always enjoyed a good sale.

And that is the reason that *Star Wars* can bring new readers—because the basic elements of the movie and of a popular form of written science fiction have so much in common.

I do not expect any one type of science fiction to dominate the market, however. There is a definite place and market for a wide diversity. A fair percentage of the science fiction readers in the colleges seem to prefer a more "literary" form of fiction—though they don't seem to object to strong stories, if properly dressed to seem a bit closer to what is being studied in school as serious literature. Many new readers of the past ten years seem to prefer a somewhat diluted element of heavy science in their stories, and that readership will probably grow, though more slowly than the adventure group. Others like all the science that can be put in a story, as shown by the enthusiasm for the works of Larry Niven and a few others.

Meantime, the many new women writers who have come to the field are beginning to have more effect. Some of these love and write exactly the same type of story as do the men writers. But others are developing their own type of fiction and the readers to go with it. (And yes, some men will like it, and some will feel at home writing similar material. Good writers can't be identified as to sex from what they write—unless they choose to be.)

The fantasy element in science fiction has been increasing for a number of years, also, and I'm sure that will continue. This gives a freedom to deal with many stories that are cramped by any requirement that they stick to even minimal science, while the ability to move across space and time freely through scientific-sounding gimmickry also permits new possibilities for fantasy.

Fantasy itself—without the science element—seems to be about to burst into new popularity. I have been watching this happen for the fantasy books I edit, and the sales of good fantasy books have already exceeded my first expectations.

There seems to be a need for a number of experiences in the world today that can only be satisfied by fiction which can get away from the here and now, from the world as we know it. This need probably has always existed; but I suspect that most readers didn't know where to turn to satisfy it. Early science fiction was not well enough written or otherwise suitable in many cases; it was tailored to the young who saw science as a key to the future, and to the hobbyist, and it had to work its way up by stages to a form more easily acceptable. Fantasy was "for children" in Victorian determinism; and Freud's heirs frowned on it for even young people. It is only just becoming respectable and accessible again.

Probably new forms will eventually emerge from the slow union of fantasy and science fiction that is beginning to take place. This will come about by evolution, and there is no way of guessing what forms will emerge. (I wish I could guess with a reasonable chance of being right; any writer or editor who could anticipate this would be in an enviable position.)

The future seems to be complex, with so many possibilities that no futurologist really has a chance at predicting it with any degree of accuracy. Men are going to go out into space again, almost certainly, and eventually I believe some way will be found to reach some habitable planet around another star, to found a colony and to fractionate the future history of the human race—soon to be races, then—to some extent.

Probably further understanding of the internal structure of the atom will lead us past the bewildering proliferation of particles that we find, to another level. When that happens—whether we call the theory after quarks or any other idea—we'll be at a new breakthrough in our accelerating progress.

Of course, in the meantime, we're beset with the question of whether our technical civilization can survive at all. We're facing what seems to be dangers of climate—either too great a warming up, or a return to an ice age, with total uncertainty about which to fear; we still haven't licked the problems of radioactive wastes and questionable power plants; we don't know how to control the size of our increasingly demanding population; and a hundred other problems seem almost impossible of solution now. Some such problems will be with us for a long time, we can be sure.

In such times, people need release, and they need myths that suit our age to support them. These are things which our fantasy and science fiction can offer, probably even better in the future. The need will continue—and I'm sure it will be answered.

It seems to me that science fiction and fantasy can look for a long and very successful future—and a highly diverse one.

And I hope the man who tries to tell the story of the world of science fiction from 1976 to 2026 will find as much satisfaction in the events he chronicles as I find in these.

Appendices

APPENDIX 1

Research and Study Material

DESPITE THE PLETHORA of recent books about science fiction, the number that contribute useful and reliable information is still somewhat limited. The best study of the literature still remains the fiction itself; for that, I've appended a list of novels, collections and anthologies, keyed to the periods of development I've used in this book. But there are a few books I have found of sufficient value to add to my library as reference material or, in a few instances, for the pleasure of having them.

Of these books, probably the various indices are most useful for the serious research into the works of a writer. They make rather poor reading, but they do enable the location of stories, the checking of the works of a writer and numerous other useful functions.

Some of these books were published in limited editions and may be out of print—in one case, long out. Nevertheless, they are available in some large libraries, or in the libraries of the colleges that are beginning to collect science fiction.

Below are those I find most useful:

1. *Anatomy of Wonder*, edited by Neil Barron. Bowker, 1976.

This contains short synopses of many of the major books of science fiction from 1870 to 1975, as well as some critical discussions of various fields of science fiction. A useful, quick guide to the literature.

2. *The Craft of Science Fiction*, edited by Reginal Bretnor. Harper & Row, 1977.

An examination by fifteen established writers of the attitudes behind the writing of science fiction. A view of the craft that should prove valuable to readers as well as writers.

3. *Extrapolation, 1959–1969*, edited by Thomas D. Clareson. Gregg Press, 1978.

A reprint of the first ten years of an academic "fanzine" devoted to critical studies of science fiction. Some material is pompous or pretentious, but this is the best source of criticism for the serious student who wishes to relate science fiction to other literature.

4. *Science Fiction Reader's Guide*, by L. David Allen. Centennial Press, 1974.

An analysis and explication of fifteen major science fiction novels, together with short essays to aid the reader in a better understanding of this type of fiction. Done with understanding by a teacher who is well versed in the field.

5. *The Visual Encyclopedia of Science Fiction*, edited by Brian Ash. Harmony Books, 1977.

Most of this is devoted to a series of articles on the development of the major themes of science fiction, with other articles on fandom, comics, television, etc. It's somewhat spotty, with some valuable articles and some far less useful; there is also a strong bias toward the modern school of British science fiction. Nevertheless, it presents a great deal of information. Illustrated.

6. *The Hills of Faraway*, by Diana Waggoner. Atheneum, 1978.

A guide to fantasy, giving theories, trends and categories. There is a fairly complete coverage of major fantasy titles, with brief summaries. At times highly opinionated, but generally useful.

7. *Who's Who in Science Fiction*, by Brian Ash. Taplinger, 1976.

Brief biographies of major writers, editors and artists. The only source of ready biographical information covering most figures in the field.

8. *A Requiem of Astounding*, by Alva Rogers. Advent, 1964.

A nostalgic review of thirty years of *Astounding Science Fiction* by a longtime fan. An article by Harry Bates gives the true history of the first days of the magazine.

9. *The Immortal Storm*, by Sam Moskowitz. ASFO Press, 1954.

An account of early fans, fan clubs and feuds, told as they seemed to the fans at the time. Reissued by Hyperion Press.

10. *All Our Yesterdays*, by Harry Warner, Jr. Advent, 1969.

This is a detailed and apparently unbiased history of science fiction fandom from its beginnings to 1950. The best all-over view of fandom available.

11. *Index to the Science Fiction Anthologies and Collections*, by William Contento. G. K. Hall, 1978.

This indexes almost 2,000 books containing 12,000 different stories by author, story title and book title, with pertinent information. A major reference book.

12. *Index to the Science Fiction Magazines, 1926–1950*, by Donald B. Day. Perri Press, 1952.

Most of the contents of the magazines are indexed by authors and titles, with publications and dates. Unfortunately, this small edition has long been out of print. Perhaps one of the major reprinters may yet discover the need for it.

13. *The Index of Science Fiction Magazines, 1951–1965*, by Norm Metcalf. J. Ben Stark, 1968.

A continuation of the Day *Index,* facilitated by the use of computer indexing and typesetting. This was further continued by the New England Science Fiction Society in a 1966–1970 *Index,* which has been kept up to date with annual supplements.

14. *The Encyclopedia of Science Fiction and Fantasy,* by Donald H. Tuck. Advent. Vol. 1, A–L, 1974; Vol. 2, M–Z, 1978.

A listing of authors, editors, artists, etc., with brief biographies. Coverage of their major work, with brief, pertinent descriptions of stories and a listing of all editions through 1968. Volume 2 lists all titles for cross-referencing to the author entries. This is a monumental work and an invaluable reference.

APPENDIX 2

A Recommended Reading List

IN ORDER TO RELATE the novels below to their proper period, I list the date of first appearance, rather than that of publication in book form. In the case of collections and anthologies, I list two dates, that of the earliest story in the book and that of the latest. Books are given by author, title and date of first appearance.

No publisher is listed, since this information would be more misleading than helpful. Most of the original hard-cover books (if there was a hard-cover edition) are now unavailable. And in paperback format, a book may be licensed for a few years to one publisher and then go to another, so that there is little hope of any accurate listing beyond the time of writing.

Probably many of the books will not be readily available in most bookstores at any given time. Yet science fiction, unlike most other fiction, has few good books that ever go permanently out of print. Within a five-year period, nearly all get reissued.

Today, there are a number of bookstores specializing in science fiction, many of which keep stocks of books not otherwise available. A search through such a store will turn up a large number of these books.

Many hard-to-find books can be obtained from the several publishers who specialize in reprinting the classics of science fiction. These are especially durable editions designed for libraries but available to interested readers. Among such publishers are Hyperion Press, Gregg Press, and Garland Publishing, Inc.

Collections and anthologies are listed separately after the novels, since they usually span more than one "age." These books of shorter works should not be neglected, since much of the best science fiction is to be found in short stories and novelettes. The Healy and McComas anthology is a huge compilation of the cream of the Golden Age; the Silverberg anthology is arranged by date and is a fascinating view of the evolution and highlights of the field. Both books are currently available in paperback format.

Most of these books are good reading, regardless of the date of appearance. In a few cases, the style and handling are dated and they are included only because of their importance in the history of science fiction. These are indicated by an asterisk (*) before the title. A few fantasies are also included and have (F) preceding the title.

Author	Title	Date
BACKGROUND: Before 1926		
J. D. Beresford	The Hampdenshire Wonder	1911
Edgar Rice Burroughs	A Princess of Mars	1912
Ray Cummings	* The Girl in the Golden Atom	1923
George Allan England	Darkness and Dawn	1912
H. Rider Haggard	(F) She	1886
A. Merritt	The Moon Pool	1919
Jules Verne	* From the Earth to the Moon	1865
H. G. Wells	The Time Machine	1895
———	The War of the Worlds	1897
THE AGE OF WONDER: 1926–1937		
Edwin Balmer and Philip Wylie	When Worlds Collide	1932
John W. Campbell	* The Black Star Passes	1930
Robert E. Howard	(F) Conan the Conqueror	1935
Aldous Huxley	Brave New World	1932
H. P. Lovecraft	(F) At the Mountains of Madness	1936
Laurence Manning	The Man Who Awoke	1933
A. Merritt	The Face in the Abyss	1931
Philip Francis Nowlan	* Armageddon 2419 A.D.	1928
Edward E. Smith, Ph.D.	* The Skylark of Space	1928
Olaf Stapledon	Odd John	1935
Jack Williamson	The Legion of Space	1934
THE GOLDEN AGE: 1938–1949		
Isaac Asimov	The Foundation Trilogy	1942
L. Sprague de Camp	Lest Darkness Fall	1939
L. Sprague de Camp and Fletcher Pratt	(F) The Compleat Enchanter	1940
Lester del Rey	Nerves	1942
L. Ron Hubbard	Final Blackout	1940
Henry Kuttner	Destination Infinity	1947
Fritz Leiber	Gather, Darkness!	1943
Clifford D. Simak	City	1944
George O. Smith	Venus Equilateral	1942
A. E. Van Vogt	Slan	1940
———	The World of Null-A	1945

THE AGE OF ACCEPTANCE: 1950–1961

Brian Aldiss	*The Long Afternoon of Earth*	1961
Poul Anderson	*The Man Who Counts*	1958
———	*The High Crusade*	1960
Isaac Asimov	*The Caves of Steel*	1953
Alfred Bester	*The Demolished Man*	1952
James Blish	*Earthman, Come Home*	1950
———	*A Case of Conscience*	1953
Ray Bradbury	*Fahrenheit 451*	1951
Arthur C. Clarke	*Childhood's End*	1953
Hal Clement	*Mission of Gravity*	1953
Lester del Rey	*The Eleventh Commandment*	1961
Gordon R. Dickson	*Dorsai*	1960
Philip José Farmer	*The Lovers*	1951
Edmond Hamilton	*City at World's End*	1950
Harry Harrison	*Deathworld*	1960
Robert A. Heinlein	*The Star Beast*	1954
———	*Double Star*	1956
———	*Stranger in a Strange Land*	1961
Frank Herbert	*Under Pressure*	1955
Walter M. Miller, Jr.	*A Canticle for Leibowitz*	1959
Edgar Pangborn	*A Mirror for Observers*	1954
Frederik Pohl and C. M. Kornbluth	*The Space Merchants*	1952
Theodore Sturgeon	*More Than Human*	1953
J. R. R. Tolkien	(F) *The Fellowship of the Ring*	1954
John Wyndham	*The Day of the Triffids*	1951
———	*The Midwich Cuckoos*	1957

THE AGE OF REBELLION: 1962–1973

J. G. Ballard	*The Crystal World*	1966
John Brunner	*Stand on Zanzibar*	1968
Anthony Burgess	*A Clockwork Orange*	1962
Arthur C. Clarke	*Rendezvous with Rama*	1973
Thomas M. Disch	*Camp Concentration*	1967
Philip José Farmer	*To Your Scattered Bodies Go*	1971
Frank Herbert	*Dune*	1963
Ursula K. Le Guin	*The Left Hand of Darkness*	1969
Anne McCaffrey	*Dragonflight*	1967
Larry Niven	*Ringworld*	1970
Andre Norton	(F) *Witchworld*	1963
———	*Victory on Janus*	1966
Edgar Pangborn	*Davy*	1964
H. Beam Piper	*Little Fuzzy*	1962

———	Space Viking	1963
———	Lord Kalvan of Otherwhen	1965
Robert Silverberg	Dying Inside	1972
Clifford D. Simak	Way Station	1963
E. C. Tubb	The Winds of Gath	1967
Roger Zelazny	Nine Princes of Amber	1970

THE FIFTH AGE: 1974–

Marion Zimmer Bradley	The Heritage of Hastur	1975
Terry Brooks	(F) The Sword of Shannara	1977
Jack Chalker	Midnight at the Well of Souls	1977
C. J. Cherryh	Brothers of Earth	1976
Samuel R. Delany	Dhalgren	1975
Stephen R. Donaldson	(F) Lord Foul's Bane	1977
Larry Niven and Jerry Pournelle	The Mote in God's Eye	1974
Frederik Pohl	Gateway	1977

COLLECTIONS

Isaac Asimov	I, Robot	1940–1950
Leigh Brackett	The Best of Leigh Brackett	1944–1956
Ray Bradbury	The Martian Chronicles	1946–1958
Arthur C. Clarke	The Nine Billion Names of God	1946–1962
L. Sprague de Camp	The Best of L. Sprague de Camp	1938–1976
Lester del Rey	The Best of Lester del Rey	1938–1964
Philip K. Dick	The Best of Philip K. Dick	1952–1974
Harlan Ellison	The Fantasies of Harlan Ellison	1956–1967
Raymond Z. Gallun	The Best of Raymond Z. Gallun	1934–1954
Robert A. Heinlein	The Past Through Tomorrow	1939–1962
Henry Kuttner	The Best of Henry Kuttner	1939–1955
Fritz Leiber	The Best of Fritz Leiber	1944–1967
Murray Leinster	The Best of Murray Leinster	1934–1956
C. L. Moore	The Best of C. L. Moore	1933–1946
Frederik Pohl	The Best of Frederik Pohl	1954–1967
Eric Frank Russell	The Best of Eric Frank Russell	1937–1959
Cordwainer Smith	The Best of Cordwainer Smith	1950–1966
Theodore Sturgeon	Not Without Sorcery	1939–1948

APPENDICES 389

Stanley G. Weinbaum	*The Best of Stanley G. Weinbaum*	1934–1937
Jack Williamson	*The Best of Jack Williamson*	1928–1976
Roger Zelazny	*Four for Tomorrow*	1963–1965

ANTHOLOGIES

Isaac Asimov, editor	*Before the Golden Age*	1931–1938
Terry Carr, editor	*Classic Science Fiction*	1940–1942
Peter Haining, editor	*Weird Tales*	1934–1952
Raymond J. Healy and J. Francis McComas, editors	*Adventures in Time and Space*	1936–1945
Sam Moskowitz, editor	*Science Fiction by Gaslight*	1891–1911
Robert Silverberg, editor	*Science Fiction Hall of Fame*	1934–1963

APPENDIX 3

The Garland Library of Science Fiction

NOTHING can be more frustrating to a science fiction reader or collector than to discover that some of the classic books are unavailable. These "lost" titles present a constant annoyance, particularly if they are considered major classics in the field.

Books can become "lost" for a number of reasons. J. D. Beresford's great early story of a superchild appeared long before the market for science fiction was created, hence its publishers simply let it go out of print. Otto Willi Gail's novel of the first scientifically correct rocket to the moon influenced a generation of writers; but it languished in the faded pages of a magazine because it was not considered right for today's market. And some of the finest science fiction novels appeared only in tiny editions, printed by amateur publishers, or bound as paperback editions (risking disintegration within a generation). As a result they were rarely stocked by most libraries.

To meet the need of readers and libraries for copies of such books, Garland Publishing, Inc., undertook the task of finding such books and reissuing them in permanent form, on acid-free paper and with exceptionally durable bindings. I was called in as editor of the series to select books deserving of permanent preservation.

My intention in selecting books was to present a cross section of science fiction, with examples of the various styles and the themes that had dominated the field. Above all, I wanted books that could be read for pleasure. Science fiction has always been a literature of entertainment, and a dull book—however worthy from a purely literary and stylistic view—has no place in a library meant to represent the field. A few of the books were chosen primarily for their importance in the history of science fiction; but even these, while perhaps lacking in some literary qualities, proved to be anything but dull. (Had they been, of course, they would hardly have influenced the field.) This aversion to dullness made me avoid the large number of books published in the eighteenth and nineteenth centuries. Some of them are quite well written and of historical value; but their basic themes are so dated that no modern reader can hope to enjoy them.

One of my tests of the suitability of a book, aside from the fact that no permanent edition existed, was that no book was to be included which I had not previously read at least twice by my own desire!

To a great extent, I feel that the resultant Library of

some forty-five books is itself a compressed world of science fiction.

THE GARLAND LIBRARY OF SCIENCE FICTION

1. Del Rey, Lester. *The World of Science Fiction, 1926–1976*
2. Beresford, J. D. *The Hampdenshire Wonder*
3. Bester, Alfred. *The Demolished Man*
4. Čapek, Karel. *The Absolute At Large*
5. Coblentz, Stanton A. *After 12,000 Years*
6. Coblentz, Stanton A. *In Caverns Below*
7. Cummings, Ray. *Tarrano the Conqueror*
8. Delany, Samuel R. *The Einstein Intersection*
9. Farmer, Philip José. *The Maker of Universes*
10. Farmer, Philip José. *Night of Light*
11. Fletcher, George U. (Fletcher Pratt). *The Well of the Unicorn*
12. Fort, Charles. *The Book of the Damned*
13. Fort, Charles. *Lo!*
14. Fort, Charles. *New Lands*
15. Fort, Charles. *Wild Talents*
16. Gail, Otto Willi (tr. from German by F. Currier). *Shot Into Infinity*
17. Hubbard, L. Ron. *Final Blackout*
18. Hubbard, L. Ron. *Return to Tomorrow*
19. Jones, Neil R. *Planet of the Double Sun*
20. Kuttner, Henry. *Destination Infinity*
21. Kuttner, Henry. *Mutant*
22. Lafferty, R. A. *Past Master*
23. Le Guin, Ursula K. *City of Illusions*

24. Le Guin, Ursula K. *Planet of Exile*
25. Le Guin, Ursula K. *Rocannon's World*
26. Pangborn, Edgar. *Davy*
27. Piper, H. Beam. *Lord Kalvan of Otherwhen*
28. Piper, H. Beam. *Space Viking*
29. Pohl, Frederik and C. M. Kornbluth. *Wolfbane*
30. Smith, Cordwainer. *You Will Never Be the Same*
31. Smith, George O. *The Brain Machine*
32. Smith, George O. *Venus Equilateral*
33. Smith, Edward E., with Mrs. Lee Hawkins Garby. *The Skylark of Space*
34. Smith, Edward E. *Skylark Three*
35. Smith, Edward E. *Skylark of Valeron*
36. Smith, Edward E. *Skylark DuQuesne*
37. Stasheff, Christopher. *The Warlock in Spite of Himself*
38. Stapledon, Olaf. *Odd John*
39. Sturgeon, Theodore. *More Than Human*
40. Taine, John (Eric Temple Bell). *The Time Stream*
41. van Vogt, A. E. *The Book of Ptath*
42. van Vogt, A. E. *Slan*
43. Williamson, Jack. *Darker Than You Think*
44. Williamson, Jack. *The Legion of Space*
45. Zelazny, Roger. *Four for Tomorrow*
46. Zelazny, Roger. *This Immortal*

INDEX

A. Merritt Fantasy (magazine), 179
Absolute at Large, The (Capek), 87
Ace Books, 171, 186, 204, 243–47, 248, 280–82, 286, 298
Ace Doubles, 205, 244
Ackerman, Forrest J., 75, 77
Actifan, 317
Action Comics, 306
"Admiral's Inspection" (Jameson), 97
Advent Publishers, 214–15, 278, 284
Adventure (magazine), 29
Adventures in Time and Space (Healy and McComas), 130, 389
"Adventures of Post and Nega" (Skidmore), 62
"Affairs of the Brains, The" (Gilmore), 55
After 12,000 Years (Coblentz), 47
After World's End (Williamson), 122
After Worlds Collide (Balmer and Wylie), 88
Afterglow, The (England), 24
Again, Dangerous Visions (Ellison), 241
Against the Fall of Night (Clarke), 121
"Agent of Vega" (Schmitz), 113
Air Wonder Stories (magazine), 49–51

"Airlords of Han, The" (Nowlan), 47, 304
Akers, Alan Burt, 282
Aldiss, Brian, 15, 176, 255, 387
Alejandro, 110
Algol (fanzine), 276, 286
All Our Yesterdays (Warner), 278, 383
All-Story Magazine, 23, 24, 26, 28
Allen, Irwin, 313
Allen, L. David, 284, 382
Alley Oop (comic strip), 305
Alternate World, 317
Amateur Press Associations, 208
Amazing Detective Tales (magazine), 51
Amazing Stories (magazine), 43–47, 49, 61–62, 63, 71–72, 80, 87, 110, 114–19, 140–42, 161, 175, 178, 188, 195, 229–30, 279–80, 300, 304
Amazing Stories Annual (magazine), 44, 178
Amazing Stories Quarterly (magazine), 45, 47, 61
American News Company, 195
American Weekly (magazine), 27
Amis, Kingsley, 359–60
Analog (magazine), 187, 219–20, 229, 233–38, 279
Analog (magazine). See also *Astounding Science Fiction* (magazine)
Analog Science Fact/Science Fiction (magazine), 186

393

394   INDEX

Anatomy of Wonder (Barron), 381
"Ancestral Voices" (Schachner), 60–61
. . . . And Call Me Conrad (Zelazny), 234, 243
And Now You Don't (Asimov), 113
. . . . And Searching Mind (Williamson), 112
. . . . And Some Were Human (Del Rey), 134
Anderson, Poul, 110, 148, 172, 184, 185–86, 187, 206, 387
Android, 317
Andromeda Strain, The (Creighton), 284
"Angel's Egg" (Pangborn), 174
Anthony, Piers, 233
Anti-gravity, 317
Anti-matter, 317
Anvil, Christopher, 183
Appleton, Victor, 19
"Arena" (Brown), 107
Argosy (magazine), 23, 28–29, 36, 123
Argosy Weekly (magazine), 28
Ariosto, Ludovico, 13, 292
Aristotelian logic, 317
Arkham House (publishers), 297
"Armageddon, 2419 A.D." (Nowlan), 46, 304, 386
Armegeddon, 2419 A.D. (Nowlan), 47
Arno Press, 281
Arrowsmith (Lewis), 4
"As Easy As A.B.C." (Kipling), 22
Ash, Brian, 282, 283
Asimov, Isaac, 4, 95, 100–101, 103, 104, 107, 109, 112, 113, 116, 125, 135, 137, 138, 148, 151–52, 173, 175, 183, 203, 218, 224, 238, 240–41, 242, 251, 324, 331, 338, 386, 387, 388, 389
See also French, Paul
Asteroid, 317
Astounding Science Fiction (magazine), 34, 53, 55, 56–57, 58–61, 65–67, 69–71, 80, 82, 91–114, 115, 116, 118, 128–30, 148–57, 162–64, 168–76, 178, 182–84, 185–86, 189, 191–94, 215, 217–19, 296, 298, 383
See also *Analog* (magazine)
Astounding Stories of Super-Science (magazine), 53
Astounding Stories (magazine). See *Astounding Science Fiction* (magazine)
At the Earth's Core (Burroughs), 26
At the Mountains of Madness (Lovecraft), 69, 386
Atlanta Science Fiction Organization Press, 214
Atlantic Monthly (magazine), 18, 21, 359
"Atomic Power" (Stuart), 68
Australian Futurian Association, 145
Authentic Science Fiction (magazine), 181
Avon Books, 127, 243
Avon Fantasy Reader (magazine), 127, 178, 300
Avon Science Fiction Reader (magazine), 178
Avon Science Fiction & Fantasy Reader (magazine), 178
Award Books, 243
Ayre, Thornton. See Fearn, John Russell

"Baby Is Three" (Sturgeon), 174
Baen, James, 280
Bailey, J. O., 263
Baird, Edward, 296
Ballantine, Betty, 247–48, 283, 301–02
Ballantine, Ian, 205–06, 225, 283, 301–02
Ballantine Books, 131, 173, 174, 205–06, 224–25, 235, 243, 245–49, 281, 283–84, 286, 301–02, 314, 372
Ballard, J. G., 243, 254–55, 387
Balmer, Edwin, 87, 309, 385
Bantam Books, 206, 243, 283
Barnaby (comic strip), 144
"Barrier, The" (Boucher), 103

Index

Barron, Neil, 381
Bates, Harry, 53–54, 56, 57, 67, 75, 98, 217, 309, 383. *See also* Gilmore, Anthony
Battle of Dorking, The (Chesney), 21
Bean, Norman. *See* Burroughs, Edgar Rice
Beetle Horde, The (Rousseau), 53
Before the Golden Age, 389
Bell, Eric Temple. *See* Taine, John
Bellamy, Edward, 342
Belmont Books, 243
Bem, 317
Benet, Stephen Vincent, 129
Bensen, Donald, 206, 248
Beresford, J. D., 20–21, 386
Bergerac, Cyrano De, 14, 278
Bergey, Earle K., 120
Berkley Books, 184, 243, 248, 281, 284, 286, 298
The Best of C. L. Moore, 388
The Best of Cordwainer Smith, 388
The Best of Eric Frank Russell, 388
The Best of Frederik Pohl, 388
The Best of Fritz Leiber, 388
The Best of Henry Kuttner, 388
The Best of Jack Williamson, 389
The Best of L. Sprague de Camp, 388
The Best of Leigh Brackett, 388
The Best of Lester del Rey, 388
The Best of Murray Leinster, 388
The Best of Philip K. Dick, 388
The Best of Raymond Z. Gallun, 388
Best of Science Fiction, The (Conklin), 129
Best Science Fiction Stories (Bleiler and Dikty), 200
The Best of Stanley G. Weinbaum, 389
Bester, Alfred, 174, 183, 211, 215, 387
Beyond Fantasy Fiction (magazine), 179, 301

Beyond Mars (comic strip), 306
Beyond the Great Oblivion (England), 24
"Beyond the Sphinx's Cave" (Leinster), 59
Beyond this Horizon (Heinlein), 102, 133
Bierce, Ambrose, 129
Big Bang, 317–18
Big Eye, The (Ehrlich), 132
"Big Front Yard, The" (Simak), 185
Big Pond Fund, 212
Billion Year Spree, The (Aldiss), 15
Binder, Eando, 116. *See also* Giles, Gordon A.
"Birth of a Salesman" (Tiptree), 236
Black Cat (magazine), 23
Black Cloud, The (Hoyle), 200
"Black Destroyer" (van Vogt), 94
Black Flame, The (Weinbaum), 121, 133
Black Hole, 318
Black Man's Burden (Reynolds), 187
Black Star Passes, The (Campbell), 48, 386
Blade, William, 116
Blaster, 318
Bleiler, E. F., 200
Blish, James, 74, 77, 125, 138, 168, 172, 175, 200, 215, 222, 225, 314, 340, 372, 387
Bloch, Robert, 74, 78, 116, 215, 300
Blowups Happen (Heinlein), 98
Blue Book (magazine), 29, 87
Blue Ribbon Publications, 122–23
"Bluff of the Hawk, The" (Gilmore), 56
BNF, 318
Bok, Hannes, 138, 298, 301
Bonestell, Chesley, 110
Bonfiglioli, Kyril, 231
Book of the Damned, The (Fort), 68, 391
"Born of Man and Woman" (Matheson), 172

"Born of the Sun"
(Williamson), 67
Boskones, 143, 278
Boucher, Anthony, 103, 170, 185, 188, 209, 217, 358
Bova, Ben, 187, 237, 241
Brackett, Leigh, 97, 125, 135, 156, 202, 262, 283, 334, 373, 388
Bradbury, Ray, 125, 156, 173, 202, 298, 387, 388
Bradbury, Walter, 201, 203
Bradley, Marion Zimmer, 168, 175, 244, 245, 262, 282, 330, 341, 388
Brave New World (Huxley), 87, 260, 345, 386
Bretnor, Reginald, 382
Breuer, Miles J., 44
Brick Bradford (comic strip), 305
Brick Moon, The (Hale), 18
"Bridle and Saddle" (Asimov), 103
"Bright Illusion" (Moore), 67, 80
Briney, Robert E., 214
"Bring the Jubilee" (Moore), 174
Bring the Jubilee (Moore), 8
British Fantasy Society, 145
British Science Fiction (magazine), 181
British Space Fiction (magazine), 181
Brooks, Terry, 302–03, 388
Brothers of Earth (Cherryh), 282, 388
Brown, Charles, 237, 239, 277, 281, 286
Brown, Dena, 239, 277, 281, 286
Brown, Fredric, 107, 121, 125, 200
Brown, Howard V., 34, 66, 120
Browne, Howard, 120, 188, 300
Brunner, John, 205, 241, 244, 275, 387
Buck Rogers (movie; 1939), 309
Buck Rogers 2429 (comic strip), 305
Buck Rogers in the 25th Century (comic strip), 46, 305

Budrys, Algis J., 175, 187, 358
Bug Jack Baron (Spinrad), 235, 252
Bulmer, Ken, 212
"Bureau of Slick Tricks" (Fyfe), 97
Burgess, Anthony, 243, 387
Burks, Arthur J., 54, 75, 122
Burn Witch Burn (Merritt), 28
Burroughs, Edgar Rice, 24–27, 28, 44–45, 246, 386
Bussard Ram-Jet, 318
But without Horns (Page), 336
"By His Bootstraps" (MacDonald), 100

Cabinet of Dr. Caligari, The (movie), 307
Calkins, Dick, 305
"Call Me Joe" (Anderson), 184
Camp Concentration, 387
Campbell, John W., Jr., 37–39, 47–49, 63, 68–71, 84, 91–114, 128–30, 132, 135, 139, 146, 148–57, 163–69, 182, 186, 188, 191, 211, 217–18, 233, 236–37, 272, 283, 295, 299, 305, 309, 322, 371, 386. See also Campen, Karl van; Stuart, Don A.
Campen, Karl van, 69. See also Campbell, John W.
Canticle for Leibowitz, A (Miller), 177, 340, 387
Capek, Karel, 87
"Captain A.V.G.," 162
Captain Future (magazine), 121
Captain Video (TV program), 312
Carnell, E. J. "Ted", 74, 128, 147, 231, 249, 251
Carr, Terry, 282, 389
Carter, Lin, 247, 297, 302
Cartmill, Cleve, 108
Case of Conscience, A (Blish), 175, 340, 387
Cavalier (magazine), 23–24, 26
Caves of Steel, The (Asimov), 175, 183, 387

CBS Playhouse (radio program), 311
Chalker, Jack, 388
Chanson de Roland, 292
Checklist of Fantastic Literature, The (Korshak and Dikty), 135
Cherryh, C. J., 282, 339, 388
Chesney, George Tomkyns, 21
Chicon (1940), 146
Chicon II (1952), 209, 274
Chicon III (1962), 274
"Child's Play" (Tenn), 110
Childhood's End (Clarke), 200, 387
Children of Dune (Herbert), 284
"Children of the Betsy B" (Jameson), 94
Children of the Lens, The (Smith), 111
Chilton Publishers, 242
Christopher, John, 185, 254
Cinvention (1949), 147
"City" (Simak), 107
City (Simak), 107, 135, 386
City and the Stars, The (Clarke), 200
City at World's End (Hamilton), 172, 387
City of Illusion (Le Guin), 244
Clareson, Thomas B., 265, 270, 360, 382
Clarion Courses, 268–69
Clarke, Arthur C., 109, 121, 135, 138, 148, 200, 206, 238, 248, 283, 310, 387, 388
"Clash by Night" (O'Donnell), 105, 111
Classic Science Fiction, 389
Clayton, William, 52, 54–58
Clayton Publications, 53, 298
Clement, Hal, 103, 113, 148, 154, 173, 175, 186, 202, 387
Clevention (1955), 211
Clifton, Mark, 175
"Cloak of Aesir" (Stuart), 94, 135
Clockwork Orange, A (Burgess), 243, 387
Clone, 318
Close to Critical (Clement), 186

COA, 318
Coblentz, Stanton A., 47, 346
'Coffin Ship, The (Gilmore), 59
Cogswell, Theodore R., 175
Cohen, Sol, 230
"Cold Equations, The" (Godwin), 176
"Coldest Place, The" (Niven), 234
Coleman, Sidney, 214
Collapsium, 323
Collier's (magazine), 202
Collier, John, 129
Color out of Space, The (Lovecraft), 44
"Colossus" (Wandrei), 66
Columbia Publications, 186, 188, 195
Columbus of Space, A (Serviss), 23–24
Comet Stories (magazine), 126
"Command, The" (de Camp), 93
"Common Sense" (Heinlein), 100
Compleat Enchanter, The (de Camp and Pratt), 299, 386
Con, 318
Conan Doyle, Arthur, 22, 130
Conan the Conqueror (Howard), 297, 386
Condé Nast Publications, 237
Conklin, Groff, 129–30, 171, 220, 358
Connecticut Yankee in King Arthur's Court, A (Twain), 19
Conquest of the Moon Pool, The (Merritt), 27
Conquest of the Planets, The (Campbell), 63
Conservative, The (magazine), 76
Contento, William, 383
Contest of the Planets, The (Campbell), 63
Contra-terrene Matter, 317
"Cooperate—or Else!" (van Vogt), 102
Corwin, Cecil, 126. *See also* Kornbluth, Cyril

398   INDEX

Cosmic Engineers (Simak), 94
Cosmic Stories (magazine), 126
Cosmos (magazine), 286
Cosmos Science Fiction & Fantasy (magazine), 179
Crabbe, Buster, 309
Craft of Science Fiction, The (Bretnor), 382
"Creator, The" (Simak), 340
Creep, Shadow (Merritt), 28
Cross, Polton. *See* Fearn, John Russell
Crown Publishers, 130
Crudzine, 319
Cryogenics, 319
"Crystal Ray, The (Gallun), 50
Crystal World, The (Ballard), 254–55, 387
Cummings, Raymond, 16, 28, 34, 54, 333, 386

Dahlgren (Delaney), 283
Dangerous Dimension, The (Hubbard), 92
Dangerous Visions (Ellison), 241
Daniken, Erich von, 8, 167
Darkness and Dawn (England), 24, 386
Darkover Series (Bradley), 244, 282, 330
Daugherty, Walter, 143
Davidson, Avram, 176
Davis, Joel, 287
Davis, Robert H., 26, 28
Davy, 387
Daw Books, 245, 281, 282, 286
Dawley, J. Searle, 307
"Dawn of Flame, The" (Weinbaum), 119–20, 121
Day, Donald B., 141, 212–13, 277, 383
Day of the Triffids, The (Wyndam), 202, 254, 387
Day the Earth Stood Still, The (movie), 98, 309
de Camp, L. Sprague, 91–93, 104, 113, 129, 134–35, 136, 148, 154, 202, 297, 299, 386, 388
"Dead Star Station" (Williamson), 7, 59

"Deadline" (Cartmill), 108
Dean, Norman L., 166
Dean Drive, 165, 319
Death Takes a Holiday (movie), 310
Deathworld (Harrington), 187, 387
Del Rey, Judy-Lynn, 248, 283, 286
Del Rey, Lester, 92, 94, 103–04, 107, 108–09, 114, 132, 134, 138, 144, 148, 151, 154, 173, 175, 203–04, 222–24, 274–75, 286, 302, 337–38, 340, 358, 386, 387, 388
Del Rey Books, 286
Delaney, Samuel B., 205, 283, 388
Dell Books, 206, 243, 246
Demolished Man, The (Bester), 174, 211, 387
Dent, Lester, 58
Denvention (1941), 146
Derleth, August, 296–97
Destination Infinity (O'Donnell), 111, 386
Destination Moon (movie), 131, 309
Detective Story Magazine, 23
De Voto, Bernard, 359
Dhalgren, 388
"Diamond Lens, The" (O'Brien), 16
"Dianetics, The Evolution of a Science" (Hubbard), 162
"Dianometry" (Hubbard), 162
Dick, Philip K., 175, 205, 244, 388
Dickson, Gordon R., 172, 186, 387
Diffin, Charles Willard, 54, 60
Dikty, T. E., 135, 200, 215, 224, 263
Dirac, P. A. M., 319
Dirac Drive, 319
Disch, Thomas M., 233, 248, 255, 256, 387
Discon II (1974), 284
Discord in Scarlet (van Vogt), 96
Disintegrator, 319

INDEX 399

Divining Rod, Standard Equipment (Yaco), 165
Doc Savage (magazine), 58
Dold, Elliott, 67, 92
Donaldson, Stephen R., 388
Door into Summer, The (Heinlein), 183, 202
Dorsai! (Dickson), 186, 387
Double Star (Heinlein), 183, 202, 387
Doubleday (publisher), 132, 135, 137, 201–03, 234, 240–42, 281
Dr. Jekyll and Mr. Hyde (movie; 1931), 308
Dracula (movie), 308
Dragonflight (McCaffrey), 235, 246, 387
Dragonquest (McCaffrey), 246
Dragonrider (McCaffrey), 235
Dream Master, The (Zelazny), 243
Drury, Alan, 8
Druse, Olga, 312
Duff, 319
Dumarest Series (Tubb), 245
Dumas, Alexandre, 199
Dune (Herbert), 233–34, 236, 242, 387
Dune Messiah (Herbert), 236, 242
Dune World (Herbert), 233
Dunsany, Lord, 29, 185, 293
Dutton (publishers), 200
Dwellers in the Mirage (Merritt), 28
Dying Inside (Silverberg), 246, 388
Dynamic Science Fiction (magazine), 179
Dynamic Stories (magazine), 122
Dyson, Freeman, 319
Dyson sphere, 319

E. T., 320
"E for Effort" (Sherred), 111, 153
E-type World, 320
Early Asimov, The (Asimov), 241
Early Del Rey, (Del Rey), 241

Eastercon (1944), 145
Eastern Science Fiction Association, 143, 208
Earthman, Come Home, 387
Eddison, E. R., 293
Egoboo, 219, 319
Ehrlich, Max, 132
Eight Stage of Fandom, The (Bloch), 215
Einstein, Albert, 5, 324, 332, 364
Electrical Experimenter (magazine), 33–34
Eleventh Commandment, The (Del Rey), 337, 387
Elias, Lee, 306
"Elixir, The" (Manning), 64
Ellery Queen's Magazine, 282
Ellis, Edward F., 18
Ellison, Harlan, 183, 222, 234, 241, 256, 313, 388
Elves, Gnomes and Little Men's Science Fiction & Chowder Society, 144, 209
Elwood, Roger, 249, 280, 281
"Emergency Refueling" (Blish), 125
Emshwiller, Ed, 224
Encyclopedia of Science Fiction and Fantasy, The (Tuck), 284, 384
End of Eternity, The (Asimov), 203
"Endochronic Properties of Resublimated Thiotimoline, The" (Asimov), 112
England, George Allan, 24, 44, 385
England Swings SF (Merril), 253
Enton, Harry, 18
Entropy, 319–20
"Epic of Posi and Nega, An" (Skidmore), 62
Equality; or a History of Lithconia (Anon.), 342
ESFA. *See* Eastern Science Fiction Association
Eshbach, Lloyd Arthur, 133–34, 185, 199, 215
"Ether Breather" (Sturgeon), 95

Ettinger, R. C. W., 167
"Eviction by Isotherm" (Jameson), 93
Exile of the Skies (Vaughan), 64
"Exodus" (Burks), 122
Exogenesis, 320
Experiment in Criticism, An (Lewis), 10
Experimenter Publishing Company, 47
Explorers of the Infinite (Moskowitz), 278
Extrapolation, 1959–1969 (Clareson), 382
Extrapolation and Science Fiction Studies (magazine), 270, 360
Eyraud, Achille, 18

F&SE. *See* Magazine of Fantasy & Science Fiction
Faan, 207, 320
Fabulous Riverboat, The (Farmer), 242–43
Face in the Abyss, The (Merritt), 27, 294, 386
Faerie Queene (Spenser), 292
Fahrenheit 451 (Bradbury), 173, 387
Fairy Chessman, The (Padgett), 109
"Faithful, The" (Del Rey), 92
Famous Fantastic Mysteries (magazine), 123–24, 177, 179, 300
Famous Science Fiction (magazine), 231
Famous Science Fiction Stories (Healy and McComas), 131
Fanac, 320
Fanscient (fanzine), 141, 213
Fanspeak, 316
Fantasies of Harlan Ellison, The, 388
Fantastic (magazine), 179, 188, 195, 280, 300. See also *Fantastic Adventures* (magazine)
Fantastic Adventures (magazine), 118–19, 127, 179, 300. See also *Fantastic* (magazine)
Fantastic Novels (magazine), 124, 179, 300
Fantastic Science Fiction (magazine), 179
Fantastic Science Fiction Stories (magazine), 300
Fantastic Stories (magazine), 300
Fantastic Stories of the Imagination (magazine), 300
Fantastic Story Magazine, 179
Fantastic Universe (magazine), 166, 179
Fantasy (magazine, 1938), 128
Fantasy (magazine, 1946), 128
Fantasy Advertiser (fanzine), 141
Fantasy Amateur Press Association (FAPA), 76, 141
Fantasy Book (magazine), 127, 179
Fantasy Book #6 (magazine), 173
Fantasy Commentator (fanzine), 141, 214
Fantasy Fan (magazine), 64
Fantasy Fiction Magazine, 179, 301
Fantasy Fiction Stories (magazine), 179
Fantasy Magazine, 75
Fantasy News 1938–1948 (fanzine), 140
Fantasy Press, 133–34, 185, 199, 215
Fantasy Writers' Guild, 222
Fanzine Index 1930–1952, 140
FAPA. *See* Fantasy Amateur Press Association
"Farewell to the Master" (Bates), 98
Farewell to the Master (Bates), 309
Farley, Ralph Milne, 78
Farmer, Philip Jose, 135, 175, 184, 242, 259, 387
Farrar, Strauss (publishers), 243
Faulkner, William, 251

Fearn, John Russell, 116
Fellowship of the Ring, The, 387
Femfan, 320
Fen, 320
Ferman, Ed, 235
Fermi, Enrico, 98
FFM. See *Famous Fantastic Mysteries* (magazine)
Fiawol, 207, 216, 320
Fiction House, 124–25, 191
Fictioneers Publication, 125
"Fifty Million Monkeys" (Jones), 106
Fijagh, 207, 320
Final Blackout (Hubbard), 97, 132, 386
"Final Command" (van Vogt), 113
"Final Triumph, The" (Schachner), 64
"Finished" (de Camp), 114
Finlay, Virgil, 124, 298
"Fireman, The" (Bradbury), 173
"First Contact" (Leinster), 109, 330
First Fandom, 74, 320
First Lensman (Smith), 133
First Men in the Moon, The (Wells), 20
Flash Gordon (comic strip), 305
Flash Gordon (movie; 1936), 309
Fletcher, George U., 293. See also Pratt, Fletcher
Flying Saucers (magazine), 162
"Fog" (Ley), 98, 103, 107
"For I Am a Jealous People" (Del Rey), 340
Forbidden Planet (movie), 309–10
Force Field, 321
Ford, Don, 209, 212
Forever War, The (Haldeman), 283
"Forgetfulness" (Stuart), 70
Forster, E. M., 345
Fort, Charles, 67, 391
Foster, Alan Dean, 314, 372

"Foundation" (Asimov), 103
Foundation Trilogy (Asimov), 203, 324, 386
Four for Tomorrow (Zelazny), 244, 389
Fourth Dimension, 321
Frank Reade and the Steam Man of the Prairies (Enton), 18
Frank Reade Jr. and His Steam Wonder (Senarens), 18
Franke, Herbert W., 275
Frankenstein (movie: 1910), 307
Frankenstein (movie; 1931), 308
Frankenstein (Shelley), 15
Franklin, H. Bruce, 265, 269, 270
Frau Im Mond, Die (movie), 308
Freas, Frank Kelly, 215, 224, 282
Frederick Fell (publisher), 200
French, Paul, 203. See also Asimov, Isaac
Friend, Oscar J., 119–20
Fringe Fan, 321
From the Earth to the Moon, 386
FTL, 321
Fugghead, 321
Fuqua, Robert, 114
Fury (O'Donnell), 111, 200
Future (magazine), 179, 186, 195
Future as Nightmare (Hillegas), 269
Future Fiction (magazine), 123
"Future History" (Heinlein), 152
Future History (Heinlein), 135
Future Perfect (Franklin), 269
Future Shock (Toffler), 10, 353
Futurian Society of Sydney, 145
Futurians, 78–79, 125, 142, 146
Futuristic Science Stories (magazine), 181
Fyfe, H. B., 97

Gafia, 208, 321
Gail, Otto Willi, 50, 389, 391

402 INDEX

Galactic Patrol (Smith), 91
Galaxy Science Fiction (magazine), 170–77, 179, 183–84, 187, 192, 195, 220, 229–30, 232–38, 248, 279–80, 301
Galaxy Science Fiction Novels (magazine), 179
Galileo (magazine), 280, 286–87
Gallagher, Galloway, 105
Gallun, Raymond Z., 50, 68, 92, 125, 388
"Game of Rat and Dragon, The" (Smith), 177
Garby, Lee Hawkins, 45
Garden City Press, 129
Garland Press, 281, 385
Garrett, Randall, 172. *See also* Gordon, David
Gas giant, 321
Gates of Ivrel, The (Cherryh), 339
Gateway, 388
Gather Darkness (Leiber), 105–06, 152, 200, 386
Gaughan, Jack, 173
Geiss, Richard E., 276, 286
Gene Pool, 321
General semantics, 321
Generation ship, 322
Genetic General, The (Dickson), 186
Genocides, The (Disch), 248, 255
Gentleman's Magazine, 21
German Rocket Society, 308
Gernsback, Hugo, 31–35, 39, 43–47, 49–51, 53, 64–66, 71, 73, 78–79, 80, 123, 211, 216–17, 343
Gerrold, David, 237
GHU, 322
Giesy, J. U., 28
Giles, Gordon A., 119. *See also* Binder, Eando
Gilgamesh, 12–13
Gillings, Walter, 74, 127
Gilmore, Anthony, 55–56, 59, 75. *See also* Bates, Harry; Hall, Desmond
Girl in the Golden Atom, The (Cummings), 16, 28, 333, 386
Glasser, Allen, 75
Gnaedinger, Mary, 123
Gnome Press, 135–37, 199, 203, 297
Goblin Reservation (Simak), 236, 242
Gods of Mars, The (Burroughs), 26
Gods Themselves, The (Asimov), 238, 242
Godwin, Francis, 14
Godwin, Tom, 176, 184
GOH, 322
Gold, H. L., 170–71, 173, 187–88, 195, 217, 301
"Gold at the Starbow's End, The" (Pohl), 237
Golden Argosy, Freighted with Treasures for Boys and Girls (magazine), 23
Goodavage, Joseph F., 167, 233
Gordon, David, 172. *See also* Garrett, Randall
Graham, Roger Philip, 142. *See also* Phillips, Rog
Gravy Planet (Pohl and Kornbluth), 174
Great Exclusion Act, 146
"Great Oil War, The" (Schachner), 64
"Green Hills of Earth, The" (Heinlein), 185
Green Man of Graypec, The (Pragnell), 64
Greenberg, Martin, 136, 168, 199
Greenberg Publishers, 200
Gregg Press, 281, 385
Grey, Clarence, 305
Grey Lensman (Smith), 95
Griffith, Mary, 342
Grosset & Dunlap, 200, 282
Guin, Wyman, 174
Guinn, Robert M., 170, 230
Guinn Publishing Company, 170, 188
"Gulf" (Heinlein), 114
Gulliver's Travels (Swift), 14–15
Gunn, James, 175, 240, 265, 284

Hadley, Thomas P., 132
Hadley Publishing Company, 132
Haggard, H. Rider, 293–94, 386
Haining, Peter, 389
Haldeman, Joe, 237, 283
Hale, Edward Everett, 18
Hall, Asaph, 15
Hall, Desmond, 59. *See also* Gilmore, Anthony
Hamilton, Edmond, 29, 45, 48, 50, 116–17, 121, 151, 156, 172, 298, 312, 387
Hamlin, Vince, 305
Hamling, William Lawrence, 140, 300
Hampdenshire Wonder, The (Beresford), 20–21, 386
Handbook of Science Fiction and Fantasy, The (Tuck), 214
Harcourt Brace (publisher), 200
Hardy, Thomas, 348
Harlequin Books, 282
Harper & Row, 200, 243, 281
Harper's (magazine), 25, 359
Harris, John W. Beynon, 202. *See also* Wyndam, John
Harrison, Harry, 4, 174, 187, 241, 346, 387
"Hawk Carse" (Gilmore), 55
Health Knowledge, Inc., 230
Healy, Raymond J., 130, 385, 389
Hector Servadac (Verne), 18
Heicon '70 International, 275
Heinlein, Robert A., 95–100, 102, 104, 114, 116, 130, 131, 133, 135, 146, 148, 150–52, 167, 173, 176, 183, 185, 201–04, 212, 215, 224, 234, 237, 242, 248, 251, 256, 285, 309, 321, 329, 336, 356, 372, 387, 388. *See also* MacDonald, Anson; Monroe, Lyle
Heisenberg, Werner, 326
"Helen O'Loy" (Del Rey), 93
Henderson, Zenna, 174
Henry Holt (publisher), 129
Herbert, Frank, 168, 175, 176, 236, 242, 284, 387
Here Gather the Stars (Simak), 234

Heritage of Hastur, The, 388
Hevelin, Rusty, 274
Hidden World, The (Hamilton), 50
Hieronymous Machine, 322
High Crusade (Anderson), 187, 387
Highways in Hiding (Smith), 176
Hillegas, Mark, 269
Hills of Faraway, The (Waggoner), 382
Hive Culture, 322
Hobbit, The (Tolkien), 294
Hodes, Robert M., 247
Hoen, Richard A., 113–14
"Hollywood on the Moon" (Kuttner), 119
Holt, Rinehart and Winston (publisher), 204
Homer, 13, 291
Hornig, Charles, 67, 74, 123, 138
Houghton Mifflin (publisher), 200
Hour of the Dragon, The (Howard), 297
Howard, Robert E., 135–36, 248, 294–95, 297–98, 386
Hoyle, Fred, 200
Hubbard, L. Ron, 93, 94, 97, 104, 132, 135, 162–64, 171–72, 386
Hugo Awards, 211, 229, 238, 283, 301
Hunter, Evan, 176, 260
Huxley, Aldous, 87, 260, 345, 386
Huxley, Thomas, 19
Hydra Club, 144, 208
Hyne, J. Cutliffe, 23
Hyperion Press, 281, 385
"Hyperpilosity" (de Camp), 92
Hyperspace, 322

"I, Robot" (Binder), 116, 388
"I Flew in a Flying Saucer" (Captain A.V.G.), 162
"I Remember Lemuria" (Shaver), 117–18
I Will Fear No Evil (Heinlein), 237, 242

Iceworld (Clement), 173
Idler (magazine), 22
If (magazine), 175, 176, 179, 188, 229–30, 232–34, 238, 276, 279
If This Goes On (Heinlein), 96–97
Iliad (Homer), 291
Imagination Science Fiction (magazine), 176, 179
Imaginative Tales (magazine), 179
Immortal Storm, The (Moskowitz), 78, 214, 383
Imperial Earth (Clarke), 283
Impulse (magazine), 231
In Search of Wonder (Knight), 214–15
Incomplete Enchanter, The (de Camp & Pratt), 129
Index to the S-F Magazines, 1951–1965 (MIT SF Society), 178, 277, 383–84
Index to the S-F Magazines, 1966–1971 (NESFS), 384
Index to the Science Fiction Anthologies and Collections (Contento), 383
Index to the Science Fiction Magazines, 1926–1950 (Day), 213, 277, 383
Inertialess Drive, 322
Infinity Science Fiction (magazine), 179
Ingher, Maurice, 75
International Science-Fiction (magazine), 230
"Interstellar Patrol" Series (Hamilton), 151
Invaders from Infinite (Campbell), 48
Invisible Little Man Award, 144
Invisible Man, The (Wells), 19
Ion Drive, 322
Iron Heel, The (London), 20
"Irrelevant, The" (Campen), 69
Isaac Asimov's Science Fiction Magazine, 287
Island of Dr. Moreau, The (Wells), 19, 337
Islands of Space (Campbell), 48
Isle of the Dead (Zelazny), 244

"Isolinguals, The" (de Camp), 92

Jack of Eagles (Blish), 168, 200
Jakes, John, 172
Jakobsson, Ejler, 126, 230, 280
Jameson, Malcolm, 93, 94, 97, 103
"Jameson Satellite, The" (Jones), 49
Jenkins, Will F., 54
Jones, Neil R., 49, 99
Jones, Raymond F., 106, 107
Jones, Robert Gibson, 115
Journey to the Center of the Earth (Verne), 16
Joyce, James, 251, 261
Jules Verne Magasinet, 127

Kafka, Franz, 251, 348
Karloff, Boris, 308
Keller, David H., 45
Kemp, Earl, 215
Kepler, Johannes, 14
"Killdozer" (Sturgeon), 107
King of Elfland's Daughter, The (Dunsany), 293
Kipling, Rudyard, 22, 350
Klass, Philip, 144, 265. *See also* Tenn, William
Knight, Damon, 74, 127, 140, 141, 176, 214, 222, 223, 225, 249, 256, 261, 268, 358
Kornbluth, Cyril, 5, 126, 172, 184–85, 206, 215, 246, 346, 387. *See also* Corwin, Cecil
Korshak, Melvin, 135
Korzybski, Alfred, 321
Krupa, Julian, 115
Kubrick, Stanley, 310
Kurtz, Katherine, 247, 302
Kuttner, Henry, 104–05, 111, 119, 121, 122, 135, 148, 152, 156, 185, 200, 206, 386, 388, 391. *See also* O'Donnell, Lawrence; Padgett, Lewis
Kyle, David A., 136, 144

L-5, 322
L. A. Con (1972), 275
Lafferty, R. A., 187

Lancer Books, 243, 248, 297
Lang, Fritz, 308
Laser Books, 281
LASFS. *See* Los Angeles Science Fantasy Society
Lasser, David, 50, 64, 87
Last and First Men (Stapledon), 87
"Last Enemy" (Piper), 172
Laumer, Keith, 186
Le Guin, Ursula K., 205, 233, 243, 262, 337, 348, 387
Lee, Tanith, 282
Left Hand of Darkness, The (Le Guin), 244, 387
"Legend of Post and Nega, A" (Skidmore), 62
Legion of Space, The (Williamson), 67, 133, 386
Legion of Time, The (Williamson), 92
Leiber, Fritz, 105–06, 148, 152, 200, 283, 386, 388
Leinster, Murray, 28–29, 44, 54, 59, 67, 69, 109, 120, 121, 152, 156, 329, 330, 332, 388
Lest Darkness Fall (de Camp), 129, 134, 386
"Let the Finder Beware" (Blish), 168
Let the Finder Beware (Blish), 200
Letterhack, 322
Levin, Ira, 295
Lewis, C. S., 10, 129
Lewis, Sinclair, 4
Ley, Willy, 37, 70, 98, 103, 107, 164, 218, 312
LeZombie (fanzine), 141
"Life-Line" (Heinlein), 95
Light Year, 323
Linebarger, Paul, 172. *See also* Smith, Cordwainer
"Little Black Bag, The" (Kornbluth), 172
Little Fuzzy, 387
Little Men, 144, 209–10
Lo! (Fort), 67, 391
LOC, 323
"Locked Out" (Eyfe), 97
Locus (fanzine), 237, 239, 277, 281, 286

Logan's Run (movie), 311
"Logic" (Anderson), 111
Loncon (1949), 145
Loncon I (1957), 211
London, Jack, 20
Long Afternoon of Earth, The, 387
Long, Frank Belknap, 241
Long Tomorrow, The (Brackett), 202, 334
Looking Backward, 2000–1887 (Bellamy), 342
"Loophole" (Clarke), 109
Lord Kalvan of Otherwhen, 388
Lord Foul's Bane, 388
Lord of the Rings (Tolkien), 238, 247, 294, 301
Los Angeles Science Fantasy Society, 143, 208
Lost Continent, The (Hyne), 23
Lost Horizon (movie), 310
Lost Legion, The (Monroe), 126, 167
Lost World, The (Conan Doyle), 22
Lost World, The (movie, 1925), 307
Lovecraft, H. P., 44, 69, 76, 135, 296–97, 386
"Lovers, The" (Farmer), 175, 259, 387
Low, Professor, 265
Lowell, Percival, 328
Lowndes, Robert A. W., 74, 123, 138, 144, 146, 188, 195, 231
Lucas, George, 370, 372–73
Lucian of Samosata, 13, 328
Lucifer's Hammer (Niven and Pournelle), 335
Lugosi, Bela, 308
Lunacon (1971), 272
Lunarians, 272

McIntosh, J. T., 172
MacDonald, Anson, 99, 100. *See also* Heinlein, Robert A.
MacFadden, Bernarr, 47
MacFadden-Bartell, 243
Machine Stops, The (Forster), 345

Mad Planet, The (Leinster), 29
Magazine of Fantasy, 127, 170
Magazine of Fantasy and Science Fiction, 170, 172, 174, 176–77, 179, 183–85, 187, 192, 195, 229, 234–36, 243, 279
Magazine of Horror, 231
Make Room! Make Room! (Harrison), 4, 241, 346
"Malice in Wonderland" (Hunter), 176, 260
Malzberg, Barry, 237
Mamoulian, Rouben, 308
Man in the Moone, The (Godwin), 14
"Man Who Ate the World, The" (Pohl), 183
Man Who Awoke, The (Manning), 64, 386
Man Who Counts, The (Anderson), 185, 387
"Mana" (Phillips), 4
Manning, Laurence, 64, 386
March, Fredric, 308
"Marching Morons, The" (Kornbluth), 173
Margulies, Leo, 146
Marlowe, Webb, 130. *See also* McComas, J. Francis
"Marooned off Vespa" (Asimov), 116
Martian Chronicles, The (Bradbury), 125, 202, 388
"Martian Odyssey, A" (Weinbaum), 64, 69
"Martian Quest" (Brackett), 97
Marvel Science Stories (magazine), 122, 179
Marvel Stories (magazine), 122
Marvel Tales (magazine), 122
Marx, Karl, 348–49
Mass, 323
"Master Shall Not Die, The" (Miller), 336, 368
Mastermind of Mars, The (Burroughs), 45
Mathematics of Magic, The (de Camp and Pratt), 299
Matheson, Richard, 172
Matter duplicator, 323

"Matter of Size, A" (Bates), 66–67
Matter transmitter, 323
McCaffrey, Anne, 168, 175, 187, 235, 246, 262, 387
McCauley, Harold, 115
McClary, Thomas Calvert, 66
McClure's Magazine, 22
McComas, J. Francis, 130, 170, 385, 389. *See also* Marlowe, Webb
McGivern, William P., 116
McIlwraith, Dorothy, 296
McIntyre, Vonda N., 262
Meek, S. P., 54
Méliès, Georges, 307
Men Like Gods (Wells), 20
Meredith, Scott, 221
"Merman, The" (de Camp), 93
Merril, Judith, 144, 222, 252–53, 256
Merritt, Abraham, 27–28, 44, 278, 294, 385, 386
Merwin, Sam, 120, 156, 174, 188
"Metal Horde, The" (Campbell), 48
Metal Monster, The (Merritt), 27
Methuselah's Children (Heinlein), 99, 242, 336
Metropolis (movie), 308
"Microscopic God" (Sturgeon), 100
Midamericon (1976), 285
"Midas Plague, The" (Pohl), 176
Midnight at the Well of Souls, 388
Midwich Cuckoos, The, 387
Mightiest Machine, The (Campbell), 68, 132–33
"Mile-Long Spaceship, The" (Wilhelm), 184
Milford Conferences, 222–23, 268
Miller, P. Schuyler, 51, 174, 220, 358
Miller, R. DeWitt, 336, 368
Miller, Walter M., Jr., 177, 340, 387
"Million-Year Picnic, The" (Bradbury), 125

"Mimsy Were the Borogoves" (Padgett), 105
Mindbridge (Haldeman), 283
Mines, Samuel, 174
Minnicon (1971), 272
Minos of Sardanes (Stilson), 27
Miracle Science and Fantasy Stories (magazine), 67
Mirror for Observers, A, 387
Mislaid Charm, The (Philipps), 134
Mission of Gravity (Clement), 175, 202, 387
MIT Science Fiction Society, 178, 277
Modern Electrics (magazine), 32–33
Modern Language Association, 270
Modern Library, 131
Modern Utopia, A (Wells), 343
Monroe, Lyle, 126, 167. *See also* Heinlein, Robert A.
Moon Is a Harsh Mistress, The (Heinlein), 234, 242
"Moon Pool, The" (Merritt), 27, 386
"Moon Waits, The" (Sullivan), 62–63
Moorcock, Michael, 231, 251–52, 255
Moore, C. L., 67–68, 80, 108, 262, 283, 388. *See also* O'Donnell, Lawrence
Moore, Robert. *See* Williams, Robert Moore
Moore, Ward, 8, 174
More Than Human (Sturgeon), 174, 387
More, Sir Thomas, 341–42
Morey, Leo, 49, 126
Morris, William, 293
Moskowitz, Sam, 74, 78, 142–43, 146, 213–14, 224, 263, 278, 281, 383, 389
Mote In God's Eye, The, 388
Mother World, The (Campbell), 63
Mule, The (Asimov), 109
Mundane, 323
Munsey, Frank A., 23, 29

Munsey Publications, 123–24
Mutant, 323
Mutant (Padgett), 109, 391

Naked Sun, The (Asimov), 4, 183
National Fantasy Fan Federation, 144
Nebula Awards, 238
Nebula Science Fiction (magazine), 181
Needle (Clement), 113
Neofan, 323
"Nerves" (Del Rey), 103, 107, 108–09, 386
NESFA. *See* New England Science Fiction Society
Neutron star, 323
Neutronium, 323
New Adam, The (Weinbaum), 336
New England Science Fiction Society, 275, 277, 384
New Fandom, 146
New Lands (Fort), 67
New Maps of Hell (Amis), 359–60
New Wave, 232, 243, 248, 252–57, 259, 374
New Worlds (British magazine), 128, 177, 181, 188, 231, 235, 251–52, 255–56
New Worlds Science Fiction (magazine), 179
New Writings in Science Fiction (Carnell), 249
Newark Science Fiction League, 143
Newton, Isaac, 14, 332, 364
NFFF. *See* National Fantasy Fan Federation
"Night of Light" (Farmer), 184
"Nightfall" (Asimov), 101
"Nightwings" (Silverberg), 236
Nightwings (Silverberg), 236
Nimoy, Leonard, 314, 371
"Nine Lives" (Le Guin), 337
Nine Billion Names of God, The, 388
Nine Princes of Amber, 388
1984 (Orwell), 129, 346

Niven, Larry, 234, 246, 335, 337, 375, 387, 388
No Blade of Grass (Christopher), 185, 254
"No Woman Born" (Moore), 108
Noname. *See* Senarens, Luis P.
Noreascon (1971), 275
North, André, 127. *See also* Norton, André
Norton (W. W.), 243
Norton, Alice Mary, 204
Norton, André, 127, 132, 387. *See also* North, André; Alice Mary
Norwescon (1950), 209, 213
Not Without Sorcery, 388
Nova Science Fiction Novels (magazine), 181
Now You See It (Asimov), 112
Nowland, Philip Francis, 46, 304, 305, 386
Nyberg, Bjorn, 297
Nycon (1939), 145
Nycon II (1956), 211, 222
Nycon III (1967), 274

Obeler, Arch, 311
Oberth, Hermann, 5, 50
O'Brien, David Wright, 116
O'Brien, Fitz-James, 16
Ocean (magazine), 23
Odd John (Stapledon), 87, 336, 386
O'Donnell, Lawrence, 105, 110, 111. *See also* Kuttner, Henry; Moore, C. L.
Odyssey (Homer), 13, 291
Odyssey Science Fiction (magazine), 280
Of World Beyond (Eshbach), 215
"Okie" (Blish), 172
Okie (Blish), 200
"Old Faithful" (Gallun), 68
Oliver, Chad, 172
Olson, Bob, 80
O'Meara, James, 215
"Omnilingual" (Piper), 184
On the Beach (Shute), 334
One Against the Legion (Williamson), 94

O'Neill, Gerard K., 322
Orban, Paul, 104, 108
Orbit (Knight), 249, 256
Orbit Science Fiction (magazine), 179
(Original) Science Fiction Stories (magazine), 180, 186, 195
Orlando Furioso (Ariosto), 13, 292
Orwell, George, 129, 346
"Other Tracks" (Sell), 333
Other Worlds, The (Strong), 129
Other Worlds Science Stories (magazine), 119, 161–62, 179
"Our Distant Cousins" (Dunsany), 29, 185
"Out of Night" (Stuart), 70–71, 94
Out of the Silent Planet (Lewis), 129
Out of this World Adventures (magazine), 179
Outer Limits (TV program), 315
Outline of History, The (Wells), 19
"Over the Top" (Del Rey), 114

Padgett, Lewis, 105, 109. *See also* Kuttner, Henry
Page, Norvell W., 336
Palmer, Raymond A., 51, 56, 74, 75, 78, 114–19, 138, 149, 161–62, 166–67, 188, 298–300
Palos of the Dog Star Pack (Giesy), 28
Pangborn, Edgar, 174, 387
Panshin, Alexei, 215
Paperback Library, 243
Parallel evolution, 323
Parallel universe, 323–24
Paratime, 324
Parsec, 324
Parthenogenesis, 324
"Passing of Ku Sui, The" (Gilmore), 56
Past through Tomorrow, The (Heinlein), 201, 242, 388

Paul, Frank R., 34, 43, 49–50, 73, 115, 126, 145
Pavane (Roberts), 255
Pearson's Magazine, 22
Pebble in the Sky (Asimov), 203
Pellegrini & Cudahy (publisher), 200
"People of the Crater, The" (North), 127
"People of the Pit, The" (Merritt), 27
Perri Press. 213
Pfeil, Donald J., 231
Philadelphia Science Fantasy Society, 78, 143
Philcon (1947), 147
Philcon II (1953), 210
Phillips, Alexander M., 134
Phillips, Peter, 4
Phillips, Rog, 142. *See also* Graham, Roger Philip
Pierce, John J., 37, 280
Pilgrims through Space and Time (Bailey), 263
Piper, H. Beam, 111, 112, 148, 172, 184, 233, 244, 324, 333, 387
"Piper's Son, The" (Padgett), 109
"Piracy Preferred" (Campbell), 48
Planet of Exile (Le Guin), 244
Planet Savers, The (Bradley), 244
Planet Stories (magazine), 124, 156, 178, 180, 182, 191, 202
Plato, 342
Platt, Charles, 255
Player Piano (Vonnegut), 346
Plunkett, Edward. *See* Dunsany, Lord
Pocket Book of Science Fiction, The (Wollheim), 129, 205
Pocket Books, 129, 135, 206, 243
Poe, Edgar Allan, 15–16, 43, 130, 211
Pohl, Frederik, 4, 5, 11, 74, 125, 138, 144, 146, 167, 174, 176, 183, 184, 187, 206, 221, 229, 232, 236, 237, 241, 246, 276, 283, 346, 387, 388. *See also* Wylie, Dirk
Polaris and the Goddess Glorian (Stilson), 27
Polaris of the Snows (Stilson), 27
"Police Operation" (Piper), 112
Popular Library, 191
Popular Publications, 29, 124, 125, 191
Portable Novels of Science Fiction (Wollheim), 129
Porter, Andrew, 276, 286
Portland Worldcon (1950), 209, 213
Pournelle, Jerry, 335, 388
Powers, Richard, 225
Pragnell, Festus, 64
Pratt, Fletcher, 129, 135, 293, 299, 386. *See also* Fletcher, George U.
Price, George W., Jr., 215, 284
Prime Press, 134, 343
Prime, Alfred, 134
Princess of Mars, A (Burroughs), 24, 25, 386
Pro, 324
Proceedings (Worldcon, 1962, 1963), 215
Prophet of Dune (Herbert), 234
"Proxima Centauri" (Leinster), 69
PSFS. *See* Philadelphia Science Fantasy Society
Psi, 324
"Psionic Machine—Type One" (Campbell), 164
Psychohistory, 343
Psychotic ("zine), 276
Publisher's Weekly (magazine), 358
Puppet Masters, The (Heinlein), 173, 202
Putnam (publisher), 201, 203, 242, 248, 249, 281
Pyramid Books, 176, 184, 206, 243, 248, 281

"QRM—Interplanetary" (Smith), 103–04
Queen of Zamba, The (de Camp), 113

Queens Science Fiction League, 142

R. U. R. (Capek), 87
Radio News (magazine), 34
Railroad Man's Magazine, 23
Ralph 124C41+ (Gernsback), 32, 343
Random House, 130, 247
Ray, 324
Raymond, Alex, 305
"Reason" (Asimov), 100
Rebirth (McClary), 66
Red Circle Magazines, 122
Red Gods Call, The, 68
"Red Mask of the Outlands, The" (Schachner), 66
"Red Plague, The" (Miller), 51
Red Planet (Heinlein), 131
Reinsberg, Mark, 140
Reiss, Malcolm, 124
Relativity, 324–25
Renaissance (Jones), 107
Rendezvous with Rama (Clarke), 238, 248, 387
"Repent Harlequin Said the Ticktockman" (Ellison), 234
Repp, Ed Earl, 50
Republic (Plato), 343
Requiem for Astounding, A (Rogers), 53, 383
"Rescue Party" (Clarke), 109
Restoree (McCaffrey), 246
"Return of Hawk Carse, The" (Bates), 56
Return to Tomorrow (Hubbard), 172
"Revolt of the Scientists, The" (Schachner), 63
Reynolds, Mack, 187
Rhodan, Perry, 245, 280
Richardson, R. S., 114
Ring around the Sun (Simak), 174
Ringworld (Niven), 246, 387
Ritt, William, 305
Riverworld (Farmer), 135
Roaring Trumpet, The (de Camp and Pratt), 299
Roberts, Keith, 255
Robeson, Kenneth, 58
Robot, 325

"Robots Return" (Williams), 93
Rocannon's World (Le Guin), 244
Rocket Ship Galileo (Heinlein), 131, 309
Rocket Stories (magazine), 180
Roddenberry, Gene, 313–14
Rogers, Alva, 53, 215, 383
Rogers, Hubert, 94, 104, 110, 113
Rogue Queen (de Camp), 202
Roman de la Rose, 292
"Romance of Posi and Nega, The" (Skidmore), 62
"Rose for Ecclesiastes, A" (Zelazny), 234
Rosemary's Baby (Levin), 295
Rostand, Edmond, 14
Rothman, Milton, 72
Rouge Moon (Budrys), 187
Round the Moon (Verne), 17
Rousseau, Victor, 53
"Rule 18" (Simak), 92
"Runaway Skyscraper, The" (Leinster), 29
Russ, Joanna, 186, 262
Russell, Eric Frank, 388

Saberhagen, Fred, 187
Santesson, Hans Stefan, 166, 224
Sargent, Pamela, 262
Satellite Science Fiction (magazine), 180
Saturday Evening Post (magazine), 29, 185
Saturn, Magazine of Fantasy & Science Fiction, 180
"Scanners Live in Vain" (Smith), 172
Schachner, Nathan, 54, 59, 60–61, 63, 66
Scheckley, Robert, 175
Schmitz, James H., 113
Schneeman, Charles, 92, 104, 113
Schuss Ins All, Der (Gail), 50
Schwartz, Julius, 75
Sci-Fi, 325
Science and Inventions (magazine), 34

INDEX   411

Science and Sanity (Korzybski), 321
Science Fantasy (magazine), 181, 188, 231
Science Fantasy Society, 145
Science Fiction (magazine), 123, 180, 186
Science Fiction Adventures (British magazine), 176, 180, 181, 231
Science Fiction Book Club, 202, 240
Science Fiction By Gaslight, 389
Science Fiction Digest (magazine), 75, 180
Science Fiction Forum (magazine), 223–24
Science Fiction Hall of Fame (Silverberg), 241, 389
Science Fiction League, 73–74, 78, 143
Science Fiction Novel, The (Symposium), 215
Science Fiction Plus (magazine), 180
Science Fiction Quarterly (magazine), 123, 180
Science Fiction Reader's Guide (Allen), 382
Science Fiction Research Association, 270
Science Fiction Review (fanzine), 276, 286
Science Fiction Shop, 286
Science Fiction Stories (magazine), 180
Science Fiction Times (fanzine), 141
Science Fiction Writers of America, 241, 261–62
Science of Life, The (Wells), 19
Science Stories (magazine), 180
Science Wonder Quarterly (magazine), 50
Science Wonder Stories (magazine), 49–50, 51
Scientific Adventures of Baron Munchausen, The (Gernsback), 33
Scientific Detective Stories (magazine), 51
Scientification (magazine), 43
Scithers, George, 287
Scoops (magazine), 127
Scortia, Thomas N., 176
Scribner's (magazine), 21
Scribner's (publisher), 131, 176, 203, 243
Seacon (1961), 212
Second Deluge, The (Serviss), 24
"Second Stage Lensman" (Smith), 101
"Secret of the Observatory" (Bloch), 116
"Seeds of the Dusk" (Gallun), 92
Seekers of Tomorrow (Moskowitz), 278
"Seesaw, The" (van Voght), 101, 104
Seetee Shock (Williamson), 306
Sell, William, 333
Senarens, Luis P., 18
Sercon, 207, 325
Serling, Rod, 312
Serviss, Garrett P., 23–24, 44
SFCON (1954), 211
Shadow, The (magazine), 58
Shadow out of Time, The (Lovecraft), 69, 296
Shasta Publishers, 135, 201, 242
Shaver, Richard S., 117
Shaver Mystery Series, 117–18, 161, 300
She (Haggard), 294, 386
Sheldon, Alice, 236. *See also* Tiptree, James, Jr.
Shelley, Mary Wollstonecraft, 15, 308
Sherred, T. L., 111, 153
Shield, 325
Ship of Ishtar, The (Merritt), 28
"Ship who Sang, The" (McCaffrey), 187
Shot into Infinity, The (Gail), 50
Shuster, Joseph, 306
Shute, Nevil, 334
"Sidewise in Time" (Leinster), 67, 152, 332
Siegel, Jerome, 306

Sigmond, 110
Signet Books, 183, 206, 243, 248
Silent Running (movies), 310–11
Silmarillion (Tolkien), 303
Silverberg, Robert, 176, 222, 236, 241, 246, 275, 362, 385, 388, 389
Simak, Clifford D., 51, 92, 94, 107, 135, 148, 151, 154, 171, 174, 185, 234, 236, 242, 338, 340, 386, 388
Simon & Schuster, 132, 171, 200, 240
Sirius (Stapledon), 129
Sixth Column (MacDonald), 99
Skidmore, Joseph W., 62
Skylark Duquesne (Smith), 235
Skylark of Space, The (Smith), 45–46, 132, 329, 386
Skylark of Valeron (Smith), 67
Skylark Three (Smith), 48
Slan! (van Voght), 97, 105, 336, 386
Slant (fanzine), 145
"Slaves of Mercury" (Schachner), 54
Sloane, T. O'Conor, 47, 62, 114
Smith, Clark Ashton, 298
Smith, Cordwainer, 172–73, 177, 388. *See also* Linebarger, Paul
Smith, Edward Elmer, 45–46, 48, 58, 63, 67, 84, 91, 94, 95–96, 101, 111, 126, 132, 133, 134, 143, 146, 154, 235, 248, 322, 329, 386
Smith, George O., 103–04, 120, 121, 134, 135, 148, 154, 176, 386
Smith, Malcolm, 115
Smith, Thorne, 295
SMOF, 325
Snide (fanzine), 141
Snow, C. P., 155, 351
"Solarite" (Campbell), 48
"Solution Unsatisfactory" (MacDonald), 99
Somnium (Kepler), 14
Sophont, 325
Soylent Green (movie), 241, 346

Space Cadet (Heinlein), 131
"Space Dwellers, The" (Gallun), 50
Space Hawk (Gilmore), 56
Space Hounds of IPC (Smith), 133
Space Merchants, The (Pohl and Kornbluth), 5, 174, 387
Space opera, 325
Space Prison (Godwin), 184
Space Science Fiction (magazine), 180
Space Stories (magazine), 180
Space Viking (Piper), 233, 388
Space Warp, 325
Space: 1999 (TV program), 315
Spaceway (magazine), 180
Spaceways (fanzine), 140
Spenser, Edmund, 292
Spinrad, Norman, 233, 235, 252
Splinter of the Mind's Eye (Foster), 372
"Stacked Deck" (Del Rey), 175
Stand on Zanzibar (Brunner), 241, 387
Standard Magazines, 65, 146, 191, 298
Stapledon, Olaf, 87, 129, 336, 386
Star Beast, The (Heinlein), 176, 387
Star gate, 325
Star Kings, The (Hamilton), 117
Star Lummox (Heinlein), 176
Star Science Fiction (magazine), 180
Star Series, 249
Star Short Novels, 340
Star Trek (TV program), 313–15, 371–73
Star Wars (movie), 311, 317, 369–74
Stardust (fanzine), 140
Stars Like Dust, The (Asimov), 173
Stars My Destination, The (Bester), 183
Startling Mystery (magazine), 231
Startling Stories (magazine), 120, 121, 142, 156, 172, 174, 175, 178, 180, 182

Steady state, 325-26
Steam Man of the Plains, The (Ellis), 18
Stellar Publishing Company, 49
Stevens, Lawrence, 124
Stewart, Will, 306. *See also* Williamson, Jack
Stilson, Charles B., 27
Stirring Science Stories (magazine), 126-27
Stockton, Frank, 130
Stong, Phil, 129
Stopa, John, 215
Strand Magazine, 22
Strange Stories (maganize), 127, 298
Strange Tales (magazine), 298
Stranger in a Strange Land (Heinlein), 201, 237, 387
Strauss, Erwin S., 277
Street & Smith Publications, 23, 34, 58, 70, 91, 106, 191, 298
Stuart, Don A., 68-69, 70, 84, 93, 94, 113, 135. *See also* Campbell, John W.
"Study of the Solar System, A" (Campbell), 69
Sturgeon, Theodore, 95, 100, 107, 114, 129, 134, 148, 154, 174, 206, 222, 387, 388
Sub-space, 322
Subjective time, 326
Sullivan, L. L. G., 62
Super-C, 321
Super Science Novels (magazine), 125
Super Science Stories (magazine)), 125, 167, 173, 180
Superman (comic book), 306
"Survival" (Burks), 122
Suspended animation, 326
Swift, Jonathan, 14-15
Sword of Aldones, The (Bradley), 244
Sword of Shannara, The (Brooks), 302-03, 388
Sykora, Will, 142, 209

Tachyon, 326
TAFF, 212, 326
Taine, John, 51

Tales of Tomorrow (magazine), 181
Tales of Wonder (magazine), 127-28
Tarrano the Conqueror (Cummings), 34
Tarzan of the Apes (Burroughs), 26
Taurasi, James V., 140-41, 142
Teck Publications, 47, 63
Ten Story Fantasy (magazine), 180
Tenn, William, 110, 144, 206, 265. *See also* Klass, Philip
"Tentacles from Below, The" (Gilmore), 55
Terraforming, 326
Terran, 326
Thing, The (movie), 93
Thing from Another World, The (movie), 309
Things to Come (movie), 309
Things to Come (Wells), 309
This Immortal (Zelazny), 234, 243
Thomas, Theodore L., 175, 233
Three Hundred Years Hence (Griffith), 343
Three Musketeers, The (Dumas), 199
Thrilling Wonder Stories (magazine), 65, 119-20, 156, 174, 178, 180, 182
"Through the Dragon Glass" (Merritt), 27
Tiger, Tiger! (Bester), 183
Time and Again (Simak), 171
Time and Time Again" (Piper), 111
Time Enough for Love (Heinlein), 100, 242
"Time Locker" (Padgett), 105
Time Machine, The (Wells), 21, 345, 386
Time Quarry (Simak), 171
"Time Ray of Jandra, The" (Palmer), 51
Time Stream, The (Taine), 51
Time Traveller, The (magazine), 75
Time Tunnel (TV program), 313
Timmins, William, 104

Tiptree, James, Jr., 236. *See also* Sheldon, Alice
To the Stars (Hubbard), 171
To Your Scattered Bodies Go (Farmer), 242, 387
Toby Press Novels (magazine), 180
Toffler, Alvin, 10, 353
Tolkien, J. R. R., 238, 247, 294, 301, 303, 387
Tom Corbett: Space Cadet (TV program), 312
Tom Swift Series (Appleton), 19
Tomorrow the Stars (Heinlein), 202
"Tomorrow's Children" (Anderson and Waldrop), 110–11
Tomorrow's World (Hunter), 176
"Too Soon to Die" (Godwin), 184
Torcon (1948), 147
Torcon (1973), 238, 275
Totipotency, 326
Train, Oswald, 77
Tramp, The (Hubbard), 93
Transatlantic Fan Fund. *See* TAFF
Treasury of Science Fiction, A (Conklin), 130
Tremaine, F. Orlin, 59–60, 66, 69–71, 80, 87, 91, 126, 157, 217, 298
"Trends" (Asimov), 95
Tricon (1966), 274
Trip from the Earth to the Moon, A (Verne), 17
Trip to the Moon, A (movie), 307
Triplanetary (Smith), 58, 63, 133
True Story, The (Lucian of Samosata), 13, 328
Trufan, 326
Trumbull, Douglas, 310
Tubb, E. C., 245, 275, 282, 388
Tuck, Donald H., 214, 284, 384
Tucker, Bob, 139, 141
Tucker, Wilson, 139
Twain, Mark, 19

Twenty Thousand Leagues under the Sea (Verne), 17
"Twilight" (Stuart), 68, 80
Twilight Zone (TV program), 312
Two Complete Science Adventure Books (magazine), 180
2001: A Space Odyssey (movie), 310
Tyrann (Asimov), 173

Uncanny Stories (magazine), 127
Uncanny Tales (magazine), 127
Uncertainty Principle, 326–27
Under Pressure (Herbert), 176, 387
Under the Moons of Mars (Burroughs), 24
Unearth (magazine), 286
Universal Publishing and Distributing Company, 230
"Universe" (Heinlein), 99, 116
Universe Science Fiction (magazine), 179, 180
Unknown (magazine), 96, 103–04, 113, 118, 127, 129, 134, 202, 295, 299
Unknown Worlds (magazine), 96, 106, 299. *See also Unknown* (magazine)
"Unparalleled Adventure of One Hans Pfaal" (Poe), 16
"Unready to Wear" (Vonnegut), 176
Utopia (More), 341–42

"Valley of Dreams" (Weinbaum), 65
Van Dongen, H. R., 173, 224
van Vogt, A. E., 94, 95, 97, 101–05, 109, 113, 135, 148, 154, 164, 167, 321, 336, 386
Vance, Jack, 121
Vanguard Amateur Press Association, 141–42
Vanguard Science Fiction (magazine), 180
Vargo Statten Science Fiction (magazine), 181
Vaughan, Richard, 64

INDEX 415

Venture Science Fiction (magazine), 180, 184, 230
Venus Equilateral (Smith), 134, 386
Verne, Jules, 16–18, 35, 43, 44, 128, 386
Verril, A. Hyatt, 44
Vertex (magazine), 231, 280
"Via Etherline" (Giles), 119
"Viagens Interplanetarias" (de Camp), 113
Victory on Janus, 387
Vincent, Harl, 50, 54
"Vintage Season" (O'Donnell), 110
Vision of Tomorrow (magazine), 231
Visual Encyclopedia of Science Fiction, The (Ash), 382
Vonnegut, Kurt, Jr., 175–76, 243, 346
"Vortex Blaster" (Smith), 126
Vortex Science Fiction (magazine), 180
"Voyage that Lasted 600 Years, The" (Wilcox), 116
"Voyage to Laputa" (Swift), 14
Voyage to the Bottom of the Sea (TV program), 313
Voyage to the Moon (Bergerac), 14
Voyage to Venus, A (Eyraud), 18

Waggoner, Diana, 382
Waldo, Bud, 134
Waldo and Magic, Inc. (Heinlein), 201–02
Waldrop, F. N., 110
Walton, Evangeline, 302
Wandrei, Donald, 66, 296
War of the Wing Men (Anderson), 186
War of the Worlds, The (Wells), 19, 23, 254, 309, 386
War of the Worlds, The (radio program; 1938), 311
War of the Worlds, The (movie), 309
Warner, Harry, Jr., 140, 215, 278, 383
Way Station (Simak), 234, 388

"We Hail" (Stuart), 113
Weapon Makers, The (van Vogt), 105, 154
"Weapon Shops, The (van Vogt), 104
"Weatherman, The (Thomas), 233
Weinbaum, Stanley G., 64–65, 69, 78, 84, 119, 121, 129, 133, 283, 336, 389
Weird Tales (magazine), 29, 68, 127, 135, 151, 177, 296, 298
Weird Tales, 389
Weisinger, Mortimer, 65, 74–75, 119, 138
Well at World's End, The (Morris), 293
Well of the Unicorn, The (Fletcher), 293
Welles, Orson, 20, 311
Wells, Herbert George, 19–20, 23, 30, 35, 43, 44, 129, 130, 152, 254, 263, 309, 337, 343, 345, 385
Wessolowski, H. W., 53, 70
"Weyr Search" (McCaffrey), 235
"What Dead Men Tell" (Sturgeon), 114
What Mad Universe? (Brown), 121
"When the Atoms Failed" (Campbell), 47–48
"When the World Screamed" (Conan Doyle), 22
When Worlds Collide (Balmer and Wylie), 87, 309, 386
When Worlds Collide (movie), 309
White, James, 175
White, Ted, 230, 274, 280
"Who Goes There?" (Stuart), 93, 135, 309
Who's Who in Science Fiction (Ash), 383
Wilcox, Don, 116, 329
Wild Talents (Fort), 67
Wilhelm, Kate, 183, 184, 262, 268
Willey, Robert. *See* Ley, Willy
Williams, James, 134

Williams, Robert Moore, 93, 115
Williamson, Jack, 29, 45, 59, 66–67, 92, 94, 104, 112, 122, 133, 135, 241, 246, 265, 306, 386, 389. *See also* Stewart, Will
Willis, Walter A., 145, 212
Wilson, Gahan, 297
Wilson, Robin Scott, 268
"Wind between the Worlds" (Del Rey), 173
Winds of Gath, The (Tubb), 245, 388
Winston (publisher), 203–04
"Witches of Karrea, The" (Schmitz), 113
Witchworld, 387
"With Folded Hands" (Williamson), 111
"With the Night Mail" (Kipling), 22
Without Sorcery (Sturgeon), 134
Wolfbane (Pohl and Kornbluth), 184–85
Wollheim, Donald A., 74, 78, 126, 129, 138, 146, 204–05, 243, 245, 248, 282, 300
Woman in the Moon, The, (movie), 308
Wonder Stories (magazine), 51, 61, 63–65, 73, 87, 180
Wonder Stories Quarterly (magazine), 61
Wonder Story Annual (magazine), 180
Wonders of the Spaceways (magazine), 181
Wood, Edward, 215, 284
World Fantasy Convention, 297
World of Adventure (magazine), 37
World of Null-A, The (van Vogt), 109, 386
World of Ptavvs, The (Niven), 246
"World of the Red Sun, The" (Simak), 51
World Publishing Company, 278
Worldcon (London, 1965), 274
Worldcon (Melbourne, 1975), 285
Worldcon (New York, 1950), 208–09
Worlds Beyond (magazine), 180
Worlds of Fantasy (magazine), 181
Worlds of Tomorrow (magazine), 230
Worm Holes, 327
Worm Ouroboros, The (Eddison), 293
Wright, Earnsworth, 296
Wright, Sewell Peaslee, 54
Wylie, Dirk, 221. *See also* Pohl, Frederik
Wylie, Philip, 87, 309, 385
Wyndam, John, 202, 254, 387. *See also* Harris, John W. Beynon

Xeno-, 327

Yaco, Murray F., 165
Young Communist League, 79

Zelazny, Roger, 205, 233, 234, 243, 388, 389
Ziff-Davis Publishing Company, 114, 195, 230, 300

For Product Safety Concerns and Information please contact our EU
representative GPSR@taylorandfrancis.com
Taylor & Francis Verlag GmbH, Kaufingerstraße 24, 80331 München, Germany

www.ingramcontent.com/pod-product-compliance
Lightning Source LLC
Chambersburg PA
CBHW071227290426
44108CB00013B/1312